STATE NAMES, FLAGS, SEALS, SONGS, BIRDS, FLOWERS, AND OTHER SYMBOLS

STATE NAMES, FLAGS, SEALS, SONGS, BIRDS, FLOWERS, AND OTHER SYMBOLS

A Study
based on historical documents giving the origin and significance of the state names, nicknames, mottoes, seals, flags, flowers, birds, songs, and descriptive comments on the capitol buildings and on some of the leading state histories, with facsimiles of the state flags and seals

Revised Edition

By

GEORGE EARLIE SHANKLE, Ph.D.

GREENWOOD PRESS, PUBLISHERS
WESTPORT, CONNECTICUT

This book was catalogued by the Library of Congress as follows:

Shankle, George Earlie.
State names, flags, seals, songs, birds, flowers, and other symbols; a study based on historical documents giving the origin and significance of the State names, nicknames, mottoes, seals, flags, flowers, birds, songs, and descriptive comments on the capitol buildings and on some of the leading State histories, with facsimiles of the State flags and seals. Rev. ed. Westport, Conn., Greenwood Press [1970]
522 p. illus. 23 cm.
Reprint of the 1938 ed.
Bibliography: p. [427]–479.
1. Names, Geographical—U. S. 2. Seals (Numismatics)—U. S. 3. Flags—U. S. 4. Capitols. 5. Mottoes. 6. State flowers. 7. State birds. 8. State songs. 9. U. S. — History, Local — Bibliography. I. Title.

E155.S43 1970	917.3	73–109842
ISBN 0-8371-4333-0		MARC
Library of Congress	71 [4]	

PUBLISHER'S NOTE

For technical reasons the flags originally illustrated in color on pages 272a-d have been converted to black and white. A color description of each flag, however, is given in the text.

Originally published in 1938 by the H. W. Wilson Company, New York

Reprinted from an original copy in the collections of the Brooklyn Public Library

Reprinted in 1970 by Greenwood Press, Inc., 51 Riverside Avenue, Westport, Conn. 06880

Library of Congress catalog card number 73-109842
ISBN 0-8371-4333-0

Printed in the United States of America

10 9 8

PREFACE

This book grew out of the desire of its author to know, about his native state, a great many facts which he found exceedingly difficult to obtain. After three years of research in the Library of Congress, he is able to give to the public this storehouse of information, which could have been gathered from no library less fertile in source material.

Not all of the data contained in this publication, however, could be found in this great assemblage of books; for much of it was gathered by means of personal letters or questionnaires sent to people whose experience or occupation enabled them to give expert information regarding certain facts which research had failed to discover.

It has long been the conviction of the writer that the public would welcome such a collection of information. People are constantly asking librarians and others in official positions for facts about the state birds, flowers, flags, seals, songs, nicknames, trees, mottoes, etc. Often these persons are unable to supply the information desired because it is not available. It was the hope of giving to the public just such data that led the writer to attempt this study.

A debt of gratitude is hereby acknowledged to the librarians and other officials of the Library of Congress for their untiring efforts to assist; to the librarians of the various state libraries; to the archivists or historians of the departments of archives and history of the several states; to the secretaries of the divers state historical societies, many of whom gave valuable information; to all others who in any way contributed suggestions, data, or source material; and to the following persons employed to assist with the clerical work: Miss Amy D. Putnam, a graduate student at the George Washington University, who in addition to typing much of the first draft of the manuscript, rendered efficient service by helping to locate portions of the reference material in the Library of Congress; Miss Hazel Parsons, a commercial student at the State Teachers College, Fredericksburg, Virginia, who typed the final draft of the manuscript; and Miss Rosalind Decker, one of the author's students at the State Teachers College, Fredericksburg, Virginia, who made pen drawings both of facsimiles of the state flags and of the impressions of the state seals.

The manuscript for this book having been completed, the author submitted the data dealing with each state to the State Librarian, the State Historian, or, as was necessary in a few instances, to the Librarian of the State University of the state under consideration. Each of the above-named persons having critically read and returned the data submitted to him or her, the author, after he had given due consideration to the criticisms and suggestions offered, arranged the final copy of the manuscript for the press.

The descriptions of the state seals and of the state flags given in the text were quoted or paraphrased from the laws adopting them, with few exceptions; but the illustrations of the seals and of the flags were printed from pen drawings of the impressions of the seals or of the facsimiles of the flags supplied to the author by the secretaries of the various states. In a few instances there occur variations between the legal descriptions and the illustrations.

TABLE OF CONTENTS

Chapter III

STATE MOTTOES: THEIR ORIGIN AND SIGNIFICANCE

Chapter IV

THE GREAT SEALS OF THE STATES OF THE UNION

The State Seals 181

Chapter V

INTERPRETATION OF THE INSIGNIA ON THE STATE SEALS

Introduction 224

The Great Seal of the United States 224

The Seals of the States 230

Chapter VI

THE FLAGS OF THE STATES

A General Discussion of Flags 257

The Flag of the United States 257

Flags of the States 264

Chapter VII

THE STATE CAPITOL BUILDINGS

Chapter VIII

THE STATE FLOWERS

Chapter IX

THE STATE TREES

Chapter X

THE STATE BIRDS

Chapter XI

THE STATE SONGS

Chapter XII

MISCELLANEOUS ITEMS

Chapter XIII

A LIST OF LEADING STATE HISTORIES

ILLUSTRATIONS

INTRODUCTION

It is the purpose of this book to record the facts about the various state names, nicknames, flowers, trees, flags, birds, songs, seals, mottoes, capitol buildings, and some of the outstanding state histories.

The chapter discussing the origin of the names of the states of the Union calls attention to the fact that the state names come from seven different languages; namely, Greek, Latin, French, Spanish, Dutch, English, and American Indian dialects. This chapter also shows, as far as possible, when, by whom, and under what conditions the states were named; for whom they were named; and traces the name itself back to its root meaning in the parent language from which it is derived, giving footnotes to show upon what authority these statements are based.

The unit dealing with the nicknames of the states and with the nicknames of the people of these states entailed an enormous amount of research, covering source material taken both from the literary and from the slang level, before it could be written up. This unit contains a systematic discussion of the origin and of the significance of the nicknames wherever it was at all possible to gather these facts, giving footnotes to the pages of the source material.

The chapters giving information about the adoption of the state seals, flags, flowers, birds, trees, and songs, are developed from data secured chiefly from the state codes or session laws officially designating them as such, from personal letters, and from other sources, all of which the footnotes indicate. In addition to these sources many of the facts about the state songs were taken from the songs themselves.

The illustrations of the seals were printed from pen drawings of the impressions of the seals which were furnished the writer by the secretaries of the various

states, with one or two exceptions. The illustrations of
the state flags were made from pen drawings of these flags
which hang in the rotunda of the Post Office building at
Washington, D.C. Miss Alice B. Sanger, Personnel Officer
of the Post Office Department, who has collected these
flags, kindly gave the writer permission to have the pen
drawings made. In the Revised Edition, the illustrations
of the flags were checked by recent facsimiles of these
supplied the author by the secretaries of the various states,
and new illustrations were made in case the facsimiles did
not agree with the illustrations in the original edition.

The section of the book giving information about the
state capitol buildings is one of the most interesting, yet
it was one of the most difficult to develop. Its purpose is
to give the following facts about each of the statehouses;
the location of the building, its dimensions, the name of
the architect who designed it, the style of architecture it
represents, the material out of which it was constructed,
and the amount of money it cost.

Probably those of a scholarly turn of mind or those
versed in classical literature will be most interested in the
chapter on the state mottoes, for research reveals the fact
that the expression of these mottoes employs seven languages: Greek, Latin, Spanish, French, Italian, American
Indian, and English. The Latin language is employed
most frequently, for twenty-three of the forty-nine states
(counting the District of Columbia as a state) write their
mottoes in Latin. For the most part, these expressions
are taken from the greater Latin writers, such as Virgil,
Cicero, Lucretius, and Seneca.

The chapter naming and discussing some of the outstanding state histories gives a great deal of helpful information to those who are not familiar with this available
material. While this unit does not propose to include all
the outstanding state histories, it calls attention to four
or more trustworthy ones dealing with the historical facts
relative to each state. For each history there are given the
name of the publisher, the place and the date of publica-

tion, and the price whenever it could be ascertained. Of course the prices listed, being those given by the publishers at the time of publication, are subject to change. An outstanding feature of this chapter is the annotations, giving a brief digest of the nature of the contents of each history.

The footnotes throughout the text give the name of the book, the name of the author, the place and the date of publication, and the page reference. This order is followed because in a book of this nature those concerned with checking the source material are interested first in getting the name of the book.

Since one of the major functions of this handbook is to supply reference material, the writer, in the matter of footnotes, has followed the library procedure in the use of abbreviations, and of figures to indicate consecutive page numbers.

Throughout the text, the writer has italicized the names of books, the names of the states, the names of the state songs, the state mottoes, the state nicknames, the nicknames of the inhabitants of the states, and many other important words; but because a great number of these expressions occur in Roman type quoted matter, the lack of consistency in the matter of typography in such instances is unavoidable.

CHAPTER I

THE ORIGIN AND THE SIGNIFICANCE OF THE NAMES OF THE STATES OF THE UNION

A fascinating study is that of the significance of names. Some of them are self-explanatory; some are so strange-sounding and forbidding-looking that they defy the investigator; some are easily broken up into their component parts and analyzed for meanings; and others yield their significance at a tremendous cost of effort.

Tracing the meanings of place-names has always been especially fascinating to men of an investigative turn of mind, so much so that in all ages they "have been favorite beasts of the chase"; game that has been eagerly sought and that has provided marvelous sport for the pursuers.

In studying the origin of the names of states and of countries, one often finds that they were named after persons, streams, mountains, that they have allegorical significance, or that they originated in some philological suggestion. Occasionally they thwart all attempts at classification or interpretation according to philological or etymological principles. In many instances they have lost all the earmarks of their identity, having dropped prefixes and suffixes, or having combined roots, stems, and terminations from two or more languages, thus forming hybrids that resemble none too closely any of the component languages. The names of states or countries generally prove to be records of the past, fraught with most interesting historical significance, explaining physical characteristics, or other outstanding features of a country, of its climate, or of its inhabitants.

When the primitive meaning of the name of a state or of a country is recovered, one often finds that it tells the story of "emigrations—immigrations—the commingling of races by war and conquest, or by the peaceful processes of commerce: the name of a district, [of a state], or of a town may speak to us of events which written history has failed to commemorate." [1] This is especially true with reference to the significance of the names of the various states of the Union. When traced to their original sources in the parent languages from which they came, they reveal a wealth of lore both interesting and instructive.

The historian is concerned chiefly with recording the events in the lives of individuals, cities, states, or nations; but the historian of names, the lexicographer, and the philologist give interesting facts about, or the origin and the significance of names.

These state names come from seven different languages; namely, Greek, Latin, French, Spanish, Dutch, English (including Anglo-Saxon, Celtic, and other early forms of the English language), American Indian dialects, and one is purely American in origin.

Eleven states derived their names from the Latin language; three, from the French; and four, from the Spanish. The name of one state, Rhode Island, is accredited with Greek origin in one interpretation and with Dutch origin in another. New York, New Jersey, New Hampshire, and Maryland in its present form are English appellations. The name Washington goes back to the Anglo-Saxon for its source, and the term New York is given by some as Celtic, by some as Anglo-Saxon, and by some as Latin, in origin.

Seven of the states were named after kings and queens; namely, Georgia, Louisiana, Maryland, North and South Carolina, Virginia, and West Virginia. The four states named for noted personages other than kings and queens are Delaware, the District of Columbia, New York, and Pennsylvania. New Hampshire and New Jersey were named after British localities.

---

[1] *Words and Places Illustrations of History, Ethnology, and Geography,* Isaac Taylor (J. M. Dent and Sons, Limited, London, 1911. The Reprint Edition was published by E. P. Dutton and Company, New York, 1927.) p. 10.

STATES NAMED AFTER KINGS AND QUEENS

Georgia

Georgia, although named for an English king, goes back for the ultimate origin of its name to the Greek language.

The grant of land in what is now the State of Georgia, made by King George I of England to Sir Robert Montgomery about 1717, was given with the proviso that if the land were not settled within three years, the grant should become void. The colony was to have been called the *Margravate of Azilia.* No settlement had been made at the end of the three years, so the land was returned to the crown. [2] In 1732 when Oglethorpe and his associates obtained from King George II a charter to settle this land, they named it *Georgia* in honor of the king. [3] The name itself, however, is much older than the founding of this colony. It is a Greek feminine noun meaning tillage or agriculture, and comes from the two words, *ge,* meaning *earth,* and *ergon,* signifying *to work.* [4]

Georgia is also the non-official name "of a region in Transcaucasian Russia, nearly corresponding to the modern governments Yelisabetpol, Kutais, and Tiflis." [5]   It

---

[2] *Georgia, Land and People,* Frances Letcher Mitchell (The Franklin Printing and Publishing Company, Atlanta, Georgia, 1900) p. 14.

[3] *Ibidem,* p. 15.

A History of Georgia from Its First Discovery by the Europeans to the Adoption of the Present Constitution in MDCCXCVIII (1798), Reverend William Bacon Stevens, M.D.   (D. Appleton and Company, New York, 1847) vol. i, p. 62-3.

Other historians giving this account of the naming of Georgia are:
First Lessons in Georgia History, Lawton Bryan Evans (American Book Company, New York, Cincinnati, and Chicago, 1929) p. 35.

A Standard History of Georgia and the Georgians, Lucian Lamar Knight   (The Lewis Publishing Company, Chicago, Illinois, 1917) vol. i, p. 4.

The History of Georgia, Containing Brief Sketches of the Most Remarkable Events up to the Present Day (1784), Captain Hugh McCall (Reprinted by A. B. Caldwell, Publisher, Atlanta, Georgia, 1909) p. 6.

[4] *A Dictionary of the Derivations of the English Language, in Which Each Word is Traced to Its Primary Root*   (G. P. Putnam's Sons, New York.   Neither the name of the author nor date of publication is given.) p. 160.

[5] *The Century Cyclopedia of Names,* edited by Benjamin E. Smith (The Century Company, New York, 1911) vol. ii, p. 432.

was conquered by Alexander the Great, but became an independent kingdom soon after his death. This kingdom
reached its greatest state of development about 1200 A.D.
It was subdivided during the fifteenth century, and "was
annexed to Russia in 1801." These Georgians are said to
be "of the purest Caucasian type."

Besides Georgia, named for an English king, there are
two states, Maryland and Virginia, named after English
queens.

Maryland

The naming of Maryland is generally attributed to
George Calvert, the first Lord Baltimore. He is said to
have drawn up the charter for the grant himself and to
have left a place in it for the inserting of the name, which
he desired to be *Crescentia*, or the *Land of Crescence*.
However, he had planned to leave the actual naming of it
to his Majesty. The King, Charles I, before signing the
charter, asked his Lordship what he should call the province. Lord Baltimore said that he had desired to designate
it in honor of his Majesty's name, but that he was deprived
of that happiness because there was already a colony "in
those parts called Carolina."

" 'Let us therefore,' says the king, 'give it a name in
honor of the Queen; what think you of *Mariana?*' To this
his Lordship expressed his dissent, it being the name of a
Jesuit, who had written against monarchy. 'Whereupon
the King proposed [the name] *Terra Mariae*, in English,
Maryland, which was concluded on and inserted in the
bill.' And thus the proposed colony was named [Land of
Maria or Maryland] in honor of Henrietta Maria, [Queen
of Charles I], daughter of Henry IV, king of France and
Navarre, and sister of Louis XIII, who was usually called
Queen Mary by writers of the day." [6] Thwaites says that

---

[6] *History of Maryland from the Earliest Period to the Present Day*,
John Thomas Scharf   (John B. Piet, Baltimore, Maryland, 1879) vol. 1,
p. 51-2.

This account, quoted in part from the Ayscough and Sloane MSS., is
also found in the *Tercentenary History of Maryland*, Matthew Page
Andrews (The S. J. Clarke Publishing Company, Chicago and Baltimore,
1925) vol. 1, p. 20.

"at the king's request the country was named Maryland, in honor of his queen, Henrietta Maria." [7]

The name *Mary,* being the same in meaning as the word *Miriam,* [8] is of Hebrew origin. This name, given to the sister of Moses, [9] means *bitter; born when parents were in sore distress, at a time of bondage, or amidst bitter trials.* [10]

"Miriam was born at the time when the Egyptians began to embitter the lives of the Israelites by imposing arduous tasks upon them (compare [Exodus] 1:14), and for this reason she was called Miriam." [11]

The word *land* is purely Teutonic in origin, and the English term is derived from the Anglo-Saxon word *lond* or *land.* [12] Both the Anglo-Saxon and the present English forms of the word mean *the solid portion of the earth's surface; or any portion of it; public or private property (real estate); ground or soil; country or territory;* and *the country, as opposed to towns and cities.* [13]

Virginia

Historians generally agree that Virginia was named by Queen Elizabeth herself in commemoration of her unmarried state. The name was given about 1584 or 1585. [14]

[7] *Epochs of American History: The Colonies, 1492-1750,* Reuben Gold Thwaites (Longmans, Green, and Company, New York, 1910) p. 82.

[8] *The Century Cyclopedia of Names,* edited by Benjamin E. Smith (The Century Company, New York, 1911) vol. 11, p. 661, 690.

[9] *The Jewish Encyclopedia* (Funk and Wagnalls Company, New York and London, 1925) vol. 8, p. 608.

[10] *Personal and Family Names,* Harry Alfred Long (Hamilton, Adams and Company, London, 1883) p. 72, 84, 232.
History of Christian Names, Charlotte M. Yonge (Parker, Son, and Bourn, London, 1863) vol. 1, p. 76-87.

[11] *The Jewish Encyclopedia* (Funk and Wagnalls Company, New York and London, 1925) vol. 8, p. 608.

[12] *The Century Dictionary and Cyclopedia* (The Century Company, New York, 1911) vol. 5, p. 3342.

[13] *A New English Dictionary,* edited by James A. H. Murray (The Clarendon Press, Oxford, England) vol. vii, p. 46-7.

[14] *Old Virginia and Her Neighbours,* John Fiske (Houghton, Mifflin and Company, The Riverside Press, Cambridge, Massachusetts, 1900) vol. 1, p. 36.
An American History, David Saville Muzzey (Ginn and Company, Boston, Massachusetts, 1920) p. 19.

Thomas Nelson Page says:

Queen "Elizabeth graciously accorded the privileges proposed by Raleigh, giving to this new land a name in honour of her maiden state, and it was called Virginia. Raleigh was knighted for his service and given the title of 'Lord and Governor of Virginia.' " [15]

As to the naming of Virginia, Henry Howe says:

"The glowing description given by the adventurers, on their return, of the beauty of the country, the fertility of the soil, and pleasantness of the climate, delighted the queen, and induced her to name the country of which she had taken possession, Virginia, in commemoration of her unmarried life." [16]

The origin of the word Virginia is accounted for as follows: It is a Latin name generally considered to be derived from the Latin word *virgo*, meaning *a virgin*, but in reality it is the feminine form of the masculine noun *Virginius* [*Verginius*], the name of a Roman gens. [17]

West Virginia

The break between Virginia and West Virginia came in 1861. In 1862 the people belonging to the separated group framed a new constitution. The newly formed state proposed to call itself *Kanawha*, but finally the name *West Virginia* was decided upon. West Virginia was admitted into the Union as a separate state on June 20, 1863. [18]

The term *West Virginia* is a combination of the Latin derivative, *Virginia*, and the English word *west*, which comes from the Old English. The Old English term in

---

[15] *The Old Dominion, Her Making and Her Manners,* Thomas Nelson Page (Charles Scribner's Sons, New York, 1908) p. 50.

[16] *Historical Collections of Virginia,* Henry Howe (W. R. Babcock, Charleston, South Carolina, 1849) p. 18.

[17] *The Century Dictionary and Cyclopedia* (The Century Company, New York, 1911) vol. 10, p. 6765.

See also: *An Etymological Dictionary of the English Language,* John Oswald (E. C. and J. Biddle, Philadelphia, Pennsylvania, 1866) p. 514.

[18] *The Encyclopedia Americana* (Americana Corporation, New York and Chicago, 1927) vol. 29, p. 215.

turn is derived through a primitive Germanic stem from the Greek word, ἕσπερος ἑσπέρα signifying *evening* or *west*. [19]

Louisiana

Louisiana and the Carolinas were named after French kings.

La Salle in 1682 named Louisiana, then including all the Mississippi valley, in honor of Louis XIV of France. [20] The origin of the word *Louisiana* is as follows: It comes from the name *Louis,* plus the suffix *iana,* (from -*ana,* the -*i* being inserted for the sake of euphony), meaning *of* or *belonging to,* a termination used by the French during the sixteenth and seventeenth centuries especially, and by the English in the beginning of the eighteenth century. [21] The final *a* means land. [22]

The names *Clovis, Chlodowig,* and *Hlūtwīc* (Ludwig) are all identical in meaning with the word *Louis.* From the Old High German term *Hlūtwīc* (Ludwig) is derived the Italian name *Ludovico,* signifying *one famous in war.* [23]

The prefix *hlod,* from which the word *Louis* came, can be traced through the Latin and Greek to the Sanscrit: the Sanscrit form of the syllable being *çru;* the Greek form being κλύω; the Latin, *cluo* or *clueo;* and the Anglo-Saxon, *hlowan.* This prefix, some think, probably originated from the noise made by the lowing of a cow. Its many forms convey a variety of meanings, but all of them embody the idea of making a noise. The Greek term

[19] *A New English Dictionary,* edited by James A. H. Murray (The Clarendon Press, Oxford, England) vol. X⁴, p. 321.

[20] *Louisiana, Comprising Sketches of Counties, Towns, Events, Institutions, and Persons, Arranged in Cyclopedic Form,* Alcée Fortier (Southern Historical Association, Atlanta, Georgia, 1909) vol. 2, p. 94.

[21] *A New English Dictionary,* edited by James A. H. Murray (The Clarendon Press, Oxford, England) vol. 1, p. 299.

[22] "The Naming of Indiana," Cyrus W. Hodgin, in the *Papers of the Wayne County, Indiana, Historical Society* (Nicholson Printing and Manufacturing Company, Richmond, Indiana, 1903) vol. 1, no. 1, p. 7.

[23] *An Etymological Dictionary of Modern English,* Ernest Weekley (John Murray, London, 1921) p. 863.

κλύτος signifies renowned. The Greek word κλέος carries
the notion of fame, and the Latin expression *clueo*
means *to be famous.* [24]

Bardsley gives several confirmations of Charlotte M.
Yonge's opinion that the Welsh used the word *Lewis* as an
Anglicism of the name *Llewelyn.* [25]

The term *Clovis* (Latin Lluduicus) has been preserved
in the French word *Louis* and in the German term *Ludwig,*
each of which has many varied forms. The English took
the forms *Ludovick, Louis,* and *Lewis;* the German, *Ludwig, Luz,* and *Lotze;* and the French took the forms *Clovis,
Louis, Looys,* and *Loys.* The provencal term *Aloys* is said
to be the first name from which the feminine form of the
word *Aloyse* or *Heloïse* was derived. By the end of the
fifteenth century *Louise,* the feminine form of the noun,
was in use at the French court. [26]

William Arthur gives the derivation of the name *Lewis*
as follows: "In the Fr. [French], *Louis;* Latin, *Ludovicus;*
Teutonic, *Ludwig* or *Leodwig,* from the Saxon *Leod,* the
people, and *wic,* a castle—the safeguard of the people." [27]

The Carolinas

Two different forms of the name of the Carolinas have
been used. This territory was first called *Carolina* by
Jean Ribault; but under the control of King Charles I, it
was named *Carolana,* and from the time of King Charles
II, it has been called *Carolina.*

Thwaites gives the following account of the naming of
the Carolinas: While on an exploring expedition in 1562,
Jean Ribaut [Ribault] left colonists on Lemon Island at

[24] *History of Christian Names,* Charlotte M. Yonge (Macmillan and
Company, London, 1878) vol. 2, p. 387-92.
[25] *A Dictionary of English and Welsh Surnames with Special American Instances,* Charles Wareing Bardsley (Henry Frowde, London, 1901)
p. 480.
[26] *History of Christian Names,* Charlotte M. Yonge (Macmillan and
Company, London, 1878) vol. 2, p. 389-91.
[27] *An Etymological Dictionary of Family and Christian Names,* William Arthur (Sheldon, Blakeman and Company, New York, 1857) p. 183.

Port Royal, and called this territory Carolina in honor of Charles IX, the boy-king of France, under whose auspices he went out.

In the grant of 1629 to Sir Robert Heath, his attorney-general, King Charles I called this country *Carolana,* or the *Province of Carolana.* In 1663 King Charles II gave *Carolina* to eight Lords Proprietors. [28]

It is definitely stated in *A Sketch of North Carolina* that King Charles I named after himself the territory granted to Sir Robert Heath:

"In 1629, a charter was granted by [King] Charles I of England to Sir Robert Heath of the Southern part of Virginia, latitudes 31 degrees to 36 degrees, under the name, in honor of that king, of Carolina. As Heath did nothing under it, a renewal was granted in 1663 to eight Lords Proprietors, and an enlargement to 36 degrees 30 seconds and 29 degrees, two years afterwards." [29]

This assertion is also borne out by Ashe in his quotation from Sir Robert Heath's patent, dated October 30, 1629, which granted the territory "between 31 and 36 degrees of north latitude" to Heath, and says: " 'Know that we . . . do erect and incorporate them into a Province, and name the same *Carolana,* or the *Province of Carolana.* ' " [30]

"The fixing of the name Carolana upon the coast and interior regions between the 31st and 36th degrees of north latitude dates from the charter granted by Charles I of England to Sir Robert Heath, his attorney general, on October 30, 1629. . . . Afterward Carolina came to be applied to the coastal domain, and Carolana to the interior as far as the Mississippi." [31]

[28] *Epochs of American History: The Colonies, 1492-1750, Tenth Edition Revised,* Reuben Gold Thwaites (Longmans, Green, and Company, New York, 1897) p. 33, 88, 89.

[29] *A Sketch of North Carolina* (The Lucas-Richardson Company, Charleston, South Carolina. No date of publication is recorded.) p. 4.

[30] *History of North Carolina,* Samuel A'Court Ashe (Charles L. Van Noppen, Greensboro, North Carolina, 1908) vol. I, p. 50.

[31] *History of South Carolina,* edited by Yates Snowden (The Lewis Publishing Company, Chicago and New York, 1920) vol. I, p. 31.

The territory was divided into North and South Carolina by the Lords Proprietors in 1665,[32] yet this division corresponded roughly to the two districts previously colonized; one by colonists from Virginia, settling at Albemarle in 1653, and the other by colonists from the English community on the island of Barbados, settling at Clarendon in 1664.[33]

As to the meaning of the word *Carolina*, W. Robertson's Dictionary says that the word *Carolina* (*Carlina*) is a Latin feminine noun meaning *the Chameleon or the white thistle*.[34]

The *New English Dictionary* derives the term *Carline*, said to be the same word as *Carolina*, from the expression *Carolus Magnus*, the Latin name of *Charlemagne*. It also gives Carline as a noun denoting *a genus of composite plants closely allied to the thistles*, and hence generally called the *Carline Thistle*.[35]

Murray further states that *Caroline* used as an adjective may mean of or pertaining to Charles; of Charles the Great (Charlemagne); and of Charles I and II of England, or their periods.[36]

The English name *Charles* is derived from the Latin term *Carolus* which is the latinized form of the German word *Carl*, meaning *strong, stout, courageous*, and *valiant*.[37]

---

[32] *The New International Encyclopaedia*, Second Edition (Dodd, Mead and Company, New York, 1930) vol. 17, p. 222.

[33] *Epochs of American History: The Colonies, 1492-1750*, Reuben Gold Thwaites (Longmans, Green, and Company, New York, 1910) p. 88-90.

[34] *Gouldman Dictionary, Latin and English: A Copious Dictionary in Three Parts*, W. Robertson (John Hayes, Printer to the University, Cambridge, England, 1674). This dictionary is not paged. See the words *Carolina* and *Carline*.

[35] *A New English Dictionary*, edited by James A. H. Murray (The Clarendon Press, Oxford, England) vol. II¹, p. 121.

[36] *Ibidem*, p. 126.

[37] *An Etymological Dictionary of Family and Christian Names*, William Arthur (Sheldon, Blakeman and Company, New York, 1857) p. 94.
For other explanations of the origin and meaning of the word *Charles*, see *An Etymological Dictionary of Modern English*, Ernest Weekley (John Murray, London, 1921) p. 282.

STATES NAMED AFTER NOTED PERSONS OTHER
THAN KINGS AND QUEENS

The District of Columbia

Both the *District of Columbia* and the *District of Alaska* are possessions of the United States with no elective franchise, directly under the control of Congress. [38]

A district to be used as the site of the National Capitol was provided for in the Constitution of the United States. This document provides, among other powers, that Congress shall "exercise exclusive Legislation in all Cases whatsoever, over such District (not exceeding ten Miles square) as may, by Cession of particular States, and the Acceptance of Congress, become the Seat of Government of the United States." [39] Thus it becomes evident that in the Constitution, the word district was first used to apply to the body of land upon which the Capital City of the Federal Government is built.

The name *Territory of Columbia* was given to the future *District of Columbia* as early as January 24, 1791. [40]

"The first mention of the name 'District of Columbia' in an Act of Congress is in the title, but not in the body, of 'An act authorizing a loan for the use of the city of Washington, in the District of Columbia, and for other purposes therein mentioned,' approved May 6, 1796." [41]

[38] *A New English Dictionary,* edited by James A. H. Murray (The Clarendon Press, Oxford, England) vol. III², p. 535.

[39] *The Constitution of the United States—1787,* article 1, section 8, sub-section 17, *United States Code, Compact Edition, Comprising the Laws of a General and Permanent Nature as Embodied in the Code of the Laws of the United States, and Supplements as Corrected, Amended and Supplemented to December 3, 1928, together with Tables and Index* (West Publishing Company, St. Paul, Minnesota, 1928) p. xvi.

[40] *History of Western Maryland,* J. Thomas Scharf (Louis H. Everts, Philadelphia, Pennsylvania, 1882) vol. I, p. 693.

[41] A letter from Danial E. Garges, Secretary to the Board of Commissioners of the District of Columbia, Washington, D.C., April 18, 1930.

The *District of Columbia* was named after Christopher Columbus, the discoverer of America. [42] The word *Columbus* is a Latin masculine noun, meaning *a male dove or pigeon*. [43] *Columba* is the feminine form of the noun *Columbus*. [44] *Columba* used figuratively as a term of endearment, signifies *my dove*. *Columbia*, a new Latin form derived from the noun *Columbus*, is a poetical name for the United States of America. [45]

The term district is derived from the Latin word *districtus*, the past participle of the verb *distringere*, denoting *to draw asunder*. District originally meant the territory under the jurisdiction of a feudal lord, but as it is used in the expression, *District of Columbia*, it signifies *a division of the country directly under the control of Congress, and having no elective franchise*. [46] The literal meaning of the name *District of Columbia* is *the territory of or belonging to the United States* (Columbia).

Pennsylvania

Pennsylvania was named by King Charles II in honor of William Penn's father. Penn gives the following account of the naming of the State in a letter to his friend Robert Turner, dated January 5, 1681:

". . . this day my country has confirmed to me under the great seal of England, with large powers and privileges, by the name of Pennsylvania; *a name the king would give it in honour of my father*. I chose New Wales, being, as this, a pretty hilly country, but Penn being Welsh for *a head*, as . . . Penn in Buckinghamshire, the

[42] *King's Handbook of the United States,* planned and edited by Moses King, text by M. F. Sweetser (Moses King Corporation, Publishers, Buffalo, New York, 1891) p. 150.

[43] *A Latin-English Dictionary,* Reverend John T. White and Reverend J. E. Riddle (Longmans, Green, Longmans Company, London, 1862) p. 332.

[44] *Ibidem,* p. 332.

[45] *The Century Dictionary and Cyclopedia* (The Century Company, New York, 1911) vol. 2, p. 1114.

[46] *A New English Dictionary,* James A. H. Murray (The Clarendon Press, Oxford, England) vol. III², p. 535.

highest land in England, [they] called this Pennsylvania, which is the *high or head woodlands;* for I proposed, when the Secretary, a Welshman, refused to have it called New Wales, *Sylvania,* and they added *Penn* to it; and though I much opposed it, and went to the King to have it struck out and altered, he said it was past, . . . nor could twenty guineas move the under secretary to vary the name; for I feared lest it should be looked upon as a vanity in me, and not as a respect in the King, as it truly was, to my father, whom he often mentions with praise." [47]

The name *Pennsylvania* is made up of two words. The first one *penn* (pen), an old Celtic term, means *a head* or *a head-land;* [48] and *sylvania,* the second one, is a Neo-Latin feminine place-name coming from the Latin word *sylvanus,* or *silvanus* meaning *relating to a forest,* which in turn is derived from the Latin name *silva,* or *sylva,* denoting *a wood forest.* [49]

Penn's interpretation of the name *Pennsylvania* as *a high* or *head woodland* is correct; but the term is commonly thought to mean *Penn's woods,* or *Penn's forest.*

Delaware

The State of Delaware was named after the Delaware river, which in turn received its name from the bay. Captain Samuel Argall, having been driven by a storm out of his course while he was on his way from England to Virginia, [50] sighted and named Delaware bay in honor of Thomas West, Lord De La Warr, or Delaware, the first governor of Virginia.

The white settlers called the native Lenape Indians the *River Indians,* but they were also called the Delawares.

[47] *William Penn, Founder of Pennsylvania,* John William Graham (Headley Brothers, Limited, London, 1917) p. 130.

[48] *The Place-Names of the English People at Home and Overseas,* Max John Christian Meiklejohn (Meiklejohn and Sons, Limited, London, 1929) p. 23.

[49] *The New International Encyclopaedia,* Second Edition (Dodd, Mead and Company, New York, 1930) vol. 18, p. 291.

[50] *A History of Delaware,* Walter A. Powell (The Christopher Publishing House, Boston, Massachusetts, 1928) p. 29-30.

These Indians gave to the river the name *Kit-hanne*, meaning *Great river*. They also called it the *Lenape-wihittuck*, signifying *river of the Lenape*. [51]

Hamilton B. Staples says that the claim that the bay and the river were named after the Delaware Indians, who in 1600 dwelt upon their shores, is unfounded. He further states that the Indian name for the Delaware river was *Lenapehittuck*, signifying *Lenape river*. [52]

Lord Delaware was descended from "an old noble family which derived its name from an estate called La Warre (or Warwick), in Gloucestershire, England." [53] Some of the varied forms of the name are: *Delaware, De La Warr, De la War*, and *De la Warre*.

War, the first part of the word *Warwick*, is a French term, the old French spelling being *werre*. The fundamental meaning of the word in the various forms through which it has passed is *strife, war, broil*, or *confusion*. The name *wick* means *a town*, and comes from the Latin word *uīcus*, signifying *a village*. [54]

Skeat gives *wick*, in connection with some place-names, as a Scandinavian or Icelandic word, one meaning of which is *a small creek, inlet*, or *bay*. [55]

Mawer says that the word *wīc* is an Old English term primarily meaning *a dwelling-place, abode*, or *quarters*. [56] In the *Publications of the English Place-Name Society*,

---

[51] *History of Delaware, Past and Present,* edited by Wilson Lloyd Bevan (Lewis Historical Publishing Company, Incorporated, New York, 1929) vol. 1, p. 20.

[52] "The Origin of the Names of the States of the Union," Hamilton B. Staples, in the *Proceedings of the American Antiquarian Society,* New Series (Press of Charles Hamilton, Worchester, Massachusetts, 1882) vol. 1, p. 369.

[53] *Appleton's New Practical Cyclopedia,* New and Revised Edition (D. Appleton and Company, New York, 1920) vol. 2, p. 162.

[54] *An Etymological Dictionary of the English Language,* New Edition, Revised and Enlarged, Reverend Walter William Skeat (The Clarendon Press, Oxford, England, 1910) p. 701.

[55] *Ibidem,* p. 714.

[56] *The Chief Elements Used in English Place-Names, Being the Second Part of the Introduction to the Survey of English Place-Names,* edited by Allen Mawer (The University Press, Cambridge, England, 1924) p. 64-5.

Volume 1, Part 2, he says that apart from the place-names "which are on estuaries or creeks or bays, there is no evidence for the existence of such a word in OE [Old English] and as these names are all capable of explanation with the ordinary *wic*, we should probably rest content with that." [56]

New York

When Governor Stuyvesant surrendered Fort Amsterdam to the English in 1664, the whole of the Dutch territory in America came into the possession of the English Crown. The King of England granted to his brother, James, Duke of York and Albany, a patent covering all this territory. The burgomasters proclaimed Richard Nicolls "deputy governor for the Duke of York; in compliment to whom he directed that the city of New Amsterdam should thenceforth be known as 'New York.'" [57]

Ignorant of the fact that the Duke of York had granted New Jersey to Berkeley and Carteret, "Nicholls gave to the region west of the Hudson the name of 'Albania,' and to Long Island that of 'Yorkshire,' so as 'to comprehend all the titles' of the Duke of York." [58]

According to *The Story Key to Geographic Names,* "New York, (nū yôrk) the state and the city, and also the city of York in Pennsylvania, were named after a county in England. It took a long while and many changes to simmer the word down to the short and snappy form it has now. To begin with it was *Eburacum,* a Celtic term related to *labar,* a word meaning muddy bottom. By and by this was changed to *Eboracum,* and then, in the Anglo-Saxon, [the name] became *Eoforwic,* which meant a 'wild-boar town.' In changing the form the original meaning was forgotten." [59] When the Danes came to England, they, finding Eoforwic clumsy to say, changed the form of the

[57] *History of the State of New York,* John Romeyn Brodhead (Harper and Brothers, New York, 1853) vol. I, p. 743.

[58] *Ibidem,* p. 745.

[59] *The Story Key to Geographic Names,* O. C. von Engeln and Jane McKelway Urquhart (D. Appleton and Company, New York, 1924) p. 63.

word to *Jorvik.* "From *Jorvik* to *York* was an easy change, and about as far as one could go in shortening the word." [59]

Other accounts of the origin of the word *York* are as follows:

"The old Romano-British name for York was *Eboracum.* The English, on getting hold of this name, made the *Eborac* into *Eoforwic,* which appeared to mean the *wīc* or *town of the wild-boar,* and from which our modern name is derived. . . . Eoforwic, pronounced hurriedly, easily slides into 'York.' . . . The Archbishop of York still signs —'Ebor.' " [60]

William Arthur, basing his information on Richard Verstegan's *A Restitution of Decayed Intelligence, in Antiquities,* derived the name of the State "from *Eure-ric* or *Eouer-ric,* of *Euere,* a wild boar, and *ryc,* a refuge; a retreat from the wild boars which were in the forest of Gautries. The Romans called the city *Eboracum;* it is memorable for the death of two emperors, Severus and Comstantius Chlorus, and for the nativity of Constantine the Great." [61]

The *New English Dictionary* traces the word through the following forms: Old English Eoforwíc, later Eferwic, Euerwic: Middle English, Everwik, also Yerk, . . . Latin Eboracum. [62]

The name *New York* is composed of the prefix *New* and the name *York.* The present form of the word *new* evidently came from the Old English *niwe, niowe, néowe.* The common Aryan stem *new(j)* appears in the Greek form νέος, the Sanscrit form *návyas* or *navas,* and in the Latin form *novus,* meaning *not existing before, of recent origin or growth, young,* or *recent.* [63]

[60] *The Place-Names of the English People at Home and Overseas,* Max John Christian Meiklejohn (Meiklejohn and Son, Limited, London, 1929) p. 8.

[61] *An Etymological Dictionary of Family and Christian Names,* William Arthur (Sheldon, Blakeman and Company, New York, 1857). p. 270.

[62] *A New English Dictionary,* edited by James A. H. Murray (The Clarendon Press, Oxford, England) vol. X⁵, p. 68.

[63] *A New English Dictionary,* edited by James A. H. Murray (The Clarendon Press, Oxford, England) vol. VI⁵, p. 113.

Washington

On March 2, 1853, the territory of Washington was named for George Washington, the first President of the United States. In a petition to Congress framed by the delegates of the citizens of northern Oregon on October 25, 1852, it was suggested that the territory be named the *Territory of Columbia*. When the bill came up for consideration in the House of Representatives on February 8, 1853, Representative Stanton of Kentucky suggested that, since there was already a *District of Columbia*, the name of the new territory be changed to Washington, saying that he desired to see "a sovereign State bearing the name of the Father of his Country." [64] A motion was made to strike out the word *Columbia* and to insert the word *Washington*, which was done.

An early form of the name *Washington* is *Wessingatun*, which seems to have been used about 946-955 A.D., [65] according to the *Publications of the English Place-Name Society*, Volume 6, Part 1. This publication discourages the idea that the words *waesc, waesse . . . wase*, denoting *marshy land*, are a part of the name *Washington*, for the English Washington, it points out, is situated on a "spur of the downs, well out of the valley below. The soil of the valley is largely sand, so that neither from the site of Washington itself nor from the neighbourhood are we justified in looking for any word waesc, *waesse*, ... or wase denoting marshy land as part of the name." [66] Mawer and Stenton also explain that the occasional variant vowel in the early forms of the word leading to the replacing of *ss* by *sh* was confused with the common words *gewaesc* and *waescan*, Middle English *wasshe, wesshe*. [67] The word Washington is composed of a personal name, *Wassa*, plus

[64] *History of the State of Washington*, Edmond S. Meany (The Macmillan Company, New York, 1924) p. 156-8.

[65] "The Place-Names of Sussex," A. Mawer and F. M. Stenton, *Publications of the English Place-Name Society* (The University Press, Cambridge, England, 1929) vol. 6, part 1, p. 240-2.

[66] *Ibidem*, p. 241.

[67] *Ibidem*, p. 241-2.

the syllable *ing,* plus the suffix *ton.* [68] The termination *ing* in place names signifies "the settlement of a family or clan community, in certain cases possibly the descendants of some one man." [69] The suffix *ton* or *tun* means "primarily a piece of ground surrounded by a hedge or [a] rough palisade, inside [of] which there might or might not be placed a dwelling." [70] It also carried the idea of a farm; [70] consequently the name *Washington* means *farm* or *settlement of the people of Wassa.* [71]

STATES NAMED AFTER ENGLISH LOCALITIES

New Hampshire

Captain John Mason gave the name *New Hampshire* to his part of the grant including the territory now contained in this State, made by the Council of Plymouth in 1629. Prior to his coming to America, Captain Mason was governor of the town of Portsmouth in Hampshire, England; therefore he named the new territory for his "office and residence in that capacity." [72]

The name Hampshire comes from an old Anglo-Saxon word *Hamtūnscīr.* [73] Hām, the first element in this word, means *a home, a dwelling, or a house;* [74] *tūn,* the second

---

[68] "The Place-Names of Sussex," A. Mawer and F. M. Stenton, *Publications of the English Place-Name Society* (The University Press, Cambridge, England, 1929) vol. 6, part 1, p. 241-2.

[69] *The Place-Names of the English People at Home and Overseas,* Max John Christian Meiklejohn (Meiklejohn and Son, Limited, London, 1929) p. 89.

[70] *Ibidem,* p. 80, 81.

[71] "The Place-Names of Sussex," A. Mawer and F. M. Stenton, *Publications of the English Place-Name Society* (The University Press, Cambridge, England, 1929) vol. 6, part 1, p. 242.

[72] *New Hampshire, Resources, Attractions, and Its People: A History,* Hobart Pillsbury (The Lewis Historical Publishing Company, Incorporated, New York, 1927) vol. 1, p. 41.
History of New Hampshire, Everett S. Stackpole (The American Historical Society, New York, 1916) vol. 1, p. 12-13.

[73] *Century Cyclopedia of Names,* edited by Benjamin E. Smith (The Century Company, New York, 1911) vol. 11, p. 478.

[74] *A Concise Anglo-Saxon Dictionary, for the Use of Students,* Second Edition, Revised and Enlarged, John Richard Clark Hall (The University Press, Cambridge, England, 1916) p. 145.

element, denotes *a garden, a field, a yard,* or *an enclos-ure;* [75] *scīr,* the final syllable of the word, means *a district, a diocese, a see, a province, a shire,* or *a parish.* [76] From the suffix *scīr* the word *shire* is derived which in turn is used as a suffix on the names of the geographical divisions of England corresponding to the county divisions of most of the states of the United States.

There are two separate Old English words which form the element *ham* or *hamp* in the English place names of today. The first is *hām,* spelled with a long *a,* meaning *home,* and pronounced as is the present Scotch word *hame.* "The other word, *hamm,* signifies *an enclosed possession or fold,* and very specially *the land enclosed in the fold of a stream.*" [77] The English word *hem,* meaning *to shut in,* is akin to the word *hamm.*

It is an evident fact that the words *ham* and *hamm* are closely related; but for all practical purposes, it is best to disregard hair-splitting distinctions and to accept the meaning common to both words, which is *a permanent dwelling place.* [78]

The etymology of the word *new* is given under the discussion of the topic *New York,* which see.

New Jersey

The naming of New Jersey is significant both to the historian and to the philologist.

"The province, now the State, of New Jersey (NL *Nova Caesarea*) was so named in 1664, in the grant to the proprietors, Lord Berkeley and Sir George Carteret, after the Island of Jersey, which Sir George Carteret had defended

---

[75] *A Concise Anglo-Saxon Dictionary, for the Use of Students,* Second Edition, Revised and Enlarged, John Richard Clark Hall (The University Press, Cambridge England, 1916) p. 302.

[76] *Ibidem,* p. 255.

[77] *The Place-Names of the English People at Home and Overseas,* Max John Christian Meiklejohn (Meiklejohn and Son, Limited. London, 1929) p. 82.

[78] *Ibidem.* p. 82-3.

against the Long Parliament." [79]   Carteret was a native of
the Isle of Jersey.

It is interesting to note that the province of New Jersey
was formerly called *New Canary,* and that its Indian name
was *Scheyichlie.* [80]

Philip Falle, basing his statement on Camden's *De
Insulis Britannicis,* page 854, gives the derivation of the
term *Jersey* as a corruption of the term *Caesarea.* He says
that in the language of the northern nations who overran
England about the eighth century A.D., *ey,* the suffix of
the word *Jersey,* meant an *island,* and that *jer* or *ger* is a
contraction of *Caesar;* [81] therefore the name Jersey means
the island of Caesar, or *Caesar's Island.* Other forms of
the name of the island are *Gersey, Gearsey, Jarsey, Jarsy,
Jarzie,* and *Jerseye.*

For the derivation of the word *new,* see the discussion
of the word under the topic *New York.*

State Names Derived from the Latin Language

Of the state names having Latin origins, the following
have been considered earlier in this chapter: the Carolinas,
the District of Columbia, Louisiana, Maryland, New
Jersey, Pennsylvania, Virginia, and West Virginia.

Montana

On February 11, 1863, the name of the State Montana,
was recommended to Senator Sumner by James M. Ashley,
Chairman of the Congressional Committee on Territories.
Senator Sumner questioned there being such a word as

[79] *The Century Dictionary and Cyclopedia* (The Century Company,
New York, 1911) vol. 5, p. 3227.

[80] *The History of New Jersey from Its Earliest Settlements to the
Present Time,* John O. Raum (John E. Potter and Company, Philadelphia,
Pennsylvania, 1877) vol. 1, p. 41.

[81] *Caesarea, or an Account of Jersey,* Philip Falle (Printed for T.
Wooton, London, 1734) p. 3.

Montana, whereupon Ashley then looked up the word and showed it to the Senator. [82]

The word *Montana* is a Latin neuter noun meaning *mountainous regions.* [83]

"The name was a happy conception, being at once euphonious and descriptive of the rugged country it was destined to designate." [84]

The name *Montana* was used ages ago by the Latin authors to designate the rocky mountainous lands of Western Europe. It is now applied to "the American Land of the Mountains," [85] thus retaining its original meaning.

STATE NAMES DERIVED FROM THE FRENCH LANGUAGE

Maine

It is difficult to trace the name of the State of Maine to a definite source, or to say why it was so named because during the period of exploration several different nations were exploring this region of the country and making grants which overlapped. [86]

The account of the discovery of Vinland by Leif Ericsson [87] about the year 1000 A.D. gives a possibility that he and his voyagers were the first to see the coast of Maine. John Cabot probably sighted its shores on his second

[82] *Contributions to the Historical Society of Montana with Its Transactions, Officers, and Members* (The Independent Publishing Company, Helena, Montana, 1907) vol. 6, p. 171.

[83] *Harper's Latin Dictionary,* Revised, Enlarged and in Great Part Rewritten by Charleton T. Lewis and Charles Short (Harper and Brothers, New York, 1879) p. 1163.

[84] *A History of Montana,* Helen Fitzgerald Sanders (The Lewis Publishing Company, Chicago and New York, 1913) vol. 1, p. 19.

[85] *Montana, Its Story and Biography,* under the editorial supervision of Tom Stout (The American Historical Society, Chicago and New York, 1921) vol. 1, p. 1.

[86] *A Gazetteer of the State of Maine with Numerous Illustrations,* George J. Varney (B. B. Russell, Boston, Massachusetts, 1881) p. 36-7.

[87] *The Encyclopaedia Britannica,* Fourteenth Edition (Encyclopaedia Britannica, Incorporated, New York, 1929) vol. 14, p. 689.

voyage in 1498. The next explorer, Giovanni da Varazzano or Verrazano, an Italian sent out by the King of France, visited this territory in 1524, and called the entire coast New France. [88]

Some time after 1497 the French, on exploring this region, called the southern part of it west of the Kennebec river *Maine* and the eastern part *Acadie*. [89]

As to the fixing of the name, William Darby states that although the English were the first to effectively colonize this territory about 1635, "the name was given by still earlier, but transient settlers from France." [90]

William Arthur states that the word *Main* or *Mayne* is derived from a French province by the same name, that the term *magne* means *great, large, rich, powerful,* and that it is the same in meaning as the Latin word *magnus*. [91]

According to the *Century Cyclopedia of Names,* the word *Maine* is derived from the French language, "perhaps from the second element of the Old Celtic name (Latin Cenomanni)," which was the name of the country of the ancient Cenomanni situated in Northern France. [92]

On August 10, 1622, [93] the Council of New England granted to Sir Ferdinando Gorges and Captain John Mason, jointly "all that part [94] of ye maine land in New England lying vpon ye Sea Coast betwixt ye rivers of Merimack & Sagadahock and to ye furtherest heads of ye said Rivers and soe forwards up into the land westward untill threescore miles be finished from ye first entrace of

[88] *Universal Cyclopaedia and Atlas,* Charles Kendall Adams (D. Appleton and Company, New York, 1905) vol. 7, p. 448.

[89] *The Penny Cyclopaedia of the Society for the Diffusion of Useful Knowledge* (Charles Knight and Company, London, 1839) vol. 14, p. 308.

[90] *View of the United States, Historical, Geographical, and Statistical,* William Darby (H. S. Tanner, Philadelphia, Pennsylvania, 1828) p. 531.

[91] *An Etymological Dictionary of Family and Christian Names,* William Arthur (Sheldon, Blakeman and Company, New York, 1857) p. 189.

[92] *The Century Cyclopedia of Names,* edited by Benjamin E. Smith (The Century Company, New York, 1911) vol. 11, p. 643.

[93] *Documentary History of the State of Maine, Volume VII, Containing The Farnham Papers, 1603-1688,* compiled by Miss Mary Frances Farnham (The Thurston Print, Portland, Maine, 1901) p. 65

[94] *Ibidem,* p. 67.

the aforesaid rivers," which they, says the grant, "with the consent of ye President & Councell intend to name ye PROVINCE OF MAINE." [95] This is said to have been the first use of the phrase *Province of Maine* in any printed document. [96]

Later, in 1639 the king confirmed this grant, specifying " 'that Gorges' "portion of the mainland" should forever hereafter be called and named the *Province* or *County of Maine,* and not by any other name or names whatsoever.' " [97]

Several authorities say that the name *Maine* was given to the mainland in contradistinction to the many islands which break up the coast, and several of the encyclopedias accept this origin of the name. [98]

William Durkee Williamson agrees with the French and with the mainland origins of the naming of the territory. [99] He implies that the names *the Main, Mayne, Mayn,* or *Meyne,* [100] were given to the mainland before the

[95] *Ibidem,* p. 68.
Maine: Resources, Attractions, and Its People: A History, Harrie Badger Coe, Editor (The Lewis Historical Publishing Company, Incorporated, New York, 1928) vol. 1, p. 24.

[96] *Origin of the Name of Maine,* Albert Matthews, reprinted from *the Publications of The Colonial Society of Massachusetts, Volume XII* (John Wilson and Son, The University Press, Cambridge, Massachusetts, 1910) p. 371.
Maine: Resources, Attractions, and Its People: A History, Harrie Badger Coe, Editor (The Lewis Historical Publishing Company, Incorporated, New York, 1928) vol. 1, p. 24.

[97] *Maine: Resources, Attractions, and Its People: A History,* Harrie Badger Coe, Editor (The Lewis Historical Publishing Company, Incorporated, New York, 1928) vol. 1, p. 25.

[98] *The New International Encyclopaedia,* Second Edition (Dodd, Mead and Company, New York, 1923) vol. 14, p. 682.
The Century Cyclopedia of Names, edited by Benjamin E. Smith (The Century Company, New York, 1911) vol. 11, p. 643.
The Encyclopedia Americana (Americana Corporation, New York and Chicago, 1929) vol. 18, p. 142.
The World Book, M. V. O'Shea, Editor-in-chief (W. F. Quarrie and Company, Chicago, New York, and Toronto, 1927) vol. 6, p. 3606.
The Universal Cyclopaedia and Atlas, Charles Kendall Adams (D. Appleton and Company, New York, 1905) vol. 7, p. 445.

[99] *The History of the State of Maine from Its First Discovery A. D. 1602, to the Separation, A. D. 1820, Inclusive,* William D. Williamson (Glazier, Masters, and Smith, Hallowell, Maine, 1839) vol. 1, p. 277.

[100] *Ibidem,* p. 277.

use of the term in the charter of 1622. He further states that in the grant of the territory in the charter of 1639, " 'all the islands and inlets within five leagues of the Main' " [101] are included. James Sullivan affirms that the name was given by Gorges in compliment to the queen of King Charles I of England, who granted the patent, the name being given in honor of the *Province of Mayne* in France, which province was a private estate of the wife of King Charles I. [102]

The best statement of a probable reconciliation of these two theories is that given by Varney who says that the province was named for the French *Province of Meyne* (now Province of Maine), but "the fishermen of New England, at the time, no doubt thought the name was an adoption of their own term of 'main,' used to distinguish a coast from the neighboring islands." [103]

D. B. Warden, along with others, says that "the old voyagers and historians gave to this country the name of *Mavoshen* or *Mavooshen*, . . . also named in honor of the wife of [King] Charles I, who had a domain of the same name in France, her native country. This wife was Henrietta Maria, daughter of Henry IV, King of France." [104]

Vermont

Historians do not agree as to who named the Territory of Vermont. It was probably named by Samuel de Champlain, for "upon the map of his discoveries which

[101] *A History of the State of Maine from Its First Discovery A.D. 1602, to the Separation, A.D. 1820, Inclusive,* Williamson D. Williamson (Glazier, Masters, and Smith Hallowell, Maine, 1839) vol. 1, p. 272.

[102] *The History of the District of Maine,* James Sullivan (Printed by I. Thomas and E. T. Andrews, Boston, Massachusetts, 1795) p. 307.

[103] *A Gazetteer of the State of Maine with Numerous Illustrations,* George J. Varney (B. B. Russell, Boston, Massachusetts, 1881) p. 7.

[104] *L'Art de Vérifier les Dates, Depuis l'Année 1770 jusqu'à nos Jours,* Quatrième Partie, D. B. Warden (Imprimerie de Bruneau, Paris, France, 1842) tome dix-septième (17) p. 440.

The original passage reads as follows: "Les anciens voyageurs et historiens donnaient à ce pays le nom de *Mavoshen* ou *Mavooshen* . . . ainsi nommé en l'honneur de l'épouse de Charles Ier, qui avait un domaine du même nom en France, son pays natal. Cette épouse était Henriette-Marie, fille du Henri IV, roi de France."

Champlain made later, he called the mountains he had seen in the east, 'Verd Mont' or Green Mountains, the name probably suggested by the dense growth of evergreen trees which covered their slopes. . . ." [105]

Ira Allen states that the name *Vermont* "was given to the district of the New Hampshire Grants, as an emblematical one, from the French of *Verd-mont,* green mountains, intended to perpetuate the name of the Green Mountain Boys, by Dr. Thomas Young, of Philadelphia, who greatly interested himself in behalf of the settlers of Vermont. . . ." [106]

The reference is to the name "Green Mountain Boys," taken by the military forces defending the New Hampshire grants when, about 1767 to 1769, the Governor of New York threatened to drive them into the Green Mountains. [107] This was at the time when the State of New York attempted to seize the Territory of New Hampshire by virtue of "a grant from King Charles II to his brother James Duke of York, containing 'all the lands from the west side of [the] Connecticut river, to the east side of the Delaware bay.' " [108]

The story of the christening of this land by the Reverend Samuel Peters [109] is denied either in part or as a whole by some of the authorities. [110]

Another mooted question in this connection is whether the words *alias Vermont* appear after the name *New Connecticut* in the Proceedings of the Convention of January 15, 1777, declaring the independence of Vermont. [111]

[105] *Vermont for Young Vermonters,* Miriam Irene Kimball (D. Appleton and Company, New York, 1904) p. 8.

[106] *The Natural and Political History of the State of Vermont,* Ira Allen (Printed by J. W. Myers, London, 1798) p. 86.

[107] *Ibidem,* p. 27.

[108] *Ibidem,* p. 22.

[109] "The Story of Vermont," John L. Heaton, *The Story of the States* (D. Lothrop Company, Boston, Massachusetts, 1889) p. 37.

[110] *History of Vermont, Natural, Civil, and Statistical, in Three Parts,* with an Appendix, Zadock Thompson (Published by the Author; Stacy and Jameson, Printers, Burlington, Vermont, 1853) part 1, chap. 1, p. 4.

[111] *Vermont Historical Society Collections* (Printed for the Society by J. and J. M. Poland, Printers, Montpelier, Vermont, 1870) vol. 1, p. 40.

Slade's State Papers quotes the document with the words inserted. [112] The *Vermont Historical Society Collections* questions the authenticity of this fact on the grounds that the name *New Connecticut* was used alone and that on the fourth of June of the following year the name was changed to Vermont. [113]

The origin of the word *Delaware* is also French, but it has been previously accounted for under the discussion of the naming of Delaware.

STATE NAMES DERIVED FROM THE SPANISH LANGUAGE

California

There is a great deal of conjecture on the part of historians as to when and by whom California was named. Greenhow says that it was named by the Spaniards in 1536, [114] the year after the discovery of the peninsula by Cortes. [115] It is the opinion of Dr. Edward Everett Hale that Cortes, when he discovered the peninsula in 1535, named it *California*. He bases his statement on Antonio de Herrera's *Historia General de los Hechos de los Castellanos,* Decade VIII, Book VI. [116]

Venegas says that the oldest use of the name *California* is that by Bernal Diaz, who applied it to the bay alone. [117]

[112] *Vermont State Papers, . . . from the Year 1779 to 1786, Inclusive,* compiled and published by William Slade (J. W. Copeland, Printers, Middlebury, Vermont, 1823) p. 70.

[113] *Vermont Historical Society Collections* (Printed for the Society by J. and J. M. Poland, Printers, Montpelier, Vermont, 1870) vol. 1, p. 40.

[114] *The Geography of Oregon and California, and the Other Territories on the North-west Coast of North America,* Robert Greenhow (Mark H. Newman, New York, 1845) p. 12.

[115] *The History of Oregon and California and Other Territories on the North-west Coast of North America,* Robert Greenhow (Charles C. Little and James Brown, Boston, Massachusetts, 1844) p. 55.

[116] "The Name of California," Edward Everett Hale, in the *Proceedings of the American Antiquarian Society* (John Wilson and Son, Boston, Massachusetts, 1862) p. 45.

[117] *Noticia de la California y de su Conquista,* Miguel Venegas (Viuda de Manuel Fernandez, Madrid, Spain, 1757) vol. 1, p. 1-2.

Later on, the name was given to the whole peninsula; and finally to what is now the State of California. [118]

Dr. Hale points out the fact that "twenty-five years before Cortes discovered the American California, [119] the name appeared, with precisely the" present-day spelling, in a Spanish romance called *Las Sergas de Esplandian*, a book written by García Ordoñez de Montalvo, and first published in 1510 or 1511. The original passage which contains this name is translated thus:

"Know that, on the right hand of the Indies, there is an island called California, very near to the Terrestrial Paradise, which was peopled with black women, without any men among them, because they were accustomed to live after the fashion of Amazons. They were of strong and hardened bodies, of ardent courage, and of great force." [120]

It is Dr. Hale's opinion that the Spanish explorers being acquainted with Montalvo's romance and believing that they had come to the island " 'on the right side of the Indies, near the Terrestrial Paradise,' " [121] named the supposed island *California*.

There is much conjecture and ingenious speculation on the part of writers about the origin and significance of the word *California*. [122]

[118] *U. S.: An Index to the United States of America,* compiled by Malcolm Townsend (D. Lothrop Company, Boston, Massachusetts, 1890) p. 54-5.

[119] "The Name of California," Edward Everett Hale, in the *Proceedings of the American Antiquarian Society* (John Wilson and Son, Boston, Massachusetts, 1862) p. 48.

[120] *Las Sergas de Esplandian,* García Ordoñez de Montalvo, in the *Biblioteca de Autores Españoles, Volume 40, Libros de Caballerías,* Don Pascual de Gayangos (M. Rivadeneyra, Madrid, Spain, 1857) chap. 157, p. 539.
The translation is that given by Dr. Hale. The passage in the original text reads as follows:
"Sabed que á la diestra mano de las Indias hubo una isla, llamada California, muy llegada á la parte del Paraíso Terrenal, la cual fué poblada de mujeres negras, sin que algum varon entre ellas hubiese, que casi como las amazonas era su estilo de vivir. Estas eran de valientes cuerpos y esforzados y ardientes corazones y de grandes fuerzas."

[121] "The Name of California," Edward Everett Hale, in the *Proceedings of the American Antiquarian Society* (John Wilson and Son, Boston, Massachusetts, 1862) p. 50-1.

[122] *U. S.: An Index to the United States of America,* compiled by Malcolm Townsend (D. Lothrop Company, Boston, Massachusetts, 1890) p. 54-5.

Some think this name is derived from the Indian words *Kali forno,* a phrase used by the Baja California natives, signifying *high hills, mountain,* or *native land.* Still another theory offered is that the name came from the old Indian word for the peninsula, *Tchalifalñi-al,* meaning *the sandy land beyond the water.* [123]

Others suppose that the word *California* is derived from one of the following Greek phrases:

Kala pho nea, Kala phora nea, Kala phor neia, Kala phorneia, Kala chora nea, and *Kalos phornia,* variously translated as *beautiful woman, moonshine* or *adultery,* and *fertile land* or *country.* [124]

Some authorities, including Dr. Hale, say that the name is derived from the Spanish word *Califa,* which in turn is derived from the Arabic name *Khalifah,* meaning *successor.* [125] This explanation fits in well with the Esplandian origin advanced by Dr. Hale, who gives the Spanish spelling of the root element of the word as *Calif,* the name of "the sovereign of the Mussulman power of the time," [126] a spelling of the word which doubtless "was in the mind of the author as he invented these Amazon allies of the Infidel power." [126]

The Latin words *calida (callida) fornax,* meaning *a hot furnace,* were the source most commonly assigned to the derivation of the word *California* before Dr. Hale's discovery. Hubert H. Bancroft suggests that this expression may signify *a hot climate,* yet he thinks that the climate of California was not as hot as that of some other places to which the explorers were accustomed. He is also of the opinion that the phrase *calida fornax* may refer to the hot baths of the natives. [127]

[123] *U.S.: An Index to the United States of America,* compiled by Malcolm Townsend (D. Lothrop Company, Boston, Massachusetts, 1890) p. 55.

[124] *Ibidem,* p. 54.

[125] *Ibidem,* p. 54.

[126] "The Name of California," Edward Everett Hale, in the *Proceedings of the American Antiquarian Society* (John Wilson and Son, Boston, Massachusetts, 1862) p. 53.

[127] *History of the Pacific States of North America,* Hubert Howe Bancroft (A. L. Bancroft and Company, San Francisco, California, 1884) vol. 13, p. 65-6.

Don Jose Campoi, giving as the roots from which the name *California* is derived the Spanish word *cala,* meaning *a little cove of the sea,* and the Latin term *fornix,* signifying *the vault of a building,* calls attention to the fact that the early explorers were familiar with both of these languages. He believes that the name was given in commemoration of the cove-like formation near San Lucas. [128]

Colorado

Historians generally agree that Colorado was named after the Colorado river. Diaz, in 1540, called the river *Rio del Tisòn,* meaning *Firebrand river,* which name he gave to this stream "from the fact that the naked Indians of that locality carried firebrands with which to warm themselves in cold weather." [129] The duration of the name *Rio del Tison* being short, the river soon came to be known by another Spanish word, *Colorado,* signifying *reddish* or *brown color.* There seems to be no record of the exact date when the name was changed; historians merely state that the change was made, and that the word *Colorado* is "descriptive of the water [of the river] and of much of the country through which it flows." [129]

Upon the authority of Leroy R. Hafen, Uribarri in 1706 took possession of the territory of eastern Colorado in the name of King Philip V of Spain and called it *Santo Domingo* (Holy Sabbath), a "favorite Spanish name." He further states that one hundred fifty-five years later the "territory was rechristened with another Spanish name, a permanent heritage from Old Spain—Colorado." [130]

[128] *Historia de la Antigua ó Baja California,* Francisco Javier Clavijero (Juan R. Navarro, Mexico City, Mexico, 1852) p. 2.

"The Name of California," Edward Everett Hale, in the *Proceedings of the American Antiquarian Society* (John Wilson and Son, Boston, Massachusetts, 1862) p. 4.7

[129] *History of Colorado, Prepared under the Supervision of The State Historical and Natural History Society of Colorado,* James H. Baker, Editor (Linderman Company, Incorporated, Denver, Colorado, 1927) vol. I, p. 261.

[130] "Coming of the White Men: Exploration and Acquisition," Leroy R. Hafen, in the *History of Colorado, Prepared under the Supervision of the State Historical and Natural History Society of Colorado,* James H. Baker, Editor (Linderman Company, Incorporated, Denver, Colorado, 1927) vol. I, chap. vi, p. 271.

The word *Colorado* is derived from the past participle of the Spanish verb *colorar*, [131] meaning *to color*. The participial form often carries the meaning of ruddy or red. Townsend suggests that the word *Colorado* may have been derived from the term Coronado, the name of the Spanish Missionary who came into this territory from Mexico in 1540; [132] but he gives no source material upon which he bases this suggestion.

Florida

Florida was named by Ponce de Leon in 1512, from the fact that he discovered it on Easter Sunday, or from the fact that the whole region which he saw was covered with flowers. Historians say that Ponce de Leon landed on "Easter Sunday (the Pascua Florida or feast of flowers of the Roman Catholic Church)," [133] that "the name Florida was given to the country by its discoverer" [133] and that it "was afterwards bestowed upon a region indefinite in extent, covering a much larger territory than the present State includes." [133]

Another writer says that "the whole country was in the fresh bloom of spring; the trees, trellised with vines, were gay with blossoms, and fragrant with delicious odors; the fields were covered with flowers; from which circumstance, as well as having discovered it on Palm Sunday (*Pascua Florida*), he [Ponce de Leon] gave it the name Florida." [134]

The word *Florida* is a Spanish feminine adjective, meaning *flowery, covered with flowers*, or *abounding in flowers*.

[131] *The Encyclopedia Americana* (Americana Corporation, New York and Chicago, 1929) vol. 7, p. 321.

[132] *U. S.: An Index to the United States of America,* compiled by Malcolm Townsend (D. Lothrop Company, Boston, Massachusetts, 1890) p. 55.

[133] *Florida: A Pamphlet Descriptive of Its History, Topography, Climate, and Soil, Resources and Natural Advantages, in General and by Counties,* prepared in the interest of immigration by the Department of Agriculture, B. E. McLin, Commissioner (T. B. Hilson, State Printer, Tallahassee, Florida, 1904) p. 5.

[134] *The History of Hernando de Soto and Florida,* Barnard Shipp (Collins, Printer, Philadelphia, Pennsylvania, 1881) p. 78.

Pascua Florida or *Pascua de Flores* means *Feast of flowers* or *Flowery Easier; Tierra Florida* means *Flowery land;* consequently the feminine form of the adjective, *Florida,* was originally used in either case.

Nevada

It is no easy undertaking to trace the naming of the State of Nevada to any one definite source, for "various persons, at various times, have claimed the honor of having proposed the present name." [135] In February, 1858, when it was decided to form a new territory out of western Utah, the name suggested for the new territory was *Sierra Nevada.*

When the bill was introduced into the House of Representatives on May 12, 1859, the proposed territory was called the *Territory of Nevada.* On the application of this territory for admission to statehood, it was suggested that the name be changed to *Washoe, Humboldt, Esmeralda, Sierra Plata,* or *Bullion;* but the state was admitted under the name *Nevada.* [136]

The word *Nevada* is a Spanish adjective, meaning *covered with snow,* or *white as snow;* or a Spanish noun, meaning *snow-fall.* [137]

According to the accounts given in some of the outstanding encyclopedias, the name of the State was taken from the expression *Sierra Nevada* applied to the range of mountains in the western part of the State, which range in turn was named after the *Sierra Nevadas* in Spain. [138]

---

[135] "History of Nevada, Colorado, and Wyoming, 1540-1888," in *The History of the Pacific States of North America,* Hubert Howe Bancroft (The History Company, San Francisco, California, 1890) vol. 20, p. 151.

[136] *Ibidem,* p. 150-1.

[137] *Ibidem,* p. 23.

[138] *Century Cyclopedia of Names,* edited by Benjamin E. Smith (The Century Company, New York, 1911) vol. 11, p. 731.

STATE NAME DERIVED FROM THE DUTCH LANGUAGE

Rhode Island

Historians disagree as to the origin of the name *Rhode Island*. One theory is that it is derived from the two Dutch words, *Roodt Eylandt*, meaning *the red island*. The Dutch navigator Adrian Block gave this name to the island to commemorate "the fiery aspect of the place, caused by the red clay in some portions of its shores." [139] Arnold believes that by means of easy transposition *Roodt Eylandt* became *Rhode Island*.

Another theory, which is questioned by a great many of the historians and accepted by others, is based on the following passage from *Verrazano's Relation*:

"We weied Ancker, and sayled toward the East, for so the coast trended, and alwayes for 50 leagues, being in the sight thereof, wee discouered an Ilande in the forme of a triangle, distant from the maine lande 3 leagues, about the bignesse of the Ilande of the Rhodes." [140]

[139] *History of the State of Rhode Island and Providence Plantations,* Samuel Greene Arnold (D. Appleton and Company, New York, 1859) vol. 1, p. 70.

[140] *The Relation of John de Verarzanus, A Florentine, of the Lande by Him Discouered in the Name of His Maiestie, Written in Dieppe the Eight of July, 1524, in Divers Voyages Touching the Discovery of America and the Islands Adjacent,* Volume 7, collected and published by Richard Hakluyt, Prebendary of Bristol, in the year 1582, edited with notes and an introduction by John Winter Jones of the British Museum (Printed for the Hakluyt Society by Richards, Printer, London, 1850) p. 63-4.

Some of the other historians agreeing with this theory are:
History of Rhode Island, Reverend Edward Peterson (John S. Taylor, New York, 1853) p. 17.
Rhode Island: A Study in Separatism, Irving Berdine Richman (Houghton, Mifflin and Company, The Riverside Press, Cambridge, Massachusetts, 1905) p. 43-4.
Some of the historians disagreeing with this theory are:
History of the State of Rhode Island and Providence Plantations, Samuel Greene Arnold (D. Appleton and Company, New York, 1859) vol. 1, p. 70.
A History of Connecticut, Its People and Institutions, George L. Clark (G. P. Putnam's Sons, New York and London, 1914) p. 4.
State of Rhode Island and Providence Plantations at the End of the Century: A History, Edward Field, Editor (The Mason Publishing Company, Boston, Massachusetts, and Syracuse, New York, 1902) vol. 1, p. 9.

This theory is that the name *Rhode Island,* suggested by Verrazano, was given to the newly discovered island because of its supposed resemblance to the Greek island *Rhodos,* or *Rhodes,* situated in the Mediterranean Sea. The Greek name means *Island of Roses.*

The general court of Aquidneck Island changed its name to the "Isle of Rhodes or Rhode Island" on March 13, 1644. [141] In 1663 the title "Rhode Island and Providence Plantations" was given to the colony. This has persisted to the present day, but it has shortened in common usage to Rhode Island. [142]

STATE NAMES DERIVED FROM THE AMERICAN INDIAN DIALECTS

It is not possible in every instance to get the primitive forms of the Indian words from which the following state names are derived, for the Indians kept no written records which might reveal the original form of the names by which they designated the rivers, lakes, fortifications, or regions of the country from which the present state names are taken. When the explorers first visited these various regions of the United States, they heard the Indians speak these different names, and each explorer recorded the Indian name in his own language as it sounded to him, spelling it by means of his own phonetic symbols; consequently there are as many forms of the primitive Indian word from which each of the state names is derived as there were different countries making explorations.

The following twenty-six states trace the origin of their names back to American Indian dialects: Alabama, Ari-

[141] *Rhode Island: A Study in Separatism,* Irving Berdine Richman (Houghton, Mifflin and Company, The Riverside Press, Cambridge, Massachusetts, 1905) p. 43.
[142] *Rhode Island: A Study in Separatism,* Irving Berdine Richman (Houghton, Mifflin and Company, The Riverside Press, Cambridge, Massachusetts, 1905) p. 44.
History of the State of Rhode Island and Providence Plantations (1636-1700), Samuel Greene Arnold (D. Appleton and Company, New York and London, 1859) vol. I, p. 70.

zona, Arkansas, Connecticut, Idaho, Illinois, Iowa, Kansas, Kentucky, Massachusetts, Michigan, Minnesota, Mississippi, Missouri, Nebraska, New Mexico, North and South Dakota, Ohio, Oklahoma, Oregon, Tennessee, Texas, Utah, Wisconsin, and Wyoming.

Alabama

The name *Alabama* first appeared in the narratives of De Soto's expedition of the year 1540. [143] Some authorities think that *Alabama* was the name of a tribe of Indians belonging to the Creek Confederacy. [143] Others say that the name was first given to the Alabama river by the French explorers in 1714. [143]

Historians rather definitely agree that the name has been applied to the river, Indian fortifications, or Indian tribes since the days of De Soto.

When the Mississippi Territory was divided in 1817, the eastern half of it became Alabama Territory, which two years later was admitted into the Union as the State of Alabama. [144]

Thomas McAdory Owen says that the Alabama river, the principal river of the State, received its name from the "aboriginal name of a Muskhogean tribe of the Creek confederacy, whose habitat, when first known to European explorers, was in Central Alabama, [and that] the State in turn was named for the river." [145]

There are several different theories as to the origin of the name *Alabama*.

It is the opinion of recent investigators [146] that the name came from the Choctaw words *alba*, denoting *a thicket or mass of vegetation*, and *amo*, a transitive verb

---

[143] *Our State, Alabama,* compiled by Marie Bankhead Owen, *Publication of the Alabama State Department of Archives and History, Historical and Patriotic Series, Number Seven* (Birmingham Printing Company, Birmingham, Alabama, 1927) p. 137.

[144] *Ibidem,* p. 137.

[145] *History of Alabama and Dictionary of Alabama Biography,* Thomas McAdory Owen (The S. J. Clarke Publishing Company, Chicago, Illinois, 1921) vol. 1, p. 15.

[146] *Ibidem,* p. 15.

signifying *to clear, to collect, to gather up, to pick, to pull, to trim, to mow, to reap;* consequently the word *Alibamo*, made up of these two component parts means thicket clearers or vegetation gatherers. [147] Some historians think that this name was given to the "Creek tribe by the Choctaw Indians, who were their neighbors on the west. . . . At this time the Choctaw Indians were still a roving, hunting tribe or nation and applied the name 'Alabama' signifying agricultural people to these first farmers of the State as a term of derision." [148]

Allen Wright, a "highly educated Choctaw" Indian, and Professor Henry Sale Halbert, both of whom have made studies of Alabama history, accept the derivation of the name as given above. [149]

Cyrus Byington in his *Dictionary of the Choctaw Language,* defines the word *alba* as meaning *vegetation, herbs, plants, weeds,* [150] and *amo* as signifying *to pick, to pull, to trim, to mow, to reap.* [151]

Dr. William S. Wyman of Tuscaloosa, reputed to be "one of the best known students of the State" is inclined to believe that the name *Alabama* is derived from the Indian word *Ullibali,* or *Ullebehalli,* which means *Mulberry people.* [152]

Judge Alexander Beaufort Meek, a former poet and legislator of Alabama, thinks that the word came from the

[147] *History of Alabama and Dictionary of Alabama Biography,* Thomas McAdory Owen (The S. J. Clarke Publishing Company, Chicago, Illinois, 1921) vol. I, p. 15.

[148] *Our State, Alabama,* compiled by Marie Bankhead Owen, *Publication of the Alabama State Department of Archives and History, Historical and Patriotic Series, Number Seven* (Birmingham Printing Company, Birmingham, Alabama, 1927) p. 137.

[149] *History of Alabama and Dictionary of Alabama Biography,* Thomas McAdory Owen (The S. J. Clarke Publishing Company, Chicago, Illinois, 1921) vol. I, p. 15.

[150] *A Dictionary of the Choctaw Language,* Cyrus Byington, *Smithsonian Institution, Bureau of American Ethnology, Bulletin Number 46* (Government Printing Office, Washington, D.C.) p. 74.

[151] *Ibidem,* p. 80.

[152] *History of Alabama and Dictionary of Alabama Biography,* Thomas McAdory Owen (The S. J. Clarke Publishing Company, Chicago, Illinois, 1921) vol. I, p. 16.

Muscogee Indian word *Alibamo*, the name of an Indian fort, the scene of a fight between De Soto and the natives. He thinks that the Indian name means *Here we rest.* [153] Marie Bankhead Owen says that Judge Meek, basing his interpretation of the word *Alabama* upon an Indian legend, gives the origin as follows: A tribe of Indians, fleeing another warlike tribe, coming to the banks of a river, said, *Alabamo*, signifying *Here we rest.* [154]

Although this account has gained common currency, and has found its way through the State motto to the State seal, it is the opinion of Marie Bankhead Owen that "the interpretation, *'Here we rest,'* which has been accepted in our times as a true interpretation, is without historical basis and is the result of a poetic legend." [155]

General Le Clerc Milfort, who lived as a member of the Creek Nation from 1776 to 1796, in his discussion of the Creek Indians mentions the Alabama Indians fighting along the Yazoo river, and refers to a river that bears their name. [156]

Writers have recorded at least thirty-one different forms of the name *Alabama*, among which are the following: *Alibamons, Alibamus, Alibamas, Alimamu,* and *Aybamos.* [157]

Arizona

The Spaniards called the mining camp in the locality of "the famous Planchas de Plata mine" *Arizona,* thus being the first to apply the word to any part of the present

[153] *Romantic Passages in Southwestern History, Including Orations, Sketches, and Essays,* Second Edition, A. B. Meek (S. H. Goetzel and Company, New York, 1857) p. 233.

[154] *Our State, Alabama,* compiled by Marie Bankhead Owen, *Publication of the Alabama State Department of Archives and History, Historical and Patriotic Series, Number Seven* (Birmingham Printing Company, Birmingham, Alabama, 1927) p. 137.

[155] *Ibidem,* p. 137.

[156] *Memoire ou Coup-D'oeil Rapide sur Mes Differens Voyages et Mon Séjour dans la Nation Crëck,* Le Gal. Milfort (L'Imprimerie de Giguet et Michaud, Paris, France, an XI, 1802) p. 229-88.

[157] *History of Alabama and Dictionary of Alabama Biography,* Thomas McAdory Owen (The S. J. Clarke Publishing Company, Chicago, Illinois, 1921) vol. I, p. 15.

State of Arizona. They probably used the primitive form
arizonac, a Pima Indian name. [158]

The region now included in the State of Arizona was
first visited in 1539 by a negro slave, sometimes called
Black Stephen, but usually known as Estevan. Close
behind him a Spanish friar, Marcos de Niza, crossed this
same region from south-west to north-east. [159]

When, in 1854, the residents of that section of the
country now known as Arizona petioned Congress to make
this district a territory, they suggested the following
names by which it might be called: *Pimeria, Gadsonia,* and
Arizona. The name *Arizona* was chosen "because it was
supposed to be the most euphonius." [160]

On August 29, 1856, [161] a memorial was sent to Congress urging that body to grant their petition of 1854. [162]
The Territory bearing the name *Arizona* [161] was officially
sanctioned by Congress on February 24, 1863; [163] and when
this Territory was admitted as a State into the Union on
February 14, 1912, [164] the name *Arizona* was retained.

[158] "Arizona and New Mexico, 1530-1888," in *The History of the
Pacific States of North America,* Hubert Howe Bancroft (The History
Company, Publishers, San Francisco, California, 1888) vol. 12, p. 520.

[159] "Arizona and New Mexico, 1530-1888," in *The History of the
Pacific States of North America,* Hubert Howe Bancroft (The History
Company, San Francisco, California, 1888) vol. 12, p. 345.

*Papers of the Archaeological Institute of America, American Series
V, Hemenway Southwestern Archaeological Expedition, Contributions to
the History of the Southwestern Portion of the United States,* Adolph
Francis Alphonse Bandelier (John Wilson and Son, Cambridge, Massachusetts, 1890) p. 24-5.

[160] *History of Arizona,* Thomas Edwin Farish (Printed for the Author
by the Filmer Brothers Electrotype Company, Typographers and Stereo-
typers, San Francisco, California, 1915) vol. 1, p. 322.

[161] *History of the Pacific States of North America,* Hubert Howe
Bancroft (The History Company, San Francisco, California, 1888) vol. 12,
p. 504.

[162] *The Resources of Arizona,* Second Edition, Enlarged and Illustrated, compiled by Patrick Hamilton (A. L. Bancroft and Company,
Printers, San Francisco, California, 1883) p. 13.

[163] *Arizona: Prehistoric, Aboriginal, Pioneer, Modern,* James H.
McClintock (The S. J. Clarke Publishing Company, Chicago, Illinois,
1916) vol. 2, p. 313.

[164] *Ibidem,* p. 375.

There are various accounts of the origin of the word *Arizona*.

James H. McClintock points out that the name would seem to come from the two Spanish words *arida,* meaning *arid, dry,* or *barren,* and *zona,* signifying *a zone;* thus making the name denote *a dry zone or country.* He further states that this origin sounds plausible, but that there are some authorities who do not agree that the name is derived from the Spanish language. [165]

Patrick Hamilton thinks that the name *Arizona* is a corruption of the term *Arizuma* used by the early Spanish explorers. He says, too, that some believe the word in the Pima Indian language means *little creek;* while others say that it comes from the two Pima words *ari,* signifying *a maiden,* and *zon,* meaning *a valley* or *country.* This origin had its beginning in the tradition of a maiden queen who once ruled the whole Pima nation. [166] Isaac D. Smith, who gathered much information about the Papago Indians, their language, and their customs, it is said, while pioneering in the Arizona country, derives the name from the two Papago words *aleh-Zon,* meaning *young spring.* [167]

Samuel Hughes "one of the oldest of Tucson's residents," derives the name from the Indian word *arisonac,* [168] meaning *a place of chastisement.* Frederick W. Hodge, an ethnologist in the Smithsonian Institution, derives the name from the Indian term *arizonac,* the name of "a former Papago rancheria situated between Guevavi and Saric, in Sonora, Mexico, just below the present southern boundary of Arizona. He believes that the word

---

[165] *Arizona: Prehistoric, Aboriginal, Pioneer, Modern,* James H. McClintock (The S. J. Clarke Publishing Company, Chicago, Illinois, 1916) vol. I, p. I.

[166] *The Resources of Arizona,* Second Edition, Enlarged and Illustrated, compiled by Patrick Hamilton (A. L. Bancroft and Company, Printers, San Francisco, California, 1883) p. 13.

[167] *Arizona: Prehistoric, Aboriginal, Pioneer, Modern,* James H. McClintock (The S. J. Clarke Publishing Company, Chicago, Illinois, 1916) vol. I, p. 3.

[168] *Arizona: Prehistoric, Aboriginal, Pioneer, Modern,* James H. McClintock (The S. J. Clarke Publishing Company, Chicago, Illinois, 1916) vol. I, p. I.

probably signified *small springs,* or *few springs.* As to the origin of the name Arizona, he further states that "in 1736-41 the finding in its vicinity of some balls of native silver of fabulous size caused a large influx of treasure seekers, and through the fame that the place thus temporarily acquired, its name, in the form Arizona, was later applied to the entire country thereabout, and, when New Mexico was divided, was adopted as the name of the new Territory." [169]

Steel derives the name *Arizona* from an Aztec word meaning *silver lining.* [170]

The weight of critical opinion seems to be in favor of deriving the name from the Papago word *ari-sonac,* meaning *little springs.* [171]

Arkansas

In tracing the origin of the name *Arkansas* to its original source, the investigator must search through an intricate maze of memoirs, journals, maps, accounts of early explorers, and historical data.

Ethnologists generally agree that the word *Arkansas* is a Gallicized form of the Indian word *Ugákhpa,* or *Quapaw* as it is found in some documents. Tradition is to the effect that the Quapaw tribe of Indians, separating from their other four allied tribes,—the Ponca, the Kansa, the Omaha, and the Osage—, at one time went down the Mississippi river and came to be called the Ugákhpa or "'those going downstream or with the current.' " [172] Josiah H. Shinn states that *Arkansa* is an Algonquin expression for the word *Kappa,* that *Arkansas* is also an Algonquin

[169] *Handbook of American Indians North of Mexico,* edited by Frederick Webb Hodge, *Smithsonian Institution, Bureau of American Ethnology, Bulletin Number 30* (Government Printing Office, Washington, D.C. 1907) part 1, p. 87.
[170] *Steel Points Junior Place Names* (Published by William Gladstone Steel. Eugenia, Oregon, 1928) vol. 4. This volume is not paged.
[171] *Arizona: Prehistoric, Aboriginal, Pioneer, Modern,* James H. McClintock (The S. J. Clarke Publishing Company, Chicago, Illinois, 1916) vol. 1, p. 1-3.
[172] *Handbook of American Indians North of Mexico,* edited by Frederick Webb Hodge (Government Printing Office, Washington, D.C. 1910) part 2, p. 334.

term, not originated by the Quapaw Indians, and that the numerous ways of spelling it are mainly due to French corruption, the latter frequently hearing the word used "among the Algonquins in Illinois." [172a] This opinion is upheld by John Gilmary Shea, who adds that *Arkansas,* in addition to being Algonquin, is also an expression of the Illinois and other Indians. [173] Hamilton B. Staples believes that the word *Arkansas* comes from aboriginal roots, but that the original word is modified by French orthoepy and enunciation. [174]

Dallas T. Herndon affirms that the word *Arkansas* is an Indian place name and traces it as such from the visit of Father Marquette, in 1673, to the founding of the Arkansas settlement by Tonti, in 1686, and the subsequent Arkansas Post. [174a] This theme is elaborated by Yancey Thomas who adds that "the name of the State, the Arkansas river, the Arkansas Post and the Territory of Arkansas were all originally derived from this tribe of Indians." [175]

The *Handbook of American Indians North of Mexico* says that the Quapaws were "a southwestern Siouan tribe, forming one of the two divisions of the Dhegiha group of Dorsey." [175a] According to James O. Dorsey, "when the Kwapa were discovered by the French they dwelt in five villages, described by the early chroniclers as the Imaha

[172a] *The History of Arkansas,* Josiah H. Shinn (Wilson and Webb, Book and Stationery Company, Little Rock, Arkansas, 1898) p. 11, 25.

[173] *Early Voyages up and down the Mississippi River by Cavelier, St. Cosme, Le Sueur, Gravier, and Guignas,* with an Introduction, Notes and Index by John Dawson Gilmary Shea (Joel Munsell, Albany, New York, 1861) p. 75, 121.

[174] "Origin of the Names of the States of the Union," Hamilton B. Staples, in the *Proceedings of the American Antiquarian Society* (Published by the Society at the Press of Charles Hamilton, Worcester, Massachusetts, 1882) New Series, vol. 1, p. 376.

[174a] *The Highlights of Arkansas History,* Dallas Tabor Herndon (Special Edition printed for distribution by The Arkansas History Commission, 1922) p. 27.

[175] *Arkansas and Its People: A History, 1541-1930,* David Yancey Thomas (The American Historical Society, Incorporated, New York, 1930) p. 8.

[175a] *Handbook of American Indians North of Mexico,* edited by Frederick Webb Hodge (Government Printing Office, Washington, D.C. 1910) part 2, p. 333.

(Imaham, Imahao), Capaha, Toriman, Tonginga (Doginga, Topinga), and Southois (Atatchasi, Ossouteouez)." [176] These Indians "were encountered in 1541 by De Soto; while in 1673 Joliet finished his voyage of discovery at their village. La Salle, Tonti, and St. Cosme all describe their villages." [176a] Pierre de Charlevoix, in his *Journal of a Voyage to North America*, says that "the Akansas [Arkansas] are reckoned to be the largest and handsomest of all the Indians of this continent, and are called by way of distinction *les beaux hommes*, or the handsome men." [177] Father Hennepin, another missionary and explorer, records that the Akansa, coming to meet them offered to "dance the Calumet of Peace to us, in order to maintain a good understanding, and trade with the French nation." [177a]

While the Quapaws were calling themselves as such, the early French chroniclers were undertaking to write the word as they were hearing it pronounced, with the result that, according to Yancey Thomas and others, there were as many as seventy odd variations. [178] Some examples are as follows:

Akansea, in *An Account of the Discovery of Some New Countries and Nations in North America*, in *1673*, Pere

[176] *Siouan Sociology*, James Owen Dorsey, *A Posthumous Paper; Extract from the Fifteenth Annual Report of the Bureau of Ethnology* Government Printing Office, Washington, D.C. 1897) p. 229.

[176a] *Journal of a Voyage to North America*, translated from the French of Pierre Xavier de Charlevois, edited by Louise Phelps Kellogg (The Caxton Club, Chicago, Illinois, 1923) vol. 2, p. 229.

[177] *Ibidem*, vol. 2, p. 231.

[177a] *A Description of Louisiana*, Father Louis Hennepin, Recollect Missionary, translated from the edition of 1683, and compared with the Nouvelle Découverte, the La Salle Documents and other Contemporaneous Papers, by John Dawson Gilmary Shea (John Dawson Gilmary Shea, New York, 1880) p. 186.

[178] *Arkansas and Its People: A History, 1541-1930*, David Yancey Thomas (The American Historical Society, Incorporated, New York, 1930) p. 8.

Centennial History of Arkansas, Dallas T. Herndon (The S. J. Clarke Publishing Company, Chicago, Illinois and Little Rock, Arkansas, 1922) vol. 1, p. 149.

Handbook of American Indians North of Mexico, edited by Frederick Webb Hodge (Government Printing Office, Washington, D.C. 1910) p. 334.

Marquette and Sieur Joliet;[178a] *Akamsea*, in *Recit des Voyages et des Decouvertes*, Pere Jacques Marquette, 1673;[179] *Akansa*, in *Récit de Nicolas de La Salle*, 1682;[179a] *Akansa*, in *A Description of Louisiana*, Father Louis Hennepin, 1683;[180] *Akanscas*, in *Letter of John Francis Buisson de St. Cosme, Missionary Priest to the Bishop* [*of Quebec*] 1699;[180a] *Akanseas*, in *Letter of Mr. de Montigny*, 1699;[181] *Akansas*, in *Relation des Événemens D'Iberville, Depuis le Départ de Brest Jusqu'au Départ du Cap Français Avec Chasteaumorant*, 1699;[181a] *Arkansas*, in *Les Premiers Postes de La Louisiane, Relation de Pénicaut*, 1700;[182] *Atcansas*, in *Autre Extrait de la Relation de Bénard de La Harpe*, 1719;[182a] *Alkansas*, in *Projets de*

[178a] *Historical Collections of Louisiana, Embracing Translations of Many Rare and Valuable Documents Relating to the Natural, Civil and Political History of that State*, compiled with Historical and Biographical Notes, and an Introduction by B. F. French (Daniels and Smith, Philadelphia, Pennsylvania, 1850) part 2, p. 296.

[179] *Discovery and Exploration of the Mississippi Valley: with the Original Narratives of Marquette, Allouez, Membré, Hennepin, Anaste Douay*, John Dawson Gilmary Shea (Redfield, New York, 1852) p. 254.

[179a] *Relation of the Discovery of the Mississippi River, Written from the Narrative of Nicolas de La Salle, Otherwise Known as the Little M. de la Salle*, the translation done by Melville B. Anderson (The Caxton Club, Chicago, Illinois, 1898) p. 18.

[180] *A Description of Louisiana*, Father Louis Hennepin, Recollect Missionary, translated from the edition of 1683, and compared with the Nouvelle Découverte, the La Salle, Documents and other Contemporaneous Papers, by John Dawson Gilmary Shea (John Dawson Gilmary Shea, New York, 1880) p. 186.

[180a] *Early Voyages up and down the Mississippi by Cavalier, St. Cosme, Le Sueur, Gravier, and Guignas*, with an Introduction, Notes, and an Index by John Dawson Gilmary Shea (Joel Munsell, Albany, New York, 1861) p. 47.

[181] *Ibidem*, p. 75.

[181a] *Découvertes et Établissements des Français Dans L'Ouest et Dans Le Sud de L'Amérique Septentrionale (1614-1754), Mémoires et Documents Originaux, Recueillis et Publiés par Pierre Margry, Membre de la Société de L'Histoire de France, Membre Correspondant des Sociétés Historiques de Massachusetts, de Pennsylvanie, de Buffalo, de Wisconsin et du Maine, Quatrième Partie (1694-1703)* (Imprimerie D. Jouaust, Rue Saint-Honoré, 338, Paris, 1880) vol. 4, p. 121.

[182] *Découvertes et Établissements des Français Dans L'Ouest et Dans Le Sud de L'Amérique Septentrionale (1614-1754), Mémoires et Documents Originaux, Recueillis et Publiés par Pierre Margry, Membre de la Société de L'Histoire de France et de Plusieurs Sociétés Historiques des États-Unis, Cinquième Partie (1683-1742)* Imprimerie de D. Jouaust, Rue Saint-Honoré, 338, Paris, 1883) vol. 5, p. 402.

[182a] *Ibidem*, vol. 6, p. 311.

*Bénard de La Harpe, Commandant le Poste des Cadoda-
quious,* Bénard de La Harpe, 1720. [183]

An interesting but improbable supposition is that the
term *Arkansas* is a derivation of the French words *arc en
sang,* meaning *bloody bow,* a phrase used by the early
French explorers when referring to a special acacia-wood
bow made by the Indians. [183a] Fay Hempstead considers
it an erroneous suggestion that the word is derived from
the expression *Kansas,* preceded by the French prefix
arc, meaning *a bow,* thus giving to the combination the
significance of *smoky bow* or *bow of smoky water.* [184]

The similarity of the sound of the word *Kansas* with
the syllable *arc* prefixed and of the word *Arkansas* is probably accidental, and the theories about the latter name's
being derived from the former are further weakened by
reading the accounts of early chroniclers and finding there
the various forms of the word *Arkansas* as listed previously. Gallatin, discussing the subdivisions of the Sioux
Indians, says that three of the southern tribes were the
Quapas or Arkansas, at the mouth of the Arkansas river,
the Osages, and the Kansas, south of the river Kansas. [185]
That there were two groups of Indians, the Kansa and the
Akansa, having similar sounding names, is further affirmed
by Marquette, who, in 1673—"the very first Frenchman to
meet them" [185a]—already found the prefix on the word
Akansa, thus making improbable the theory that it was a
later addition; the word is found also in the language of
the nearby Choctaws.

[183] *Ibidem,* vol. 6, p. 241.

[183a] "The Contributors Club," in *The Atlantic Monthly* (Houghton
Mifflin Company (The Riverside Press, Cambridge, Massachusetts, May,
1881) vol. 47, p. 733.

[184] *A Pictorial History of Arkansas from Earliest Times to the Year
1890,* Fay Hempstead (N. D. Thompson Publishing Company, St. Louis
and New York, 1890) p. 18-19.

[185] *Archeologia Americana: Transactions and Collections of the
American Antiquarian Society* (Printed for the Society at the University
Press, Cambridge, Massachusetts, 1836) vol. 2, p. 126.

[185a] *A Pictorial History of Arkansas from Earliest Times to the
Year 1890,* Fay Hempstead (N. D. Thompson Publishing Company,
St. Louis and New York, 1890) p. 19.

On June 27, 1806, the legislature of the Territory of Louisiana formed a new territory out of the lower part of the New Madrid district which they called the *District of Arkansaw.* [186]

The forming of the Arkansaw Territory was officially sanctioned by an act of Congress on March 2, 1819, and this territory was admitted into the Union as the State of Arkansas on June 15, 1836. [186a]

Judge U. M. Rose, a prominent citizen of Arkansas and an able authority on Arkansas history, thinks that in the earliest books and records the name did not have the final *s*, but that it was most likely added in later writings by the French to make up such phrases as *les pays des Arkansas* and *la rivière des Arkansas.* He further states that after the cession of this territory by France to the United States in 1803, the question of the final *s* was still unsettled. [187]

The confusion in the pronunciation of the name doubtless is due to the facts that the French in their records added the *s* to the original word to form the plural and that they added a silent *s* on the end of words terminating in *a* to give it a broader sound. Judge Rose says that "it is absolutely certain that the name as pronounced by the Indians was the same as if [it were] spelled in our language Arkansaw." [188] He finds no evidence that the name was pronounced with the accent on the second syllable until about the time of the admission of Arkansas to statehood in 1836, and at that time it was unusual enough to be regarded as an innovation. [188a]

[186] *A Pictorial History of Arkansas from Earliest Times to the Year 1890,* Fay Hempstead (N. D. Thompson Publishing Company, St. Louis and New York, 1890) p. 134.

[186a] *History of Arkansas: Historical Review of Arkansas: Its Commerce, Industry and Modern Affairs,* Fay Hempstead (The Lewis Publishing Company, Chicago, Illinois, 1911) vol. I, p. 82.

[187] *Proceedings of the Legislature and of the Historical Society of The State of Arkansas, and the Eclectic Society of Little Rock, Arkansas, Fixing the Pronunciation of the Name Arkansas* (Printed by Kellogg Printing Company, for the Eclectic Society, Little Rock, Arkansas, 1881) p. 13-14.

[188] *Ibidem,* p. 13-14.

[188a] *Ibidem,* p. 13.

Fay Hempstead says that the people of the State pronounced their State name *Arkansaw;* [188b] but that those living outside of the State pronounced it Arkansas, [as the spelling would seem to indicate].

The confusion in the pronunciation of this State name finally led to legislation on the matter. The *State Historical Society* and the *Eclectic Society of Little Rock* having agreed upon what they considered to be the correct pronunciation of the State name, based on historical data and on the early usage of the American immigrants, the State Legislature in 1881, following their recommendation, passed a law that the name should be pronounced in three syllables, with the final *s* silent, the *a* in each syllable being pronounced as is Italian *a*. This law specifies that the first and last syllables of the word shall carry the accents, and that the pronunciation with the accent on the second syllable with the *a* in this syllable sounding short as it does in the word man, and sounding the final *s*, is to be discouraged. [188c]

Connecticut

To endeavor to ascertain just who named the State of Connecticut is much like attempting to pass through a labyrinth or to untie the Gordian knot, for one soon loses himself in the intricate details of letters, journals, records of the early explorers, colonial documents, and historical data.

Adrian Block, a Dutch navigator, in 1614 explored the Connecticut river, which he named *Versch,* signifying *fresh water river,* because he perceived that there was a strong

[188b] *History of Arkansas: Historical Review of Arkansas: Its Commerce, Industry and Modern Affairs* (The Lewis Publishing Company, Chicago, Illinois, 1911) vol. 1, p. 5.

[188c] *Acts of Arkansas, 1881: Acts and Resolutions of the General Assembly of the State of Arkansas, Passed at the Session Held at the Capitol, in the City of Little Rock, Arkansas, Commencing on the 10th Day of January, 1881, and Ending on the 19th Day of March, 1881,* by authority (Mitchell and Bettis, State Printers, Little Rock, Arkansas, 1881) p. 216-17.

downward current a very short distance above the mouth of the river. [189]

The natives called the river *Connittecock* or *Quonehtacut*, which "aboriginal appelation survives to the present day in the name of the river and [of] the State of Connecticut." [190]

Trumbull, who is probably one of the best authorities on Indian names, says that the Indian word *Quonehtacut*, or *Connecticut*, means *the long river.* [191]

The State of Connecticut was named after the river, which had previously been named by the natives. [192]

Connecticut was the home of Nathan Hale, the patriot martyr, Roger Sherman, the only man who signed "all the four of the fundamental documents establishing our country," Oliver Ellsworth, William Samuel Johnson, and Governor Jonathan Trumbull. General George Washington, Count de Rochambeau, Governor Jonathan Trumbull, and "their distinguished official associates in May, 1781" formulated the plans for the siege of Yorktown in the Webb House at Wethersfield, Connecticut.

[189] *History of the State of New York, First Period, 1609-1664,* John Romeyn Brodhead (Harper and Brothers, New York, 1853) vol. 1, p. 56-7.

Connecticut as a Colony and as a State, Forest Morgan, Editor-in-chief (The Publishing Society of Connecticut, Hartford, Connecticut, 1904) vol. 1, p. 47.

A History of Connecticut: Its People and Institutions, George L. Clark (G. P. Putnam's Sons, New York and London, 1914) p. 4.

The Memorial History of Hartford County, Connecticut, 1633-1884, edited by J. Hammond Trumbull (Edward L. Osgood, Publisher, Boston, Massachusetts, 1886) vol. 1, p. 11.

History of the Indians of Connecticut from the Earliest Known Period to 1850, John W. De Forest (William James Hamersley, Hartford, Connecticut, 1853) p. 70.

[190] *History of the State of New York, First Period, 1609-1664,* John Romeyn Brodhead (Harper and Brothers, New York, 1853) vol. 1, p. 57.

A Complete History of Connecticut, Civil and Ecclesiastical, from the Emigration of Its First Planters from England in the Year 1630 to the Year 1764, Benjamin Trumbull (Maltby Goldsmith and Company, and Samuel Wadsworth, T. G. Woodward, Printer, Hartford, Connecticut, 1818) vol. 1, p. 32.

[191] *Ibidem,* vol. 1, p. 32.

[192] *The Historical, Statistical and Industrial Review of the State of Connecticut, Part One* (W. S. Webb and Company, New York, 1883) p. 65.

The historic Charter Oak stood on the Wyllys place at Hartford, Connecticut. It is too well known to students of history to need discussion as to its significance and importance. The Charter Oak, which is supposed to have been upwards of one thousand years of age, was blown down during a thunder storm on August 21, 1856.

Connecticut, says George S. Godard, "is the land of steady habits, sound finance, and skilled industries. It is the mother of constitutions, the home of higher education, and the exponent of practical idealism. The diversity of its interests is amazing. It has within its borders the insurance center of the Nation; the brass manufacturing center of the world; the hardware city of the Union; the silver manufacturing center of the country; and a hat center of national repute." [192a]

Idaho

The word *Idaho* was first applied to the locality of Idaho Springs in 1859. It was next used by the Washington Legislature in 1862 to designate a county in what was then a part of the State of Washington, but in what is now a part of the State of Idaho. The name *Idaho* was given to the Idaho Territory created by Congress on March 3, 1863. [193] When the bill for organizing this territory was before Congress, the word *Montana* [194] was suggested as being a suitable name for the proposed territory, but through the influence of Senator Henry Wilson of Massa-

---

[192a] The *Response* which George S. Godard as representative of Governor Wilbur L. Cross made for the State of Connecticut at the formal exercises of the Yorktown Sesquicentennial, Yorktown, Virginia, in 1932. The complete response may be found in *The Yorktown Sesquicentennial: Proceedings of the U.S. Yorktown Sesquicentennial Commission . . .* (Prepared by S. O. Bland, Washington, D.C. 1932) p. 133-5. This material was sent to the writer by George S. Godard, Connecticut State Librarian, in a communication from the State Library, Hartford, Connecticut, September 13, 1933.

[193] A full discussion of these details is found in *History of the State of Idaho*, C. J. Brosnan (Charles Scribner's Sons, New York, Chicago, and Boston, 1918) p. 117, 120, 121, 122.

chusetts the territory was named *Idaho* rather than
Montana. [194]

Joaquin Miller says that he was probably the first
person to use the word *Idaho* as it is spelled today; however he does not claim to have originated the word. His
account of how he came to use the name is as follows:

"On my return to Lewiston I wrote a letter containing
a brief account of our trip and of the mines, and it was
published in one of the Oregon papers, which one I have
now forgotten. In that account I often mentioned E-dah-
hoe, but spelt it *Idaho,* leaving the pronunciation unmarked
by any diacritical signs." [195]

He says: " 'The distinction of naming Idaho certainly
belongs to my old friend Colonel Craig (since deceased) of
Craig's Mountain, Nez Percé County. As for some fellow
naming it in Congress—bah! The name was familiar in
5,000 men's mouths as they wallowed through the snow in
'61, on their way to Oro Fino mines long before Congress,
or any man of Congress, had ever heard of the new
discovery.' " [196]

Idaho is a contraction of the Shoshoni Indian exclamation *Ee-dah-how,* [197] denoting in English "It is sunup!"

[194] *Idaho: Facts and Statistics Concerning Its Mining, Farming, Stock-Raising, Lumbering, and Other Resources and Industries, together with Notes on the Climate, Scenery, Game and Mineral Springs. Information for the Home-Seeker, Capitalist, Prospector, and Traveler,* James L. Onderdonk, Territorial Controller (A. L. Bancroft and Company, Book and Job Printers, San Francisco, California, 1885) p. 10.
See also: *History of the State of Idaho,* C. J. Brosnan (Charles Scribner's Sons, New York, Chicago, and Boston, 1913) p. 122.

[195] *Idaho: Facts and Statistics Concerning Its Mining, Farming, Stock-Raising, Lumbering, and Other Resources and Industries together with Notes on the Climate, Scenery, Game and Mineral Springs. Information for the Home-Seeker, Capitalist, Prospector, and Traveler,* James L. Onderdonk, Territorial Controller (A. L. Bancroft and Company, Book and Job Printers, San Francisco, California, 1885) p. 10.

[196] *Ibidem,* p. 10.

[197] "Idahho," Joaquin Miller, in *The Continent, an Illustrated Weekly Magazine,* conducted by Albion W. Tourgee, Vol. 3, January to June, 1883 (Our Continent Publishing Company, Philadelphia, Pennsylvania) May 30, 1883, p. 689.
History of the State of Idaho, C. J. Brosnan (Charles Scribner's Sons, New York, Chicago, and Boston, 1918) p. 121.

The word consists of three component parts,[198] the first
Ee conveys the idea of *coming down,* which word, when
properly translated into English, means *water coming
down,* or *snow coming down.* The second syllable is *dah,*
the Shoshoni stem signifying both *sun* and *mountain.* The
syllable, *how,* is an exclamation. The Shoshoni word is
Ee-dah-how and the Indian thought thus conveyed, when
literally translated into English, means "Behold! the sun
coming down the mountain."

" 'Idaho' has been so nicely explained and elaborated
[upon] so profusely by the poetical and idealist[ic], that
Idahoans feel proud of a name which signifies such a noble
and expressive thought as the 'Gem of the Mountains' ";[199]
the popular conception of the meaning of the word.

While this common interpretation of the meaning of
the word *Idaho* as *gem of the mountains,* or *mountain gem,*
is not a literal translation of the Indian word, yet it is one
that is known and loved by most of the Idahoans. This
popular conception is accounted for as follows:

"From his teepee, through the clear, exhilarating morning air, the Shoshoni Indian beheld a lustrous rim of light
shining from the mountain top. This radiant mountain
crown or diadem was likened to a gem glittering from a
snowy peak. In this way 'Ee-dah-how' came to have attributed to it the popular and beautiful signification, 'Mountain Gem' or 'Gem of the Mountains.' "[200]

[198] *Idaho—Its Meaning, Origin and Application,* John E. Rees, printed
from the *Oregon Historical Quarterly,* vol. 18, No. 2, 1917 (The Ivy
Press, Portland Oregon, 1917) p. 4.

[199] *Ibidem,* p. 3.

[200] *History of the State of Idaho,* C. J. Broshan (Charles Scribner's
Sons, New York, Chicago, and Boston, 1926) p. 121.

For other clear-cut discussions of the meaning of the word Idaho,
see *An Illustrated History of the State of Idaho :* or *Idaho, The Gem of
the Mountains.* The author's name is not given. (The Lewis Publishing
Company, Chicago, Illinois, 1899) p. 5-6.

*Idaho : Facts and Statistics Concerning Its Mining, Farming, Stock-
Raising, Lumbering, and Other Resources and Industries, together with
Notes on the Climate, Scenery, Game and Mineral Springs. Information
for the Home-Seeker, Capitalist, Prospector, and Traveler,* James L.
Onderdonk, Territorial Controller (A. L. Bancroft and Company, Book
and Job Printers, San Francisco, California, 1885) p. 10.

Illinois

La Salle, having sailed along the Illinois river from its mouth in 1679, named it after the tribe of Indians which he found dwelling along its banks. [201]

The Territory of Illinois, having been organized on February 3, 1809, [202] was admitted into the Union as the State of Illinois on December 3, 1818. [203]

Both the river and the State were called Illinois, a native name, "given by the French to a confederate tribe of Indians and [to] the country which they inhabited" [204] along the Mississippi Valley. [205]

The name *Illinois* is derived "from the Algonquin Indian word Inini, which the French pronounced Illini," signifying *the men, perfect and accomplished.* "The suffix *ois* is purely French, and denotes tribe." [206] Thus the word *Illinois* in its original meaning signifies *a tribe of men, men perfect and accomplished,* or as it is often given, *a tribe of superior men.*

This combination of Indian and French elements used to form a new word "is a symbol of how the two races—the French and the Indians—were intermixed during the early history of the country." [207]

[201] *Illinois, Historical and Statistical,* John Moses (Fergus Printing Company, Chicago, Illinois, 1889) vol. I, p. 17.
The New International Encyclopaedia, Second Edition (Dodd, Mead and Company, New York, 1930) vol. II, p. 772.

[202] *The New International Encyclopaedia,* Second Edition (Dodd, Mead and Company, New York, 1930) vol. II, p. 773.
The Encyclopaedia Britannica, Fourteenth Edition (Encyclopaedia Britannica, Incorporated, New York, 1929) vol. 12, p. 91.
The Encyclopedia Americana (Americana Corporation, New York and Chicago, 1929) vol. 14, p. 691.

[203] *The Encyclopedia Americana* (Americana Corporation, New York and Chicago, 1929) vol. 14, p. 691.

[204] *Illinois, Historical and Statistical,* John Moses (Fergus Printing Company, Chicago, Illinois, 1889) vol. I, p. 17.

[205] *The Past and Present of La Salle County, Illinois.* The name of the author is not given. (H. F. Kett and Company, Chicago, Illinois, 1877) p. 13.

[206] *Illinois, Historical and Statistical,* John Moses (Fergus Printing Company, Chicago, Illinois, 1889) vol. I, p. 17.

[207] *The Past and Present of La Salle County, Illinois.* The name of the author is not given. (H. F. Kett and Company, Chicago, Illinois, 1877) p. 13.

Iowa

It is the opinion of some of the leading Iowa historians that the origin and meaning of the name *Iowa* are uncertain. [208] Investigation reveals the truthfulness of the statement made by L. F. Andrews, who says that "words have been twisted, distorted and corrupted until they bear little or no orthographic relation to that which the tradition-searchers have reached in their quest." [209]

Johnson Brigham, the State Historian of Iowa, calls attention also to the great part speculation plays in determining the origin and meaning of the name Iowa. "Is it," he asks, "(1) a tribal designation; or (2) a place name; or (3) a name descriptive of some characteristic of the region?" [210] He presents a mass of scholarly research in which he cites annals, journals, and historical records, dating from the year 1676. He closes his introductory remarks by saying that "it is evident from these divergent views that this [the origin and the significance of the name *Iowa*] must ever remain one of the open questions confronting the student of Iowa history." [211]

Historians generally agree that both the Iowa river and the State were named after a powerful tribe of Indians which in primitive times lived in that part of the United States now comprising the State of Iowa. [212]

[208] *Iowa: Its History and Its Foremost Citizens,* Johnson Brigham (The S. J. Clarke Publishing Company, Chicago, Illinois, 1915) vol. 1, p. 7-8.
      The Red Men of Iowa, A. R. Fulton (Mills and Company, Des Moines, Iowa, 1882) p. 423-4.

[209] "The Word 'Iowa'—What it Means," L. F. Andrews, in the *Annals of Iowa, A Historical Quarterly,* Third series, Vol. 2, edited by Charles Aldrich (Published by The Historical Department of Iowa, C. F. Byrkit, Printer, Des Moines, Iowa) July, 1896, p. 465.

[210] *Iowa: Its History and Its Foremost Citizens,* Johnson Brigham (The S. J. Clarke Publishing Company, Chicago, Illinois, 1915) vol. 1, p. 7.

[211] *Ibidem,* p. 8.

[212] *The Red Men of Iowa,* A. R. Fulton (Mills and Company, Des Moines, Iowa, 1882) p. 423.
      Iowa: The First Free State in the Louisiana Purchase from Its Discovery to the Admission of the State into the Union, 1673-1846, William Salter (A. C. McClurg and Company, Chicago, Illinois, 1905) p. 277-9.

Of the various writers giving the meaning of the word *Iowa*, some affirm that it signifies *beautiful* or *the beautiful land;* [213] others say that the word means *this is the place.* [214] Augustus C. Dodge, former United States Senator from Iowa, and other authorities say that the name means *none such;* [215] and again others state that the term *Iowa* in the Dakota language denotes *" 'something to write or paint with—a pen or pencil.' "* [216] The weight of critical opinion seems to justify the conclusion that the word *Iowa* means *this is the place.* [217]

Probably the chief reason for the origin and the significance of the primitive Indian word for Iowa's being so difficult to ascertain is the fact that its original form has been lost in the records of the French and Spanish explorers, or the other early travelers, or of the fur traders, and in the mass of historical data which has grown up later. Some of the forms of the word found in these documents are: *Ayouas, Aiouez, Ayavois, Ainovines, Aiodais, Aiouas, Aiouways,* and *Ioways.* [218]

[213] *The Red Men of Iowa*, A. R. Fulton (Mills and Company, Des Moines, Iowa, 1882) p. 423-4.

"Indian Tribes In Iowa before 1846," J. L. Pickard, in the *Annals of Iowa, A Historical Quarterly*, Third series, vol. 2, edited by Charles Aldrich (Published by the Historical Department of Iowa, C. E. Byrkit, Printer, Des Moines, Iowa, 1895-1897) July to October, 1895, p. 174.

"A Memoir of Indian Names in Iowa," Samuel Storrs Howe, in the *Annals of Iowa, A Historical Quarterly* (Edited and published by Samuel Storrs Howe, Iowa City, Iowa, January, 1882) vol. 1, p. 4.

[214] *The Red Men of Iowa*, A. R. Fulton (Mills and Company, Des Moines, Iowa, 1882) p. 424.

[215] "A Memoir of Indian Names in Iowa," Samuel Storrs Howe, in the *Annals of Iowa, A Historical Quarterly* (Edited and published by Samuel Storrs Howe, Iowa City, Iowa, January, 1882) vol. 1, p. 4.

[216] *The Red Men of Iowa*, A. R. Fulton (Mills and Company, Des Moines, Iowa, 1882) p. 425.

[217] *Ibidem*, p. 424.

Annals of Iowa, A Historical Quarterly, New series, no. 1, January, 1882 (edited and published by Samuel Storrs Howe, Iowa City, Iowa, 1882) vol. 1, p. 4.

The Annals of Iowa, A Historical Quarterly, Third series, edited by Charles Aldrich (Published by the Historical Department of Iowa, C. E. Byrkit, Printer, Des Moines, 1895-1897) July to October, 1895, vol. 2, p. 556.

[218] *Iowa: Its History and Its Foremost Citizens*, Johnson Brigham (The S. J. Clarke Publishing Company, Chicago, Illinois, 1915) vol. 1, p. 7, 29.

Mr. Brigham points out the fact that the early French explorers spelled the name *Ayouas;* the Spanish, *Ajoues;* and the English, *Ioways.* [219] He also states that the first appearance of the modern spelling of the name, *Iowa,* is found in *Morse's American Gazetteer* of 1804, "in which it was applied to the river along which Iowa Indian towns were located." [220]

Fulton says that it should be remembered that the word is of Dakota origin and that it had great varieties of orthography until finally the word *Ioway* was commonly used, and then the form *Iowa* "was adopted and the name applied by the whites to the Territory and the State where the tribe had so long made their home." [221]

Kansas

Robert Hay having consulted about eighty different authorities and having found about twenty-four spellings of the name *Kansas,* notes that very few of the writers whom he consulted thought "it worth while to dwell on the matter of orthography." [222]

In the State Constitution of 1858, the name of the Territory is spelled *Kansas* [223] and the act of Congress admitting the Territory to statehood in 1861 spells the name of the State *Kansas.* [224] The State was named after the river, which in previous times had been named after a tribe of Indians who lived along its banks towards the mouth. [225]

[219] *Iowa: Its History and Its Foremost Citizens,* Johnson Brigham (The S. J. Clarke Publishing Company, Chicago, Illinois, 1915) vol. 1, p. 8.

[220] *Ibidem,* p. 8.

[221] *The Red Men of Iowa,* A. R. Fulton (Mills and Company, Des Moines, Iowa, 1882) p. 425.

[222] "Kaw and Kansas: A Monograph on the Name of the State," Robert Hay, in the *Transactions of the Kansas State Historical Society,* 1905-1906, vol. 9, edited by George W. Martin, Secretary (State Printing Office, Topeka, Kansas, 1906) p. 523-5.

[223] *The Annals of Kansas,* New Edition, 1541-1885, Daniel Webster Wilder (T. Dwight Thacher, Kansas Publishing House, Topeka, Kansas. 1886) p. 217.

[224] *Ibidem,* p. 231-2, 310-11.

[225] *History of Kansas from the First Exploration of the Mississippi Valley to Its Admission into the Union,* John N. Holloway (James, Emmons and Company. Lafayette. Indiana, 1868) p. 87.

William E. Connelley, Secretary of the Kansas State Historical Society, points out that the word *Kansa* (the Kansas of our day) is an old word of the Siouan language, meaning *Wind People, Small-wind, People of the South Wind, South-wind People, Makes-a-breeze-near-the-ground,* or *Camp-behind-all.* [226] He is also of the opinion that to the Indians of the old time it probably meant more than is expressed in these phrases, for the word has been embedded in the social organization of the Siouan tribe from prehistoric times.

Kentucky

It probably will never be definitely known just who first applied the name *Kentucky* in its present form to the State now so designated; for the facts of the matter are so concealed by legends, traditions, early records, and historical data that it seems that no one has been able to ferret them out

Perhaps the first mention of the word *Kentucky* with its present spelling in a public document is found in a letter [227] from a leading trader, Major William Trent, to Governor Hamilton, dated April 10, 1753.

Just who was the first white man to visit what is now the State of Kentucky is a disputed matter; some say that La Salle in 1669 went down the Ohio river to the present site of Louisville, [228] being probably the first white man to see Kentucky; others affirm that La Salle perhaps never saw the Ohio river, [229] but that Gabriel Arthur, a Cherokee-

[226] *A Standard History of Kansas and Kansans,* William Elsey Connelley (The Lewis Publishing Company, Chicago and New York, 1918) vol. I, p. 193-6.

[227] "John Findley: The First Pathfinder of Kentucky," Lucien Beckner, in *The History Quarterly,* vol. I, no. 3, published quarterly by the Filson Club and the University of Louisville (Press of John P. Morton and Company, Louisville, Kentucky, April, 1927) p. 114-15.

[228] *The Encyclopedia Americana* (Americana Corporation, New York and Chicago, 1929) vol. 20, p. 615.

[229] *The First Explorations of the Trans-Alleghany Regions by the Virginians, 1650-1674,* Clarence Walworth Alvord and Lee Bidgood (The Arthur H. Clark Company, Cleveland, Ohio, 1912) p. 24.

Shawnee captive, in 1674 traversed the eastern part of the State. [230]

About 1774, Colonel Richard Henderson of North Carolina was instrumental in purchasing from the Cherokee Indians for ten thousand pounds the greater part of the country called *Cane-tuck-ee*. [231]

"In 1780 Kentucky, still a province of Virginia, was divided into three counties"; [232] namely, Jefferson, Fayette, and Lincoln.

"In 1790 Kentucky became a territory, and on June 1, 1792," it was admitted as a State into the Union. [233]

The name *Kentucky* has passed through various forms, including the words, *Cantucky, Kain-tuck-ee,* and *Kentuckee.*

The most common meaning attributed to the name is *dark and bloody ground.* General George Rogers Clark says that the word *Ken-tuck-e* means *the river of blood,* which meaning refers to the tradition that a race of prehistoric inhabitants was driven out by the Indians, [234] thereby causing much bloodshed. Others think that this meaning commemorates the struggles among the different tribes of Indians who came to hunt on this territory, but the *Encyclopaedia Britannica* states that these Indian combats were between the Iriquois and the Cherokees. [235]

The Encyclopedia Americana derives the expression *Kentucky* from a Cherokee word, meaning *prairie,* or *the barrens,* and not *dark and bloody ground.* [236] *Appleton's*

---

[230] *Tales of the Dark and Bloody Ground,* Williard Rouse Jillson, State Geologist of Kentucky (C. T. Dearing Printing Company, Louisville, Kentucky, 1930) p. 2, 4.

[231] "The Story of Kentucky," Emma M. Connelly, in *The Story of the States* (D. Lothrop Company, Boston, Massachusetts, 1890) p. 15.

[232] *Ibidem,* p. 77.

[233] *Werner Encyclopaedia* (The Werner Company, Akron, Ohio, 1909) vol. 14, p. 46.

[234] *The Prehistoric Men of Kentucky,* Colonel Bennett H. Young, *Filson Club Publications,* No. 25 (John P. Morton and Company, Incorporated, Printers to the Filson Club, Louisville, Kentucky, 1910) p. 3-5.

[235] *The Encyclopaedia Britannica,* Fourteenth Edition (Encyclopaedia Britannica, Incorporated, New York, 1929) vol. 13, p. 335.

[236] *The Encyclopedia Americana* (Americana Corporation, New York and Chicago, 1929) vol. 16, p. 363.

New Practical Cyclopedia derives the name *Kentucky* from the Iriquois word, *Kentake,* meaning *prairie* or *meadow land,* which word was applied by these Indians to the large prairie, or treeless region, situated in the south-central part of the State. [237]

Yet another authority says that the name *Kentucky* is derived from the Wyandot (Iroquoian) name *Ken-tah-teh,* signifying *to-morrow,* or *the land of to-morrow.* [238]

Massachusetts

The State of Massachusetts retained the name of the colony, which received its designation from the bay, which in turn derived its name from the Massachusetts Indians who peopled its shores in primitive times. [239]

The word Massachusetts is supposedly derived from two Indian words: *massa,* meaning *great,* and *wachusett,* signifying *a mountain place.* John Cotton has defined the word as meaning *a hill in the form of an arrowhead,* but Roger Williams thought that "the Massachusetts were so called from the *blue hills.*" [240]

Dr. Edward Everett Hale says that the bay was named by a tribe of Indians living around *the great hills,* "which are now known as the Blue Hills, in Milton, Quincy and Braintree." He also says that *chuset* or *wachuset* meant *a hill,* that *matta* meant *great;* that *Mattachusetts* meant in the Indian dialect *the great hills,* and that the harsh double *t* soon yielded to the sibilant double *s,* thus giving the present form of the name. [241]

---

[237] *Appleton's New Practical Cyclopedia,* edited by Marcus Benjamin, New and Revised Edition (D. Appleton and Company, New York, 1920) vol. 3, p. 453.

[238] *The World Almanac and Book of Facts for 1931,* edited by Robert Hunt Lyman (The New York World, New York, 1931) p. 523.

[239] *The Story of Massachusetts,* Edward Everett Hale (D. Lothrop Company, Boston, Massachusetts, 1891) p. 146.

[240] *A Gazetteer of the State of Massachusetts,* Reverend Elias Nason, Revised and Enlarged by George J. Varney (B. B. Russell, Boston, Massachusetts, 1890) p. 11.

[241] *The Story of Massachusetts,* Edward Everett Hale (D. Lothrop Company, Boston, Massachusetts, 1891) p. 146.

James Hammond Trumbull affirms that in composition the Algonkin Indian word *adchu* always meant *mountain* or *hill;* the suffix *set* denoted location and meant *near* or *in the vicinity of;* that the adjective *massa* meant *great;* and that from these forms in combination is made up the word *Mass-adchu-set,* meaning *near* [or *in the vicinity of*] *the great mountain.* *Mass-adchu-set* now has the form Massachusetts. [242]

Michigan

It would be a noteworthy accomplishment indeed, to be able to say authoritatively just who first gave the name *Michigan* to the Territory which now forms the State of Michigan, and from what exact Indian word it came. Hulda T. Hollands says that "the most northern point of the southern Peninsula of Michigan, and the island near it, were given their names by the Red men long before the white men knew anything about the place." [243] If this be the case, the word they used was *Mishi-maikin-nac,* which meant to them *"a swimming tortoise, or turtle."* It is said that this part of the country, "both the Island and the elevated point of the main land, when seen from a distance on the water, resemble a turtle in outline." [244]

Perry F. Powers says that " 'the word Michigan first appears as applied to land area in the congressional proceedings of 1804, culminating in the act of January 11, 1805, establishing the Territory of Michigan . . . The name Michigan applied to the territory and state, unquestionably was taken from the lake, and that, in turn, had emerged in its present form after many vicissitudes, and was the survival of differing forms and other names.' " [245]

[242] "The Composition of Indian Geographical Names, Illustrated from the Algonkin Languages," James Hammond Trumbull, in the *Collections of the Connecticut Historical Society,* Vol. 2 (Printed by Case, Lockwood and Brainard, Hartford, Connecticut, 1870) p. 20.

[243] *When Michigan Was New,* Hulda T. Hollands (A. Flanagan Company, Chicago, Illinois, 1906) p. 72.

[244] *Ibidem,* p. 72.

[245] *A History of Northern Michigan and Its People,* Perry F. Powers (The Lewis Publishing Company, Chicago, Illinois, 1912) vol. 1, p. 89-90.

James H. Lanman affirms that "the State of Michigan derives its name, it is said, from the Indian words *Mitchi-sawgyegan,* which mean, in English, a great lake, a term which has been given to the territory from the position it occupies." [246]

The territory comprising practically what is now the State of Michigan, was formed out of the then Indiana Territory on June 30, 1805, at which time it was designated as the Michigan Territory. [247] This territory was admitted into the Union as the State of Michigan on January 26, 1837. [248]

Minnesota

Most of the authorities agree that the name *Minnesota* was given first to the river, next to the Territory when it was established on March 3, 1849, [249] and last to the State.

When the territorial bill was before the United States Congress in 1846, for the new Territory, the following names were proposed: *Itasca, Algonquin, Chippewa, Washington, Jackson,* and *Minnesota.* [250] Through the influence of Honorable Morgan L. Martin, Honorable Henry Hastings Sibley, [251] and H. L. Dousman, the word *Minnesota* was chosen as the name of the Territory because "of its geographical fitness and because of the beauty of the name." [252]

[246] *History of Michigan from Its Earliest Colonization to the Present Time,* James H. Lanman (Harper and Brothers, Publishers, New York, 1855) p. 15.
[247] *The Encyclopedia Americana* (Americana Corporation, New York and Chicago, 1929) vol. 19, p. 27.
[248] *The Encyclopaedia Britannica,* Fourteenth Edition (Encyclopaedia Britannica, Incorporated, New York, 1929) vol. 15, p. 423.
[249] "Last Days of Wisconsin Territory and Early Days of Minnesota Territory," Honorable Henry L. Moss, in the *Collections of the Minnesota Historical Society,* Vol. 8 (Published by The Society, St. Paul, Minnesota, 1898) p. 77-81.
Minnesota, The North Star State, William Watts Folwell (Houghton Mifflin Company, The Riverside Press, Cambridge, Massachusetts, 1908) p. 1.
[250] *Collections of the Minnesota Historical Society* (Printed by Ramaley, Chaney and Company, Printers, St. Paul, Minnesota, 1872) vol. 1, p. 482-3.
[251] *Collections of the Minnesota Historical Society* (Published by The Society, St. Paul, Minnesota, 1898) vol. 8, p. 76-7.
[252] "A History of the City of Saint Paul, and of the Country of Ramsey, Minnesota," by J. Fletcher Williams, in the *Collections of the*

At the Stillwater Convention in August, 1848, instructions were given to the delegate who was chosen to represent the interests of the convention at Washington "that the name of the Territory should be written *Min-ne-so-ta,* and not *Mi-ne-so-ta,*" [253] as it was written and pronounced by many at that time.

It is the consensus of historical opinion that the word *Minnesota* is a Dakota Indian name, [254] composed of the two words [minni] *minne,* meaning *water,* and *sota,* about which there is some difference of opinion. Edward Duffield Neill says that the latter term signifies "the peculiar appearance of the sky on certain days," and that the interpretation of the term Minnesota as meaning *sky-tinted water,* the interpretation given by Gideon H. Pond, an outstanding Dahkotah scholar, has been adopted by the Historical Society Publications. [255] Some authorities give the meaning of the word *sota* as *clouded;* some, as *turbid;* some, as *clear;* the idea implied in all these interpretations seems to be water that reflects the sky. [256]

William Watts Folwell gives two pages and one-half to the discussion of the meaning of the word *sota,* after which he concludes by saying that in spite of criticism, Gideon Pond's "sky-tinted water" will hold its place. [257]

"An illustration of the meaning of the word is told to Dr. Warren Upham, of the State Historical Society, by Mrs. Moses N. Adams, the widow of the venerable missionary to the Dakotas. She states that at various times the Dakota women explained it to her by dropping a little milk

Minnesota Historical Society. Vol. 4 (Published by The Society, Pioneer-Press Company, Book and Job Printers, St. Paul, Minnesota, 1876) p. 156.

[253] *Annals of the Minnesota Historical Society,* prepared by Edward D. Neill, Secretary of the Society (Joseph R. Brown, Territorial Printer, St. Paul, Minnesota, 1856) p. 3.

[254] *Ibidem,* p. 3.

[255] *The History of Minnesota: from the Earliest French Explorations to the Present Time,* Second Edition, Edward Duffield Neill (J. B. Lippincott and Company, Philadelphia, Pennsylvania, 1873) Introduction, li.

[256] *Collections of the Minnesota Historical Society* (Ramaley, Chaney and Company, Printers, St. Paul, Minnesota, 1872) vol. 1, p. 197.
Our Minnesota, Hester McLean Pollock (E. P. Dutton and Company, New York, 1917) p. 1-2.

[257] *A History of Minnesota,* William Watts Folwell (Published by the Minnesota Historical Society, Saint Paul, Minnesota, 1921) vol. 1, p. 455-7.

into water and calling the whitishly clouded water 'min-ne-sota.' " [258]

Mississippi

The Mississippi river was named by the Indians, and the State in turn was named after the river. *Mississippi*, like most other Indian names, has been written in various forms in imitation of the sound of the name as it was pronounced by the Indians. Dunbar Rowland points out that the name was spelled *Missisippi* by the French [explorers], and *Misisipi* by the Spanish [explorers], pronounced by both *Meeseeseepee* in imitation of the Indian spoken words. [259]

Franklin L. Riley says that it is not known when the present spelling of the word Mississippi was first used. [260] Dunbar Rowland, the State historian, says that "the present spelling is adapted from the French and the Spanish spelling, the consonants being doubled to indicate the short sound of *i*." [261]

Historians do not generally agree as to what tribe of Indians the original name belonged, but most of them say that the term is made up of the two words *meeche* or *mescha*, [262] meaning as an adjective, *great*, and *cebe* signifying *river;* consequently the name *Mississippi* as applied by the Indians to the river, meant *the great river*, or probably *the great water*.

---

[258] *Minnesota: Its Story and Biography*, Henry Anson Castle (The Lewis Publishing Company, Chicago and New York, 1915) vol. 1, p. 105.

[259] *Mississippi: Comprising Sketches of Counties, Towns, Events, Institutions, and Persons, Arranged in Cyclopedic Form*, planned and edited by Dunbar Rowland (Southern Historical Publishing Association, Atlanta, Georgia, 1907) vol. 2, p. 254.

[260] *School History of Mississippi*, Franklin L. Riley (B. F. Johnson Publishing Company, Richmond, Virginia, 1900) p. 349.

[261] *Mississippi: Comprising Sketches of Counties, Towns, Events, Institutions, and Persons, Arranged in Cyclopedic Form*, planned and edited by Dunbar Rowland (Southern Historical Publishing Association, Atlanta, Georgia, 1907) vol. 2, p. 254.

[262] "A Description of the English Province of Carolana, by the Spaniards Called Florida, and by the French, La Louisiane," in the *Historical Collections of Louisiana*, compiled by Benjamin French (Daniels and Smith, Philadelphia, Pennsylvania, 1850) part 2, p. 224.

Missouri

Research confirms the opinion of the historians who say that "the real Indian meaning of [the name] Missouri will probably remain a mystery." [263]

The river was first called Missouri in commemoration of a tribe of Indians who lived along its borders. It is not certain that the name *Missouri* means *muddy water*, as is often asserted. It is certain, however, that the Indian name of the river was *Pekitanoui*, or *Pekitanou*, which did mean *muddy water*, and that this river was called Missouri about 1712. [264]

Walter Williams says that Colonel W. F. Switzler, Editor of the Boonville Democrat, in the issue of October 22, 1897, pointed out the error in the belief of those who had believed and taught that the word *Missouri* meant *muddy water*. He says that the name *Missouri* was at first applied to the Indian tribe inhabiting the territory near the mouth of the river and not to the river itself. He also states that Marquette gave the river the name *Pe-kit-a-noui*, an Indian name meaning *muddy water*, that "the name given by Marquette prevailed until the time [about 1712] of the Jesuit missionary to the Illinois nation, Father Gabriel Marest, who called the river 'Missouri.' "

He further states that the name *Missouri* "does not and never did mean 'muddy water' but 'Wooden Canoe,' [and that] it belongs to the Illinois dialect of the Algonquin

[263] *Our State of Missouri,* Thomas J. Walker and Luther Hardaway (The Macmillan Company, New York, 1928) p. 102-3.
[264] *The History of Missouri from the Earliest Times to the Present.* Revised Edition, Perry S. Rader (The Hugh Stephens Printing and Stationery Company, Jefferson City, Missouri, 1922) p. 13.
Some of the writers who discuss the meaning of the name *Missouri* as *muddy water* are:
Our State of Missouri, Thomas J. Walker and Luther Hardaway (The Macmillan Company, New York, 1928) p. 102.
The Origin of Certain Place Names in the United States, Second Edition, Henry Gannett, Department of the Interior, United States Geological Survey, Charles W. Walcott, Director, Bulletin No. 258, Series F, Geography, 45 (Government Printing Office, Washington, D.C., 1905) p. 210.
A History of Missouri from the Earliest Explorations and Settlements until the Admission of the State into the Union, Louis Houck (R. R. Donnelley and Sons Company, Chicago, Illinois, 1908) vol. 1, p. 1-2.

Indian language, the language which was generally spoken (as maintained by many historians) by the various aboriginal tribes between the Mississippi River and Delaware Bay." [265]

Williams concludes his article by saying, "Let us remember in [the] future, therefore, the name given to the great State of Missouri has nothing to do with 'muddy' or any other category of water, but means—'The town of the large canoes.' "

G. W. Featherstonhaugh explains how the Nahcotah Indians called the Missouri river and the country lying beyond it, *Minnay Shóshóh Chhráy,* which meant "Water muddy Hill." [266] Featherstonhaugh also says that by "abbreviating the first word, 'Minnay,' of its last four letters, and afterwards the others, according to the practice of the French, the word Mi-sho-ray is produced." [267] It is probable, he says, that the word *Missouri* came into existence in this way, and that the French adventurers named the river.

Nebraska

The word *Nebraska* probably appeared in print for the first time in the report of John C. Fremont, who was sent by the United States Government in 1842 "to explore the [western] plains and the Rocky Mountains." [268] Fremont used the word in speaking of the Nebraska river.

In his annual report, dated November 30, 1844, William Wilkins, Secretary of War, recommended that the section of the country called Nebraska Country be organized as a

---

[265] *Missouri, Mother of the West,* Walter Williams and Floyd Calvin Shoemaker, assisted by an Advisory Council (The American Historical Society, Incorporated, Chicago and New York, 1930) vol. I, p. 3-4.

[266] *A Canoe Voyage up the Minnay Sotor,* G. W. Featherstonhaugh (Richard Bentley, London, England, 1847) vol. I, p. 402-3.

[267] *Ibidem,* p. 403.

[268] *History and Stories of Nebraska,* Addison Erwin Sheldon (The University Publishing Company, Chicago, Illinois, and Lincoln, Nebraska, 1913) p. 232.

territory, "and that it should be called **Nebraska** on account of the great river which bisected it." [269]

The Douglas Bill, bringing into existence the two new territories, Kansas and Nebraska, was passed and received the signature of President Franklin Pierce on May 30, 1854. [270]

Authorities differ as to the original Indian word from which the name *Nebraska* is derived. Some say that it is a French version of the Omaha name *ni-ubthatka,* the first part of the word, *ni,* signifying *water,* and the second part *bthatka,* meaning *spreading.* Others affirm that the State name comes from the word *"Niobrara,* the name of a river in the northern part of the state," which is an approximation of the "Omaha name *Niubthatka,* meaning *spreading river."* [271]

Addison E. Sheldon, the Secretary of the Nebraska State Historical Society, implies that Nebraska was probably named after the Platte river, and that the name was derived from *Nebrathka,* meaning *flat water,* the Otoe Indian name for that river. It may be seen that the correct meaning of the Indian words, in whatever forms they are found, is the same as that of the name of the Platte river, signifying *flat* or *spreading water.* [272]

New Mexico

The name *New Mexico* is said to be older than any other state name except that of Florida. The first known record of the name is found in the narrative of Antonio de Espejo in 1583, the name "having been given by Espejo to

[269] *Collections of the Nebraska State Historical Society,* edited by Albert Watkins (The Nebraska State Historical Society, Lincoln, Nebraska, 1911) vol. 16, p. 27.

[270] *History and Stories of Nebraska,* Addison Erwin Sheldon (The University Publishing Company, Chicago, Illinois, and Lincoln, Nebraska, 1919) p. 236.

[271] *Publications of the Nebraska State Historical Society,* edited by Albert Watkins (Published by the Nebraska State Historical Society, Lincoln, Nebraska, 1919) vol. 19, p. 134.

[272] *History and Stories of Nebraska,* Addison Erwin Sheldon (The University Publishing Company, Chicago, Illinois, and Lincoln, Nebraska, 1919) p. 233.

the fifteen provinces he discovered." Gonzales de Mendoza says that Espejo named this territory New Mexico " 'because it is similar in many things to the other Mexico already discovered.' "[273]

Alvar Nuñez Cabeza de Vaca and his three companions in 1535 or 1536 were the first aliens to enter what is now New Mexico.[274] Benjamin M. Read says that Espejo did not give the name to this country, but that the name he gave was *Nueva Andalucia*[275] [or New Spain].

Paul A. F. Walter says that the name *New Mexico* was first applied in 1568, "to the region which then covered part of the present State of New Mexico, included what is now Arizona, [a] part of Colorado and extended as far north as Yellowstone Park and east to Louisiana,"[276] the name being given by Francisco del Cano sent north by Ibarra to discover "another Mexico." Twitchell thinks that the name *New Mexico* may have been "applied in later years to a country Governor Ibarra had never seen."[277]

New Mexico was ceded to the United States by the *Treaty of Guadalupe Hidalgo* on February 2, 1848. It became a Territory on September 9, 1850. Congress passed the *Enabling Act* for its statehood on June 20, 1910, but on account of the difficulty encountered by those framing the proposed State Constitution, New Mexico was not admitted as a State into the Union until January 6, 1912.[278]

[273] *A Concise History of New Mexico*, Second Edition, L. Bradford Prince (The Torch Press, Cedar Rapids, Iowa, 1914) p. 13.

[274] "Historical Sketch of New Mexico," Paul A. F. Walter, in *New Mexico, the Land of Opportunity* (Board of Exposition Managers, A. E. Koehler, Junior, Editor and Publisher, San Diego, California, 1915) p. 13.

[275] *An Illustrated History of New Mexico*, Benjamin M. Read, translated into English under the direction of the author by Eleuterio Baca (Printed by the New Mexican Printing Company, Las Vegas, New Mexico, 1912) p. 187.

[276] "Historical Sketch of New Mexico," Paul A. F. Walter, in *New Mexico, the Land of Opportunity* (Board of Exposition Managers, A. E. Koehler, Junior, Editor and Publisher, San Diego, California, 1915) p. 13.

[277] *The Leading Facts of New Mexican History*, Ralph Emerson Twitchell (The Torch Press, Cedar Rapids, Iowa, 1911) vol. i, p. 283-4.

[278] "Historical Sketch of New Mexico," Paul A. F. Walter, in *New Mexico, the Land of Opportunity* (Board of Exposition Managers, A. E. Koehler, Junior, Editor and Publisher, San Diego, California, 1915) p. 16.

Historians generally agree that New Mexico was named after Old Mexico in honor of the Spanish adventurers who explored it, or that it was named in honor of three Franciscan missionaries, Fray Augustine Rodrigues or Ruis, Fray Francisco Lopez, and Juan de Santa Maria, who went into this territory from Mexico [279] in 1581-1582, and lost their lives in an effort to convert the Indians to Christianity.

Ladd says that Niça first discovered New Mexico, and called it the kingdom of San Francisco. [280]

Many historians do not endeavor to trace the word *Mexico* to its original source; but those who do agree that it is derived from the name of the Mexican god *Mexitli* or *Mexitl*. [281] This deity was also called *Uitzilopochtli*. [282]

Co, the final syllable of the word Mexico, comes from the Sanscrit term *ku*, and signifies *land*; [283] therefore the name Mexico means *the land of Mexitli or Mexitl*.

For the derivation of the word *new*, see the discussion of the name of New York State.

The Dakotas

Alfred Barnaby Thomas says that Coronado in 1541 went "beyond the Arkansas River" [284] into "the Kansas of today." Paul A. Jones in *Quivira* on page 13, records evidence that Coronado went into the Indian village, Quvira, four miles west of Lyons, Kansas. Afterwards the Spaniards of Mexico went up the *Big Muddy* to the Dakotas. In 1738 Verendrye and his party came from the Great Lakes and stopped near the present site of Minot. In 1804 the Lewis and Clark Expedition explored, for the United States Government, the territory now included in the

[279] "The Story of New Mexico," Horatio O. Ladd, in *The Story of the States* (D. Lothrop Company, Boston, Massachusetts, 1891) p. 77-84.
[280] *Ibidem*, p. 84.
[281] *A Mexican-Aryan Comparative Vocabulary*, T. S. Denison (T. S. Denison, Publisher, Chicago, Illinois, 1909) p. 53.
[282] *Ibidem*, p. 53.
[283] *Ibidem*, p. 35.
[284] *After Coronado: Spanish Exploration Northeast of New Mexico, 1696-1727, Documents from the Archives of Spain, Mexico, and New Mexico*, translated and edited by Alfred Barnaby Thomas (University of Oklahoma Press, Norman, Oklahoma, 1935) p. 5.

Dakotas, [285] which region had previously been explored both by the Spanish and by the French as has been stated above.

In 1857 people from Saint Paul came and located claims in the region lying around Sioux Falls, calling their territory Dakota. [286]

"On March 2, 1861, President Buchanan signed the bill creating Dakota Territory." [287] About 1871 the Territory of Dakota began petitioning Congress to divide it into two parts. These petitions continued until November 2, 1889, [288] when North Dakota and South Dakota were admitted into the Union as separate states with their present boundaries.

The Dakotas were named after the Dahkota or Dakota Indians. These Indians called themselves *Lakotas* or *Dakotas,* which name in their language meant *friends* or *allies.* Their enemies applied to them as a term of contempt, the name Sioux, a sort of nickname, which is "a French-Canadian abbreviation of the Chippewa *Nadowe-is-iw,* a diminutive of *nadowe,* "an adder," hence "an enemy." *Nadoweisiw-eg* is the diminutive plural. The diminutive singular and plural were applied by the Chippewa to the Dakota, and to the Huron to distinguish them from the Iroquois proper, the true "adders" or "enemies." According to Chippewa tradition the name was first applied to a body of Indians living on an island somewhere

---

[285] *A Brief History of North Dakota,* Herbert Clay Fish and R. M. Black (American Book Company, New York, 1926) p. 20, 22, 32, 33.

[286] *History of North Dakota: Early History of North Dakota,* Clement A. Lounsberry (Liberty Press, Washington, D.C., 1919) p. 216.

[287] *Collections of the State* [North Dakota] *Historical Society,* O. G. Libby, Editor (Printed by Normanden Publishing Company, Grand Forks, North Dakota, 1923) vol. 5, p. 171.

[288] *A Brief History of North Dakota,* Herbert Clay Fish and R. M. Black (American Book Company, New York, 1926) p. 131, 143.
  History of South Dakota: South Dakota, Sui Generis, Stressing the Unique and Dramatic in South Dakota History, Doane Robinson, with *South Dakota Biography,* by a Separate Staff of Special Writers, issued in three volumes, illustrated (American Historical Society, Incorporated, Chicago and New York, 1930) vol. 1, p. 316.

east of Detroit." [289] Some authorities say that the name Sioux is an Ojibway word meaning foes. Their enemies used this nickname so constantly that it almost replaced the name Dakotas, the real name of the tribe.

The word *Dahkota* means to be "allied or joined together in friendly compact, and is equivalent to 'E pluribus unum,' the motto on the seal of the United States." [290]

Ohio

The State of Ohio was named after the Ohio river, which forms its southern boundary. [291] The section of the country now known as Ohio was explored by the French. This territory became a state with its present name and boundaries on February 19, 1803. [292]

The Shawanoese Indians called the Ohio river, *Kis, ke, pi, la Sepe,* meaning *eagle river.* The Wyandot word, *O, he, zuh,* as the French pronounced it, was *Ohio.* This word is thought to have been employed by the French voyagers in their boat songs, the French equivalent being *la belle rivière,* meaning in English, *the fair and beautiful river.* The Wyandot word *O, he, zuh* meant *great, grand, fair to look upon.* [293]

Townsend suggests several Indian words from which the name *Ohio* may have been derived, among which are: the Iroquois word *Oheo,* denoting *beautiful,* spelled by the

[289] *Handbook of American Indians North of Mexico,* edited by Frederick Webb Hodge, Smithsonian Institution, Bureau of American Ethnology, Bulletin No. 30 (Government Printing Office, Washington, D.C., 1907) part I, p. 376.

[290] *The History of Minnesota from the Earliest French Explorations to the Present Time,* Second Edition, Revised and Enlarged, Edward Duffield Neill (J. B. Lippincott and Company, Philadelphia, Pennsylvania, 1873) p. 50.

[291] *U. S.: An Index to the United States of America,* compiled by Malcolm Townsend (D. Lothrop Company, Boston, Massachusetts, 1890) p. 61.

[292] *Ohio: First Fruits of the Ordinance of 1787,* Rufus King (Houghton Mifflin and Company, New York, 1891) p. 293.

[293] *Historical Collections of Ohio,* Henry Howe (Published for the author by Derby, Bradley and Company, Cincinnati, Ohio, 1847) p. 574.

French *O-y-o*, and the name *Ohuipeekhanne*, meaning *a stream very white with froth.* [294]

Gregory and Guitteau derive the name *Ohio* from the Iroquois word *Ohion-hiió*, signifying *beautiful river.* [295]

Hanna says: "The Delaware Indian name *Kittanning* means '*at the Great River,*' great river being the equivalent of the Iroquois word *Ohio*. As to the Great River of the Senecas, the name, *Ohio*, was at first applied to this river by the Iroquois from the sources of the Allegheny to the mouth of the Mississippi. The secondary meaning of *io*, as 'grand,' or 'beautiful,' came to be applied to the Ohio only after the discovery of the upper Mississippi by the French." [296]

Oklahoma

The bill creating the Territory of Oklahoma was signed on May 2, 1890. On November 16, 1907, President Theodore Roosevelt issued a proclamation declaring Oklahoma a State. [297]

Historians agree [298] that the name *Oklahoma* is derived from the two Choctaw words, *okla,* signifying *people,* and *humma* or *homma,* meaning *red;* consequently the name signifies *red people.* Byington [299] gives the meanings of *okla* as *a people, a tribe, a nation, citizens, folks, persons, men,* and *population.* For *humma* [or *homma*] he gives the meanings *red, crimson, redness, rouge,* and *scarlet.* [300]

[294] *U. S.: An Index to the United States of America,* compiled by Malcolm Townsend (D. Lothrop Company, Boston, Massachusetts, 1890) p. 61-2.

[295] *History and Geography of Ohio,* William Mumford Gregory and William Backus Guitteau (Ginn and Company, Boston, Massachusetts, 1929) p. 5.

[296] *The Wilderness Trail,* Charles A. Hanna (G. P. Putnam's Sons, New York and London, 1911) vol. 1, p. 290.

[297] *A Standard History of Oklahoma,* Joseph B. Thoburn (The American Historical Society, Chicago and New York, 1916) vol. 2, p. 648, 857.

[298] *The Story of Oklahoma,* Muriel Hazel Wright (Webb Publishing Company, Oklahoma City, Oklahoma, 1929) p. 164.

[299] *A Dictionary of the Choctaw Language,* Cyrus Byington, printed in Bulletin No. 46 of the Bureau of American Ethnology (Government Printing Office, Washington, D.C., 1915) p. 297

[300] *Ibidem,* p. 170.

Joseph B. Thoburn, the present Curator of the Oklahoma Historical Society, tells how the State of Oklahoma was named. He obtained the facts about the naming of the State from a friend and neighbor of the late Reverend Allen Wright, with whom he discussed the matter in detail. Allen Wright represented the Choctaws in the proceedings before Congress which officially created the Indian Territory. During the proceedings "the Commissioner of Indian Affairs rather abruptly asked: 'What would you call your territory?' To this inquiry, Reverend Allen Wright, a Choctaw delegate, impulsively replied 'Okla homa!' Whereat, several of the Cherokee delegates were said to have shown signs of displeasure" considering themselves as an elder brother and entitled to be heard first. The matter was dropped then, but "Wright wrote the name 'Territory of Oklahoma' into the Choctaw-Chickasaw treaty with the United States Government as that of the 'proposed new territory.' " [301] The expression *Indian Territory* was used as the name of the division admitted as a territory at that time, and Oklahoma was afterwards employed for the Territory, now the State of Oklahoma. When the bill for the organization of the Indian Territory came up before the Forty-first Congress, "the name 'Oklahoma' is said to have been suggested to the House Committee on Indian Affairs by Col. Elias C. Boudinot, of the Cherokee Nation, out of deference to the clause in the Choctaw-Chickasaw Treaty of 1866 which specified that the proposed intertribal commonwealth should be called 'The Territory of Oklahoma.' " [302]

Oregon

The name *Oregon* was first applied to the Columbia river, next to a vast undefined territory, known as "the

[301] A letter from Joseph B. Thoburn, Curator of the Oklahoma Historical Society, Oklahoma City, Oklahoma, April 15, 1930.

[302] *A Standard History of Oklahoma,* Joseph B. Thoburn (The American Historical Society, Chicago and New York, 1916) vol. 2, p. 462.

countries of the Columbia," [303] later to the Territory of Oregon, and last to the State.

Jonathan Carver first used the name *Oregon* [304] in a document entitled *Travels through the Interior Parts of North America,* published in London in 1778. Authorities think that Carver's use of the word *Oregon* is a corruption of the name *Ouragon* or *Ourigan,* "which was communicated to him by Major Robert Rogers, the English commandant of the frontier military and trading post at Mackinac, Michigan, during the years (1766-1767) of Captain Carver's journey to the Upper Valley of the Mississippi river and to lake Superior." It is thought that Rogers obtained the word *Ouragon* or *Ourigan* from French Canadian voyageurs and traders, [305] but Rees suggests that Jonathan Carver heard the word spoken by the Sioux Indians. [306]   The French word *Ouragan* is supposed to be the source of the present English word *hurricane.* [305]

T. C. Elliott says that "recent research established the fact that the name Oregon is a corruption or variation by Jonathan Carver of the name Ouragon, or Ourigan." [307] The Oregon river about 1765 was supposed to rise "in Western Minnesota and to flow westward" through a tornado region, and its name, *Ouragon,* is thought to be "practically the same as" the French word *ouragan,* meaning then, "windstorm, hurricane, or tornado." [308]

In his poem *Thanatopsis,* published in 1812, William

---

[303] *The History of Oregon and California,* Robert Greenhow (Charles C. Little and James Brown, Boston, Massachusetts, 1844) p. 20, 142, 359.

[304] "The Origin of the Name Oregon," T. C. Elliott, in the *Quarterly of the Oregon Historical Society* vol. 22, June, 1921, no. 2 (The Ivy Press, Portland, Oregon, 1921) p. 93.

[305] *Oregon: Her History, Her Great Men, Her Literature,* John B. Horner (The J. K. Gill Company, Portland, Oregon, 1921) p. 19.

[306] "Oregon: Its M aning, Origin, and Application," John E. Rees, in the *Quarterly of the Oregon Historical Society,* Vol. 21, December, 1920, No. 4 (The Ivy Press, Portland, Oregon, 1920) p. 310.

[307] "The Origin of the Name Oregon," T. C. Elliott, in the *Quarterly of the Oregon Historical Society,* Vol. 22, June, 1921, No. 2 (The Ivy Press, Portland, Oregon, 1921) p. 91.

[308] Ibidem. p. 99.

Cullen Bryant used the word *Oregon* as the name of the Oregon river, and did much to popularize the name.

John F. Rees says that "the word *Oregon* is derived from the Shoshoni Indian expression, meaning *The River of the West,* originating from the two Shoshoni words *'Ogwa,'* [denoting] *River,* and 'Pe-on,' [meaning] West," [309] the complete Shoshoni word being *ogwa pe-on.* Rees also points out that the first syllable in the word *ogwa* means *undulations,* and that this syllable, in the original Indian language, was "the basis of such words as *'river,' 'snake,' 'salmon,'* or anything having a *wavy motion.*" He further states that the sound *pah,* given to the second syllable of the word, *ogwa,* meant *water;* consequently, the Indian word *ogwa peon* [*pe-ah*] signified *undulating water.*

William G. Steel, the first President of the Oregon Geographic Board, says that "it is claimed that [the word] 'Oregon' " is derived from the Shoshoni word *oyer-un-gon,* denoting *a place of plenty.* [310]

Bishop Blanchet thinks the name *Oregon* came from the term *orejones,* the plural form of the Spanish word *orejone,* meaning *big ears.* It is also his opinion that the term was applied by the Spaniards to the tribes of Indians whose warriors had enlarged their ears by "loads of ornaments." [311]

Tennessee

From its beginning to the time that it was admitted as a State into the Union, Tennessee had a long and checkered career. It was a part of the original territory granted by King Charles II to the Lords Proprietors of Carolina in 1665. It was known as the *Washington District* from 1775 to 1776. It was formed into the *State of Franklin* on August 23, 1784, and existed as such until 1788. It was

[309] "Oregon: Its Meaning, Origin, and Application," John E. Rees, in the *Quarterly of the Oregon Historical Society,* December, 1920, no. 4, vol. 21 (The Ivy Press, Portland, Oregon, 1920) p. 319.

[310] *Oregon: Her History, Her Great Men, Her Literature,* John B. Horner (The J. K. Gill Company, Portland, Oregon, 1921) p. 20.

[311] *Ibidem,* p. 20.

formed into the *Territory South of the Ohio* in 1790, and on June 1, 1796, it became the State of Tennessee. [312]

The word *Tennessee*, like most other state names derived from the American Indian dialects, cannot be definitely traced to any specific parent Indian word since there are several Indian words from which historians claim it originated; but the consensus of critical opinion seems to be that the State name is derived from the Indian word *Tenassee, Tanasi, Tanassee,* or *Tansi,* the name of the ancient capital of the Cherokee tribe which dwelt "on the west bank of the present Little Tennessee River, a few miles above the mouth of Tellico, and afterwards gave the name to the Tennessee river and to the State." [313]

Historians say that the first mention of the name *Tennessee* [314] (*Tanassee*) was by Alexander Cummings, who, in 1730, "had been sent by Great Britain to meet the chiefs at all the Cherokee towns at Nequassee, near the present town of Franklin in North Carolina." [315]

The name *Tennessee* is derived from the name of the Indian town *Tenassee, Tanasi, Tanassee* or *Tansi,* the meaning of which is not known. Hodge says that this name "has lost its meanings, all the so-called derivations being fanciful." [316]

[312] *The Encyclopedia Americana* (Americana Corporation, New York and Chicago, 1929) vol. 26, p. 428-30.

The New International Encyclopaedia, Second Edition (Dodd, Mead and Company, New York, 1930) vol. 22, p. 101-2.

[313] *The Annals of Tennessee to the End of the Eighteenth Century,* James Gattys McGregor Ramsey (Walker and James, Charleston, South Carolina, 1853) p. 47.

"The Volunteer State, Tennessee, as a Seceder," Susie Gentry, in the *North Carolina Booklet* (E. M. Uzzell and Company, Printers and Binders, Raleigh, North Carolina, July, 1903) vol. 3, no. 3, p. 7.

[314] *The Annals of Tennessee to the End of the Eighteenth Century,* James Gattys McGregor Ramsey (Walker and James, Charleston, South Carolina, 1853) p. 47.

Tennessee: The Volunteer State, 1769-1923, John Trotwood Moore and Austin P. Foster (The S. J. Clarke Publishing Company, Chicago and Nashville, 1923) vol. 1, p. 51.

[315] *Tennessee: The Volunteer State, 1769-1923,* John Trotwood Moore and Austin P. Foster (The S. J. Clarke Publishing Company, Chicago and Nashville, 1923) vol. 1, p. 51.

[316] *Handbook of American Indians North of Mexico,* edited by Frederick Webb Hodge, Smithsonian Institution, Bureau of American Ethnology, Bulletin No. 30 (Government Printing Office, Washington, D.C., 1910) part 2, p. 729.

Some of the fanciful derivations of the original name
are *river with a big bend,* and *a curved spoon.* [317]
There were several names suggested for the State when
the matter of naming it came up, one of which was
Cherake, the old Indian name for what is now the Tennessee river. The river, however, had been called the
Tennessee for a long time, and the whole Southwest Territory was often called the *Tennessee country;* [318] therefore
Tennessee was adopted as the name of the State.

Texas

The name *Texas* was probably first applied to such
tribes of Indians as banded themselves together for mutual
protection. This name was first given to the region
occupied by these Indians, known as "The Texas Province"
about the year 1690. [319]

Texas was a republic from March 2, 1836, until Anson
Jones, the last President of the Republic of Texas, turned
over the executive authority of the republic to James
Pinkney Henderson, the newly elected Governor of the
State of Texas on February 19, 1846. [320]

The name *Texas* is derived from the Indian name
Texia [321] or from the Spanish form *Tejas,* signifying *allies,
friends,* or *confederates,* a name commonly applied to
Indian tribes that allied themselves together for mutual
protection. [322] While this origin is generally considered

[317] *U. S.: An Index to the United States of America,* compiled by
Malcolm Townsend (D. Lothrop Company, Boston, Massachusetts, 1890)
p. 63.

[318] *A School History of Tennessee,* S. E. Scates (World Book Company, Chicago and New York, 1925) p. 200-1.

[319] *The History and Geography of Texas as Told in County Names,*
Zachary Taylor Fulmore (The Press of E. L. Steck, Austin, Texas, 1915)
p. vii.

[320] *Historical Review of South-East Texas,* Honorable Dermot H.
Hardy and Major Ingham S. Roberts, Associate Editors (The Lewis
Publishing Company, Chicago, Illinois, 1910) vol. i, p. 141-63.

[321] *The History of the Pacific States of North America,* Hubert Howe
Bancroft (A. L. Bancroft and Company, San Francisco, California, 1883)
vol. 10, p. 391.

[322] *The History and Geography of Texas as Told in County Names,*
Zachary Taylor Fulmore (The Press of E. L. Steck, Austin, Texas, 1915)
p. vii.

correct, J. M. Morphis says that "at an early day some Spaniards travelling the Camino del Rey, between San Antonio and the Hondo, camped on the Neches, and their commander, in the morning, beholding many spider-webs between himself and the rising sun, all spangled with dew drops and glittering like diamonds, joyfully exclaimed: *'Mira las tejas!'*—that is to say, 'Look at the spider webs!'—and named the land Texas." [323]

Utah

The first organization of what is now the State of Utah was effected in 1849, and called the *Provisional State of Deseret*. The passage of the *Omnibus Bill* on September 9, 1850, brought the Territory of Utah into official existence. However, it was not until April 5, 1851, that the *Provisional State of Deseret,* dissolving itself, agreed to become a territory of the United States. [324]   The proclamation admitting Utah as a State into the Union was signed on January 4, 1896. [325]

The Utah nation of the Shoshones contained many tribes.   The name *Utah* in early times was variously spelled as follows: *Youta, Eutah, Utaw,* and *Utah.* [326]

The Indian name *Utah,* a corruption of the word *Eutaw,* means " 'in the tops of the mountains,' " or, as the Indians themselves expressed it, *high-up.*   Other meanings given to the word include *the land of the sun* and *the land of plenty,* but "most of the Utes and Paiutes who remember the traditions of their fathers speak of their people (as those) who live on the heights." [327]

[323] *History of Texas from Its Discovery and Settlement,* J. M. Morphis (United States Publishing Company, New York, 1874), p. 10.
[324] *Utah and the Nation,* Leland Hargrave Creer, *A University of Washington Publication in the Social Sciences,* Vol. 7, July, 1929 (University of Washington Press, Seattle, Washington, 1929) p. 63, 87, 93.
[325] *The Encyclopaedia Britannica,* Fourteenth Edition (Encyclopaedia Britannica, Incorporated, New York, 1929) vol. 22, p. 913.
[326] *History of Utah,* Hubert Howe Bancroft (The History Company, San Francisco, California, 1890) p. 34-5.
[327] *The Founding of Utah,* Levi Edgar Young (Charles Scribner's Sons, New York, 1923) p. 3-4.

Wisconsin

After having been successively a part of the Northwest Territory, of Indiana, Illinois, and of Michigan territories, Wisconsin became a territory in her own name in 1836. [328] On May 29, 1848, Wisconsin was admitted as a state into the Union by an act of Congress. [329]

Historians generally agree that the aboriginal word from which the present name, *Wisconsin,* is derived is not known. Reuben Gold Thwaites says that "the meaning of the aboriginal word . . . is now unknown, [that] popular writers declare that it signifies 'gathering of the waters,' or 'meeting of the waters,' having reference, possibly, to the occasional mingling of the divergent streams over the low-lying watershed at Fox-Wisconsin portage; but [that] there is no warrant for this." [330]

The Wisconsin Magazine of History in its section called *The Question Box* says that "Wisconsin is named for its principal river, but [that] the origin of that name has never been satisfactorily determined [and] that it had over twenty spellings on the early maps ranging from 'Miscous' to the ordinary French form 'Ouisconsin,' anglicized as 'Wisconsin.' " [331]

Three or more writers state that the name, *Wisconsin,* is of Chippewa origin, [332] and Alfred Brunson says that

[328] *Wisconsin in Three Centuries* (*1634-1905*), Henry C. Campbell (The Century History Company, New York, 1906) vol. 2, p. 159.

[329] *Appleton's New Practical Cyclopedia,* edited by Marcus Benjamin (D. Appleton and Company, New York, 1920) vol. 6, p. 427.

[330] "Wisconsin, the Americanization of a French Settlement" in *American Commonwealths,* Reuben Gold Thwaites (Houghton Mifflin Company, Boston and New York, 1908) p. 233.

[331] *The Wisconsin Magazine of History: Publications of the State Historical Society of Wisconsin,* Joseph Schafer, Superintendent, Milo M. Quaife, Editor (Published Quarterly by the State Historical Society of Wisconsin at the Collegiate Press of the George Banta Publishing. Company, Menasha, Wisconsin) vol. 3, no. 3, March 1920, p. 364.

[332] "Wisconsin Geographical Names, "Alfred Brunson, in *Wisconsin Historical Society Collections: First Annual Report and Collections of the State Historical Society of Wisconsin, for the Year 1854* (Beriah Brown, Printer, Madison, Wisconsin, 1855) vol. 1, p. 111.

"Early History of Education in Wisconsin," Honorable W. C. Whitford, President of Milton College, in *Wisconsin Historical Society Collections: Report and Collections of the State Historical Society of* "the State derives its name from the principal river which runs centrally through it." [333] He further states upon the authority of an Indian trader, that "the Chippewas upon its head waters call this river *Wees-kon-san* which signifies 'the gathering of the waters.'" [333]

According to Brunson, the original idea of the name refers to the fact that at its head, several streams gather to make up the Wisconsin river, which flows for a great ways with practically no more tributaries. The French changed the form of the word to Ouisconsin, which brings the first syllable nearer to the Indian sound of the original word than does the present day word *Wis.* He further states that the last syllable, *sin*, "is evidently a derivation from" the original term in both the French and the English forms.

One finds in the records of the early French explorers several forms of the name, Wisconsin, some of which are: *Ouisconsin,* [333a] or *Misconssin,* [333a] *Misconsing,* [333b] and *Mesconsin.* [333c] Louise Phelps Kellogg, Research Asso-

Wisconsin, for the Years, 1867, 1868, and 1869 (Atwood and Rublee, State Printers, Journal Office, Madison, Wisconsin, 1868) vol. 5, p. 351. "Traditions and Recollections of Prairie Du Chien," related by Honorable B. W. Brisbois: noted down and annotated by Lyman C. Draper, in *Wisconsin Historical Society Collections: Report and Collections of the State Historical Society of Wisconsin, for the Years 1880, 1881, and 1882* (David Atwood, State Printer, Madison, Wisconsin, 1882) vol. 9, p. 301.

[333] "Wisconsin Geographical Names," Alfred Brunson, in *Wisconsin Historical Society Collections: First Annual Report and Collections of the State Historical Society of Wisconsin, for the Year 1854* (Beriah Brown, Printer, Madison, Wisconsin, 1855) vol. 1, p. 111.

[333a] *A New Discovery of the Vast Country in America,* Father Louis Hennepin, Reprinted from the Second London Issue of 1698, with Facsimiles of the Original Title-pages, Maps, and Illustrations, and the Addition of Introduction, Notes, and Index by Reuben Gold Thwaites (A. C. McClurg and Company, Chicago, Illinois, 1903) vol. 1, p. 221.

[333b] "Details sur le Voyage de Louis Jolliet," in the *Première Partie, Voyages des Français sur les Grands Lacs et Découverte de L'Ohio et du Mississippi (1614-1684),* in *Découvertes et Établissements des Français dans L'Ouest et dans le Sud de L'Amérique Septentrionale (1614-1754) Mémoires et Documents Originaux Recuellis et Publiés* par Pierre Margry, Membre de la Société de l'Histoire de France, Membre Correspondant des Sociétés Historiques de Massachusetts, de Pennsylvanie et de Buffalo (Imprimerie D. Jouaust, Rue Saint-Honoré, 383, Paris, France, 1876) vol. 5, p. 259.

[333c] *A New Discovery of the Vast Country in America,* Father Louis Hennepin, Reprinted from the Second London Issue of 1698, with Fac-

ciate of the State Historical Society of Wisconsin, says that the names *Meskousing* and *Miskous*, by which the guides of Marquette designated the Wisconsin river, were changed by Pierre Margry to *Misconsing* "in a report appearing under Jolliet's name," [333d] the *n* being a typographical error for *u*. One finds in the records of Hennepin that the following forms of the name appear: *Misconsing*, [334] *Mesconsin*, *Misconsin*, and *Ouisconsin:* [334a] thus it is seen that the initial *ou* of the word began to appear very early in the French documents.

Brunson says that "an attempt was made, a few years since, to restore the second syllable of this name to its original Indian sound by substituting *k* for *c*": but that the legislature decided that the name should be spelled *Wisconsin*. [334b]

The name, *Wisconsin*, was given in the act establishing the territorial government of Wisconsin, dated April 20, 1836. [334c]

Various other spellings of this name are: *Ouisconsin*, *Misconsing*, *Ouisconching*, *Ouiskensing*, *Wiskonsan*, and *Wiskonsin*. [334d]

similes of the Original Title-pages, Maps, and Illustrations, and the Addition of Introduction, Notes, and Index by Reuben Gold Thwaites (A. C. McClurg and Company, Chicago, Illinois, 1903) vol. 2, p. 643.

[333d] "The French Regime in Wisconsin and the Northwest," Louise Phelps Kellogg, in the *Publications of the State Historical Society of Wisconsin*, edited by Joseph Schafer, Superintendent of the Society (Published by the State Historical Society of Wisconsin, composed, printed and bound by The Collegiate Press of the George Banta Publishing Company, Menasa, Wisconsin, 1925) p. 195.

[334] *A New Discovery of the Vast Country in America*, Father Louis Hennepin, Reprinted from the Second London Issue of 1698, with Facsimiles of the Original Title pages, Maps, and Illustrations, and the Addition of Introduction, Notes, and Index by Reuben Gold Thwaites (A. C. McClurg and Company, Chicago, Illinois, 1903) vol. 2, p. 621, 643.

[334a] *Ibidem*, vol. 1, p. 221.

[334b] "Wisconsin Geographical Names." Alfred Brunson, in *Wisconsin Historical Society Collections: First Annual Report and Collections of the State Historical Society of Wisconsin, for the Year 1854* (Beriah Brown, Printer, Madison, Wisconsin, 1855) vol. 1, p. 112.

[334c] *The Public Statutes at Large of the United States of America*, edited by Richard Peters (Charles C. Little and James Brown, Boston, Massachusetts, 1846) Statute 1, vol. 5, p. 10.

[334d] *The Wisconsin Blue Book, 1927*, edited by Fred L. Holmes (Democrat Printing Company, State Printer, Madison, Wisconsin, 1927) p. 2.

The State was named *Wisconsin* by Congress, the name *Wiskonsin* having been suggested by Judge James Duane Doty "in honor of its principal river." [334e]

Wyoming

The country which now forms the State of Wyoming was originally a part of the territory ceded to the United States under the Louisiana Purchase in 1804. [335]

The Territory of Wyoming was organized on July 25, 1868, [335a] and it was admitted as a state into the Union by an act of Congress on July 10, 1890. [336]

The Territory of Wyoming came near being called *Cheyenne*. [337] As early as 1865 James M. Ashley, a member of Congress from Ohio, introduced into the House of Representatives a bill " 'to provide a temporary government for the Territory of Wyoming.' " [338] It was this name which finally was applied to the Territory, and which the State still bears today.

The name *Wyoming* is "supposed to be a corruption of the Indian word *Maughwauwame*," [339] meaning the *large plains* or the *large meadows*. The Indians had given this name to a broad, beautiful valley in Pennsylvania where the tribe once lived. The name *Wyoming* was popularized

---

[334e] "The Story of Wisconsin," in the *Story of the States*, Reuben Gold Thwaites (Lothrop Publishing Company, Boston, Massachusetts, 1899) p. 197.

[335] *History of Natrona County, Wyoming, 1888-1922,* Alfred James Mokler (R. R. Donnelley and Sons Company, The Lakeside Press, Chicago, Illinois, 1923) p. 1.

[335a] *Ibidem,* p. 1.

[336] *The State of Wyoming,* edited and published under the direction of Bryant B. Brooks, Governor (Sheridan Post Company, Printers, Sheridan, Wyoming, 1905) p. 9.

[337] "History of Nevada, Colorado, and Wyoming, 1540-1888," Hubert Howe Bancroft, in *The History of the Pacific States of North America,* vol. 20 (The History Company, San Francisco, California, 1890) p. 740.

[338] *History of Wyoming,* Ichabod S. Bartlett, Editor (The S. J. Clarke Publishing Company, Chicago, Illinois, 1918) vol. 1, p. 164-5.

[339] *History of Natrona County, Wyoming, 1888-1922,* Alfred James Mokler (R. R. Donnelley and Sons Company, The Lakeside Press, Chicago, Illinois, 1923) p. 1.

by its use in a romantic tale by the poet, Thomas Campbell, called *Gertrude of Wyoming,* which tale had its setting in the Wyoming valley in Pennsylvania. This name became so popular that it was applied to several localities in various parts of the United States. Frederick Webb Hodge says that the original form of the Delaware word is *M'cheuwómink,* [340] meaning *upon the great plain.*

STATE NAME DERIVED FROM THE AMERICAN LANGUAGE

Indiana

From 1787 to 1800 what is now the State of Indiana was a part of the Northwest Territory. [341] On July 4, 1800, [342] it became Indiana Territory; and on December 11, 1816, [343] it became the State of Indiana.

Thomas Hutchins' old map, published in 1778, applied the name *Indiana* to the territory lying within the "triangle formed by the Little Kanawha and the Ohio rivers and the western ranges of the Alleghany Mountains," [344] and the company which exploited this region was called the Indiana Land Company as early as 1776. [345]

This land company probably received its name from the Territory called *Indiana*—Indian land, which was ceded to the Philadelphia Trading Company by the Six Nations of the Iroquois Confederacy in 1768. [346]

[340] *Handbook of American Indians North of Mexico,* edited by Frederick Webb Hodge, Smithsonian Institution, Bureau of American Ethnology, Bulletin No. 30 (Government Printing Office, Washington, D. C., 1910) part 2, p. 978.

[341] *The Encyclopedia Americana* (Americana Corporation, New York and Chicago, 1929) vol. 15, p. 37.

[342] *Centennial History and Handbook of Indiana,* George S. Cottman (Max R. Hyman, Indianapolis, Indiana, 1015) p. 42.

[343] *Ibidem,* p. 71.

[344] *Ibidem,* p. 41.

[345] "The Naming of Indiana," Cyrus W. Hodgin, in the *Papers of the Wayne County, Indiana, Historical Society* (Nicholson Printing and Manufacturing Company, Richmond, Indiana, 1903) vol. 1, no. 1, p. 8.

[346] *Ibidem,* p. 6-7.

The name Indiana, meaning *the land of the Indians,* is a Neo-Latin word. [347] It is formed from the word *Indian,* plus the termination *a,* a Latin place-suffix, meaning land. [348] This name *Indiana* is modelled according to the same linguistic law as the words Bulgaria, Andalusia, Virginia, Carolina, Georgia, Louisiana, and Pennsylvania, [348] thus producing another euphonious state name.

The word *India* goes back for its origin through many varied forms to the Sanscrit word *sindhu,* meaning *river.* [349] This Sanscrit name was originally applied to the river now known as the *Indus,* and then to the territory bordering on the river. The early explorers of America, thinking that they had found India, called the natives Indians; thus it becomes evident that Indiana is indebted to the Sanscrit for the original root form upon which her state name is built. [349]

Indiana is the only state name having an American origin as distinguished from those derived from the American Indian dialects.

[347] *Century Cyclopedia of Names,* edited by Benjamin E. Smith (The Century Company, New York, 1911) vol. ii, p. 527.

[348] "The Naming of Indiana," Cyrus W. Hodgin, in the *Papers of the Wayne County, Indiana, Historical Society* (Nicholson Printing and Manufacturing Company, Richmond, Indiana, 1903) vol. i, no. i, p. 7.

[349] *A New English Dictionary,* edited by James A. H. Murray (The Clarendon Press, Oxford, England) vol. v¹, p. 204.

CHAPTER II

THE NICKNAMES OF THE STATES AND OF THEIR INHABITANTS

The origin of the word *nickname* is interesting to those of a philological turn of mind. The word is a hybrid formed by the union of the Anglo-Saxon word *eke,* meaning *besides, in addition,* and the modern English word *name.* The present form, nickname, was made up by the liaison of the expression *an ekename,* the *a* being lost and the *n* attaching itself to the following word, which in the course of time took its present form. The expression *neke name* or *eke name* appears in the English language as early as 1440. [1] The *Americana* says that "possibly the name came from nick, to cut; for the nickname is primarily a cutting of the full name, such as Ned for Edward, Bess for Elizabeth, Nick for Nicholas." [1]

According to the standard lexicographers, as well as to the general usage of the word, "a nickname is a name or appelation added to or substituted for, the proper name of a person, place, [2] [animal, or object,] usually implying ridicule or reproach, often being an approbrious or contemptuous appellation." In many instances, especially in the case of children or young animals, the nickname is a diminutive of the real name.

A nickname frequently condenses into a single word meaning that it would take much space to express otherwise. It has been said that the meaning of nicknames is

[1] *The Encyclopedia Americana* (Americana Corporation, New York and Chicago, 1929) vol. 20, p. 323.

[2] *A New English Dictionary,* edited by Sir James A. H. Murray (The Clarendon Press, Oxford, England vol. VI, p. 132.

The Century Dictionary and Cyclopedia (The Century Company, New York, 1911) vol. VI, p. 3987.

sometimes a mystery. "Often they are apparently mean-
ingless and incapable of any rational explanation; yet they
are probably due, in such cases, to some subtle, impercep-
tible analogy of which even their authors were hardly
conscious." [3]

Nicknames doubtless are as old as the human race.
There are few persons who do not have one or more of
these sobriquets. Personal nicknames differ from national
nicknames in the respect that they are generally given to
individuals by others, while national nicknames as a rule
are first applied by the people constituting the citizenship
of the individual nation to which the nickname is attributed. The nicknames were given to the states of the
Union by their inhabitants or by others to commemorate
some characteristic, industry, or trait of character of the
inhabitants, to emphasize physical features of the states,
or for historical reasons.

Judge Charles E. Flandrau says that State nicknames
"never originate by any recognized authority. They arise
from some event that suggests them, or from some important utterance that makes an impression on the public
mind." [4]

The people comprising the citizenship of the states of
the Union, as well as the states themselves, have various
nicknames. Some of these are amusing; some are mirth-
producing; and others are characteristic of the people or
of their occupations.

ALABAMA

Alabama is the possessor of four nicknames: *The
Cotton Plantation State,* the *Cotton State,* the *Lizard
State,* and the *Yellowhammer State.* Leopold Wagner says
that "Alabama is called *The Cotton Plantation State,* just

[3] *A Book of Nicknames,* John Goff (Courier-Journal Job Printing
Company, Louisville, Kentucky, 1892) p. 8.

[4] *The History of Minnesota and Tales of the Frontier,* Judge Charles
E. Flandrau (Published by E. W. Porter, St. Paul, Minnesota, 1900)
p. 242.

as the cotton-producing states generally in the South are referred to under the name of Cottonia and Cottondom." [5] The name, the *Cotton State*, designates that its possessor is the central state in the cotton belt. [6] During the earlier times along Alabama's streams lizards were numerous. The people lived along the borders of these streams or hidden in the woods nearby in which respects their lives were analogous to those of the lizards; [7] consequently, the State came to be called the *Lizard State*. The *Yellowhammer State* became a nickname of Alabama during the War between the States because the gray uniforms of the Confederate soldiers, having been home-dyed, had a yellowish tinge. [8]

The Alabamians are called *Lizards* and *Yellowhammers*. These nicknames were given to the people of Alabama for the reasons that the State was called the *Lizard State* and the *Yellowhammer State*, which have been accounted for in the discussion above.

ARIZONA

Arizona has seven nicknames: The *Apache State*, the *Aztec State*, the *Baby State*, the *Copper State*, the *Italy of America*, the *Sand Hill State*, the *Sunset State* or the *Sunset Land*, and the *Valentine State*. The nickname, the *Apache State*, was applied to Arizona, doubtless, from the great numbers of Apache Indians originally inhabiting this territory. The *Americana* says that for nearly ten years the Territory of Arizona "was the scene of one of the most awful Indian wars in history." [9] Arizona is called the *Aztec State*, [10] probably, from the fact that many

[5] *More About Names*, Leopold Wagner (T. Fisher Unwin, London, 1893) p. 28.
[6] *The New International Encyclopaedia*, Second Edition (Dodd Mead and Company, New York, 1930) vol. 21, p. 463.
[7] *U. S.: An Index to the United States of America*, compiled by Malcolm Townsend (D. Lothrop Company, Boston, Massachusetts, 1890) p. 75.
[8] A letter from Marie B. Owen, Director of the Department of State Archives and History, Montgomery, Alabama, March 18, 1930.
[9] *The Encyclopedia Americana* (Americana Corporation, New York and Chicago, 1929) vol. 2, p. 51.
[10] *A Book of Nicknames*, John Goff (Courier-Journal Job Printing Company, Louisville, Kentucky, 1892) p. 13.

of the old ruins in the Gila river and the Salt river valleys and in other parts of Arizona have Aztec names, and were erroneously considered by some to have been built by the Aztecs. [11] The *Baby State* refers to Arizona's being next to the last state to come into the Union. It, the forty-seventh state, was admitted to statehood on February 14, 1912.

The sobriquet, the *Copper State,* [11a] has been applied to Arizona because it produces more copper than any other state in the Union.

Arizona is nicknamed the *Italy of America* from the facts that so much of the State is mountainous and that it contains some of the most beautiful scenic regions of America, consisting of mountain peaks, canyon cuts, mountain spurs, buttes, cones of extinct volcanoes, and the Grand Canyon, one of the most gorgeous of all nature's pictorial scenes.

Arizona is designated as the *Sand Hill State,* perhaps, from the facts that the Mexican Cordilleras divide the State diagonally into two regions, and from the desert-like appearance of many regions of the State. "The whole State, however, is mountainous in the form of short, isolated ranges having a general northwest-southeast trend, which are abrupt sterile, and gashed by deep canyons and dry watercourses." [12]   The nickname, the *Sunset State* or the *Sunset Land,* was probably given to Arizona because of her elaborate sunsets, especially those in the Grand Canyon, or because of the varied colorings of the Canyon at different times of the day.

Patrick Hamilton said that "there is no region on the globe, not even excepting the Italian peninsula, that can show such grand effects of light and shade, such gorgeousness of coloring, or such magnificent sun-bathed land-

[11] *Arizona, the Youngest State*: Arizona, Prehistoric—Aboriginal—Pioneer—Modern, The Nation's Commonwealth within a Land of Ancient Culture, James H. McClintock (The S. J. Clarke Publishing Company, Chicago, Illinois, 1916) vol. 1, p. 6, 7.

[12] *The New International Encyclopaedia,* Second Edition (Dodd. Mead and Company, New York, 1930) vol. 2, p. 116.

[11a] *The World Book Encyclopedia* (W. F. Quarrie and Company, Chicago, Illinois, 1935) vol. 1, p. 394.

scapes. When the banks of clouds around the western horizon look like masses of burnished gold set in a sea of silver, then is presented a picture to which neither pen nor pencil can do justice. And when the last ray has disappeared, and the western sky is yet blushing with the mellow radiance of the last glorious caress, the stars begin to peep out from the clear, blue canopy, and in a short time the vault of heaven's dome is lit up by the brilliant beams from the countless creations that gem the firmament." [13]

Arizona is often called the *Valentine State* "because she was admitted to statehood on February the fourteenth." [14]

The only nickname applied to the residents of the State of Arizona by people living outside of the State is *Sand Cutters*, [15] but the writer was unable to ascertain how the sobriquet originated.

ARKANSAS

Arkansas is known as the *Bear State,* the *Bowie State,* the *Hot Water State,* the *Guinea Pig State,* the *Toothpick State,* and *The Wonder State.*

The nickname, the *Bear State,* was given to Arkansas because of the vast number of bears which in pioneer days abounded within the limits of the present State. [16] It should also be noted that this name was pronounced as though it were *Bär State.*

The *Bowie State* was a nickname applied to Arkansas because of the prevalence of bowie-knives [17] throughout that section of the country during its frontier times.

[13] *The Resources of Arizona,* Third Edition, Patrick Hamilton (A. L. Bancroft and Company, Printers, San Francisco, California, 1884) p. 141.

[14] *Our Arizona,* Ida Flood Dodge (Charles Scribner's Sons, New York and Boston, 1929) p. 134.

[15] *A Book of Nicknames,* John Goff (Courier-Journal Job Printing Company, Louisville, Kentucky, 1892) p. 19.

[16] *Americanisms; The English of the New World,* M. Schele De Vere (Charles Scribner and Company, New York, 1872) p. 658.

[17] *Ibidem,* p. 322.

The sobriquet, the *Hot Water State*, attributed to Arkansas, doubtless alludes to the hot water supplied by natural sources at Hot Springs, Arkansas.

Because the people of Arkansas were willing for this State to become "a proving ground" for the experiments of the Agricultural Department of the Federal Government during the Administrations of President Franklin Delano Roosevelt, it has recently been called *The Guniea Pig State.* [17a]

In Arkansas bowie-knives, that could be shut up into handles, were ironically designated as Arkansas tooth-*picks,* [18] from which fact the fifth nickname, the *Toothpick State,* is derived.

Arkansas accepted the name, *The Wonder State,* adopted by Senate concurrent resolution number two, on January 26, 1923. The reasons stated in the law for accepting this nickname are given as follows:

"Whereas, it is an admitted fact that the State of Arkansas excels all others in natural resources, and

"Whereas, the publicity campaign of the Arkansas Advancement Association has so indelibly stamped upon the mind of the world that Arkansas is 'The Wonder State,' and

"Whereas, this title is so befitting, while the old one, 'The Bear State' is a misnomer, and leads to a false impression, while 'The Wonder State' is accurate and is deserving of special recognition:

"Now, Therefore,

"Be It Resolved by the Senate of the State of Arkansas, the House of Representatives Concurring:

"That we accept the name, 'The Wonder State,' given us by this patriotic association which has done much to acquaint the world with Arkansas and its wealth of resource, and we hereby specially proclaim that hereafter Arkansas shall be known and styled 'The Wonder State.' " [19]

[17a] *The Washington Post,* Washington, D.C., February 6, 1935, col. 3, p. 8.

[18] *Americanisms; The English of the New World,* M. Schele De Vere (Charles Scribner and Company, New York, 1872) p. 322.

[19] *Acts of Arkansas, 1923: General Acts and Joint and Concurrent Resolutions and Memorials and Proposed Constitutional Amendments of the Forty-fourth General Assembly of the State of Arkansas, Passed at*

The people of Arkansas were formerly called *Toothpicks*. The nickname *Toothpicks* referred to the bowie-knives which the early settlers carried, and Fay Hempstead says that outsiders jestingly spoke of the natives as using them for toothpicks; regardless now of its disuse, the name is still remembered by the public.[20] This nickname, which grew out of a playful allusion, is mentioned by Moses King in his *Handbook of the United States*,[20a] and by Leopold Wagner in his *More About Names*.[21]

CALIFORNIA

California was first called the *El Dorado State* because of the discovery of gold there, and later the nickname was "applied to regions where gold and other precious metals were thought to be plentiful."[22]

The *Century Dictionary and Cyclopedia* says that El Dorado "was used with specific reference to California for some years after the discovery of gold there in 1848."[23] Townsend says that California is called the *Golden State* on account of "its being the most important gold producing region in the world."[24] California is designated as the *Grape State* in commemoration of the vast quantities of grapes grown there yearly. There are more than three hundred thousand tons[24a] of grapes grown in California

the Session at the Capitol, in the City of Little Rock, Arkansas, Commencing on the 8th Day of January, 1923, and Ending on the 18th Day of March, 1923, by authority (Democrat Printing and Lithographing Company, Little Rock, Arkansas, 1923) p. 803, 804.

[20] *A Pictorial History of Arkansas*, Fay Hempstead (N. D. Thompson Publishing Company, St. Louis and New York, 1890) p. 212.

[20a] *King's Handbook of the United States*, M. F. Sweetser, planned and edited by Moses King (Moses King Corporation, Publishers, Buffalo, New York, 1891-1892) p. 61.

[21] *More About Names*, Leopold Wagner (T. Fisher Unwin, London, 1893) p. 31.

[22] *Spanish and Indian Place Names of California, Their Meaning and Their Romance*, Nellie Van De Grift Sanchez (A. M. Robertson, San Francisco, California, 1914) p. 300, 303.

[23] *The Century Dictionary and Cyclopedia* (The Century Company, New York, 1906) vol. 3, p. 1865.

[24] *U. S.: An Index to the United States of America*, compiled by Malcolm Townsend (D. Lothrop Company, Boston, Massachusetts, 1890) p. 66.

[24a] *King's Handbook of the United States*, planned and edited by Moses King, text by M. F. Sweetser (Moses King Corporation, Publishers, Buffalo, New York, 1891) p. 84.

annually and more than seventeen millions gallons [25] of grape wine produced each year; therefore California richly merits her sobriquet, the *Grape State.*

California's nickname, *The Land of Gold,* doubtless originated in the fact that California produces such enormous quantities of gold. California is also referred to as the *Eureka State* in commemoration of the State motto, *Eureka.*

The inhabitants of California are called *Gold Diggers* and *Gold Hunters* in commemoration of the *Forty-niners,*[26] whose business it was to hunt and dig for gold.

COLORADO

Colorado is known by five nicknames: *The Buffalo Plains State,* the *Centennial State,* the *Lead State,* the *Silver State,* and the *Switzerland of America.* Wagner says: "As the bison is no longer found on the plains, its . . . name, *The Buffalo Plains State,* is now rarely heard." [27] It was called the *Centennial State* because it was admitted into the Union on August 1, 1876, [28] one hundred years after the Declaration of Independence was signed. Colorado is designated the *Lead State,* doubtless, because of the large quantity of lead mined there. "In 1926 were produced 34,494 short tons, in value $5,519,024." [29] The output reached its peak during the World War. Colorado is now seldom spoken of as the *Silver State;* but it

[25] *King's Handbook of the United States,* planned and edited by Moses King, text by M. F. Sweetser (Moses King Corporation, Publishers, Buffalo, New York, 1891) p. 84.

[26] *U. S.: An Index to the United States of America,* compiled by Malcolm Townsend (D. Lothrop Company, Boston, Massachusetts, 1890) p. 75.

[27] *More About Names,* Leopold Wagner (T. Fisher Unwin, London, 1893) p. 34.

[28] *U. S.: An Index to the United States of America,* compiled by Malcolm Townsend (D. Lothrop Company, Boston, Massachusetts, 1890) p. 66.

[29] *The New International Encyclopaedia,* Second Edition (Dodd, Mead and Company, New York, 1930) vol. 5, p. 612.

was given that name at the time of the great silver agitation during the year 1896, and thereabout. [30]

The nickname, the *Switzerland of America,* is attributed to Colorado because of its magnificent natural beauty. It contains some of the most attractive scenery in the western part of the United States. Thousands of tourists visit Colorado annually to enjoy its splendid scenery. It has been said that this State "is the Mecca of hundreds of thousands of sightseers every summer." [31]

The people of Colorado are sometimes designated as *Silverines, Rovers,* and *Centennials.* The first nickname alludes to the great silver mines in the State, from which many Coloradans amassed fortunes. The second commemorates the roving disposition of the "settlers at the time of the Pike's Peak gold fever." [32] The inhabitants of Colorado are named *Centennials* for the same reason that the State is called the *Centennial State,* which fact has been explained in the previous discussion.

CONNECTICUT

The sobriquet, the *Nutmeg State,* is applied to Connecticut because its early inhabitants had the reputation of being so ingenious and shrewd that they were able to make and sell wooden nutmegs. Sam Slick (Judge Halliburton) seems to be the originator of this story. Some claim that wooden nutmegs were actually sold, but they do not give either the time or the place.

The State Librarian says that "probably the inventive and manufacturing abilities of the inhabitants were the reasons for Connecticut's getting the name. The people have not generally resented the nickname, but have used

---

[30] A letter from Albert R. Sanford, Assistant Curator of History, State Historical Society, State Museum, Denver, Colorado, March 24, 1930.

[31] *The Making of Colorado: A Historical Sketch,* Eugene Parsons (A. Flanagan Company, Chicago, Illinois, 1908) p. 6.

[32] *U. S.: An Index to the United States of America,* compiled by Malcolm Townsend (D. Lothrop Company, Boston, Massachusetts, 1890) p. 75.

the wooden nutmegs as souvenirs and emblems with a certain amusement." [33]

A letter from the Connecticut State Librarian gives the origin of the nickname, the *Constitution State,* in brief, as follows:

"Connecticut, The Constitution State, was given as a motto on a charter oak, frame and tablet, exhibited in the Connecticut State building, at the Louisiana Purchase Exposition, in 1904. There seems to be some authority for this nickname in various historical works. In 1639, at Hartford, the Fundamental Orders were drawn up, largely the work of Thomas Hooker, called by John Fiske, the father of American democracy. These orders are stated to be the first written constitution drawn up by the people, and the Constitution of the United States is said by John Fiske 'to be in lineal descent more nearly related to that of Connecticut than that of any others of the thirteen colonies.' . . . Many of the features of the Federal Constitution were constructed on the lines of the Connecticut model." [33]

Connecticut was nicknamed the *Blue Law State* in commemoration of "the unenviable fame acquired by the first government of New Haven Plantation, in framing the famous Blue Laws of that colony." [34] These laws were said to have been compiled from a General History of Connecticut, by Reverend Samuel A. Peters, a Tory minister, who had charge of the English churches in Hartford and Hebron, and who had to flee from the colonies to England at the outbreak of the Revolutionary War. His history was published in England in 1781. [35]

Connecticut was formerly nicknamed, and is now frequently called by people outside of the state, the *Brown-*

[83] A letter from George S. Godard, Librarian, Connecticut State Library, Hartford, Connecticut, March 18, 1930.

[84] *A New Dictionary of Americanisms,* Sylva Clapin (Louis Weiss and Company, Publishers, New York, 1903 (?)) p. 61.

[85] *The New International Encyclopaedia,* Second Edition (Dodd, Mead and Company, New York, 1930) vol. 3, p. 425.

stone State because of the brownstone quarries at Portland, which although very important at a former period of time, have now ceased to exist, and the *Freestone State* because of her freestone quarries which were formerly valuable. *The Land of Steady Habits* is another sobriquet applied to Connecticut because of "the alleged staid deportment and excellent morals of its inhabitants." [36]

The nicknames *Nutmegs* and *Wooden Nutmegs,* applied to the inhabitants of Connecticut, have the same origin as Connecticut's nickname, the *Nutmeg State,* discussed above.

DELAWARE

Delaware, though next to the smallest state in the Union, possesses four nicknames: the *Blue Hen's Chickens State,* or the *Blue Hen State,* the *Diamond State, New Sweden (Nya Sveriga),* and *Uncle Sam's Pocket Handkerchief.*

The name, the *Blue Hen's Chickens State,* or the *Blue Hen State,* originated during the Revolutionary War. "Captain Caldwell of Colonel Haslet's regiment from Kent County, Delaware, took with his company two game cocks of the breed of a certain blue hen, well known in Kent County for their fighting qualities. When put in the ring, these cocks flew at each other with such fury and fought so gamely that a soldier cried,—'We're sons of the Old Blue Hen and we're game to the end.' Thus these Delaware regiments came to be known as 'Blue Hen's Chickens.' " [37] Later this name came to be state wide in its application.

Delaware gets the nickname, the *Diamond State,* from the fact that it is small in size but great in importance. [38] The State was nicknamed *New Sweden (Nya Sveriga)* because Peter Minuit having been sent out in 1638 by Queen Christina built a fort on the present site of

[36] *A New Dictionary of Americanisms,* Sylva Clapin (Louis Weiss and Company, Publishers, New York, 1903 (?)) p. 254.

[37] *A History of Delaware,* W. A. Powell (The Christopher Publishing House, Boston, Massachusetts, 1928) p. 155.

[38] *A New Dictionary of Americanisms,* Sylva Clapin (Louis Weiss and Company, Publishers, New York, 1903 (?)) p. 158.

Wilmington, named it after the Queen, and garrisoned it with Swedes and Finns, after which for many years the peninsula was under Swedish rule. [39] Delaware is sometimes called *Uncle Sam's Pocket Handkerchief*, [40] probably from the fact that it is so small; but the writer was unable to find out why the State is thus designated.

Delawareans are called *Blue Hen's Chickens* and *Muskrats*. They are proud of the sobriquet *Blue Hen's Chickens* because of its historical association as stated in the foregoing narrative. Muskrats were very numerous in Delaware in the early days. From this fact and from the smallness of the physical surface of the State, it was humorously asserted that only muskrats could get a foothold there; [41] consequently the people of this State became known as *Muskrats*.

THE DISTRICT OF COLUMBIA

The District of Columbia is frequently designated the *Nation's State*, presumably because it is not a separate state; but is "owned and administered by the United States Government." [42]

FLORIDA

Florida is called the *Alligator State*, [43] doubtless from the fact that numerous alligators are found in its various streams and swamps; the *Everglade State*, from the fact that vast numbers of everglades [44] are prevalent through-

---

[39] *King's Handbook of the United States*, planned and edited by Moses King, text by M. F. Sweetser (Moses King Corporation, Publishers, Buffalo, New York, 1891) p. 143.

[40] *Manual of Useful Information*, J. C. Thomas (The Werner Company, Chicago, Illinois, 1893) p. 22.

[41] *U. S.: An Index to the United States of America*, compiled by Malcolm Townsend (D. Lothrop Company, Boston, Massachusetts, 1890) p. 75.

[42] *The Encyclopedia Americana* (Americana Corporation, New York and Chicago, 1929) vol. 9, p. 193.

[43] *A Book of Nicknames*, John Goff (Courier-Journal Job Printing Company, Louisville, Kentucky, 1892) p. 13.

[44] *More About Names*, Leopold Wagner (T. Fisher Unwin, London, 1893) p. 28.

out the greater part of the State; the *Flower State* or the *Land of Flowers,* from the fact that wild flowers grow in such abundance within its borders, which fact also gave the State its name; the *Orange State,* [45] because it has such great numbers of orange groves, in which it vies with California; the *Peninsula State,* [46] because most of its area is included in the Peninsula of Florida; and the *Gulf State,* from the fact that the Gulf of Mexico borders it for such a great distance.

Floridians are nicknamed *Alligators, Crackers,* and *Fly-up-the-Creeks.* They are called *Alligators* for the reason that the State was nicknamed the *Alligator State* as previously explained. The nickname *Crackers* is applied to the people of Florida, tradition says, because the planters during the early days cracked their whips so loudly over the backs of their mules. [47]   See this topic under *Georgia.*

The fly-up-the-creeks are a variety of green heron (*Butorides virescens*), common along the marshy shores [48] of the streams throughout the State; consequently the name was applied to the inhabitants of the State as a sobriquet.   Leopold Wagner says that the Floridians at one time were called *Fly-up-the-Creeks* "doubtless from their 'retiring disposition' on the appoach of strangers." [49]

GEORGIA

Georgia is known by five nicknames: the *Buzzard State,* the *Cracker State,* the *Goober State, The Empire State of the South,* and the *Yankee Land of the South.* The nickname, the *Buzzard State,* was formerly given to Georgia in commemoration of "a very strict law enacted in that State

[45] *A Book of Nicknames,* John Goff (Courier-Journal Job Printing Company, Louisville, Kentucky, 1892) p. 13.
[46] *Ibidem,* p. 13.
[47] The writer obtained this information from an old gentleman who lives in Florida.
[48] *U. S.: An Index to the United States of America,* compiled by Malcolm Townsend (D. Lothrop Company, Boston, Massachusetts, 1890) p. 75.
[49] *More About Names,* Leopold Wagner (T. Fisher Unwin, London. 1893) p. 28.

for the protection of the buzzards," [50] because they were then so necessary as scavengers.

Georgia's nickname, the *Cracker State,* was derived from the sobriquet, the *Crackers,* given to worthless, boastful immigrants into Georgia from Virginia, North Carolina, and other colonies, such persons having previously brought the nickname with them from England. This sobriquet signifies *a boaster* or *a braggart.* [51] *The London Chronicle* of 1748 speaks of the crackers as overrunning the back settlements of Maryland. In 1783 Anthony Stokes said: "Georgia is also subjected to another disagreeable circumstance beyond any other of the Thirteen States, which is this: The Southern Colonies are overrun with a swarm of men from the western parts of Virginia and North Carolina, distinguished by the name of Crackers." [52] A. B. Bernd, Literary Editor of the *Macon Telegraph,* [53] is of the opinion that the English crackers were the ancestors of the Georgia and other American crackers. Although the Georgians do not resent being called the *Crackers,* the nickname cannot be applied literally to the excellent people of Georgia today.

Georgia is nicknamed the *Goober State* [54] from the fact that goobers or peanuts are very commonly grown throughout the State.

Georgia is known as *The Empire State of the South,* "in allusion to its rapid and enterprising industrial development." [55] It stands in the foremost rank of the southern states for the number and value of its manufactures.

[50] *A New Dictionary of Americanisms,* Sylva Clapin (Louis Weiss and Company, Publishers, New York, 1903 (?)) p. 89.

[51] *A New English Dictionary,* edited by James A. H. Murray (The Clarendon Press, Oxford, England) vol. 2^2, p. 1124.

[52] *A View of the Constitution of the British Colonies in North-America and the West Indies,* Anthony Stokes (Printed for the author and sold by B. White, London, 1783) p. 140.

[53] A letter from A. B. Bernd, Literary Editor of the Macon Telegraph, Macon, Georgia, May 10, 1934.

[54] *A Book of Nicknames,* John Goff (Courier-Journal Job Printing Company, Louisville, Kentucky, 1892) p. 13.

[55] *King's Handbook of the United States,* planned and edited by Moses King, text by M. F. Sweetser (Moses King Corporation, Publishers, Buffalo, New York, 1891) p. 179.

The nickname, the *Yankee Land of the South,* is also applied to Georgia. Olmsted in speaking of this nickname quotes a letter from a native Alabamian to *The New York Times* as follows:

" 'Georgia has the reputation of being the *Yankee Land of the South,* and it is well deserved. She has the idea of doing—the will and the hand to undertake and accomplish—and you have only to be abroad among her people to see that she intends to lead the way in the race of Southern empire. . . .' " [56]

The people of the State of Georgia are designated by the sobriquets: *Buzzards, Crackers, Goober-grabbers,* and *Sand-hillers.* The Georgians were nicknamed *Buzzards* and *Crackers* for the reasons that the State was called the *Buzzard State* and the *Cracker State* embodied in the text above.

The sobriquet *Goober-grabbers* is applied to the people of Georgia and Alabama from the fact that the *goobers* are so common throughout these states. [57] The Georgians were formerly called *Sand-hillers* from a class of poor and illiterate white people "mainly found in the 'pine barrens' where they" [58] are said to have lived an idle and wretched life.

IDAHO

Idaho, doubtless, gets her nickname, the *Gem State* or the *Gem of the Mountains,* [59] from the popular conception of the meaning of the State name, which is *Gem of the Mountains;* and *Little Ida* [60] from the fact that the size of the State is small in comparison to many of the other western states.

[56] *A Journey in the Seaboard Slave States, with Remarks on Their Economy,* Frederick Law Olmsted (Dix and Edwards, New York, 1856) p. 530.
[57] *A New Dictionary of Americanisms,* Sylva Clapin (Louis Weiss and Company, New York, 1903 (?)) p. 208.
[58] *Ibidem,* p. 346.
[59] *Americanisms; The English of the New World,* M. Schele De Vere (Charles Scribner and Company, New York, 1872) p. 18.
[60] *A Book of Nicknames,* John Goff (Courier-Journal Job Printing Company, Louisville, Kentucky, 1892) p. 13.

The Idahoans were nicknamed *Fortune-seekers,*[61] probably in allusion to the vast number of people who came to Idaho during pioneer days for the sake of amassing fortunes by mining gold and silver.

ILLINOIS

The State of Illinois has five sobriquets: the *Corn State, Egypt,* the *Garden of the West,* the *Prairie State,* and the *Sucker State.* Illinois is called the *Corn State* because it is one of the most important states in the corn belt, producing in 1926 three hundred twelve million, nine hundred seventy thousand bushels of corn.[62]

The sobriquet *Egypt*[63] was given to the State of Illinois, in all probability, both on account of the fertility of the soil in and around Cairo, Illinois, which resembles that around Cairo, Egypt, after the Nile has flooded, and on account of the fact that the people of southern Illinois are dark-complexioned; thus resembling the inhabitants of Egypt. The similarity of the names of the two cities Cairo probably had something to do with fixing the State nickname.

The State is nicknamed the *Garden of the West,*[64] doubtless, from the appearance of its rolling prairies and its vast cultivated fields.

Illinois is designated as the *Prairie State* because so much of its area is composed of prairie lands. The nickname, the *Sucker State,* is generally applied to Illinois. There is much conjecture as to the origin of this sobriquet. Townsend says that it is related that the term originated at the Galena Lead Mines in 1822, at which time there was a great exodus of Illinois men returning home from the mines. An old miner said to them: " 'Ye put me in [the]

[61] *A Manual of Useful Information,* compiled under the direction of J. C. Thomas (The Werner Company, Chicago, Illinois, 1893) p. 23.
[62] *The Encyclopedia Americana* (Americana Corporation, New York and Chicago, 1929) vol. 14, p. 686.
[63] *More About Names,* Leopold Wagner (T. Fisher Unwin, London, 1893) p. 32.
[64] *King's Handbook of the United States,* planned and edited by Moses King, text by M. F. Sweetser (Moses King Corporation, Publishers, Buffalo, New York, 1891) p. 203.

mind of suckers, they do go up the river in the spring, spawn, and all return down ag'in in the fall.' " [65]

Townsend gives as another possible origin the fact that in many places the western prairies were filled with crawfish holes out of which the early travellers by means of long reeds would suck up the pure water from beneath. When a traveller would find one of the craw-fish holes, he would call " 'a sucker! a sucker!,' " [66] meaning thereby a reed; and in this way the name probably originated.

The inhabitants of Illinois are given the sobriquets: *Egyptians, Sand-hillers,* and *Suckers.* The people of the southern part of the State are nicknamed *Egyptians* for the reason that the State was called *Egypt* accounted for in the text previously. The sobriquet *Sand-hillers* was probably first attributed to those citizens who live on the gradually sloping hills or the broken sandy plains of the State. The name *Suckers* was applied "throughout the West to a native of Illinois," from the facts given as the source of the sobriquet *Sucker State* explained in the text above.

INDIANA

The origin of Indiana's nickname, the *Hoosier State,* or *Hoosierdom* is a mooted question. Jacob Piatt Dunn suggests that probably the original form of the word was *Hoozer,*[67] signifying *hill dweller* or *highlander,* and that it was brought over by the settlers of Indiana or by their immediate forebears from Cumberland County, England.

Another explanation is that the nickname *Hoosier* was given to the settlers, who were so proverbially inquisitive and gruff in speech that they could never pass a house without pulling the latchstring and crying out, "Who's

[65] *U. S.: An Index to the United States of America,* compiled by Malcolm Townsend (D. Lothrop Company, Boston, Massachusetts, 1890) p. 67.

[66] *Ibidem,* p. 67-8.

[67] *Indiana and Indianans,* Jacob Piatt Dunn (The American Historical Society, Chicago and New York, 1919) vol. 2, p. 1146.

here?" [68]   The Kentuckians are said to have given this explanation of the origin of the name.

Still another account is that the early boatmen of Indiana were strong and great fighters, and that one of them on a certain occasion on the levee at New Orleans, successfully fought several individuals at one time, after which, springing up and speaking in a foreign accent, he exclaimed, "I'm a Hoosier!" The New Orleans papers printed an account of the affair, and afterwards applied the name to all boatmen from Indiana, and finally to the citizens of the State. According to the story, the word *Hoosier* means *husher*, or one who can hush his man. [68]

Indiana has been designated by those in charge of the State Department of Conservation *The Playground of the Middle West* [69] because its lakes, streams, state parks, and other outdoor features attract numerous tourists, vacationists, and sportsmen.

The Indianans are called *Hoosiers* for the same reason that the State is nicknamed the *Hoosier State* cited in the foregoing discussion.

IOWA

According to some authorities, [70] the *Hawkeye State* came to be applied as a sobriquet to Iowa from the Indian chief Hawkeye, who was once the terror of travelers along the border, in early days. The nickname, the *Land of the Rolling Prairie*, was given to Iowa because of the vast expanses of rolling prairies within the limits of the State.

The New International Encyclopaedia says that the sobriquet, the *Hawkeye State*, was attributed to Iowa in

---

[68] *Americanisms—Old and New*, John S. Farmer (Privately printed by Thomas Foulter and Sons, London, 1889) p. 304.

[69] *Indiana State Parks* (Indiana Department of Conservation, Division of State Parks, Lands, and Waters, Indianapolis, Indiana, 1937) p. 28.

[70] *Ibidem*, p. 291.

A New Dictionary of Americanisms, Sylva Clapin (Louis Weiss and Company, New York, 1903 (?)) p. 223.

King's Handbook of the United States, planned and edited by Moses King, text by M. F. Sweetser (Moses King Corporation, Buffalo, New York, 1891) p. 255.

More About Names, Leopold Wagner (T. Fisher Unwin, London, 1893) p. 30.

allusion apparently "to J. G. Edwards, familiarly known as 'Old Hawkeye,' editor of the Burlington *Patriot,* now the *Hawkeye and Patriot.*" [71]

The sobriquet *Hawkeyes,* applied to the Iowans, has the same origin as the State nickname, *Hawkeye State,* explained in a previous paragraph.

KANSAS

Kansas is known by eight nicknames as follows: the *Central State,* the *Cyclone State,* the *Garden State,* the *Garden of the West,* the *Grasshopper State,* the *Jayhawker State,* the *Squatter State,* and the *Sunflower State.*

Because it occupies a more-or-less central position among the states of the Union, Kansas is designated as the *Central State.*

The origin of the nickname, the *Cyclone State,* attributed to Kansas, is self explanatory when one considers that "the great cyclone area of the United States is the central Mississippi Valley, notably in Kansas." [72]

The sobriquet, the *Garden State,* is frequently applied to Kansas "from the beautiful appearance of rolling prairies and vast cultivated fields which abound in that fertile region." [73]

Kansas is also called the *Garden of the West* because of its fertile lands and mild climate, and because of its perfect irrigation produced by its many watercourses. [74]

It is nicknamed the *Grasshopper State* apparently from the fact that the "Rocky Mountain grasshopper (*Melanoplus spretus*) damaged the grain crops of Colorado, Nebraska, and neighboring states in the years 1874 to 1876

---

[71] *The New International Encyclopaedia,* Second Edition (Dodd, Mead and Company, New York, 1930) vol. 21, p. 463.

[72] *The Encyclopedia Americana* (Americana Corporation, New York and Chicago, 1929) vol. 8, p. 362.

[73] *Americanisms; The English of the New World,* M. Schele De Vere (Charles Scribner and Company, New York, 1872) p. 659.

[74] *U. S.: An Index to the United States of America,* compiled by Malcolm Townsend (D. Lothrop Company, Boston, Massachusetts, 1890) p. 68.

to an extent of hundreds of millions of dollars and reduced thousands of families almost to starvation." [75]

The *Jayhawker State* is a term derisively applied to Kansas in reference to James Montgomery and his men, who were connected with many of its territorial troubles. [76] The *Standard History of Kansas and Kansans* says: "The term, 'Jayhawker' was applied along the border at the beginning of the (Civil) war to irregular troops and pillaging bands on both sides. It was accepted by some of the Kansas soldiers, and soon came to be the name by which all of them were known. . . . The origin of the name is unknown. . . . The name was in use in Texas and the West many years before Kansas was a territory." [77]

Kansas is occasionally designated as the *Squatter State,* "from the pertinacity with which squatter-sovereignty was discussed there [about 1854], and settlers poured in by the two contesting parties." [78]

The name, the *Sunflower State,* has been applied to Kansas because of the "prolific growth of sunflowers" [79] it produces.

The Kansans are nicknamed *Grasshoppers, Jayhawkers,* and *Sunflowers.* They received the first sobriquet in commemoration of a great plague of grasshoppers that in 1874 almost destroyed the crops of Kansas and her neighboring states. The people of Kansas are called *Jayhawkers* in reference to the term *Jayhawker,* signifying an armed man, not a soldier. [80] Sylva Clapin gives the follow-

[75] *The New International Encyclopaedia,* Second Edition (Dodd, Mead and Company, New York, 1930) vol. 10, p. 263.

[76] *Ibidem,* vol. 21, p. 463.

[77] *A Standard History of Kansas and Kansans,* William E. Connelley (Lewis Publishing Company, Chicago and New York, 1918) vol. 2, p. 742

[78] *Americanisms; The English of the New World,* M. Schele De Vere (Charles Scribner and Company, New York, 1872) p. 659, 660.

[79] *The Encyclopedia Americana* (Americana Corporation, New York and Chicago, 1929) vol. 26, p. 37.

[80] *U. S.: An Index to the United States of America,* compiled by Malcolm Townsend (D. Lothrop and Company, Boston, Massachusetts, 1890) p. 76.

ing account of the origin of the word *jayhawker:* "A term applied, during the Kansas troubles of 1856, to bushrangers and guerillas, then perpetuated during the Civil War, and subsequently borne by political marauders and pillagers in general. The term is doubtless derived from 'jayhawk' (a ferocious bird, delighting in killing from mere love of sport), and is said to have first come from Australia, where it was originally coined to mean a thief by nature, who could be also, according to occasion, a murderer and pillager." [81] This sobriquet is also said to have originated in the fact that "Colonel Jennison [of New York] and his soldiers," once stationed in one of the forts of Kansas, were called *Gay Yorkers,* [82] which gradually emerged as *Jayhawkers.*

Kansas is known as the *Sunflower State* because of the "abundance and luxuriance" [83] of sunflowers it produces. The people of Kansas are designated as *Sunflowers* as a result of this fact.

KENTUCKY

The five sobriquets by which Kentucky is designated are: the *Blue Grass State,* the *Corn-cracker State,* the *Dark and Bloody Ground State,* the *Hemp State,* and the *Tobacco State.*

Kentucky is called the *Blue Grass State* from the abundant growth of blue grass on its rich limestone soil, [84] especially in the vicinity of Louisville and Lexington.

The nickname, the *Corn-cracker State,* applied to Kentucky, was given in allusion to the poorer class of white people living in the mountainous regions of this and

[81] *A New Dictionary of Americanisms,* Sylva Clapin (Louis Weiss and Company, New York, 1903 (?)) p. 243.

[82] *U. S.: An Index to the United States of America,* compiled by Malcolm Townsend (D. Lothrop and Company, Boston, Massachusetts, 1890) p. 76.

[83] *King's Handbook of the United States,* planned and edited by Moses King, text by M. F. Sweetser (The Matthews-Northrup Company, Buffalo, New York, 1896) p. 265.

[84] *A New Dictionary of Americanisms,* Sylva Clapin (Louis Weiss and Company, New York, 1903 (?)) p. 60.

other southern States. [85] Another authority says that the name is a corruption of corn-crake, a species of crane, found frequently in Kentucky. The peculiar craking sound [86] uttered by this fowl caused it to be called the corn-crake. See this topic under *Georgia.*

Kentucky was given the nickname, the *Dark and Bloody Ground,* from the fact that her territory was formerly the battleground between the northern and southern Indian tribes. [87] *Dark and Bloody Ground* is also said to be the meaning of the word Kentucky.

Because "Kentucky has always been the foremost State in the cultivation of hemp," [88] it is known as the *Hemp State.*

This State is also called the *Tobacco State* from the fact that she produces about two-thirds of the annual American tobacco crop.

Kentuckians are called *Bears, Corn-crackers,* and *Red Horses.* The nickname *Bears,* applied to the inhabitants of Kentucky, probably alludes to the Commonwealth's being called the *Bear State,* [89] which sobriquet was formerly given to the State on account of the prevalence of bear found there in pioneer days. The origin and the significance of the term *Corn-crackers,* applied to the Kentuckians, has been explained in connection with the origin of the nickname, *Corn-cracker State.* The sobriquet *Red Horses,* given to the people of Kentucky, probably alludes to a kind of fish, a large red sucker (*Castostomus*

[85] *Dictionary of Americanisms,* John Russell Bartlett, Fourth Edition (Little, Brown, and Company, Boston, Massachusetts, 1877) p. 147.

[86] *U. S.: An Index to the United States of America,* compiled by Malcolm Townsend (D. Lothrop Company, Boston, Massachusetts, 1890) p. 68.

[87] *Dictionary of Americanisms,* John Russell Bartlett, Fourth Edition (Little, Brown, and Company, Boston, Massachusetts, 1877) p. 168.

[88] *King's Handbook of the United States,* planned and edited by Moses King, text by M. F. Sweetser (Moses King Corporation, Publishers, Buffalo, New York, 1891) p. 279.

[89] *Americanisms; The English of the New World,* M. Schele De Vere (Charles Scribner and Company, New York, 1872) p. 660.

dequesnii), commonly found in the Ohio river and its
tributaries. [90]

LOUISIANA

The five nicknames which have been applied to Louisiana are: *The Child of The Mississippi River,* the *Creole State, The Holland of America,* the *Pelican State,* and the *Sugar State.*

The recent sobriquet, *The Child of the Mississippi River,*[91] testifies that geologists affirm that Louisiana was formed by the Mississippi river's depositing silt in the Gulf of Mexico during previous ages.

The *Creole State*[92] signifies that a part of the citizens of Louisiana are creoles of French and Spanish descent.

The Holland of America[91] commemorates the fact that Louisiana has numerous canals and extensive trucking industries.

The *Pelican State* became the sobriquet of Louisiana because of the numerous pelicans throughout the state and because this bird is depicted on the State Coat of arms.

Louisiana's numerous sugar plantations and refineries caused it to be nicknamed the *Sugar State.*

The Louisianians are designated the *Creoles* and the *Pelicans* for the same reasons that the State was nicknamed the *Creole State* and the *Pelican State* given in the discussion above.

MAINE

The following are the nicknames of Maine: the *Border State,* the *Lumber State,* the *Old Dirigo State,* the *Pine Tree State,* the *Polar Star State,* and *The Switzerland of America.*

Maine is called the *Border State,* apparently, because it is a border state between the United States and Canada, and also a border state on the Atlantic Ocean.

[90] *A New Dictionary of Americanisms,* Sylva Clapin (Louis Weiss and Company, New York, 1903 (?)) p. 333.
[91] *Compton's Pictured Encyclopedia* (F. E. Compton, Chicago, Illinois, 1933) vol. 8, p. 204.
[92] *A New Dictionary of Americanisms,* Sylva Clapin (Louis Weiss and Company, New York, 1903 (?)) p. 145.

The nickname, the *Lumber State,* was applied to Maine from the fact that she is still one of the twenty-two states in the Union which produces the bulk of the lumber for the United States. De Vere says that the occupation the pine forests "afford to a large number of inhabitants . . . has made it also known as the *Lumber State.*"[93]

According to tradition, Maine came to be called the *Old Dirigo State* because the State motto is *Dirigo.*

Maine is named the *Pine Tree State* because extensive pine forests cover its northern and central parts, and because the pine tree is one of the symbols on the State seal. Sweetser says in this connection that "the mast pine, an evergreen of towering height, is the pride of the Maine forests, and gives rise to the popular name of *The Pine-Tree State.*"[94]

Harrie Badger Coe says that "Maine is widely known as the *Switzerland* of America."[95] Its mountainous scenery and abundant snowfalls doubtless gave rise to this nickname.

Because Maine is the most northern State of the Union, and because the State coat of arms pictures the North Star, she is called the *Polar Star State.*

Maine folk are called by the following nicknames: *Down Easters, Foxes, Lumberjacks, Lumbermen, Main Staters* or *State of Mainers,* and *Pine Trees.*

The sobriquet, *Down Easters,*[96] commonly applied by various people to the inhabitants of New England in general and specially to the Maine people, was originated and attributed to the inhabitants of Maine by the Bostonians and other people of Massachusetts while Maine was a part of the latter state from about 1652 until Maine became a

---

[93] *Americanisms; The English of the New World,* M. Schele De Vere (Charles Scribner and Company, New York, 1872) p. 660.

[94] *King's Handbook of the United States,* planned and edited by Moses King, text by M. F. Sweetser (Moses King Corporation, Publishers, Buffalo, New York, 1891) p. 312.

[95] *Maine, Resources, Attractions, and Its People: A History,* Harrie B. Coe, Editor (The Lewis Historical Publishing Company, Incorporated, New York, 1928) vol. 1, p. 6.

[96] *Compton's Pictured Encyclopedia* (F. E. Compton and Company, Chicago, Illinois, 1933) vol. 9, p. 37.

state in 1820, the nickname having grown out of the parent relation of Massachusetts to Maine.

The nickname, *Foxes,* [97] originated during the earlier days in Maine when many of the inhabitants lived and worked in the pine forests in which foxes [98] were abundant. Lumbering's being one of the chief occupations of the people of Maine gave rise to the use of the sobriquets, *Lumberjacks* and *Lumbermen.* The inhabitants of Maine are called *Pine Trees* [97] because Maine is nicknamed the *Pine-tree State.*

The sobriquets, *Maine Staters* or *State of Mainers,* were originated probably by journalists in their attempts to find a general name to apply to the people of Maine. Questionnaires sent by the author to people living in various states in the East, South, and West give evidence to the fact that the inhabitants of these various sections have frequently heard the nicknames, *Foxes, Lumberjacks, Lumbermen,* and *Pine Trees* applied to the Maine people.

MARYLAND

Maryland is known as: the *Cockade State,* the *Monumental State,* the *Old Line State,* the *Oyster State,* and the *Queen State.*

With regard to the use of *Cockade* as a nickname for the State of Maryland, King says that the Old Maryland Line was largely made up of patrician young men, who "among their other equipment wore brilliant cockades"; [99] consequently, Maryland later became known as the *Cockade State.*

[97] *A Book of Nicknames,* John Goff (Courier-Journal Job Printing Company, Louisville, Kentucky, 1892) p. 19.
The Lincoln Library of Essential Information, Thoroughly Revised at Each New Printing (The Frontier Press Company, Buffalo, New York, 1936) p. 2068.
The Volume Library (Educators Association, New York, 1935) p. 365.
[98] *U.S.: An Index to the United States of America,* compiled by Malcolm Townsend (D. Lothrop and Company, Boston, Massachusetts, 1890) p. 76.
[99] *King's Handbook of the United States,* planned and edited by Moses King, text by M. F. Sweetser (Moses King Corporation, Publishers, Buffalo, New York, 1891) p. 324.

Maryland is called the *Monumental State*, doubtless from the fact that Baltimore is known as the *Monumental City* because it contains so many superior monumental trophies. [100]

Under the topic, the *Old Line State*, the *Americana* says that it is "a popular name for the State of Maryland, which in the early Colonial days was the dividing line between the Crown land grants of William Penn and [those of] Lord Baltimore." [101]

Again it is stated that the State of Maryland is called the *Old Line State* "from the 'Old Line' regiments contributed by Maryland during the War of the Revolution, she being then the only State that had regular troops of 'the line.' " [102] Sweetser says, in this connection, that "the old Maryland Line ranked among the finest bodies of troops in the Continental army," and that they were "held in admirable discipline." [103]

Maryland's nickname, the *Oyster State*, refers to the very large oyster fisheries in the State. No satisfactory explanation of the use of the term, the *Queen State*, seems available. A probable one is the fact that the State was named for Henrietta Maria, who was the queen of Charles I of England.

Marylanders have two sobriquets, *Craw-thumpers* and *Oysters*. The fishermen of Maryland probably first used the expression *Craw-thumpers* as a nickname for lobsters, after which the fishermen themselves, and later the inhabitants of Maryland, were designated as *Craw-thumpers*. This term is composed of the words *craw*, a corruption of the word *claw*, and *thumper*, signifying in the patois of the

---

[100] *Americanisms—Old and New*, John S. Farmer (Privately printed by Thomas Poulter and Sons, London, 1889) p. 371.

[101] *The Encyclopedia Americana* (Americana Corporation, New York and Chicago, 1929) vol. 20, p. 655.

[102] *A New Dictionary of Americanisms*, Sylva Clapin (Louis Weiss and Company, New York, 1903 (?)) p. 293.

[103] *King's Handbook of the United States*, planned and edited by Moses King, text by M. F. Sweetser (Moses King Corporation, Publishers, Buffalo, New York, 1891) p. 324.

local fishermen, *a banger*[104] or *a slammer*. The whole phrase refers to the thumping, banging noise made by the pincers of the lobsters, or by the falling around of the lobsters themselves, as they crawl about in a boat or other receptacle. The people of Maryland are called *Oysters*[105] in allusion to the fact that oyster fishing is one of Maryland's chief industries.

MASSACHUSETTS

The nicknames of Massachusetts are: the *Baked Bean State*, the *Old Colony State*, the *Old Bay State*, or the *Bay State*, and the *Puritan State*.

Massachusetts is called the *Baked Bean State* because Boston is so famous for baked beans. In the early Puritan days brown bread and baked beans were served as the regular Sunday meal because they could be prepared on the Saturday before.[106]

The sobriquet, the *Old Colony State*, is applied to that part of Massachusetts which was included within the limits of the original Plymouth Colony, which was settled sometime before Massachusetts Bay Colony.[107]

The *Bay State* and the *Old Bay State* were given as nicknames to the State of Massachusetts originally from Cape Cod bay where early settlements were made.

The *Puritan State* was given as a nickname to Massachusetts because it was settled by the Puritans.

The people of Massachusetts are called *Baked Beans, Bay Staters*,[108] and *Puritans*. The origin and significance of these nicknames may be traced to the same source as

[104] *U. S.: An Index to the United States of America*, compiled by Malcolm Townsend (D. Lothrop and Company, Boston, Massachusetts, 1890) p. 76.
[105] *A Book of Nicknames*, John Goff (Courier-Journal Job Printing Company, Louisville, Kentucky, 1892) p. 19.
[106] *U. S.: An Index to the United States of America*, compiled by Malcolm Townsend (D. Lothrop Company, Boston, Massachusetts, 1890) p. 69-70.
[107] A Letter from Edward H. Redstone, Librarian, State Library, Boston, Massachusetts, March 18, 1930.
[108] *A Dictionary of American Slang*, Maurice H. Weseen (Thomas Y. Crowell Company, New York, 1934) p. 306.

the sobriquets, the *Baked Bean State* and the *Puritan State,* explained in the previous narrative.

MICHIGAN

Michigan is known by four names as follows: the *Auto State,* the *Lady of the Lakes,* the *Lake State,* and the *Wolverine State.*

The *Auto State* is a nickname recently given to the State of Michigan on account of her numerous plants manufacturing automobiles,—especially those at Detroit.

The sobriquet, the *Lady of the Lakes,* has been appropriately given to Michigan, it may be inferred, on account of the vast number of lakes along and within the limits of the State. The name was probably suggested by Sir Walter Scott's poem, *The Lady of the Lake.*

The nickname, the *Lake State,* is very appropriate for Michigan, which is almost surrounded by four of the five Great Lakes on the northern border: [109]   Lake Superior, Lake Michigan, Lake Huron, and Lake Erie.

Michigan was nicknamed the *Wolverine State,* De Vere says, "from the number of wolverines (literally, little wolves) which used to abound in the peninsula, and gave the inhabitants their name of Wolverines, by which they are still generally known." [110]

The name *Wolverines* is applied as a sobriquet to the people of the State of Michigan. It is told how Conrad Tan Eyck, a tavern keeper, about 1800, made a specialty of wolf steaks. After a person had eaten a lamb chop, or a beef steak, he would ask, "Well, how did you enjoy your wolf steak?" The nickname grew out of the reply of a young girl, who having been told that she had eaten wolf steak, replied, "Then I suppose I am a Wolverine?" This name is said to have been given first to those who had eaten at this inn, and afterwards it was applied to the inhabitants of the state. [111]

---

[109] *Americanisms; The English of the New World,* M. Schele De Vere (Charles Scribner and Company, New York, 1872) p. 660.

[110] *Ibidem,* p. 660.

[111] *Detroit Free Press,* November 30, 1918.

MINNESOTA

Various sobriquets are attributed to Minnesota; namely, the *Bread and Butter State*, the *Gopher State*, the *Lake State*, the *New England of the West*, the *North Star State*, and the *Wheat State*.

The *Bread and Butter State* is applied to Minnesota as a sobriquet to commemorate "its wheat and dairy products." [112] Warren Upham, in speaking to this point, says: "Another epithet for our fertile commonwealth more recently came into use from the Pan-American Exposition at Buffalo, N.Y., in 1901, where the superior exhibits of wheat, flour, and dairy products of Minnesota caused her to be called 'the Bread and Butter state.'" [113]

With regard to Minnesota's nickname, the *Gopher State*, the first volume of *Minnesota in Three Centuries* says: "Minnesota received its most widely known sobriquet, 'The Gopher State,' from the striped gopher, a common species throughout our prairie region." [114]

Judge Charles Eugene Flandrau says that as early as 1854 or 1855 the settlers discussed whether they would call Minnesota the *Beaver State* or the *Gopher State*. The name *Beaver State*, he states, "seemed to have the greatest number of advocates, but it was always met with the objection that the beaver, although quite numerous in some of our streams, was not sufficiently so to entitle him to characterize the territory by giving it his name. While this debate was in progress the advocates of the beaver spoke of the territory as the beaver territory, but it never reached a point of universal adoption. It was well known that the gopher abounded, and his name was introduced as a competitor with the beaver; but it being a rather insignificant animal, and his nature being destructive, and

[112] *The New International Encyclopaedia*, Second Edition (Dodd, Mead and Company, New York, 1930) vol. 21, p. 463.

[113] "Minnesota Geographical Names," Warren Upham, in the *Collections of the Minnesota Historical Society* (Published by the Minnesota Historical Society, Saint Paul, Minnesota, at Colwell Press, Incorporated, Minneapolis, Minnesota, 1920) vol. 17, p. 4.

[114] *Minnesota in Three Centuries, 1655-1908, Semi-Centennial Edition*, Warren Upham (The Publishing Society of Minnesota, 1908, Printed by the Free Press Printing Company, Mankato, Minnesota, 1908) vol. 1, p. 75.

in no way useful, he was objected to by many, as too use-
less and undignified to become an emblem of the coming
great state,—for we all had, at that early day, full confidence that Minnesota was destined to be a great and
prominent state. Nothing was ever settled on this subject
until after the year 1857. As I have before stated, in that
year an attempt was made to amend the constitution by
allowing the state to issue bonds in the sum of $5,000,000
to aid in the construction of the railroads which the United
States had subsidized with land grants, and the campaign
which involved this amendment was most bitterly fought.
The opponents of the measure published a cartoon to bring
the subject into ridicule, which was very generally circu-
lated throughout the state, but failed to check the enthu-
siasm in favor of the proposition. . . . This cartoon, coming just at the time the name of the state was under
consideration, fastened upon it the nickname of 'Gopher,'
which it has ever since retained. The name is not at all
inappropriate, as the animal has always abounded in the
state." [115]

The sobriquet, the *Lake State*, was given to Minnesota
because of "its myriad of interior lakes." [116]

The *New England of the West* came to be applied as a
sobriquet to Minnesota because great numbers of people
from New England are to be found there. [117]

The designation, the *North Star State*, attributed to
Minnesota, alludes to the fact that the State seal has on it
the motto, *L'Etoile du Nord* [118] (the star of the north),
chosen by Governor Henry H. Sibley.

Minnesota's nickname, the *Wheat State*, commemorates
its vast wheat crops.

[115] *The History of Minnesota and Tales of the Frontier*, Judge Charles
Eugene Flandrau (E. W. Porter, Saint Paul, Minnesota, 1900) p. 242-4.

[116] *King's Handbook of the United States,* planned and edited by
Moses King, text by M. F. Sweetser (Moses King Corporation, Publishers, Buffalo, New York, 1891) p. 421.

[117] *Americanisms; The English of the New World*, M. Schele De Vere
(Charles Scribner and Company, New York, 1872) p. 660.

[118] *King's Handbook of the United States,* planned and edited by
Moses King, text by M. F. Sweetser (Moses King Corporation, Publishers, Buffalo, New York, 1891) p. 421.

The Minnesotans have been designated as *Gophers,* a humorous appellation suggested by the word gopher, the name of a large mole which is commonly found on the prairies of the state.

MISSISSIPPI

Mississippi has seven nicknames: the *Bayou State,* the *Border-eagle State,* the *Eagle State,* the *Ground-hog State,* the *Magnolia State,* the *Mud-cat State,* and the *Mud-waddler State.*

It is called the *Bayou State* because of "the number of its bayous (rivulets)," and of the word, bayou, on state maps. [119]

The sobriquet, the *Border-eagle State,* was attributed to Mississippi, Wagner says, because the State coat of arms depicts the American eagle. [120]

Mississippi is designated as the *Eagle State* from the fact that its coat of arms consists of an American spread eagle on a silver circular field.

John Goff says that Mississippi is nicknamed the *Ground-hog State,* [121] but he fails to tell why. The name supposedly commemorates the fact that ground hogs were or are numerous in Mississippi.

The *Magnolia State* is given as a nickname to Mississippi because of the great number of magnolia trees growing within the State.

De Vere says that "Mississippi is occasionally spoken of humorously as the *Mud-cat State,* the inhabitants being quite generally known as Mud-cats, a name given to the large catfish abounding in the swamps and the mud of the rivers of the state." [122]

[119] *The New International Encyclopaedia,* Second Edition (Dodd, Mead and Company, New York, 1930) vol. 21, p. 463.

[120] *More About Names,* Leopold Wagner (T. Fisher Unwin, London, 1893) p. 30.

[121] *A Book of Nicknames,* John Goff (Courier-Journal Job Printing Company, Louisville, Kentucky, 1892) p. 14.

[122] *Americanisms; The English of the New World,* M. Schele De Vere (Charles Scribner and Company, New York, 1872) p. 660.

Mississippi's sobriquet, the *Mud-waddler State,* is given by John Goff, [123] who does not explain its origin or significance.

Mississippians are, or have been called *Mudcats, Mud-waddlers,* and *Tadpoles. Mudcats* is a humorous appellation sometimes applied to the people of this State. It had its origin in the same source as the nickname the *Mud-cat State,* discussed in the narrative above. The writer is unable to account for the origin or significance of the sobriquet *Mud-waddlers* [124] applied to the Mississippians. As to *Tadpoles,* Townsend says that the nickname is "equivalent to the expression Young Frenchmen. The Frenchmen [Parisians] were called *Crapauds* (frogs) from their ancient heraldic device, 'three toads erect saltant. . .' "; [125] but he does not tell why the Mississippians were so called.

MISSOURI

There are seven sobriquets attributed to Missouri; namely, the *Bullion State,* the *Iron Mountain State,* the *Lead State,* the *Ozark State,* the *Pennsylvania of the West,* the *Puke State,* and the *Show Me State.*

Missouri's nickname, the *Bullion State,* is derived from the sobriquet *Old Bullion,* "applied to Senator Thomas Hart Benton of that State" [126] because of the stand that he took on the question of gold and silver currency. He was in favor of the establishment of a currency of gold and silver only.

This State gets its nickname, the *Iron Mountain State,* from the name of the Iron Mountain in St. Francois County, which in turn is so called from the very large veins of iron ore which it contains. [127]

[123] *A Book of Nicknames,* John Goff (Courier-Journal Job Printing Company, Louisville, Kentucky, 1892) p. 14.
[124] *Ibidem,* p. 19.
[125] *U. S.: An Index to the United States of America,* compiled by Malcolm Townsend (D. Lothrop and Company, Boston, Massachusetts, 1890) p. 76.
[126] *The New International Encyclopaedia,* Second Edition (Dodd, Mead and Company, New York, 1930) vol. 21, p. 463.
[127] A letter from Floyd C. Shoemaker, Secretary of the State Historical Society of Missouri, Columbia, Missouri, March 25, 1930.

The *Lead State,* the third sobriquet of Missouri, refers to the very productive lead mines situated in the southeastern part of the State. [128]

The nickname, the *Ozark State,* was given to Missouri, doubtless, from the name of the Ozark Mountains. In all probability, Missouri is called the *Pennsylvania of the West* because of her similarity to Pennsylvania in mining interests, manufacturing, and foreign-born population.

Concerning Missouri's nickname, the *Puke State,* Townsend says that "this inelegant application took place in 1827 at the Galena Lead Mines, where throughout the mining craze so many Missourians had assembled, that those already there declared the State of Missouri had taken a 'puke.' " [129]

Missouri is called the *Show Me State* from the expression *Show Me* commonly associated with Missouri or Missourians. The origin of the expression *Show Me* is generally attributed to the late Willard D. Vandiver, former Representative from Missouri. "The late Speaker Champ Clark credited Vandiver with originating the expression in an impromptu humorous address as a Member of Congress before the Five O'Clock Club in Philadelphia in 1899. 'I come from a country that raises corn, cotton, cockleburs, and Democrats,' Vandiver said in the address. 'I'm from Missouri, and you've got to show me.' " [130]

With regard to the origin of the nickname *Pukes,* formerly applied to the natives of Missouri, Leopold Wagner says that "the natives of Missouri are universally styled *Pukes,* a corruption of the older name *Pikes,* which still obtains in California as the description of the migratory whites from the South owing to the idea that these originally came from Pike County, Missouri." [131]

[128] *The New International Encyclopaedia,* Second Edition (Dodd, Mead and Company, New York, 1930) vol. 13, p. 665.

[129] *U. S.: An Index to the United States of America,* compiled by Malcolm Townsend (D. Lothrop Company, Boston, Massachusetts, 1890) p. 71.

[130] *The Washington Post,* May 31, 1932.

[131] *More About Names,* Leopold Wagner (T. Fisher Unwin, London, 1893) p. 28-9.

MONTANA

Montana has the three following nicknames: the *Bonanza State,* the *Stubtoe State,* and the *Treasure State.* Concerning the origin of these sobriquets, the State Librarian affirms that "the names *Bonanza* and *Treasure* are typical of the mining area of the State, and *Stubtoe* of the mountainous nature of the western section of the State; but there is no official reason to give for their adoption."[132]

King says that "the pet name, *The Bonanza State,* on account of its many bonanza mines, was given to Montana by Judge John Wasson Eddy, and has been very generally accepted."[133]

NEBRASKA

The nicknames given to Nebraska are as follows: the *Antelope State,* the *Blackwater State,* the *Bug-eating State,* the *Tree Planters State,* and the *Corn Huskers State.*

Mr. Addison E. Sheldon states that "the name *Antelope State* was applied to Nebraska about 1870 in allusion to the great abundance of those beautiful creatures upon our prairies."[134]

Nebraska is sometimes called the *Blackwater State* from the black color of its streams, "darkened by the rich black soil,"[135] which they bear in solution.

The *Bug-eating State* is a sobriquet applied to Nebraska from the fact that it has numerous bull bats (*Caprimulgus europaeus*)[136] locally named bug-eaters because they feed on bugs.

[132] A letter from David Hilger, Librarian of the Historical Society of Montana, Helena, Montana, April 18, 1930.

[133] *King's Handbook of the United States,* planned and edited by Moses King, text by M. F. Sweetser (Moses King Corporation, Publishers, Buffalo, New York, 1891) p. 510.

[134] A letter from Addison E. Sheldon, Secretary and Superintendent of the Nebraska State Historical Society, Lincoln, Nebraska, March 20, 1930.

[135] *King's Handbook of the United States,* planned and edited by Moses King, text by M. F. Sweetser (Moses King Corporation, Publishers, Buffalo, New York, 1891) p. 522.

[136] *U. S.: An Index to the United States of America,* compiled by Malcolm Townsend (D. Lothrop Company, Boston, Massachusetts, 1890) p. 77.

The nickname, the *Tree Planters State,* was adopted by an act of the Nebraska legislature, approved on April 4, 1895. [137] The law says:

"Whereas, The state of Nebraska has heretofore, in a popular sense been designated by names not in harmony with its history, industry, or ambition; and Whereas, The State of Nebraska is preëminently a tree planting state; and

"Whereas, Numerous, worthy, and honorable state organizations have by resolution designated Nebraska as the 'Tree Planters State,' Therefore,

"Be it Resolved by the Legislature of the State of Nebraska:

"That Nebraska shall hereafter in a popular sense be known and referred to as the 'Tree Planters State.' "

"The name 'Cornhuskers' arose within the past thirty years as an epithet for the University of Nebraska football team, and it was extended to include the state" [138]; consequently the State came to be designated as the *Corn Huskers State.*

The nickname *Bug-eaters,* attributed to the people of Nebraska, originated in the same source as the sobriquet the *Bug-eating State,* explained in the previous text. Sylva Clapin says that the origin of the term comes from "the poverty-stricken appearance of many parts of the State. Indeed, so they say, if one living there were to refuse to eat bugs, he would, like Polonius, soon be 'not where he eats, but where he is eaten.' " [130]

NEVADA

Nevada's nicknames are: the *Battle-born State,* the *Mining State,* the *Sage State,* or the *Sage-brush State,* the *Sage-hen State,* and the *Silver State.*

[137] *Laws of Nebraska, 1895: Laws, Joint Resolutions, and Memorials Passed by the Legislative Assembly of the State of Nebraska at the Twenty-fourth Session, Begun and Held at the City of Lincoln, January 1, 1895,* published by authority (Omaha Printing Company, State Printers. Omaha, Nebraska, 1895) p. 441.

[138] A letter from Addison E. Sheldon, Secretary and Superintendent of the Nebraska State Historical Society, Lincoln, Nebraska, March 20, 1930.

[139] *A New Dictionary of Americanisms,* Sylva Clapin (Louis Weiss and Company, New York, 1903 (?)) p. 81.

The sobriquet, the *Battle-born State,* commemorates the fact that Nevada was admitted into the Union during the Civil War. [140]

Nevada was called the *Mining State* and the *Silver State* in recognition of one of its most important industries and the chief product of that industry. [141]

The *Sage State* and the *Sage-brush State* were given as nicknames to Nevada because of the prevalence of wild sage (*Artemisia tridentata*) growing throughout the State. [142]

The *Sage-hen State* was attributed as a sobriquet to Nevada from the fact that this fowl was formerly common throughout the State.

Diggers, Miners, and *Sagehens* are sobriquets applied to the inhabitants of Nevada. The first two nicknames refer to the mining industries of the State. The people of Nevada are called *Sagehens* for the reason that the State is called the *Sage-hen State* cited in the discussion above

NEW HAMPSHIRE

Four sobriquets are attributed to New Hampshire; namely, the *Granite State,* the *Mother of Rivers,* the *White Mountain State,* and the *Switzerland of America.*

New Hampshire is called the *Granite State* in commemoration of her extensive granite quarries. [143]

In speaking of New Hampshire's nickname, the *Mother of Rivers,* Frank West Rollins says: "One of the numerous titles of honor given this commonwealth is that of the 'Mother of Rivers' and the tribute is well deserved, for five of the great rivers of New England have their origin among the mountains of New Hampshire." [144]

[140] *King's Handbook of the United States,* planned and edited by Moses King, text by M. F. Sweetser (Moses King Corporation, Publishers, Buffalo, New York, 1891) p. 533.
[141] *Ibidem,* p. 533.
[142] *More About Names,* Leopold Wagner (T. Fisher Unwin, London, 1893) p. 35.
[143] *Ibidem,* p. 27.
[144] *The Tourists' Guide-Book to the State of New Hampshire,* published by Frank West Rollins, Second Edition (The Romford Press, Concord, New Hampshire, 1902) p. 5.

The name, the *White Mountain State*, is given to New Hampshire in allusion to the White Mountains, which lie in the northern part of this State, "covering 1,300 square miles, in several short ranges, largely clad with . . . forest, the main peaks rising above the timber-line, and crowned with storm-worn rocks." [145]

The nickname, the *Switzerland of America*, is applied to New Hampshire in recognition of her beautiful mountain scenery.

The people of New Hampshire were called *Granite Boys* [146] in allusion to the fact that many of them live among the mountains from which granite is quarried, or, as others suggest, from the fact that they live in the *Granite State*.

NEW JERSEY

People call New Jersey : the *Camden and Amboy State* or the *State of Camden and Amboy*, the *Clam State*, the *Foreigner State*, the *Garden State*, the *Jersey Blue State*, the *Mosquito State*, *New Spain*, the *State of Spain*, and the *Switzerland of America*.

New Jersey was designated as the *State of Camden and Amboy* during the time when the "Camden and Amboy Railroad influence held a dominating power." [147]

The immense quantities of clams, taken from the Atlantic Ocean and the Delaware bay in New Jersey and shipped out, give rise to the use of the nickname, the *Clam State*.

This State is sometimes called the *Foreigner State*, *New Spain*, and the *State of Spain* because when the fortunes of the Bonaparte family fell, Joseph Bonaparte, then King of Spain, fled to New Jersey about 1812 and bought fourteen hundred acres of land at Bordentown,

[145] *King's Handbook of the United States,* planned and edited by Moses King, text by M. F. Sweetser (Moses King Corporation, Publishers, Buffalo, New York, 1891) p. 539.
[146] *Manual of Useful Information,* compiled under the direction of J. C. Thomas (The Werner Company, Chicago, Illinois, 1893) p. 23.
[147] *King's Handbook of the United States,* planned and edited by Moses King, text by M. F. Sweetser (Moses King Corporation, Publishers, Buffalo, New York, 1891) p. 551.

upon which he built a palatial mansion, "where he dwelt until 1832, entertaining many illustrious Frenchmen." King says in this connection that the "Philadelphians were rather jealous of the good luck of New Jersey in securing such distinguished residents, and called the State, Spain, with good-humored raillery reading it out of the Union. Hence arose the gibe that this domain is in some sense a foreign land; and the people were long called foreigners and Spaniards, since their social leader was the King of Spain." [148]

New Jersey has many very extensive truck farms producing agricultural and floral products, especially in the valley of the Delaware river, catering particularly to the New York and Philadelphia metropolitan areas; consequently she is called the *Garden State.*

The *Jersey Blue State,* given as a sobriquet to New Jersey, commemorates the fact that the Revolutionary Militia of the colony wore blue uniforms, or probably the name goes back for its origin to the Blue Laws of the State.

"We get the scornful title, the *Mosquito State,*" says the State Librarian, "because we seem to have our share of these industrious and bloodthirsty insects. As a matter of fact, however, a considerable number of other states have fully as many, if not more, of the pests." [149]

New Jersey is often called the *Switzerland of America,* probably, because of its mountain scenery in the northwestern part of the State, occasioned by the Kittatinny range of mountains and by the ranges of the Watchung, Sourland and the Pickle mountains of the southeast. "The most famous of these is the Palisades, a line of wonderful basaltic precipices extending along the Hudson River from Staten-Island Sound to Ladentown (N.Y.), and looking down on the crowded streets of New York." [150]

[148] *King's Handbook of the United States,* planned and edited by Moses King, text by M. F. Sweetser (Moses King Corporation, Publishers, Buffalo, New York, 1891) p. 551.
[149] A letter from Charles R. Bacon, Librarian, New Jersey State Library, Trenton, New Jersey, March 24, 1930.
[150] *King's Handbook of the United States,* planned and edited by Moses King, text by M. F. Sweetser (Moses King Corporation, Publishers, Buffalo, New York, 1891) p. 552-3.

The New Jerseyans are designated as *Clam-catchers, Clams, Foreigners, Jersey Blues,* and *Spaniards.* The nicknames mentioned above originated in the same sources as those given in the previous discussion of the nicknames of the State, the *Clam State,* the *Foreigner State,* the *Jersey Blue State,* and the *State of Spain.*

NEW MEXICO

The following sobriquets are attributed to New Mexico: the *Cactus State* or *Land of the Cactus, The Land of the Delight-makers, The Land of Heart's Desire, The Land of Opportunity,* the *Land of Sunshine* or the *Sunshine State,* and the *Spanish State.*

New Mexico is designated as the *Cactus State* or the *Land of the Cactus* because there is such a profusion of cactus growing along the Mexican border and on the plains of the State. [151]

George Wharton James calls New Mexico *The Land of the Delight-makers.* This phrase was suggested to him by the title of Adolf Bandelier's novel, *The Delight Makers.* James says that New Mexico should be designated the *Land of the Delight-makers* because of the influence it has had upon literature and art, and because "it is also the home of the first real field-school of American Archaeology in America." [152]

It is very fitting that New Mexico should be named the *Land of Heart's Desire* because: (1) it is situated midway between the Gulf of Mexico and the Pacific Ocean; (2) its climatic conditions are ideal; and (3) it is yet in the early stages of its development. [153]

New Mexico is designated as the *Land of Opportunity* because of: (1) its natural beauty; (2) its ideal climatic

[151] *The New International Encyclopaedia,* Second Edition (Dodd, Mead and Company, New York, 1930) vol. 4, p. 271.

[152] *New Mexico, The Land of the Delight Makers,* George Wharton James (The Page Company, Publishers, Boston, Massachusetts, 1920) p. 6, 7.

[153] "The Land of Heart's Desire," Paul F. Walter, in *New Mexico, The Land of Opportunity* (A. E. Koehler, Jr. Editor and Publisher, Commissioner of Publicity, New Mexico's Board of Exposition Managers, Santa Fe, New Mexico, 1915) p. 17.

conditions; (3) the newness of its civilization; (4) its free lands; and (5) its industries. Paul Walter says it "offers sufficient range in climatic conditions, in resources, and in opportunities, to fulfill the hopes of its early conquerors who were in search of a new Eldorado." [154]

From the high percentage of sunshiny weather that it affords, New Mexico well deserves the title of the *Sunshine State*. It gets its nickname, the *Spanish State*, doubtless, because of its nearness to Mexico, and because of the number of people within the State who speak the Spanish language.

The inhabitants of New Mexico were called *Spanish Indians*, [155] doubtless, from the fact that so much of its earliest population consisted of Indians or Mexican Spaniards from Mexico.

NEW YORK

The *Empire State* and the *Excelsior State* are the sobriquets applied to New York.

This State is called the *Empire State* in allusion to its "commanding position," "vast wealth," and the enterprise of its people. [156] New York's nickname, the *Excelsior State*, commemorates the fact that the State motto is *Excelsior*.

New Yorkers are known both as *Excelsiors* and as *Knickerbockers*. The origin and the significance of the first sobriquet is explained in the foregoing narrative dealing with the nickname the *Excelsior State*. The second alludes to "the wide breeches worn by the early Dutch settlers of New York City, or rather New Amsterdam." [157] The word *Knickerbocker* was used by Washington Irving in the name of the character Diedrich Knickerbocker, found in his *Knickerbocker History of New York*. The

---

[154] "The Land of Heart's Desire," Paul F. Walter, in *New Mexico, The Land of Opportunity* (A. E. Koehler, Jr. Editor and Publisher, Commissioner of Publicity, New Mexico's Board of Exposition Managers, Santa Fe, New Mexico, 1915) p. 17.

[155] *Manual of Useful Information*, compiled under the direction of J. C. Thomas (The Werner Company, Chicago, Illinois, 1893) p. 23.

[156] *More About Names*, Leopold Wagner (T. Fisher Unwin, London, 1893) p. 27.

[157] *Ibidem*, p. 27.

term is German, not Dutch, being composed of two words, *knicker*, meaning a *box*, and *bock*, meaning a *he-goat*. [158] The modern application of the nickname *Knickerbockers* to the New Yorkers may be traced to Washington Irving's use of the word in the history named above.

NORTH CAROLINA

North Carolina has five nicknames: the *Land of the Sky*, the *Old North State*, the *Rip Van Winkle State*, the *Tarheel State*, and the *Turpentine State*.

The expression, the *Land of the Sky*, [159] is applied to North Carolina because of its many lofty mountain peaks.

The term, the *Old North State*, is generally applied to North Carolina in allusion to its being the more northerly of the two Carolinas after the original state was divided. C. J. Thomas's *Manual of Useful Information* on page 22, records without explaining North Carolina's sobriquet, the *Rip Van Winkle State*.

The name *Tarheels* was "given in derision by Mississippians to a brigade of North Carolinians, who, in one of the great battles of the Civil War, failed to hold their position on a certain hill. The former taunted the latter with having forgotten to tar their heels that morning, and hence the cant name." [160] The North Carolina soldiers picked up the term, and it has stuck, so that now North Carolina is still called the *Tarheel State*.

W. A. Clark gives the following account of the origin of this nickname: "The following, familiar to all the army of Northern Virginia, illustrates the complacent pride with which the North Carolina soldiers adopted the distinctive sobriquet of Tar Heels, first banteringly given them. . . . Thus after one of the fiercest battles, in which their supporting column was driven from the field and they

[158] *U. S.: An Index to the United States of America,* compiled by Malcolm Townsend (D. Lothrop Company, Boston, Massachusetts, 1890) p. 78.

[159] *King's Handbook of the United States,* planned and edited by Moses King, text by M. F. Sweetser (Moses King Corporation, Publisher, Buffalo, New York, 1891) p. 650.

[160] *Americanisms—Old and New,* John S. Farmer (Privately printed by Thomas Poulter and Sons, London, 1889) p. 528.

successfully fought it out alone, in the exchange of the compliments of the occasion the North Carolinians were greeted with the question from the passing derelict regiment: 'Any more tar down in the Old North State, boys?' Quick as thought came the answer: 'No; not a bit; old Jeff's bought it all up.' 'Is that so; what is he going to do with it?' was asked. 'He is going to put it on you'ns heels to make you stick better in the next fight.' " [161]

North Carolina is designated as the *Turpentine State* from the fact that vast quantities of turpentine are produced from its pine forests.

The North Carolinians are called *Tar-heelers* and *Tuckoes*. The first nickname had its origin in the same source as the sobriquet the *Tarheel State* cited in a previous paragraph. The name Tuckoes is a corruption of the common term *Tuckahoe*, or *Tuck-a-hoe*, derived from the word *Tauquauh*, an Indian word of the Mochican dialect meaning *bread*. This word was used by the early settlers for the *Schlerotium giganteum*, [162] called Indian bread, a curious truffle-like growth formerly used by the poor people of the State for food when poverty drove them to it. It is said to grow several feet under the ground and to have neither stems nor leafy appendages. In appearance it resembles a brown loaf of coarse bread. This nickname is applied both to the North Carolinians and to the Virginians.

NORTH DAKOTA

The sobriquets of North Dakota are: the *Flickertail State*, the *Great Central State*, and the *Sioux State* or *Land of the Dakotas*.

North Dakota is called the *Flickertail State* from the word flickertail, the nickname of the Richardson ground

---

[161] *Histories of the Several Regiments and Battalions from North Carolina in the Great War 1861-'65*, edited by Walter Clark (Nash Brothers, Book and Job Printers, Goldsboro, North Carolina, 1901) vol. 3, p. 376.

[162] *U. S.: An Index to the United States of America*, compiled by Malcolm Townsend (D. Lothrop Company, Boston, Massachusetts, 1890) p. 79.

A New Dictionary of Americanisms, Sylva Clapin (Louis Weiss and Company, New York, 1903 (?)) p. 409.

squirrel (*Citellus richardsonii*) which is so called because it flicks or jerks its tail in a characteristic manner while running, or just before entering its burrow. North Dakota is the only state in the Union in which this squirrel is found. [163]

The *Great Central State* is given as a sobriquet to North Dakota supposedly because it is in the center of the great western wheat belt and contains "several of the Bonanza wheat-farms of the Red River valley."

The nicknames, the *Sioux State* and the *Land of the Dakotas,* were given to North Dakota in commemoration of the fact that the territory now comprising this state was once the home of the Dakota Indians, who were called *Sioux* by their enemies.

OHIO

Ohio's nicknames are as follows: the *Buckeye State,* the *Modern Mother of Presidents,* and the *Yankee State.*

Ohio was called the *Buckeye State* from the following historical incident. The first court conducted by the native settlers of Ohio was located at Marietta in a large wooden fortress known as the Campus Martius. On September 2, 1788, while the judges were marching in a body to this fortification, "Colonel Sproat, who led the procession with glittering sword, was a very tall, erect man—six feet, four inches in height. It was he who so impressed a group of onlooking Indians that they shouted 'Hetuck, hetuck,' meaning Big Buckeye. It was from that incident, coupled with the abundance of the buckeye tree (*Aesculus glabra*), which caused the sobriquet 'Buckeye State' to be applied to Ohio." [164]

William M. Farrar says that "the name [*Buckeye*] never became fully crystallized until 1840, when in the crucible of what is known as the 'bitterest, longest, and most extraordinary political contest ever waged in the United States,' the name Buckeye became a fixed sobriquet

[163] A letter from Mrs. Florence H. Davis, Librarian, State Historical Library, Bismarck, North Dakota, March 20, 1930.
[164] *Ohio the Beautiful and Historic,* Charles Edwin Hopkins (L. C. Page and Company, Boston, Massachusetts, Printed by the Colonial Press, Incorporated, Boston, Massachusetts, 1931) p. 256.

of the State of Ohio and its people, known and understood
wherever either is spoken of, and likely to continue as long
as either shall be remembered or the English language
endures." [165] It cannot be definitely determined just when
the nickname *Buckeye* first began to be applied to Ohio
and Ohioans, but Cyrus P. Bradley in his journal of 1835
makes mention of its use.

The nickname, the *Modern Mother of Presidents,* was
given to Ohio because, during the last few years, she has
been furnishing some of the Presidents of the United
States.

M. F. Sweetser says that "before 1820 Ohio was generally called *The Yankee State* by the Kentuckians and
Virginians, mainly on account of its free institutions. [166]

The nickname *Buckeyes,* attributed to the inhabitants
of Ohio, commemorates the abundance of buckeye trees
within the State. This tree commonly found in Ohio gets
its name from the resemblance of the nut or fruit of the
tree to the eye of a buck. [167]

OKLAHOMA

The *Boomer's Paradise* and the *Sooner State* are the
sobriquets applied to Oklahoma.

M. F. Sweetser says that "for years the region [of
Oklahoma] has been known as the Boomer's Paradise," [168]
because when President Harrison opened up this territory
for settlement April 22, 1889, "great processions of
'boomers' poured into the new territory." [169]

The sobriquet, the *Sooner State,* was given to Oklahoma
from the fact that "when the lands of Oklahoma were

[165] "Why Is Ohio Called the Buckeye State?" William M. Farrar in
the *Historical Collections of Ohio, . . . an Encyclopedia of the State,*
The Ohio Centennial Edition, Henry Howe (Henry Howe and Sons,
Columbus, Ohio, 1890) vol. I, p. 202.
[166] *King's Handbook of the United States,* planned and edited by
Moses King, text by M. F. Sweetser (Moses King Corporation, Pub-
lishers, Buffalo, New York, 1891) p. 665.
[167] *Americanisms; The English of the New World,* M. Schele De
Vere (Charles Scribner and Company, New York, 1872) p. 661.
[168] *King's Handbook of the United States,* planned and edited by
Moses King, text by M. F. Sweetser (Moses King Corporation, Publishers,
Buffalo, New York, 1891) p. 693-4.

opened to settlement at a given hour, those who did not await the appointed time but who slipped in clandestinely ahead of time, were dubbed 'sooners' because they did not wait as required by law, but tried to gain an unfair advantage by entering the forbidden precincts too soon." [169]

The Oklahomans are called *Sooners*. This sobriquet originated in the fact that when the territory now embracing the State of Oklahoma was opened for settlement, some of the waiting settlers "became so anxious that they disregarded the conditions set forth in the rules prescribed for the opening of the lands to settlement and, eluding the vigilance of the cordon of troops by which the bounds of the district were patrolled, slipped in and concealed themselves at points conveniently near to the best lands so that they would not have far to go when the legal hour of opening arrived." [170]

OREGON

The following sobriquets are attributed to Oregon: the *Beaver State*, the *Hard-case State* or the *Land of Hard-cases*, the *Sunset State*, and the *Web-foot State*.

Oregon "is sometimes called the Beaver State, on account of the association of the little fur-bearing animal with the early history of the Oregon Country, as well as because of its intelligence, industry, ingenuity and other admirable qualities." [171]

The sobriquet, the *Hard-case State* or the *Land of Hard-cases*, attributed to Oregon, has reference to the rough and hardy life led by the early settlers [172] of the State.

[169] A Letter from Joseph B. Thoburn, Curator, Oklahoma Historical Society, Oklahoma City, Oklahoma, April 15, 1930.

[170] *A Standard History of Oklahoma*, Joseph B. Thoburn (The American Historical Society, Chicago and New York, 1916) vol. 2, p. 632.

[171] *History of Oregon*, Charles Henry Carey (The Pioneer Historical Publishing Company, Chicago and Portland, 1922) p. 808.

[172] *U. S.: An Index to the United States of America*, compiled by Malcolm Townsend (D. Lothrop Company, Boston, Massachusetts, 1890) p. 79.

Oregon is known as the *Sunset State,* "because it reaches a more westerly point than any other American commonwealth, except Washington." [173]

It is called the *Web-foot State,* because, due to the excessive rainfall during the winter months, "the climate at that season is best appreciated by the 'web-foot' animals." [174]

Beavers, Hard Cases, and *Web-feet* are the three sobriquets applied to the Oregonians. The previous discussion of the nicknames, the *Beaver State,* the *Hard-case State,* and the *Web-foot State,* explain the origin and the significance of these three sobriquets.

Beadle says, "We were among the 'Web-feet' at last, and a comely race they are, if I may judge from the plump forms and fresh, clear complexions I saw on this part of the route. The climate has no suggestions of extra dampness; the sky was clear and the air cool and dry, with the general features of Indian Summer in Ohio." [175] Beadle also says that "the rural 'web-foot', as the residents are called, in ironical allusion to the climate, is *sui generis.*" [176]

PENNSYLVANIA

Five nicknames are given to the State of Pennsylvania; namely, the *Coal State,* the *Keystone State,* the *Oil State,* the *Quaker State,* and the *Steel State.*

The *Coal State,* the *Oil State,* and the *Steel State* are sobriquets suggestive of the three greatest industries of this large state. The name, the *Keystone State,* is accounted for in two different ways: (1) When the Government was moved to Washington, D.C., in building the

---

[173] *King's Handbook of the United States,* planned and edited by Moses King, text by M. F. Sweetser (Moses King Corporation, Publishers, Buffalo, New York, 1891) p. 699.
[174] *U. S.: An Index to the United States of America,* compiled by Malcolm Townsend (D. Lothrop Company, Boston, Massachusetts, 1890) p. 72.
[175] *The Undeveloped West: or Five Years in the Territories,* J. H. Beadle (National Publishing Company, Philadelphia, Pennsylvania; Chicago, Illinois; Cincinnati, Ohio; St. Louis, Missouri, 1873) p. 759.
[176] *Western Wilds, and The Men Who Redeem Them, an Authentic Narrative,* J. H. Beadle (J. C. Chilton Publishing Company, Detroit, Michigan, 1882) p. 400.

Pennsylvania Avenue Bridge over Rock Creek to the old city of Georgetown, the initials of the name of the State of Pennsylvania were put on the thirteenth, or key stone of the arch, the initials of the names of six states being carved on the stones on either side; [177] and (2) John Morton, of Pennsylvania, is said to have voted last for the issuance of the Declaration of Independence. By voting for it, he decided the issue for his state, which is, therefore, called " 'The Keystone State,'—the thirteenth State,—the block of the arch." [178]

The nickname, the *Quaker State*, commemorates the fact that William Penn, a member of the Society of Quakers, was made proprietor of the colony in 1680, and was instrumental in causing many Quakers to settle there.

The inhabitants of Pennsylvania are variously called *Leatherheads, Pennamites*, and *Quakers*. The first nickname alludes to the great hide and tanning industries of Pennsylvania, particularly those in the Northwest part of the State. [179] *Pennamites* is a cant name for the followers or admirers of William Penn. [180] The sobriquet *Quakers* refers to the religion of Penn and of the early settlers of Pennsylvania, and to that of many of their descendants even to this day. The people in the western settlements of Pennsylvania were "called Cohees, in consequence of their addiction to the old-fashioned phrase, 'Quoth he,' generally corrupted into *Qho'he*." [181]

RHODE ISLAND

The Land of Roger Williams, Little Rhody, The Southern Gateway of New England, and the *Plantation State* are the nicknames applied to Rhode Island.

[177] *A History of the Origin of the Appellation Keystone State*, John S. Morton (Claxton, Remsen and Haffelfinger, Philadelphia, Pennsylvania, 1874) p. 13-14.

[178] *Ibidem*, p. 16.

[179] *U. S.: An Index to the United States of America*, compiled by Malcolm Townsend (D. Lothrop Company, Boston, Massachusetts, 1890) p. 80.

[180] *Ibidem*, p. 80.

[181] *More About Names*, Leopold Wagner (T. Fisher Unwin, London, 1893) p. 24.

The sobriquet, *The Land of Roger Williams*, [182] commemorates the fact that Roger Williams founded Providence Plantation when he settled at Providence in 1636. *Little Rhody* signifies that Rhode Island is the smallest state in the Union.

The Southern Gateway of New England [182] designates that Rhode Island is the most southern of the New England States which has harbors sufficient to admit ocean-going vessels bearing in and carrying out both New England raw materials and finished products and raw materials and finished products from other parts of the United States and foreign countries.

The nickname, the *Plantation State*, is applied to Rhode Island from its official title, *The State of Rhode Island and Providence Plantations*.

The people of Rhode Island are nicknamed *Gun-flints*. Townsend says that the sobriquet was "applied through the use of fire arms by its citizens at the time of the Dorr Rebellion of 1842, the arms being mostly of the old gun-flint pattern, the resource being those taken from the garrets where they had lain for years." [183]

SOUTH CAROLINA

The sobriquets of South Carolina are: the *Iodine State*, the *Keystone of the South Atlantic Seaboard*, the *Palmetto State*, the *Rice State*, the *Sand-lapper State*, and the *Swamp State*.

South Carolina is designated as the *Iodine State* from the fact that the plants grown in this State contain a great percentage of iodine. [184]

The fact that South Carolina is wedge shaped and that it is located so that the point of its wedge extends into the

[182] *Know Rhode Island: Facts Concerning the Land of Roger Williams*, Sixth Edition, compiled and distributed by the Office of the Secretary of State (State of Rhode Island and Providence Plantations, Providence, Rhode Island, 1936) p. 5.
[183] *U. S.: An Index to the United States of America*, Malcolm Townsend (D. Lothrop Company, Boston, Massachusetts, 1890) p. 80.
[184] *Legislative Manual of the Seventy-ninth General Assembly of South Carolina*, J. Wilson Gibbs, Clerk of the House of Representatives (The State Company, Columbia, South Carolina, 1931) p. 207.

Appalachian Mountains and its base extends to the Atlantic Ocean has caused it to be called *The Keystone of the South Atlantic Seaboard.* [184a]

The palmetto grows abundantly in South Carolina, especially along the coast, and is pictured on her coat of arms; consequently it has given the nickname, the *Palmetto State,* to the State. [185]

South Carolina is also called the *Rice State* from the enormous quantities of rice it produces and handles each year.

The *Sand-lapper State* is given as a nickname to South Carolina, probably, from the fact that some of its poorer inhabitants live on the sandy ridges which are covered with scrubby pine forests, it being humorously said that they lap up sand for sustenance.

The *Swamp State* is applied to South Carolina in reference to the lands where the rice is grown and other swampy lands.

The South Carolinians have six nicknames; namely. *Clay-eaters, Palmettoes, Rice-birds, Sand-hillers, Sand-lappers,* and *Weasels.* These are mostly derogatory terms given to the classes of poorer white people. *Clay-eaters* refers to the fact that certain classes of poor white people living in some of the remoter districts are said to have eaten abundantly of the white, aluminous clay found in these parts of the State when they could get no more substantial food. [186] For the origin and the significance of the sobriquets, *Palmettoes* and *Sand-lappers,* see the previous narrative dealing with the nicknames, the *Palmetto State* and the *Sand-lapper State.* *Rice-birds* is a nickname given to the well-to-do rice planters and those people living in the rich rice sections of the State. The country surrounding Beaufort, South Carolina, " 'embraces the best rice fields of the South, so proverbially so indeed that

[184a] *Compton's Pictured Encyclopedia* (F. E. Compton Company, Chicago, Illinois, 1933) vol. 13, p. 212.
[185] *A New Dictionary of Americanisms,* Sylva Clapin (Louis Weiss and Company, Publishers, New York, 1903 (?)) p. 299.
[186] *Ibidem,* p. 121.

the irrelevant "up country" are accustomed to call the aristocratic inhabitants of the region *rice-birds*.' " [187] *Sand-hillers* was applied especially to the poor descendants of the laboring white people who were driven out of the pine woods on the sandy hills of South Carolina when slave labor was introduced,[188] and there became skinny and cadaverous-looking. They are said to have skins the color of the sand of their habitat. [189] The name might have been derived from the sand-hill crane (*Grus canadensis*), a longlegged species [190] found commonly in the sections of the country in which these people live. *Sand-lappers* is a jesting nickname given to those people living in the pine barrens, whom William Gilmore Simms calls a "Sand-lapper or a Clay-eater." The *Sand-lappers* are generally described as being little, dried up, and jaundiced. Simms in *The Forayers* speaks of a woman as being "the fattest and yellowest sandlapper of a woman I ever saw." [191] The people living in the out-of-the-way sections of the State are called *Weasels*. [192]

South Dakota

South Dakota has the following nicknames: the *Artesian State*, the *Blizzard State*, the *Coyote State*, the *Land of Plenty*, and the *Sunshine State*.

The great number of artesian wells in South Dakota cause it to be named the *Artesian State*.

The sobriquet, the *Blizzard State*, was given to South

[187] *U. S.: An Index to the United States of America*, compiled by Malcolm Townsend (D. Lothrop Company, Boston, Massachusetts, 1890) p. 80.

[188] *More About Names*, Leopold Wagner (T. Fisher Unwin, London, 1893) p. 26.

[189] *A Journey in the Seaboard Slave States with Remarks on Their Economy*, Frederick Law Olmsted (Dix and Edwards, New York, 1856) p. 506.

[190] *U. S.: An Index to the United States of America*, compiled by Malcolm Townsend (D. Lothrop Company, Boston, Massachusetts, 1890) p. 80.

[191] *The Forayers*, William Gilmore Simms (Redfield, New York, 1855) p. 391.

[192] *U. S.: An Index to the United States of America*, compiled by Malcolm Townsend (D. Lothrop Company, Boston, Massachusetts, 1890) p. 80.

Dakota because occasionally "terrific northerly gales" laden with fine snow sweep over portions of the State.

The great number of coyotes or small wolves on the territorial prairies gave the name, the *Coyote State,* to South Dakota.

In discussing the expression, the *Land of Plenty,* Johnson says that "with an average of over four hundred acres of land for every family in the state, having ability to support in comfort several times the present population, South Dakota certainly deserves the title, 'Land of Plenty.' " [193]

South Dakota is known as the *Sunshine State* because of the great percentage of sunshiny weather it has during the year. North and South Dakota together are frequently called *The Twin Sisters.*

TENNESSEE

The following are the nicknames of Tennessee: the *Big Bend State,* the *Lion's Den State, The Hog and Hominy State, The Mother of South-western Statesmen,* and the *Volunteer State.*

The first of these, no doubt, originated in the expression *The River with the Big Bend,* which is the Indian name for the Tennessee River. [194]

J. C. Thomas gives the sobriquet, the *Lion's Den State,* [195] applied to Tennessee; but he does not say how it originated. Probably its origin and application to this State are in some way connected with the life and activities of Andrew Jackson.

"The corn and pork product of Tennessee reached such great proportions between 1800 and 1840, that the land received the designation (now obsolete) of *The Hog and Hominy State.*" [196]

[193] *South Dakota: A Republic of Friends,* Willis E. Johnson (The Capital Supply Company, Pierre, South Dakota, 1917) p. 13.
[194] *Origin and History of the American Flag,* George Henry Preble (Nicholas L. Brown, Philadelphia, Pennsylvania, 1917) vol. 2, p. 638.
[195] *Manual of Useful Information,* J. C. Thomas (The Werner Company, Chicago, Illinois, 1893) p. 22.
[196] *King's Handbook of the United States,* planned and edited by Moses King, text by M. F. Sweetser (The Matthews-Northrup Company, Buffalo, New York, 1896) p. 797.

Tennessee, having furnished the United States three presidents and a number of distinguished statesmen, has come to be designated as *The Mother of South-western Statesmen.*

With regard to the sobriquet, the *Volunteer State,* Governor Brown on May 26, 1847, called for three regiments of soldiers to serve in the Mexican War. Thirty thousand volunteered at once; consequently Tennessee was nicknamed the *Volunteer State.* [197]

The Tennesseeans are nicknamed *Big-benders, Butternuts, Mud-heads,* and *Whelps.* The first nickname is derived from the fact that the Tennessee river is called the river with a big bend, referring in all probability to the Moccasin bend at the foot of Lookout Mountain at Chattanooga, Tennessee. The name *Butter-nuts* was first given to the soldiers of Tennessee during the Civil War from the tan color of their uniforms, [198] and later it came to be applied to the people of the entire State. *Mud-heads* [199] is given as a nickname to the Tennesseeans by more than one writer, but its origin and significance are not explained. The sobriquet *Whelps* [200] applied to the Tennesseeans is not generally accepted by the people of the State, and the writer is unable to account for its origin and significance.

TEXAS

The State of Texas is designated as: the *Banner State,* the *Beef State,* the *Blizzard State,* the *Jumbo State,* and the *Lone Star State.*

The sobriquet, the *Banner State,* is applied to Texas, probably, from the fact that she polls a large vote in national elections. Norton says under the name *Banner*

---

[197] *Tennessee, The Volunteer State, 1796-1923,* John Trotwood Moore and Austin P. Foster (The S. J. Clarke Publishing Company, Chicago, Illinois and Nashville, Tennessee, 1923) vol. I, p. 437.

[198] *U. S.: An Index to the United States of America,* compiled by Malcolm Townsend (D. Lothrop Company, Boston, Massachusetts, 1890) p. 80.

[199] *Americanisms—New and Old,* John Stephen Farmer (Privately Printed by Thomas Poulter and Sons, London, 1889) p. 376.

[200] *U. S.: An Index to the United States of America,* compiled by Malcolm Townsend (D. Lothrop Company, Boston, Massachusetts, 1890) p. 81.

State: "The state, county, town, or other political subdivision that gives the largest vote for a party candidate is termed the 'banner state.' . . ." [201]

The *Beef State* is attributed as a sobriquet to the State of Texas in commemoration of the fact that she has been, and still is, noted for her cattle raising, producing yearly about one-seventh of the beef of the United States.

The nickname, the *Blizzard State,* was given to Texas undoubtedly on account of the frequent wind storms which sweep over the State.

The origin of the sobriquet, the *Jumbo State,* attributed to Texas, is as follows: Barnum and Bailey bought the largest African elephant ever kept in captivity and brought him from London to America to be used in their circus. The fact that this elephant's name was Jumbo has caused all unusually large things to be called Jumbo. Texas is the largest State in the Union; therefore it acquired the nickname the *Jumbo State.*

De Vere says that Texas is called the *Lone Star State* because she was "once a province of Mexico, then an independent republic, bore a single star in its coat of arms, and being for a time left to struggle unaided against the whole power of her formidable enemy, became then honorably known as the *Lone Star State*—a name which she has ever since retained." [202]

The Texans are called *Beef-heads,* [203] *Blizzards,* [204] *Cowboys,* [204] and *Rangers.* [204] The appellation *Beef-heads* is easily accounted for by the fact that Texas is a great cattle-raising country, and this fact gives an insight into the origin of the nicknames *Cowboys* and *Rangers.* The Texans are called *Blizzards* for the same reason the State is nicknamed the *Blizzard State.*

[201] *Political Americanisms,* Charles Ledyard Norton (Longmans, Green and Company, New York and London, 1890) p. 10.
[202] *Americanisms; The English of the New World,* M. Schele De Vere (Charles Scribner and Company, New York, 1872) p. 661.
[203] *U. S.: An Index to the United States of America,* compiled by Malcolm Townsend (D. Lothrop Company, Boston, Massachusetts, 1890) p. 81.
[204] *A Book of Nicknames,* John Goff (Courier-Journal Job Printing Company, 1892) p. 20.

UTAH

Utah is known as: the *Bee Hive State*, the *Deseret State*, the *Land of the Mormons*, the *Land of the Saints*, the *Mormon State*, and the *Salt Lake State*.

The *Bee Hive State* commemorates the fact that the coat of arms of Utah depicts "a conical beehive, with a swarm of bees round it, emblematical of the industry of the people." [205]

The sobriquet, the *Deseret State*, gives an insight into the fact that the Mormons first called their settlement the State of Deseret, this being the official name of the colony from 1849 to 1850, at which time the territory of Utah was organized. The word Deseret, meaning *the honeybee*, is taken from the *Book of Mormons*.

Utah is called the *Land of the Mormons* because a great percentage of the Mormons of the United States live there; the *Land of the Saints* because the Mormons called themselves Latter-Day Saints; and the *Mormon State*, from the fact that it was founded by the Mormons.

The term, the *Salt Lake State*, refers to the fact that the Great Salt Lake is located in Utah.

The people of Utah were formerly called *Polygamists* [206] from the fact that until recent years polygamy was permitted to be practiced throughout the State. The sobriquets *Mormons* and *Saints* are both applied to the people of Utah from the fact that this State was settled by the Mormons, whose church is officially known as *The Church of Jesus Christ of the Latter-Day Saints*. [207]

VERMONT

De Vere says that "*Vermont* is generally, by simple translation of the original name given by the French settlers, called the *Green Mountain State*, the principal

[205] *More About Names*, Leopold Wagner (T. Fisher Unwin, London, 1893) p. 36.
[206] *A Manual of Useful Information*, compiled under the direction of J. C. Thomas (The Werner Company, Chicago, Illinois, 1893) p. 23.
[207] *Political Americanisms*, Charles Ledyard Norton (Longmans, Green and Company, New York and London, 1890) p. 64.

ridge of mountains within its boundaries being known by that name." [208]

Vermonters are called *Green Mountain Boys* from the fact that many of the inhabitants of the State live among the Green Mountains. [209]

VIRGINIA

Virginia is nicknamed the *Ancient Dominion,* the *Cavalier State, Down Where the South Begins,* the *Mother of Presidents,* the *Mother of States,* the *Mother of Statesmen,* and *The Old Dominion.*

The names, the *Ancient Dominion* and *The Old Dominion,* are still widely applied to Virginia, having originated in Colonial days. About the year 1663, after Charles Stuart had become King of England, he quartered the Arms of Virginia on his royal shield; thus ranking Virginia along with his other four dominions, England, Scotland, France, and Ireland. Historians say that the new king elevated Virginia to the position of a dominion "by quartering its arms (the old seal of the Virginia Company) on his royal shield with the arms of England, Scotland, and Ireland, [and that] the burgesses were very proud of this distinction and, remembering that they were the oldest as well as the most faithful of the Stuart settlements in America, adopted the name of 'The Old Dominion.' " [210] Colonel Richard Lee, of the Colony of Virginia, is said to have visited Charles Stuart while he was in exile in the city of Brussels, about 1658. Charles was proclaimed King Charles II of England on May 8, 1660, and the Virginians accepted him as their king on September the 20th following his ascension. [211] This pleased King Charles so much that he referred to the people of this

[208] *Americanisms; The English of the New World,* M. Schele De Vere (Charles Scribner and Company, New York, 1872) p. 662.

[209] *U. S.: An Index to the United States of America,* compiled by Malcolm Townsend (D. Lothrop Company, Boston, Massachusetts, 1890) p. 81.

[210] *An American History,* David Saville Muzzey (Ginn and Company, New York, 1929) p. 32-3.

[211] *Old Virginia and Her Neighbors,* John Fiske (Houghton, Mifflin and Company, Boston and New York, 1897) vol. 2, p. 20-1.

colony as "the best of his distant children," [212] and elevated the colony of Virginia to the position of a dominion.

Fiske says that "after the restoration of Charles II, a new seal for Virginia, adopted about 1663, has the same motto [*En dat Virginia quintam*] the effect of which was to rank Virginia by the side of his Majesty's other four dominions, England, Scotland, 'France,' and Ireland. We are told by the younger Richard Henry Lee that in these circumstances originated the famous epithet 'Old Dominion.' " [213]

Virginia's nickname, the *Cavalier State,* is derived from the name of the Cavaliers who came over and settled there during, and shortly after the time of Charles I.

Because Virginia is the most southern of the Middle Atlantic States, located south of the Potomac river, radio broadcasters call it *Down Where the South Begins.* [213a]

Her sobriquet, the *Mother of Presidents,* alludes to the fact that so many of the early presidents of the United States were native Virginians.

Virginia was called the *Mother of States* because she was the first of the states to be settled. [214]

The original territory of Virginia was split up to make West Virginia, Ohio, Kentucky, Illinois, Indiana, Wisconsin and a part of Minnesota; hence she came to be known as the *Mother of States.* Because she has produced such a great number of statesmen, she is called *The Mother of Statesmen.*

The Virginians are nicknamed *Beagles* or *Beadles,* *Cavaliers,* *F. F. V.'s,* *Sorebacks,* and *Tuckahoes.* The sobriquet *Beadles* or *Beagles* originated during colonial days, due to the fact that the Virginians, following the

[212] *An American History,* David Saville Muzzey (Ginn and Company, New York, 1929) p. 32.
[213] *Old Virginia and Her Neighbours,* John Fiske (Houghton, Mifflin and Company, Boston and New York, 1897) vol. 2, p. 22-3.
[213a] *Virginia,* comp. and ed. by Charlotte Allen (Published by the Department of Agriculture and Immigration of the State of Virginia under the direction of George W. Koiner, Commissioner, Department of Purchase and Printing, Richmond, Virginia, 1937) p. 13.
[214] *The New International Encyclopaedia* (Dodd, Mead and Company, New York, 1930) vol. 21, p. 464.

English custom, used beadles in their courts. [215] The second nickname, *Cavaliers,* alludes to Virginia's English Cavalier settlers, and *F. F. V.'s* stands for the *First Families of Virginia,* of which the people of the State have been and are very proud. "The abbreviation was of northern origin, and was in common use prior to the Civil War." [216]

Tradition gives two accounts of the origin of the nickname *Sorebacks* applied to Virginians. One is that the Virginians are so hospitable that they slap one another on the backs until their backs become sore; the other is that the people in the southern part of the state raise so much cotton that it makes their backs sore to pick it. The North Carolinians seem to be the originators of this account. The nickname *Tuckahoes* was originally applied only to the poorer white people living in the lower part of the State. This nickname was often heard during the Civil War because poverty often drove these Virginians to eat tuckahoe. [217]

WASHINGTON

The inhabitants of the State of Washington have been nicknamed *Clam Grabbers* [217a] doubtless from the fact that they gather vast quantities of clams annually from the shallow waters of Puget Sound and of Wallapa Harbor.

The *Chinook State* was given as a nickname to the State of Washington because it was formerly the home of the "principal tribe of the Lower Chinook division of North American Indians." [218]

The sobriquet, the *Evergreen State,* suggests the continual green of the State of Washington. The big firs are always green and the grass grows all the winter.

[215] *A New Dictionary of Americanisms,* Sylva Clapin (Louis Weiss and Company, New York, 1903 (?)) p. 43.
[216] *Political Americanisms,* Charles Ledyard Norton (Longmans, Green and Company, New York and London, 1890) p. 43.
[217] *A New Dictionary of Americanisms,* Sylva Clapin (Louis Weiss and Company, New York, 1903 (?)) p. 409.
[217a] *The Lincoln Library of Essential Information,* Thoroughly Revised at Each New Printing (The Frontier Press Company, Buffalo, New York, 1937) p. 2068.
[218] *The Century Cyclopedia of Names,* edited by Benjamin E. Smith (The Century Company, New York, 1914) vol. II, p. 246.

WEST VIRGINIA

West Virginia merits the distinction of being designated as the *Mountain State* because more than one-third of the area of the state is a high plateau of the Allegheny Mountains. It is also known as the *Panhandle State* on account of the resemblance of the shape of the state to a pan with a handle on it. The region representing the handle is called the *Panhandle Section,* or simply the *Panhandle of West Virginia.* [219]

The *Switzerland of America* is applied to West Virginia from the picturesqueness of her mountain scenery.

The use of the sobriquet *Pan-handleites,* applied to West Virginia folk, has the same origin and significance as that of the nickname the *Panhandle State.*

WISCONSIN

The origin of Wisconsin's sobriquet, the *Badger State,* is as follows: This term was applied to the early lead miners, who on first coming to a new location dug in the side of a hill and lived under ground much as the badger digs in his burrow. Reuben Gold Thwaites speaks of Wisconsin as the "land of the Badgers." [220] This sobriquet had its origin in the early mining days of Wisconsin at the lead mines located near that corner of Wisconsin where the three states—Wisconsin, Illinois and Iowa—meet. Moses M. Strong, in a letter published in the *Madison State Journal* for December 10, 1879, says: "The term 'Badger'—according to tradition—was first applied to the occupants of these temporary subterranean residences in derision;—as the term 'Sucker' was applied to the migratory inhabitants of Southern Illinois, who, like the fish of the carp family, came to the 'mines' in the spring, and returned on the approach of winter;—and afterward to all the inhabitants of the lead-mine region, and by a not

---

[219] *U. S.: An Index to the United States of America,* compiled by Malcolm Townsend (D. Lothrop Company, Boston, Massachusetts, 1890) p. 81.

[220] "The Story of Wisconsin" in *The Story of the States,* Reuben Gold Thwaites (D. Lothrop Company, Boston, Massachusetts, 1890) p. 205.

unnatural adaptation, has been applied to the people of the State and to the State itself." [221]

Wisconsin's nickname, the *Copper State* refers to the copper mines in the northern part of the State.

The people of Wisconsin are frequently called *Badgers.* Professor James D. Butler, in speaking of these early miners says: "Those from Southern Illinois went home to winter; those from the east could not, but dodged the cold in such dug-outs as they could hurry up. The eastern men were hence nicknamed *Badgers,* as if burrowing in similar holes with those animals. This jocose appellation became the badge of all the Wisconsin tribe; and it will remain indelible forever." [222]

WYOMING

Wyoming has been nicknamed *The Wonderland of America* [223] because of its magnificent scenic beauty.

Wyoming is known as the *Equality State* because it was a pioneer in woman suffrage.

The sobriquet, the *Sagebrush State,* applied to Wyoming, refers to the fact that wild sage (*Artemisia tridentata*) grows on the desert sections of this State.

STATES WHOSE INHABITANTS DO NOT POSSESS NICKNAMES

The people of the following states have no nicknames: Montana, North Dakota, South Dakota, and Wyoming.

[221] "Wisconsin's Emblems and Sobriquets," Reuben Gold Thwaites, in the *Proceedings of the State Historical Society of Wisconsin at Its Fifty-fifth Annual Meeting Held November 7, 1907* (Published by the Society, Democrat Printing Company, State Printers, Madison, Wisconsin, 1908) p. 304.

[222] "Tay-Cho-Pe-Rah—The Four Lake Country—First White Foot-Prints There," Professor James D. Butler, in *Report and Collections of the State Historical Society of Wisconsin, for the Years 1883, 1884, and 1885* (Democrat Printing Company, State Printers, Madison, Wisconsin, 1888) vol. 10, p. 79.

For a similar account of the origin of this nickname, see also "The Cornish in Southwest Wisconsin," Louis Albert Copeland, in *Collections of the State Historical Society of Wisconsin* (Democrat Printing Company. Madison, Wisconsin, 1898) vol. 14, p. 305.

[223] *The World Book Encyclopedia* (The Quarrie Corporation, Chicago, Illinois, 1937) vol. 18, p. 7906.

CHAPTER III

STATE MOTTOES: THEIR ORIGIN AND SIGNIFICANCE

A motto is a word, a phrase, or a sentence, often chosen for its euphony or meaning, representing the expression of a moral or religious feeling, a war cry or heroic exclamation, a declaration of allegiance and faith, or a boast referring to some special occasion.

The custom of using mottoes may be traced back as far as there are available records, the oldest forms, perhaps, being those of a religious nature, or those designated as patriotic cries or sentiments employed by the Hebrews, the Greeks, and the Romans. Such mottoes, however, were not written, but they were generally used only for some special occasion, after which they were discarded and often forgotten. Written mottoes or inscriptions are found on monuments, tombs, and other remains of the earliest forms of civilization.

During the Middle Ages mottoes were used as war cries. Later they were emblazoned on coats of arms. A few mottoes originated from remarks or boasts such as the famed expression of Richard I at the Battle of Gisors, *"Dieu et Mon Droit";* but the majority of them were chosen "deliberately for their meaning and euphony."

European nations, in many instances, have adopted the mottoes of their reigning families or of the chivalric orders of these.

Practically all nations have made use of mottoes. They are found written in Hebrew, Greek, Latin, French, German, Italian, Cornish, Welsh, Irish, Spanish, and English.

It is interesting to note that Scotch mottoes "are characterized by great piety of feeling," as are those of the German-speaking countries. Irish mottoes may be described as "witty and jocular"; Dutch mottoes are

quaint, often to the point of grotesqueness; but those of
the English-speaking people are more cosmopolitan in their
character and significance.

Mottoes may be classified as religious invocations,
patriotic appeals, those describing the characteristics of
the people using them, enigmatical expressions, canting or
punning allusions to family names, heraldic sentiments,
and those inspired by special accomplishments or occasions.

Mottoes are employed by almost every division of
organized society, ranging from individuals, families,
chivalric orders, organizations, schools, labor unions,
armies, and towns, to counties, states and nations.

The states of the Union are cosmopolitan in the
linguistic expression of their mottoes, employing seven
languages; namely, Greek, Latin, Spanish, French, Italian,
American Indian, and English. The preference, however,
seems to be for Latin, twenty-three of the forty-nine states
—that is counting the District of Columbia as a state—
using Latin mottoes. Some of the states, in addition to
their adopted mottoes, have other mottoes on their seals,
expressed either in the same language as that of their
adopted mottoes or in a different language.

The four states having both Latin and English mottoes
are Arkansas, Missouri, Wisconsin, and Wyoming.

Both Wisconsin and Michigan have on their seals the
motto, *E Pluribus Unum,* taken in all probability from the
Great Seal of the United States. This phrase came
originally from Virgil's *Morctum,* line 103, [1] or from the
title page of the *Gentleman's Magazine,* Volume 1, 1731. [2]

It is noteworthy that the Latin mottoes, for the most
part, are taken from great Latin writers. Three were
taken from the *Latin Vulgate Version of the Bible.* Five

---

[1] The Virgilian passage reads as follows: *Color est e pluribus unus.*
[2] The title page of the *Spectator,* no. 148, August 20, 1711, displays
the following passage taken from Horace's *Second Epistle,* line 212:
Exempta juvat spinis e pluribus una, freely translated, *Better one thorn
plucked out, than all remain.* The passage in the text of Horace reads:
Quid te exempta levat spinis de pluribus una?, literally translated, *"What
good does it do you to pluck out a single one from many thorns?"*

were taken from Virgil's works; three from the *Aeneid,* one from the *Eclogues,* and one from the *Georgics.* Cicero's writings supplied three, each coming from a different work; one from *De Amicitia,* one from *De Officiis,* and one from *De Legibus.* Lucretius and Seneca each have furnished one. Four were taken from different individual mottoes, coats of arms, or inscriptions, and six seem to be made-up Latin.

THE STATE MOTTOES EXPRESSED IN THE LATIN LANGUAGE

Arizona

Arizona's motto, *Ditat Deus,* meaning *God enriches,* is probably an abbreviation of Genesis, Chapter 14, verse 23, of the *Latin Vulgate Version of the Bible.*

Arkansas

The motto of Arkansas is *Regnat Populus,* signifying *The people rule.* The original source of this expression cannot be accounted for by the writer. Arkansas's motto was originally *Regnant Populi;* but the General Assembly of the State of Arkansas on May 23, 1907, passed a resolution changing the motto from *Regnant Populi* to *Regnat Populus.* [8]

Colorado

Colorado's motto, *Nil Sine Numine,* meaning *Nothing without the Deity,* is an adaptation from Virgil's *Aeneid,* Book II, line 777.   In the Latin text the line reads:

. . . . . non haec sine numine devûm
Eveniunt.

"After the organization of the Territory of Colorado and William Gilpin had been duly installed as the first

---

[8] *Arkansas Laws, 1907: Public and Private Acts and Joint and Concurrent Resolutions and Memorials of the General Assembly of the State of Arkansas, Passed at the Session Held at the Capital, in the City of Little Rock, Arkansas, Commencing on the 14th Day of January, 1907, and Ending on the 14th Day of May, 1907,* by authority (Democrat Printing and Lithographing Company, Little Rock, Arkansas, 1907) p. 988.

governor, the design of a seal was entrusted to the Secretary of the Territory, L. C. Weld, with instructions to submit his rough draft to Governor Gilpin. It appears that the Governor approved the suggestions Weld had incorporated but said there should be a suitable and appropriate motto. Weld, according to the story, said, 'Well, Governor, what would you suggest?' Gilpin thought a moment and replied, in his own peculiar style, 'Nil Sine Numine.' " [4]

The motto of Colorado, *Nil Sine Numine,* should not be translated *Nothing without God,* but *Nothing without the Deity,* as is indicated by the fact that it is thus translated in the Joint Resolution approved November 6, 1861, adopting the Territorial seal upon which the motto is first found. [5]

Connecticut

Connecticut's motto, *Qui Translulit Sustinet,* means *He who transplanted continues to sustain.* It is an adaptation of *Psalms,* Chapter 79, verse 3, of the *Latin Vulgate Version of the Bible.* "The vines [on the State Seal] symbolize the Colony brought over and planted here in the wilderness. We read in the 80th Psalm: 'Thou has brought a vine out of Egypt: Thou hast cast out the heathen, and planted it':—in Latin, *'Vineam de AEgypto transtulisti, Ejicisti gentes et Plantasti eam';* and the motto expresses our belief that He who brought over the vine continues to take care of it—*Qui transtulit sustinet."* [6]

---

[4] A letter from Albert B. Sanford, Assistant Curator of History, State Historical Society of Colorado, State Museum, Denver, Colorado, March 17, 1930.

[5] *Laws of Colorado, 1861: General Laws, Joint Resolutions, Memorials, and Private Acts, Passed at the First Session of the Legislative Assembly of the Territory of Colorado, Begun and Held at Denver, Colorado Territory, September 9th, 1861* (Thomas Gibson, Colorado Republican and Herald Office, Denver, Colorado, 1861) p. 514.

[6] "The Public Seal of Connecticut," Charles J. Hoadly, in the *Connecticut State Register and Manual, 1889: Register and Manual of the State of Connecticut,* prepared pursuant to Section 320 of the General Statutes by the Secretary of the State (The Case, Lockwood and Brainard Company, Printers, Hartford, Connecticut, 1889) p. 441.

The District of Columbia

The motto of the District of Columbia, *Justitia Omnibus,* denoting *Justice to all,* the Secretary of the Board of Commissioners states, "may have been suggested by the fact that all classes of male citizens of the District of Columbia had then [1871] but recently, been vested with an equal right to vote on municipal matters here; and that the laws generally had been made correspondingly impartial. Until a short time before, persons of Negro descent had been excluded from the right to vote here." [7]

Idaho

The State motto of Idaho, *Esto Perpetua,* meaning *Mayest thou endure forever!,* is "the supposed dying apostrophe of Pietro Sarpi (Fra Paolo) in speaking of his beloved Venice." [8]   Miss Emma Edwards of Boise, now Mrs. Emma Edwards-Greene, who designed the State seal, says that the words *Esto Perpetua* " 'breathe the prayer that the bounty and blessing of this land may forever benefit its people.' " [9]

Kansas

The motto of Kansas is *Ad Astra Per Aspera,* signify ing *To the stars through difficulties.* "The idea represented by the motto itself is very old, and occurs frequently in classical poetry, in German set phrases and quotations, and in the feudal mottoes of the European nobility." [10] The nearest embodiment of the idea of this motto, as John S. Dawson points out, is the idea of "Caius Silius Italicus,

---

[7] A letter from Daniel E. Garges, Secretary to the Board of Commissioners of the District of Columbia, Washington, D. C., April 18, 1930.

[8] *Classical and Foreign Quotations,* W. Francis H. King (J. Whitaker and Sons, Limited, London, 1904) p. 90.

[9] *History of Idaho: The Gem of the Mountains,* James H. Hawley, Editor (The S. J. Clarke Publishing Company, Chicago, Illinois, 1920) vol. 1, p. 229.

[10] "The Great Seal of Kansas," Robert Hay, in the *Transactions of the Kansas State Historical society, 1903-1904,* vol. 8, edited by George W. Martin, Secretary (George A. Clark, State Printer, Topeka, Kansas, 1904) p. 297.

a Latin poet of the early part of the Second Century"
expressed as follows:

" 'Explorant adversa viros; per (que) aspera [11]
duro Nititur ad laudem virtus interrita clivo.' "

This motto was probably formed by the fusion of the
ideas and the words in two passages from Virgil's *Aeneid,*
forming the exact motto, *Ad Astra Per Aspera.* The
Virgilian passages are: *sic itur ad astra,* the *Aeneid,* Book
IX, line 641; and *opta ardua pennis astra sequi,* the
Aeneid, Book XII, lines 892-3.

As to the origin of this motto, Richard Cordley states
that Mrs. Josiah Miller told him that Judge Josiah Miller
"was a member of the Committee on seal. He was in his
room when the idea came to him; he was studying on the
motto. At last he brightened up and said: 'I have it—
Ad astra per aspera.' They talked it over, and agreed
that it could not be improved. He suggested it to the
committee and it was adopted without question." [12]

Maine

Dirigo, meaning *I direct* or *I guide,* is the State motto
of Maine. The resolves, adopting the seal upon which this
motto appears, say, "as the Polar Star has been considered the mariner's *guide* and *director* in conducting
the ship over the pathless ocean to the desired haven, and
as the center of magnetic attraction; as it has been figuratively used to denote the point, to which all affections turn,
and as it is here intended to represent the State, it may be
considered the citizens' *guide,* and the object to which the
patriot's best exertions should be *directed.*" [13]

[11] *Ibidem,* p. 297.
[12] "The Great Seal of Kansas," Robert Hay, in the *Transactions of
the Kansas State Historical Society, 1903-1904,* vol. 8. edited by George W.
Martin, Secretary (George A. Clark, State Printer, Topeka, Kansas,
1904) p. 299.
[13] *Resolves of the Legislature of the State of Maine, Passed at its
Session Which Commenced on the twenty-first day of May and Ended on
the twenty-eighth day of June, one thousand eight hundred twenty,* Published Agreeably to the Resolution of June 28, 1820 (Printed by Francis
Douglas, State Printer, Portland. Maine. 1820) p. 22.

Maryland

The motto on the reverse of the State seal of Maryland is *Scuto Bonae Voluntatis Tuae Coronasti Nos,* signifying *With the shield of thy good-will thou hast covered us.* This may be found in the *Latin Vulgate Version of the Bible, Psalms,* Chapter 5, line 12. On the same side of the seal is an Italian motto: *Fatti Maschii Parole Femine,* meaning *Manly deeds, womanly words;* or more strictly, *Deeds are males; words, females.* This is the Calvert motto.

Massachusetts

Massachusetts has as a State motto: *Ense Petit Placidam Sub Libertate Quietem,* signifying *With the sword she seeks peace under liberty.* This is attributed to Algernon Sydney (Sidney), an English political writer (1622-1683). His father writes to him: "It is said that the University of Copenhagen brought their album unto you, desiring you to write something therein; and that you did *'scribere in albo'* these words:

'. . . Manus haec inimica tyrannis
Ense petit placidam sub libertate quietam.' " [14]

Michigan

The State motto of Michigan, *Si Quaeris Peninsulam Amoenam Circumspice,* meaning *If you seek a pleasant peninsula, look around you,* is said to have been suggested to Lewis Cass, Michigan's second Territorial Governor, by the mural inscription on the north door of St. Paul's Cathedral in London. The mural inscription *Si Monumentum Requiris Circumspice* means *If you require a monument [for me] look around you,* [15] and commemorates the architect, Sir Christopher Wren, referring to the

[14] *Life and Memoirs of Algernon Sydney,* prefixed to his *Discourses on Government* (Printed for Richard Lee by Deare and Andrews, New York, 1805) vol. 1, p. 28.

[15] *Michigan History Magazine,* George N. Fuller, Editor, Teachers Number (Published by the Michigan Historical Commission, Lansing, Michigan, 1929) vol. 13, p. 663-4.

cathedral itself, the product and best monument of his genius. Governor Cass and his father, General Cass, having observed the "peninsular character" of Michigan, modified the motto on St. Paul's to read *Si Quaeris Peninsulam Amoenam Circumspice.* "The word *Tuebor* on the arms of Michigan is not original. It is the motto on the arms of the Viscount Torrington, an English nobleman who lived near Maidstone in Kent County, England." [16] *Tuebor* signifies *I will defend.* This Latin word has "reference to the frontier position of the State of Michigan. She lies close to the British territory, and on her devolves the defense not only of her soil, but also of the States south and east and west of her. She is the northern guard of the Union, and she says upon the shield, 'I will defend' the frontier against all enemies. In this view the word has a beautiful and brave significance, and should never be changed while our position is thus in the forefront of exposure." [17]

Mississippi

The State motto of Mississippi, *Virtute Et Armis,* meaning *by valor and arms,* was suggested by the Honorable James Rhea Preston of Virginia, who was at the time Superintendent of Education in the State of Mississippi. [18] This may have been suggested to him by the motto of Lord Gray De Wilton, *Virtute Non Armis Fido.*

Missouri

The State motto of Missouri, *Salus Populi Suprema Lex Esto,* signifying *Let the welfare of the people be the supreme law,* may be found in Cicero's *De Legibus,* Book

[16] A letter from G. N. Fuller, Secretary and Editor of the Michigan Historical Commission, State Office Building, Lansing, Michigan, March 17, 1930.

[17] *Michigan History Magazine,* George N. Fuller, Editor, Teachers Number (Published by the Michigan Historical Commission, Lansing, Michigan, 1929) vol. 13, p. 664.

[18] A letter from Dunbar Rowland, State Historian and Director of the Department of Archives and History of the State of Mississippi, Jackson, Mississippi, March 17, 1930.

III, part 3, subdivision 8, the last line of this subdivision. *United We Stand, Divided We Fall,* the other motto, in all probability was taken from George P. Morris's poem, *The Flag of Our Union.*

New Mexico

New Mexico's State motto, *Crescit Eundo,* meaning *It grows as it goes,* may be found in Lucretius's *De Rerum Natura,* Book VI, line 341.

New York

New York uses one Latin word, *Excelsior,* signifying *Higher,* as its motto. It is the comparative of the adjective *Excelsus,* meaning *high* or *lofty.* This term was first used with reference to the physical; but it has now come to include spiritual, mental, and moral progress.

North Carolina

North Carolina's motto, *Esse Quam Videri,* signifying *To be rather than to seem,* may be found in Cicero's *De Amicitia,* Section 26, line 16. The sense in which Cicero used this expression in the *De Amicitia* is different from that in which the motto is understood today. Cicero says:

Virtute enim ipsa non tam multi praediti esse quam videri volunt,

meaning thereby, *The truth is that virtue is a quality which not so many wish to possess as desire to seem to possess,* or signifying, when literally translated, *For indeed not so many wish to be endowed with virtue as wish to seem to be.* The words of the motto, *To be rather than to seem,* "are a suitable recognition of the honest, sturdy, unpretending character of our people," [19] affirms the State Librarian. The figures on the State seal are the *Goddess of Liberty* and the *Goddess of Plenty* and the people of the State "prefer to be free and prosperous rather than merely to seem to be so." [19]

[19] A letter from Carrie L. Broughton, Librarian, North Carolina State Library, Raleigh, North Carolina, March 18, 1930, giving a brief synopsis of an article entitled *Our State Motto and Coat of Arms* by Judge Walter Clark, published in the *North Carolina Teacher,* vol. 10, April, 1893.

Ohio

Between the years 1866 and 1868, the State of Ohio had as a motto *Imperium In Imperio,* signifying *An empire within an empire.* [20] Since the repeal, in 1868, [21] of the law providing this motto, the State has had no motto.

Rush R. Sloane says that this motto, "gave offense to great numbers of our people," [22] that "these acts [providing the motto] were passed by a Republican Legislature, and were repealed by the Democratic Legislature of 1868, and only remained in force about two years," [22] and that "they were repealed none too soon." [22]

The expression, *Imperium In Imperio,* is used in James Anthony Froude's *Life and Times of Thomas Becket* in the following passage: "The Church, an *imperium in imperio,* however corrupt in practice, was aggressive as an institution, and was encroaching on the State with organized system." [23] Professor Walter A. Montgomery says that "it is the opinion of some scholars that the phrase *Imperium in Imperio* did not come into existence until the time of the Holy Roman Empire, and that it was an expression of the papal feeling of the relationship of the Holy Roman Empire to the separate nations, which was a new idea, and did not agree at all with the old Roman ideas of empire." [24]

[20] *Ohio Laws, 1866: General and Local Laws and Joint Resolutions Passed by the Fifty-seventh General Assembly of the State of Ohio, at Its First Session, Begun and Held in the City of Columbus, January 1, 1866, and in the Sixty-fourth Year of Said State* (Richard Nevins, State Printer, Columbus, Ohio, 1866) vol. LXIII, p. 185 6.

[21] *Ohio Laws, 1868: General and Local Laws and Joint Resolutions Passed by the Fifty-eighth General Assembly of the State of Ohio, at Its First Session, Begun and Held in the City of Columbus, January 6, 1868 and in the Sixty-sixth Year of Said State* (L. D. Myers and Brother, State Printers, Columbus, Ohio, 1868) vol. LXV, p. 175, 176.

[22] *Our Centennial Celebration, 1903: Ohio Centennial Anniversary Celebration at Chillicothe, May 20-21, 1903, Under the Auspices of the Ohio State Archaeological and Historical Society,* edited by E. O. Randall (Published by the Society at the Press of Fred J. Heer, Columbus, Ohio, 1903) p. 117.

[23] *Life and Times of Thomas Becket,* James Anthony Froude (Scribner, Armstrong and Company, New York, 1878) p. 19.

[24] A letter from Walter A. Montgomery, Professor of Ancient Languages, University of Virginia, Charlottesville, Virginia, March 10, 1930.

Oklahoma

Labor Omnia Vincit, meaning *Labor conquers all things*, the State motto of Oklahoma, is found in Virgil's *Georgics*, Book 1, line 145. The Virgilian passage reads as follows: *Labor omnia vicit.*

Oregon

Oregon's motto, *Alis Volat Propriis*, signifying *She flies with her own wings*, was the motto of the Territory of Oregon. This seems to come from, or to be a corruption of lines 1141 and 1142 of Seneca's *Hippolytus*, Act IV. The Latin passage read as follows:

Volat ambiguis
Mobilis alis hora.

This motto implies self-reliance. [25]

South Carolina

South Carolina is credited with two mottoes: (1) *Animis Opibusque Parati*, meaning *Ready in soul and re-source*, found in Virgil's *Aeneid*, Book II, line 799, and (2) *Dum Spiro, Spero*, signifying *While I breathe, I hope*, was the motto of the Irish Viscounts Dillion. The latter motto refers to the figure of Hope on the State seal. Two more Latin mottoes appear on the State seal: (1) *Quis Separabit?* meaning *Who shall separate us?*, and (2) *Meliorem Lapsa Locavit*, freely translated signifies *He has planted a better than the fallen.* Charles B. Galbreath says that the motto *Meliorem Lapsa Locavit* was a Latin inscription on the Seal of the Northwest Territory. He says that it with the coiled snake, the boats, the rising sun, the felled forest tree, and the apple tree laden with fruit, "all combine forcibly to express the idea that the wild and savage condition is to be superseded by a higher and better organization." [26]

[25] *Oregon, Her History, Her Great Men, Her Literature*, Revised and Enlarged Edition, John B. Horner (The J. K. Gill Company, Portland, Oregon, 1921) p. 121.
[26] *History of Ohio*, Charles B. Galbreath (The American Historical Society, Incorporated, Chicago and New York, 1925) vol. I, p. 553.

Virginia

Virginia's motto is *Sic Semper Tyrannis*, meaning *Thus ever to tyrants*. This is the original motto recom-mended for the seal of Virginia by George Mason to the Virginia Convention in 1776. It was probably made up by him and his associates. [27]

The obverse of the seal of Virginia has *Virtus* with her foot on a prostrate tyrant, and the motto suggests that all tyrants will meet with such treatment. Robert Hay in speaking of Virginia's seal said: "Its motto, *Sic semper tyrannis*, so appropriate for Richard Henry Lee, had a melancholy fame in connection with the murder of Lincoln." [28]

On the exergon of the reverse of the first seal of Virginia adopted by the convention of delegates held at Williamsburg in July 1776, [28a] appeared the motto, *Deus Nobis Pace Olim Fecit*. This motto is found in Virgil's *Eclogues*, Book 1, line 6. It means *God gave us this freedom*. The motto was changed to the word *Perse-verando* by an act of the General Assembly passed in October 1779. [28b]

West Virginia

The motto of West Virginia is *Montani Semper Liberi*, meaning *Mountaineers are always freemen*. The design of the seal was drawn by Joseph H. Diss Debar of Doddridge County, an Alsatian, who came from Switzerland to Amer-ica in 1842, and "became interested in the sale of lands to Swiss and French immigrants in Western Virginia. [29] The

[27] A letter from H. R. McIlwaine, State Librarian, Virginia State Library, Richmond, Virginia, March 19, 1930.
[28] *Kansas Historical Collections, 1903-1904: Transactions of the Kansas State Historical Society, 1903-1904*, edited by George W. Martin, Secretary (George A. Clark, State Printer, Topeka, Kansas, 1904) vol. 8, p. 293.
[28a] *History of the Flags of the United States of America*, George Henry Preble, Second Revised Edition (A. Williams and Company, Boston, Massachusetts, 1880) p. 624-5.
[28b] *Acts Passed at a General Assembly, Begun and Held at the Capitol in the City of Williamsburg, on Monday the Fourth Day of October, in the Year of Our Lord, One Thousand Seven Hundred and Seventy-nine* (Printed by John Dixon and Thomas McOlson, Williamsburg [Virginia] 1779) p. 3.
[29] *West Virginia School Journal*, November 19, 1929.

motto seems to have been a favorite saying of the Swiss people. [30] On the reverse of the State seal of West Virginia appear the words: *Libertas Et Fidelitate.* This phrase means *Freedom and loyalty* and indicates that the liberty and independence of West Virginia "are the result of faithfulness to the Declaration [of Independence] and the National Constitution." [31]

Wyoming

The State motto of Wyoming, *Cedant Arma Togae,* signifying *Let arms yield to the gown,* is found in Cicero's *De Officiis,* Book 1, chapter 22, line 41. The motto *Equal Rights* also appears on the State seal, and refers to the political position of women in the State.

The State Motto Expressed in the Greek Language

California

The State motto of California is the Greek word *Eureka,* meaning *I have found it.* This is "the reputed exclamation of Archimedes when, after long study, he discovered a method of detecting the amount of alloy in King Hiero's crown . . .; hence, an exclamation of triumph at a discovery or supposed discovery. It was adopted as the motto of the State of California, in allusion to the discovery of gold there." [32]

[30] A letter from Clifford R. Myers, State Historian and Archivist, Department of Archives and History, Charleston, West Virginia, May 17, 1930.

[31] *The West Virginia Encyclopedia,* Phil Conley, Editor-in-chief (West Virginia Publishing Company, Charleston, West Virginia, 1929) First Edition, p. 863.

N.B. The Latin motto *Libertas Et Fidelitate* is sometimes given as *Libertas E Fidelitate,* meaning *Liberty from Loyalty.* For this form of the motto, see *Heraldry in America,* Eugene Zieber (Published by the Department of Heraldry of The Bailey, Banks and Biddle Company, Philadelphia, Pennsylvania, 1895) p. 194.

[32] *Century Dictionary and Cyclopaedia* (The Century Company, New York, 1906) vol. 3, p. 2030.

THE STATE MOTTO EXPRESSED IN THE FRENCH LANGUAGE

Minnesota

Minnesota has a French motto: *L'Etoile du Nord,* signifying *The star of the north.* According to tradition, Governor Sibley desired to have the north star appear on the Territorial seal; but it was left off in the cause of simplicity. He chose this motto from the French patois, which was said by some to have been the only kind of French he knew. [33]

Minnesota's seal carrying the motto *Quo Sursam Velo Videre* [34] was adopted June 25, 1858. [35] "For some unexplainable reason this State seal, which had been legally adopted, was never used" [36]; but Governor Sibley, seemingly acting upon his own initiative, changed the seal as follows: "(1) the title, 'The Great Seal of Minnesota, 1849' was replaced by 'The Great Seal of the State of Minnesota, 1858,'; (2) the outside diameter was reduced from three to two inches; (3) the drawing was reversed so as to show the Indian riding westward toward the setting sun and the Farmer—in boots—plowing eastward; (4) the absurd Latin motto was erased and the French words for the North Star, 'L'Etoile du Nord' were inserted." [37]

[33] *A History of Minnesota,* William Watts Folwell, President of the Minnesota Historical Society and President Emeritus of the University of Minnesota (Published by the Minnesota Historical Society, Saint Paul, Minnesota, 1924) vol. 2, p. 360.

[34] *Minnesota in Three Centuries, 1655-1908.* Lucius F. Hubbard and Return I. Halcombe, Semi-Centennial Edition (The Publishing Society of Minnesota, Printed by the Free Press Printing Company, Mankato, Minnesota, 1908) vol. 3, p. 475.

[35] *Journal of the House of Representatives, During the First Session of the Legislature of the State of Minnesota, Begun and Held at St. Paul on Wednesday, the 3d Day of December One Thousand Eight Hundred and Fifty-seven* (Earle S. Goodrich, State Printer, Pioneer and Democrat Office, Saint Paul, Minnesota, 1858) p. 742.

[36] *Minnesota in Three Centuries, 1655-1908,* Lucius F. Hubbard and Return I. Halcombe, Semi-Centennial Edition (The Publishing Society of Minnesota, Printed by the Free Press Printing Company, Mankato, Minnesota, 1908) vol. 3, p. 477.

[37] *A History of Minnesota,* William Watts Folwell, President of the Minnesota Historical Society and President Emeritus of the University of Minnesota (Published by the Minnesota Historical Society, Saint Paul, Minnesota, 1924) vol. 2, p. 360.

THE STATE MOTTO EXPRESSED IN THE SPANISH LANGUAGE

Montana

Montana has a Spanish motto, *Oro Y Plata,* meaning *Gold and silver.* This was chosen because it was typical of the period, as mining was the chief industry in Montana in 1865 at the time a committee was appointed by the council in 1865 to designate and to select the motto for the seal of the Territory. [38]

THE STATE MOTTO EXPRESSED IN AN AMERICAN INDIAN DIALECT

Washington

Washington takes its motto *Alki,* signifying *by and bye* from an American Indian dialect. This word is taken from the Chinook jargon. Alki Point was at first called Point Roberts. It was first settled in 1841; but on November 13, 1851, this point was favored by the landing of the Denny colony, out of which Seattle grew. The Denny colony designated the place New York. "As the one little store and the few cabin homes grew so slowly, they added a hyphen and the Indian jargon word *Alki,* meaning 'by and bye.' . . . New York-Alki meant that it was to become the metropolis of the Pacific Coast in the near future." [39] It is probable that this first use of the word influenced its selection as the State motto.

THE STATE MOTTOES EXPRESSED IN THE ENGLISH LANGUAGE

Alabama

Alabama's State motto, *Here We Rest,* is closely bound up with the meaning of the name of the State. According to one interpretation of the origin of the name, it came

---

[38] A letter from David Hilger, Librarian, Historical Society of Montana, March 21, 1930.
[39] *Origin of Washington Geographic Names,* Edmond S. Meany (University of Washington Press, Seattle, Washington, 1923) p. 4.

from the Alibamu Indians, who, fleeing a warlike tribe, coming to the banks of the river, said, *Alabama,* meaning *Here we rest.* [40] The river came to be called the Alabama river, which in turn gave its name to the State, and the English equivalent of the Indian name came to be used as the motto of the State.

Arkansas

The State of Arkansas, besides her Latin motto, *Regnat Populus,* has the words *Mercy and Justice* on her seal. No information seems available as to the origin of this Latin motto, or as to the special significance of the English phrase.

Colorado

The State seal of Colorado, besides the Latin motto, *Nil Sine Numine,* has the words *Union and Constit* [Constitution], left over from the Territoritorial seal. This was adopted in 1861, [41] during the Civil War period, when the questions of states' rights and national union were uppermost in the minds of the people.

Delaware

Delaware's State motto is *Liberty and Independence.* It would seem that this motto was given because these two ideas were uppermost in the thoughts of the citizens during the formative period of the State.

Florida

Florida's motto, *In God We Trust,* was evidently taken from the inscription on the American silver dollar. The origin and the significance of this motto are very interesting to those of an historical turn of mind. The suggestion that the Deity be recognized on the coins of the United States was made by Reverend M. R. Watkinson of Ridleyville, Pennsylvania, to Honorable Salmon P. Chase, Secre-

[40] A letter from Marie B. Owen, Director of the Department of Archives and History of the State of Alabama, Montgomery, Alabama, March 18, 1930.

[41] *History of Colorado,* Wilbur Fisk Stone, Editor (The S. J. Clarke Publishing Company, Chicago, Illinois, 1918) vol. i, p. 226.

tary of the Treasury, in a communication dated November 13, 1861. "If the republic should be shattered beyond recognition," Watkinson reasoned, "the antiquaries of succeeding centuries would rightly conclude that America had been a heathen nation" if there were no mention of God on our coins. By mentioning God on the coins, he further states, the United States would relieve itself from the ignominy of heathenism, and place itself openly under Divine protection. His suggestions for placing the name of the Deity on the nation's coins are as follows:

"Instead of the Goddess of Liberty we shall have next inside the thirteen stars a ring inscribed with the words *'Perpetual Union'*; within this ring the all-seeing eye, crowned with a halo; beneath this eye the American flag, bearing in its field stars equal to the number of the States united; in the folds of the bars the words 'God, Liberty, Law.' "

The Secretary of the Treasury, Honorable S. P. Chase, under date of November 20, 1861, addressed a letter to James Pollock, Esquire, Director of the Mint, at Philadelphia, in which he stated that "no nation can be strong except in the strength of God, or safe except in His defense. The trust of our people in God should be declared on our national coins." He requested that a device should be prepared "with a motto expressing in the fewest and tersest words possible this national recognition." A law passed January 18, 1837, prescribed the mottoes and devices to be placed on the coins of the United States, so nothing could be done without legislative action. In December, 1863, Mr. Pollock submitted to the Secretary of the Treasury for his approval designs for new one, two, and three cent pieces, proposing to place on them one of the two following mottoes: *"Our country; our God"; "God, our Trust."* In a letter written to Mr. Pollock on December 9, 1863, Mr. Chase says: "I approve your mottoes, only suggesting that on that with the Washington obverse the motto should . . . read *'Our God and our country,'* and on that with the shield, it should be changed so as to read: *'In God we trust.'* "

The coinage of two cent pieces was authorized by an act passed April 22, 1864, and it was on the bronze two cent piece that the motto "*In God we trust*" first appeared. Two acts, those of March 5, 1865, and of February 12, 1875, have authorized the placing of the motto "*In God we trust*" on all such coins as admit of the inscription thereon. Thus the motto was placed on the eagle, the double eagle, and the half eagle, as well as on the dollar, the half dollar, and the quarter dollar, in the latter half of the year 1865, and today it is inscribed on those coins whose size admits of such a motto. [42]

Georgia

The three words, *Wisdom, Justice, and Moderation,* on the obverse of the State seal of Georgia, with *Constitution* forming the arch supporting the three pillars on which they are inscribed, are emblematic of the Constitution, upheld by three columns representing, in order, the legislative, judicial, and executive branches, symbolized by Wisdom, Justice, and Moderation. [43]

Illinois

The State motto of Illinois as used on the seal of the State, is *State Sovereignty—National Union.* It reads as given, upward, and thus would seem to emphasize national union, as it is the last and uppermost on the seal. In designing the State seal of Illinois, those planning it took the United States Seal, "erased the image of the federal caesar" and its superscription, "then they proudly wrote in its stead '*State Sovereignty, National Union.*'" [44] This

[42] The data for this brief account of the history of the origin of the phrase *In God we trust* and of its being inscribed on the coins of the United States were furnished to the writer by Mr. R. J. Grant, Director of the Mint, in a letter written at Washington, D. C. on November 4, 1930.

[43] *Code of the State of Georgia, 1911: The Code of the State of Georgia, Adopted August 15, 1910,* prepared by John L. Hopkins (Foote and Davis Company, Atlanta, Georgia, 1911) vol. 1, p. 67.

[44] "Great Seal of Illinois: First Complete History of the State Symbol," Brand Whitlock, in *Journal of the Illinois State Historical Society* (Published Quarterly by the Illinois State Historical Society, Springfield, Illinois. Printed by the Illinois State Journal Company, State Printers, Springfield, Illinois, 1913) vol. 5, no. 4, January, 1913, p. 435.

motto seems to have been inspired by the fact that on the escutcheon of the United States Seal, "the pieces, paly represent the several states all joined in one compact entire, supporting a Chief which unites the whole and represents Congress."[45]   Brand Whitlock says that "the Motto alludes to the Union."[45]

Indiana

Indiana's State motto or slogan, *The Crossroads of America*, was adopted by house concurrent resolution number six, appoved on March 2, 1937. The resolution says: "Section 1. Be it resolved by the House of Representatives of the General Assembly of the State of Indiana, the Senate concurring, that the expression 'The Crossroads of America' is hereby designated and adopted as the official State motto or slogan for the State of Indiana."[45a]

JRoy Strickland in his column, "Paragraphy," in *The Evansville Courier*, published at Evansville, Ind., was largely instrumental in arousing the people of Indiana to the fact that they had no State motto, in securing suggested mottoes, and in getting those suggested before the members of the General Assembly. In regard to these matters he says: "in my column, Paragraphy, I started a campaign for suggestions for a motto for Indiana. In a period of two or three weeks, I received three hundred and twenty-four suggestions. These were printed in folder form, without the names and the addresses of the senders, and forwarded to the State legislature then in session at Indianapolis. A committee of three from the House and two from the Senate took this list of mottoes and selected

---

[45] "Great Seal of Illinois: First Complete History of the State Symbol," Brand Whitlock, in *Journal of the Illinois State Historical Society* (Published Quarterly by the Illinois State Historical Society, Springfield, Illinois. Printed by the Illinois State Journal Company, State Printers, Springfield, Illinois, 1913) vol. 5, no. 4, January 1913, p. 440.

[45a] *Acts, 1937, Indiana: Laws of the State of Indiana, Passed at the Eightieth Regular Session of the General Assembly, Begun on the Seventh Day of January, A.D., 1937*, by authority, August G. Mueller, Secretary of State (Fort Wayne Printing Company, Contractors for State Printing and Binding, Fort Wayne, Indiana, 1937) concurrent resolution, number 6, p. 1389.

[45b] A letter from JRoy Strickland, Evansville, Indiana, March 7, 1937.

'The Crossroads of America.' " [45b] Mr. Strickland did not state why this particular motto was selected, but its wording suggests that the roads to and from the various parts of America intersect within the boundaries of Indiana.

Iowa

A committee of the State Senate selected the motto of Iowa, *Our Liberties We Prize and Our Rights We Will Maintain.* It, no doubt, referred to the difficulties encountered while the Iowans were establishing their statehood.

Kentucky

The State motto of Kentucky, *United We Stand, Divided We Fall,* was probably taken from George P. Morris's poem, *The Flag of Our Union.* This idea was prevalent during the period of time from the beginning to the close of the Revolutionary War. A very famous expression of it is Franklin's remark to John Hancock, at the signing of the Declaration of Independence, "We must all hang together, or assuredly we shall all hang separately." The *Register,* the official organ of the Kentucky State Historical Society, states that the motto is said to have been suggested by the chorus of an old British song by John Dickinson, written before the Revolutionary war, which reads:

> " 'Come join hand in hand
> Comrades all—
> By uniting we stand,
> By dividing we fall.' " [46]

The *Register* says also that "Governor Isaac Shelby, in giving directions for the design of the seal of the State, December 20, 1792, had the idea tersely expressed—like a wreath around the seal."

Louisiana

The State of Louisiana has for her State motto the words, *Union, Justice and Confidence.* These must have

[46] *Register of Kentucky State Historical Society,* Mrs. Jennie C. Morton, Editor (The Globe Printing Company, Louisville, Kentucky, 1907) vol. 5, no. 14, May, 1907, p. 102.

seemed the three most important aspects of statehood to those who designed the seal.

Missouri

Missouri has on her seal the expression: *United We Stand, Divided We Fall,* which is the State motto of Kentucky, under which state its origin is given. The State motto of Missouri, *Salus Populi Suprema Lex Esto,* meaning *The welfare of the people is the supreme law,* is discussed under Latin mottoes above.

Nebraska

The State motto of Nebraska, *Equality before the Law,* is depicted on the State seal. Mr. Isaac Wiles, a Representative in the Second Legislature, is said to have originated the legend, which act was prompted perhaps by his being a strong partisan for the abolition of slavery. However, there is an old legal maxim which closely parallels this maxim, " 'All men are equal before the natural law.' " [47]

Nevada

With regard to the State motto of Nevada, V. M. Henderson, the State Librarian, says: *"All for Our Country* was the motto recommended to be placed on the State seal at the time of its adoption. Nevada was admitted during the Civil war without slaves, and the motto testifies to that fact." [48]

New Hampshire

New Hampshire has no State motto.

New Jersey

The State motto of New Jersey, *Liberty and Prosperity,* does not appear on the State seal. It was informally adopted in 1821 as the best of several suggested mottoes. [49]

---

[47] *Nebraska History and Records of Pioneer Days,* edited by Addison E. Sheldon, vol. 3, no. 1, January-March, 1920, p. 3.
[48] A letter from V. M. Henderson, Librarian, Nevada State Library, Carson City, Nevada, March 25, 1930.
[49] A letter from Charles R. Bacon, State Librarian, Trenton, New Jersey, March 24, 1930.

Zieber says, in speaking of the motto, "A variety of mottoes occur; but among the earliest is that used in the Joseph Justice edition of the laws (1821), wherein the words 'Liberty and Prosperity' are found. This is now the recognized motto of New Jersey when such is used." [50]

North Dakota

Daniel Webster's *Reply to Hayne* supplied the motto for North Dakota: *Liberty and Union, Now and Forever, One and Inseparable.* This was probably suggested by the fact that North Dakota was organized as a territory during the period of struggle for the preservation of the Union. [51] Its Territorial motto was taken over when it became a state. William M. Wemett says in speaking of the seal, that "in the sky forty-two stars are seen, representing the forty-two states then in the Union, one of the two things on the seal which recognizes the nation of which this state is an inseparable part. The other is the phrase just above them, 'Liberty and Union, Now and Forever, One and Inseparable.' " [52]

Oregon

Oregon has the motto, *The Union,* on the obverse side of her seal.

The motto, *Alis Volat Propriis,* signifying *She flies with her own wings,* was the Territorial motto of Oregon and is generally given as the State motto. It implies self reliance. [53] The State motto is *The Union,* which "divides the escutcheon into an upper and a lower section." [54] Both reflect the sentiments and problems of the Civil War period.

[50] *Heraldry in America,* Eugene Zieber (Published by the Department of Heraldry of The Bailey, Banks and Biddle Company, Philadelphia, Pennsylvania, 1895) p. 160.
[51] A letter from Mrs. Florence H. Davis, Librarian, State Historical Society, Bismarck, North Dakota, March 20, 1930.
[52] *The Story of the Flickertail State,* William M. Wemett (W. H. Wemett, Valley City, North Dakota, 1923) p. 313-14.
[53] *Oregon: Her History, Her Great Men, Her Literature,* Revised and Enlarged, John B. Horner (The J. K. Gill Company, Portland, Oregon, 1921) p. 121.
[54] *Ibidem,* p. 164.

Pennsylvania

Pennsylvania's State motto, *Virtue, Liberty, and Independence,* is specified in the original description of the obverse of the seal as being inscribed on a streamer held in the eagle's beak. It does not appear on the present seal however. "Virtue is a tradition of Pennsylvania's, dating from the time when the province passed out of the hands of the profligate Charles II of England into the possession of the magnificent character, William Penn." [55] Pennsylvania has always been active in the struggle for freedom, hence the motto *Liberty* and *Independence.*

Rhode Island

Rhode Island has her motto, *Hope,* above the anchor on her seal. This probably signifies the attitude of those struggling to frame their own form of government in the face of royalist opposition. [56]

Howard M. Chapin says that the word *Hope* was the motto of the Colony of Rhode Island, and that it first appeared on the Seal of the Colony adopted on May 4, 1664. He states that "it is not known why 'Hope' was adopted as the motto, but probably because of the biblical association of 'hope' and the 'anchor' in the phrase 'hope we have as an anchor of the soul.' " [57] This phrase may be found in Hebrews, Chapter 6, verse 19.

South Dakota

South Dakota's State motto, *Under God the People Rule,* "was suggested to the Constitutional Convention held at Sioux Falls in 1885, by Reverend Joseph Ward, founder and first president of Yankton College, Yankton,

[55] *The Seal and Arms of Pennsylvania,* James Evelyn Pilcher (The State of Pennsylvania, William Stanley Ray, State Printer, Harrisburg, Pennsylvania, 1902) p. 21.

[56] *State of Rhode Island and Providence Plantations at the End of the Century: A History,* edited by Edward Field (The Mason Publishing Company, Boston and Syracuse, 1902) vol. 1, p. 145-7.

[57] *Illustrations of the Seals, Arms and Flags of Rhode Island with Historical Notes* by Howard M. Chapin and an Introduction by Norman M. Isham (Printed for the Rhode Island Historical Society, Providence, Rhode Island, MCMXXX) p. 5.

South Dakota." [58]   South Dakota is one of the comparatively few states which expresses a religious sentiment in the wording of its motto. Willis E. Johnson in speaking of this motto, says: "We all recognize that there is a Power in the world which is mightier than that of man. The people should regulate all public affairs as in the presence of God. In former times governments were not carried on by the people or for the people. Even in our own country today, laws are often passed to protect some private interest instead of for the public good. Our state motto should ever inspire us to make our government more free from the control of selfish interests and more consecrated to the good of all." [59]

Tennessee

The State motto of Tennessee, *Agriculture and Commerce,* is explained as follows: Agriculture denotes "that the first reliance of the state should be upon products of the soil . . .," [60] and Commerce indicates "that the prosperity of all may be promoted through this means." [60]

Texas

Friendship was adopted as the State motto of Texas in February, 1930. It was adopted because: (1) the Indian [Spanish] word *Tejas* from which the name Texas was taken meant *Friendship;* (2) it is emblematic of the universal spirit existing in Texas; and (3) it reflects the spirit that has at all times influenced the people of Texas. [61]

Utah

The State motto of Utah, *Industry,* naturally grows out of the use of the beehive as the symbol of industry, and

[58] A letter from Lawrence K. Fox, State Historian and Superintendent of the State Department of History, Pierre, South Dakota, March 26, 1930.
[59] *South Dakota: A Republic of Friends,* Willis E. Johnson (The Capital Supply Company, Pierre, South Dakota, 1911) p. 20.
[60] *The Origin and History of the American Flag,* George Henry Preble (Nicholas L. Brown, Philadelphia, Pennsylvania, 1917) vol. 2. p. 638.
[61] *House Journal of the Fourth Called Session of the Forty-first Legislature of Texas,* p. 516.

out of the fact that the early settlers named their settlement *Deseret,* which they said meant *honey bee.* Deseret was first suggested as the name for the State.

Vermont

Vermont's State motto is *Freedom and Unity,* and it appears in large letters at the bottom of her seal. It was selected by Ira Allen and had reference to national relations with England and also to Vermont's resisting "the jurisdiction of New York." [62]

Wisconsin

The State motto of Wisconsin is *Forward.* Governor Nelson Dewey in 1851 took the sketch for the new seal with him to New York, to have it engraved. . . "Being in the State of New York, her motto, 'Excelsior,' doubtless came most prominently to mind, and of this idea was born the correlative *'Forward'—'Upward'* and *'Onward'* having first been considered, but rejected in favor of the adopted word." [63]

Wyoming

Wyoming has for her State motto *Equal Rights,* "suggesting the political position of women in this State." [64]

---

[62] *Vermont Legislative Directory, Biennial Session, 1915,* prepared pursuant to law by Guy W. Bailey, Secretary of State (St. Albans Messenger Print, St. Albans, Vermont, 1915) p. 369.

[63] "Wisconsin's Emblems and Sobriquet," Reuben Gold Thwaites, in *Proceedings of the Historical Society of Wisconsin at Its State Fifty-fifth Annual Meeting Held November 7, 1907* (Published by the Society, Democrat Printing Company, State Printer, Madison, Wisconsin, 1908) p. 301.

[64] *History of Wyoming,* Ichabod S. Bartlett, Editor (The S. J. Clarke Publishing Company, Chicago, Illinois, 1918) vol. 1, p. 221.

CHAPTER IV

THE GREAT SEALS OF THE STATES OF THE UNION

The suggestion has been made that the idea of using seals may have been obtained from the impress left on the naked body of man after he had leaned against a stone in which devices or symbols were cut.

It is impossible to fix any exact date or period of time for the origin of the use of seals. All nations and all races from the Orient to the Occident have made use of them— The Hebrews, the Babylonians, the Chinese, and the Greeks. They have been used for sealing State papers, national messages, the communications of individuals, loaves of bread, money bags, and box cars; to seal up tombs; to designate victims set apart for sacrifice; to identify personal property; to seal granaries and rooms, vessels and wine cellars. They are used as insignia of the royalty and nobility; of families; of societies and institutions; of governmental departments; and of private persons.

The use of seals, no doubt, was brought to America from Europe by the colonists. The state seals are artistically designed, depict scenery native to the states in many instances, record historical data, and inscribe mottoes, some of which are taken from the most noted classical authors.

The pictorial illustrations of the Great Seals of the various states shown in this chapter were printed from cuts made from pen drawings of these seals, sketched by Miss Rosalind Decker, one of the writer's students at the State Teachers College, Fredericksburg, Virginia, or by Mr. Willard Webb, of the Library of Congress. These drawings were made from the impressions of the seals supplied by the secretaries of the various states.

ALABAMA

William Wyatt Bibb, the Territorial Governor of Alabama, suggested to the First Territorial Legislature the design for the First Territorial Seal. This design, consisting of a map of the Territory showing the river courses, was adopted as the Territorial Seal by the First Territorial Legislature which met at St. Stephens on January 19, 1818.

The First State Legislature in 1819 re-adopted that seal as the State seal which remained in use until the adoption of the seal in use today.

The present seal of Alabama was adopted by an act of the State legislature approved on December 29, 1868. [1] The law prescribes that the seal shall be circular in form, having a diameter two and a quarter inches, and that "near the edge of the circle shall be the word 'Alabama,' and [that] opposite this word, at the same distance from the edge, shall be the words 'Great Seal.' " [1] This act also says that "in the center of the seal there shall be a representation of an eagle and a shield, and upon such part of the seal as the governor may direct, there shall be the words, 'Here we rest.' . . ."

ARIZONA

The Constitution of the State of Arizona, adopted in 1911, says: "The seal of the State shall be of the following design: In the background shall be a range of mountains, with the sun rising behind the peaks thereof, and at the right side of the range of mountains there shall be a storage reservoir and a dam, below which in the middle distance are irrigated fields and orchards reaching into the foreground, at the right of which are cattle grazing. To

---

[1] *Alabama Laws, 1868: Acts of the Sessions of July, September, and November 1868, of the General Assembly of Alabama, Held in the City of Montgomery, Commencing July 13th, September 16th, and November 2nd* (John G. Stokes and Company, State Printers, Montgomery, Alabama, 1868) p. 477.

the left in the middle distance on a mountain side is a quartz mill in front of which and in the foreground is a miner standing with pick and shovel. Above this device shall be the motto: 'Ditat Deus.' In a circular band surrounding the whole device shall be inscribed: 'Great seal of the State of Arizona,' with the year of admission of the State into the Union." [2]

ARKANSAS

The present seal of the State of Arkansas was approved by an act of the State legislature on May 23, 1907. This act amended the act of May 3, 1864, by changing the word-ing of the motto from *Regnant Populi* to *Regnat Populus*. [3] The law specifies that the seal of the State of Arkansas "shall present the following impressions, devices and emblems, to wit: An eagle at the bottom, holding a scroll in its beak, inscribed 'Regnat Populus,' a bundle of arrows in one claw and an olive branch in the other; a shield covering the breast of the eagle, engraved with a steamboat at [the] top, a bee-hive and [a] plow in the middle, and a sheaf of wheat at the bottom; the Goddess of Liberty at the top, holding a wreath in her right hand, a pole in the left hand, surmounted by a liberty cap and surrounded by a circle of stars, outside of which is a circle of rays; the figure of an angel on the left, inscribed 'Mercy,' and a sword on the right hand, inscribed 'Justice,' surrounded with the words 'Seal of the State of Arkansas.' " [4]

[2] *The Revised Code of Arizona, 1928,* F. C. Struckmeyer (The Manufacturing Stationers, Incorporated, Phoenix, Arizona, 1928) Constitution of Arizona, article 22, section 20, p. cviii.

[3] *Arkansas Laws, 1917: Public and Private Acts and Joint and Concurrent Resolutions and Memorials of the General Assembly of the State of Arkansas, 1907* (Democrat Printers and Lithographers Company, Little Rock, Arkansas, 1907) p. 988.

[4] *Digest of the Statutes of Arkansas, 1916: A Digest of the Statutes of Arkansas Embracing All Laws of a General Nature, in Force at the Close of the Session of the General Assembly of One Thousand Nine Hundred and Fifteen, Including the Primary Election Law Adopted at the Election Held November 7, 1916* (William F. Kirby and John T. Castle, Little Rock, Arkansas, 1916) p. 2185.

CALIFORNIA

The State seal of California "was submitted to a committee September 29, 1849, and adopted October 2, 1849, [5] by the Convention which framed the Constitution of the State of California." The design of the seal consists of a figure of "Minerva, with the Golden Gate, and a ship in full sail in the foreground, and the Sierra Nevada range [of mountains] in the background, with the word 'Eureka' above." [5a] "Around the bend of the ring are represented thirty-one stars, being the number of States of which the Union will consist upon the admission of California. The foreground figure represents the Goddess Minerva, having sprung full grown from the brain of Jupiter. She is introduced as a type of the political birth of the State of California, without having gone through the probation of a territory. At her feet crouches a grizzly bear feeding upon the clusters from a grapevine, emblematic of the peculiar characteristics of the country. A miner is engaged with his rocker and bowl at his side, illustrating the golden wealth of the Sacramento, upon whose waters are seen shipping, typical of commercial greatness; and the snow-clad peaks of the Sierra Nevada make up the background, while above is the Greek motto "Eureka" (I have found it), applying either to the principle involved in the admission of the State, or the success of the miner at work."

COLORADO

The seal of Colorado was adopted by an act of the State legislature on March 15, 1877, the law going into effect on June 13, 1877. [6]

[5] *California State Flag, Flower, etc.* (California State Printing Office, Harry Hammond, State Printer, Sacramento, California, 1932) p. 1-2.

[5a] *California Blue Book or State Roster* 1909, compiled by Charles Forrest Curry, Secretary of State (State Printing Office, Sacramento, California, 1909) p. 723-6.

[6] *Colorado General Statutes, 1883: The General Statutes of the State of Colorado, 1883, . . . Authorized by the Fourth General Assembly* (Times Steam Printing and Publishing House, Denver, Colorado, 1883) p. 913-14.

The seal is circular in form, "two and one-half inches in diameter, with the following device inscribed thereon: An heraldic shield bearing in chief ,or upon the upper portion of the same, upon a red ground, three snow-capped mountains; above, surrounding clouds; upon the lower part thereof, upon a golden ground, a miner's badge, as prescribed by the rules of heraldry; as a crest above the shield, the eye of God, being golden rays proceeding from the lines of a triangle; below the crest and above the shield, as a scroll, the Roman fasces, bearing upon a band of red, white and blue the words, 'Union and Constitution': below the whole the motto, *Nil Sine Numine';* the whole to be surrounded by the words, 'State of Colorado,' and the figures '1876.' " [7]

CONNECTICUT

The seal of Connecticut has been modified or altered several times from the days of the Colony to the present time, the dates of modification being: the Seal of 1689; the Seal of 1711; the Seal of 1784; the Seal of 1842; the Seal of 1864; the Seal of 1882; and the Seal of 1931.

Roger Wolcott in his *Memoir Relating to Connecticut* says that George Fenwick gave to the Connecticut Colony its first seal about 1644. [8] At that time the people of the Colony bought from him Saybrook Fort. This seal having a beaded border was slightly oval in form. It represented a vineyard "of fifteen vines, supported and bearing fruit. Above the vines a hand issuing from clouds holds a label with the motto SUSTINET QUI TRANSTULIT." [9]

[7] *Colorado General Statutes, 1883: The General Statutes of the State of Colorado, 1883, . . . Authorized by the Fourth General Assembly* (Times Steam Printing and Publishing House, Denver, Colorado, 1883) p. 913-14.

[8] "Memoir Relating to Connecticut," George Wolcott in *Collections of the Connecticut Historical Society* (Published for the Society by The Case, Lockwood and Brainard Company, Printers and Binders, Hartford, Connecticut, 1895) vol. 3, p. 328.

[9] *Connecticut State Register and Manual, 1889: Register and Manual of the State of Connecticut, 1889,* prepared pursuant to section 320 of the General Statutes by Secretary of the State (The Case, Lockwood and Brainard Company, Printers, 1889) p. 438.

The first General Assembly of the Colony in October 1662 adopted the Colonial seal as the State seal. This seal was delivered to Sir Edmund Andros by the Secretary (John Allyn) in October 1687. What became of the seal is not known.

On October 25, 1711, the Governor and Council adopted a State seal two and one-eighth inches in length and one and three-fourths inches in breadth. This seal had, instead of the fifteen grapevines used on the former seal, three vines, and a hand about midway on the right side pointing to them. Below the vines was a label bearing the motto QUI TRANSTULIT SUSTINET around the circumference of this seal were the words, SIGILLUM COLONIAE CONNECTICENSIS.

The General Assembly in October 1774 voted to change the public seal of the Colony from an oval to a circular shape, and to correct such mistakes as were found in the spelling and lettering of the inscription of the former seal, but this seems never to have been done. In October 1784 by vote of the General Assembly a new seal was made and ordered. This seal was a reproduction of the former seal, except that the oval upon which the design was cut was two and three-eighths inches in length and one and seven-eighths inches in breadth. Yale College today possesses the silver shield upon which this seal was engraved.

In October 1842, the General Assembly ordered that a seal for sealing with wax or wafer be procured similar to the one then in use. "The resolution as originally drawn up provided that the new seal might be [of] smaller dimensions and circular instead of oval; but these provisions were struck out in the House of Representatives, probably upon constitutional grounds, and the seal was made, similar in form and size to the preceding one, except that it is a trifle broader; the workmanship also is better; there are three clusters of grapes on each vine, whereas the old one had four on each of the upper and five on the lower one. It is engraved on brass. The hand had been omitted from the seal of 1784. The other seal is used for making an impression upon paper without the use of wax or other tenacious substance, which mode was declared, by an act, passed in 1851, to be a sufficient sealing. This seal is supposed to have been procured in 1882, under authority of a resolve passed in 1864." [9a]

The Public Acts of the State of Connecticut for 1931 says: [9b]

"The great seal of the state shall conform to the following description. It shall be a perfect ellipse with its major axis two and one-half inches in length and its minor axis two inches in length, the major axis being vertical. Within such ellipse shall appear another ellipse with its major axis one and fifteen-sixteenths inches in length and its minor axis one and one-half inches in length. The inner ellipse is separated from the outer ellipse only by a line two points one thirty-sixth of an inch in width and with the space between the two ellipses, being seven thirty-seconds of one inch, forming a border. In said space shall appear, letter spaced and in letters one-eighth inch in height and of twelve point century Roman, the words "SIGILLUM REIPUBLICAE CONNECTICUTENSIS," beginning and ending one inch and one-sixteenth of an inch apart in the lower space along such border. In the center of the inner ellipse shall be three grape vines, two above and one below, each with four leaves and three clusters of grapes intertwined around a support nine-sixteenths of one inch high, and the base of the supports of the two upper vines one inch from the base of the inner ellipse and eleven-sixteenths of one inch apart. The base of the lower support shall be nine-sixteenths of one inch from the base of the inner ellipse and half-way between said bases shall appear the motto "QUI TRANSTULIT SUSTINET," in number three, six point card Roman letters, or engraver's Roman letters, on a ribbon gracefully formed, with the ends of the ribbon turned upward and inward and cleft. A draw-

[9a] *The Connecticut State Register and Manual, 1889: Register and Manual of the State of Connecticut, 1889,* prepared pursuant to section 320 of the General Statutes, by the Secretary of the State (The Case, Lockwood and Brainard Company, Printers, Hartford, 1889) p. 441.

[9b] *Public Acts of the State of Connecticut, January Session, 1931, Cumulative Supplement to the General Statutes, Revision of 1930* (Published by the State, Hartford, Connecticut, 1931) chap. 5, sec. 14a (N), p. 5.

ing of said seal shall be filed in the office of the secretary of the state and shall be the official drawing of said seal. Said seal, whether in imprint or in facsimile form, shall be used only by or under direction of said secretary."

DELAWARE

The Great Seal of the State of Delaware, agreed upon by both houses of the State legislature, was adopted on January 17, 1777.[10] The act reads as follows:

"Resolved, N. C. D., That Mr. McKean be a committee to employ skillful workmen to make a silver seal of the diameter of three inches and of a circular form, and that there be engraven thereon a Sheaf of Wheat and an ear of Indian Corn, and an Ox, in full stature, in a shield with a river dividing the wheat sheaf and ear of Indian corn from the Ox, which is to be cut in the nether part of the shield below the river; that the supporters be an American Soldier, under arms, in the right, and an Husbandman, with a Hoe in his hand, on the left, and that a Ship be the Crest; and that there shall be an inscription around the same, near the edge or extremity thereof, in the words following, in capital letters: 'THE GREAT SEAL OF THE DELAWARE STATE, *with the figures, 1777;* which shall, from and after the delivery thereof to the President and Commander-in-Chief, be the Great Seal and deemed the Arms of this State.

"Resolved, That the Seal of the County of New Castle shall be deemed and held to be the Great Seal of this State *pro tempore* until the above described Great Seal is made and delivered to the President and Commander-in-Chief, and no longer."

Revisions of this seal were made in 1793, 1847, 1871, and in 1907.

An act of the Delaware legislature, approved on February 25, 1907, says:[10a]

---

[10] *Papers of the Historical Society of Delaware, Minutes of the Council of the Delaware State, from 1776 to 1792* (The Historical Society of Delaware, Wilmington, Delaware, 1887) vol. 6, p. 45-6.

[10a] *Delaware Laws, 1907: Laws of the State of Delaware, Passed at a Special Session of the General Assembly, Commenced and Held at Dover on Thursday, May 31st, A. D., 1906, and in the Year of the Independence of the United States the One Hundred and Thirtieth* (The Delaware Print, Dover, Delaware, 1907) vol. 24, pt. 1, p. 171.

"Section 1. That the Secretary of State be, and he is hereby authorized to procure a new seal and press, to be used as the Great Seal of the State of Delaware, which said seal shall not exceed three inches in diameter, and shall be emblazoned as follows: Party per fess, or and argent, the first charged with a garb (wheat sheaf) in bend dexter; and an ear of maize (Indian corn) in bend sinister, both proper; the second charged with an ox stantant, ruminating, proper; fess, wavy azure-supporters on the dexter, a husbandman with a hilling hoe, on the sinister, a rifleman armed and accoutred, at ease. Crest, on a wreath azure and argent, a ship under full sail, proper; with the words 'Great Seal of the State of Delaware,' and also, the words 'Liberty and Independence engraved thereon."

THE DISTRICT OF COLUMBIA

The Legislative Assembly of the District of Columbia on August 3, 1871, [11] adopted the seal of the District. The act adopting the seal does not give a description of it; but Eugene Zieber in his *Heraldry in America* quotes a description of the seal as follows: " 'The device to the left of the figure, looking at its face, appears to be a sunrise, and a train of cars on a bridge over a stream leading from a larger body of water in the foreground. Back of the eagle's wing is a barrel on its side, a sheaf of wheat, another barrel on end, and two bags of grain. To the right, from the same point of view, is the Capitol, with the Potomac River in the background, and the heights on the right bank of the river on the horizon. The legend on the scroll is "Justitia Omnibus." The date within the wreath is 1871, and the letters on the side of the book in the arms of the female figure are those of the word "Constitution," arranged in three lines of four letters each. The left hand of the male figure rests on a fasces representing the union of the States, and his right hand on a sword.' " [11a]

[11] *District of Columbia Laws, 1871-1872: Laws of the District of Columbia, 1871-1872* (Chronicle Publishing Company, Washington, D. C. 1872) pt. 2, chap. 21, p. 24.
[11a] *Heraldry in America*, Eugene Zieber (Published by the Department of Heraldry of The Bailey, Banks and Biddle Company, Philadelphia. Pennsylvania, 1895) p. 125-6.

FLORIDA

The Great Seal of Florida was adopted by legislative action on August 6, 1868. [12] The law says that the seal shall be "the size of the American silver dollar, having in the centre thereof a view of the sun's rays over a highland in the distance, a cocoa tree, a steamboat on water, and an Indian female scattering flowers in the foreground, encircled by the words: 'Great Seal of the State of Florida: In God We Trust.' "

"Be it further resolved, That when the new great seal herein provided for shall be completed and received by the Secretary of State, it shall be used in place of the present great seal in all cases where the use of the great seal of the State is required; and it shall be the duty of the Governor and the Secretary of State to see to it that the present great seal is destroyed.

"Be it further resolved, That all laws and parts of laws in conflict with this joint resolution, or any part hereof, be and the same are hereby repealed."

The symbols of the Great Seal are thus described in an official publication issued from the State Department of Agriculture: "The sun is the emblem of glory and splendor; in heraldry, its meaning is absolute authority. The highland and water are typical of the state, and the steamboat of its commerce and progress. Flowers are the symbol of hope and joy, and the Indian scattering them shows the influence of the Indian nation over the state. The cocoa or palm tree, is the emblem of victory, justice and royal honor." [12a]

The scenery imaged on the Florida State Seal represents the tropical South, but critical writers have commented unfavorably upon the Indian woman depicted on the obverse of the seal.

[12] *Florida Laws, 1868: The Acts and Resolutions adopted by the Legislature of Florida at Its First Session (1868), under the Constitution of A. D. 1868,* published by authority of Law under the direction of the Attorney-General (Printed at the Office of the Tallahassee Sentinel, Tallahassee, Florida, 1868) joint resolution no. 2, p. 183.

[12a] *History of Florida, Past and Present, Historical and Biographical,* Preface signed: H. G. Cutler, Research Historian (The Lewis Publishing Company, New York, 1923) vol. I, p. 155-6.

GEORGIA

The present State seal of Georgia, adopted by legislative action on August 17, 1914, [13] is a facsimile of the former State seal, adopted by an act of the State legislature on February 8, 1799, [13a] except that the date was changed from 1799 to 1776. The act says:

"2. The device on one side is, a view of the seashore, with a ship bearing the flag of the United States riding at anchor near a wharf, receiving on board hogsheads of tobacco and bales of cotton, emblematic of the exports of this State; at a small distance a boat, landing from the interior of the State, with hogsheads, etc., on board, representing her internal traffic; in the back part of the same side a man in the act of plowing, and at a small distance a flock of sheep in different pastures, shaded by a flourishing tree; the motto thereon, 'Agriculture and Commerce, 1799.' "

The device on the other side pictures an arch, three pillars symbolically engraved, and a man with a drawn sword. On February 23, 1937 a resolution adopted by legislative action provided for recasting and reengraving the Great Seal of the State.

IDAHO

The seal of Idaho was approved by legislative action on March 14, 1891. [14] The law says that "the design drawn and executed by Miss Emma Edwards, of Boise City, and reported and recommended by the select joint committee to devise a great seal for the state with the Latin motto 'Esto Perpetua,' be adopted, and is hereby made the great seal of the State of Idaho."

[13] *Code of the State of Georgia, 1911: The Code of the State of Georgia, Adopted August 15, 1910,* prepared by John L. Hopkins (Foote and Davies Company, Atlanta, Georgia, 1911) volume I, p. 67.
[13a] *Acts and Resolutions of the General Assembly of the State of Georgia, 1914,* compiled and published by authority of the State (Charles P. Byrd, State Printer, Atlanta, Georgia, 1914) part iv, p. 1247.
[14] *Idaho Laws, 1890-91: General Laws of the State of Idaho, Passed at the First Session of the State Legislature, Convened on the Eighth Day of December, A. D. 1890, and Adjourned on the Fourteenth Day of March, A. D. 1891, at Boise City,* published by authority (Statesman Printing Company, Boise City, Idaho, 1891) p. 215-16.

Miss Edwards' description of the design is as follows: " 'The question of Woman Suffrage was being agitated somewhat, and as leading men and politicians agreed that Idaho would eventually give women the right to vote, and as mining was the chief industry, and the mining man the largest financial factor of the state at that time, I made the figure of the man the most prominent figure in the design, while that of the woman, signifying justice, as denoted by the scales, liberty, as denoted by the liberty cap on the end of the spear, and equality with man as denoted by her position at his side, also signifies freedom. The pick and shovel held by the miner, and the ledge of rock beside which he stands, as well as the pieces of ore scattered about his feet, all indicate the chief occupation of the State. The stamp mill in the distance, which you can see by using [a] magnifying glass, is also typical of the mining interests of Idaho. The shield between the man and woman is emblematic of the protection they unite in giving the State. The large fir or pine tree in the foreground in the shield refers to Idaho's immense timber interests. The husbandman plowing on the left side of the shield, together with the sheaf of grain beneath the shield, are emblematic of Idaho's agricultural resources, while the cornucopias, or horns of plenty, refer to the horticultural. Idaho has a game law, which protects the elk and moose. The elk's head, therefore rises above the shield. The State flower, the wild syringa or mock orange, grows at the woman's feet, while the ripened wheat grows as high as her shoulder. The star signifies a new light in the galaxy of states. The translation of the Latin motto is, 'It is perpetuated,' or, 'It is forever.' The river depicted in the shield is our mighty Snake or Shoshone river, a stream of great majesty.' " [15]

ILLINOIS

Illinois by an act of her legislature, approved on March 7, 1867, adopted the present Great Seal of the State. It

[15] *Idaho State Historical Society Bulletin,* Admission Number (Published Quarterly by the State Historical Society at Boise, Idaho) vol. 1, no. 2, July 1, 1908, p. 15-16.

ALABAMA

ARIZONA

ARKANSAS

CALIFORNIA

COLORADO

CONNECTICUT

DELAWARE

DISTRICT OF COLUMBIA

FLORIDA

GEORGIA

REVERSE OF GEORGIA'S SEAL

IDAHO

ILLINOIS

STATE SEALS

INDIANA

IOWA

KANSAS

KENTUCKY

LOUISIANA

MAINE

MARYLAND

MASSACHUSETTS

MICHIGAN

MINNESOTA

MISSISSIPPI

MISSOURI

MONTANA

STATE SEALS

STATE SEALS

SOUTH CAROLINA

SOUTH DAKOTA

RHODE ISLAND

TEXAS

UTAH

TENNESSEE

VIRGINIA

REVERSE OF VIRGINIA'S SEAL

VERMONT

WEST VIRGINIA

REVERSE OF WEST VIRGINIA'S SEAL

WASHINGTON

STATE SEALS

WISCONSIN

WYOMING

being the renewal of a former seal, has the following design: " '[an] American eagle on a boulder in [a] prairie —the sun rising in [the] distant horizon' and [a] scroll in [the] eagle's beak, on which shall be inscribed the words: 'State Sovereignty,' 'National Union,' to correspond with the original seal of [the] state, in every particular." [16]

INDIANA

The State seal of Indiana is not officially described either in the constitution or in the statutes of the state. Article xv of the present state constitution says that "there shall be a seal of the State, kept by the Governor, for official purposes, which shall be called the Seal of the State of Indiana." [17] The Yearbook of the State of Indiana for the year 1919 says that "at the first session of the General Assembly, an act was passed authorizing the Governor to provide a seal and appropriating the sum of $100 to defray any expenses thereby incurred. Neither this law nor any law subsequently enacted sets forth the design of the seal, although there is a description of the contemplated seal given in the House Journal of 1816 which probably represented the design preferred by the early legislators and was at one state of the proceedings incorporated in the bill. This description is as follows: " 'A forest and a woodman felling a tree, a buffalo leaving the forest and fleeing through a plain to a distant forest and the sun setting in the West with the word Indiana.' " [18]

[16] *Illinois Laws Public: Public Laws of the State of Illinois, Passed by the Twenty-fifth General Assembly, Convened January 7, 1867* (Baker, Bailhache and Company, Springfield, Illinois, 1867) p. 36-7.

[17] *Burns Annotated Indiana Statutes, 1926,'Watson's Revision: Annotated Indiana Statutes, Containing All Indiana Statutes of General and Public Nature, in Force January 1, 1926, Including also the Constitutions of the United States and the State of Indiana All Completely Annotated, 1926,* edited by Harrison Burns, revised and annotated by Benjamin F. Watson (The Bobbs-Merrill Company, Indianapolis, Indiana, 1926) vol. 1, p. 142.

[18] *Year Book of the State of Indiana for the Year 1919,* compiled and published under the direction of James P. Goodrich, Governor, by the Legislative Reference Bureau, Charles Kettleborough, Director (Fort Wayne, Indiana, 1920) p. 952.

IOWA

The legislature of Iowa adopted the State seal on February 25, 1847. The law prescribes that the seal shall be "two inches in diameter, upon which shall be engraved the following device, surrounded by the words, 'The Great Seal of the State of Iowa'—a sheaf and field of standing wheat, with a sickle and other farming utensils, on the left side near the bottom; a lead furnace and pile of pig lead, on the right side; the citizen soldier, with a plow in his rear, supporting the American flag and liberty cap with his right hand, and his gun with his left, in the center and near the bottom; the Mississippi river in the rear of the whole, with the steamer Iowa under way; an eagle near the upper edge, holding in his beak a scroll, with the following inscription upon it: *Our liberties we prize, and our rights we will maintain.*" [19]

KANSAS

Kansas, by an act of her legislature, approved May 25, 1861, adopted the Great Seal of the State.

The device and design of this seal are as follows:

"The east is represented by a rising sun on the right hand corner of the seal; to the left of it, commerce is represented by a river and a steamboat; in the foreground, agriculture is represented as the basis of future prosperity of the State, by a settler's cabin and a man plowing with a pair of horses; beyond this, is a train of ox wagons going west; in the background is seen a herd of buffalo, retreating, pursued by two Indians on horseback; around the top, is the motto: 'Ad Astra per Aspera'—and beneath a cluster of thirty-four stars; the circle is surrounded by the words 'Great Seal of the State of Kansas, January 29, 1861.' " [20]

[19] *Iowa Laws, 1846-7: Acts and Resolutions Passed at the First Session of the General Assembly of the State of Iowa, Which Convened at Iowa City, on the Thirteenth Day of November, A. D. 1846*, published by authority (A. H. Palmer, Printer, Iowa City, Iowa, 1847) p. 164.

[20] *Kansas Laws, 1861: General Laws of the State of Kansas, Passed at the First Session of the Legislature, Commenced at the Capital, March 26, 1861, . . .* published by authority (*Kansas State Journal* Steam Power Press Print, Lawrence, Kansas, 1861) p. 275.

KENTUCKY

Kentucky, by an act of the General Assembly of the Commonwealth, approved on December 20, 1792, empowered and required the governor to procure a great seal for the Commonwealth. The act says: [20a]

"Be it enacted by the General Assembly, that the governor be empowered and he is required, to provide, at the public charge, a seal for this Commonwealth; and procure the same to be engraved with the following device, viz: two friends embracing with the name of the state over their heads; and around them, the following motto 'United We Stand, Divided We Fall.' "

An act of the General Assembly of the Commonwealth of Kentucky, approved on April 6, 1893, says that "the seal of the Commonwealth of Kentucky shall have upon it the device, two friends embracing each other, with the words 'Commonwealth of Kentucky' over their heads, and around about them the words, 'United we Stand, Divided we Fall.' " [21]

LOUISIANA

Governor W. W. Heard, complying with Section 3471 of the Revised Statutes of the State of Louisiana, "in order to establish uniformity in the State seal and its use amongst the various departments of government," [22] on April 30, 1902, "directed the Secretary of State to use a Seal," which is now the official seal of the State. The description of the seal is as follows:

[20a] *Littell's Laws of Kentucky: The Statutes Laws of Kentucky with Notes, Praelections, and Observations, on the Public Acts, Comprehending also, the Laws of Virginia and Acts of Parliament in Force in This Commonwealth; The Charter of Virginia, The Federal and State Constitutions, and so much of The King of England's Proclamation in 1763 as relates to the Titles to Land in Kentucky, Together with a Table of Reference to the Cases Adjudicated in the Court of Appeals, in three volumes,* William Littell, Esq. (Printed by and for William Hunter, Frankfort. Kentucky, 1809) vol. 1, p. 136.

[21] *Kentucky Laws, 1891-93: Acts of the General Assembly of the Commonwealth of Kentucky, . . . 1892* (E. Polk Johnson, Public Printer and Binder, Frankfort, Kentucky, 1893) p. 739.

[22] *Report of the Secretary of State to His Excellency W. W. Heard. Governor of the State of Louisiana, May 12th, 1902* (Baton Rouge News Publishing Company, State Printers, Baton Rouge, Louisiana, 1902) p. 15

"A Pelican, with its head turned to the left, in a nest with three young; the Pelican, following the tradition, in act of tearing its breast to feed its young; around the edge of the Seal to be inscribed 'State of Louisiana.' Over the head of the Pelican to be inscribed 'Union, Justice', etc.; under the nest of the Pelican to be inscribed 'Confidence.' " [23]

MAINE

The first legislature of Maine on June 9, 1820, adopted the seal of the State. [24] As specified in the law this seal consists of "a shield, argent charged with a *Pine Tree; a Moose Deer*, at the foot of it, recumbent. Supporters; on the dexter side, an *Husbandman*, resting on a scythe; on sinister side, a *Seaman*, resting on an anchor. In the foreground, representing sea and land, and under the shield, the name of the State in large Roman Capitals, to wit: MAINE. The whole surmounted by a Crest, the North Star. The motto, in small Roman Capitals, in a label interposed between the shield and the Crest, VIZ: DIRIGO."

MARYLAND

The Great Seal of the State of Maryland was adopted by the House of Delegates on March 18, 1876. [25] Zieber says that " '. . . by the adoption of this seal in 1876 the arms of Maryland were finally restored in their integrity to the Great Seal of the State. . .' " [26]

This seal is described as follows:

" 'The first and fourth quarters represented the arms of the Calvert family, described in heraldic language as *paly*

[23] *Report of the Secretary of State to His Excellency W. W. Heard, Governor of the State of Louisiana, May 12th, 1902* (Baton Rouge News Publishing Company, State Printers, Baton Rouge, Louisiana, 1902) p. 15.

[24] *Resolves of the Legislature of the State of Maine, Passed at Its Session Which Commenced on the Twenty-first Day of May, and Ended on the Twenty-eighth Day of June, one thousand eight hundred and twenty.* Published agreeably to a Resolution of June 28, 1820 (Printed by Francis Douglas, State Printer, Portland, Maine, 1820) p. 21.

[25] *Journal of the House of Delegates of Maryland, January Session, 1876* (John F. Wiley, State Printer, Annapolis, Maryland, 1876) p. 865.

[26] *Heraldry in America,* Eugene Zieber (Published by the Department of Heraldry of The Bailey, Banks and Biddle Company, Philadelphia, Pennsylvania, 1895) p. 141.

of six pieces, or and *sable, a bend counterchanged.* The second and third quarters showed the arms of the Crossland family which Cecilius inherited, from his grandmother, Alicia, daughter of John Crossland, Esquire of Crossland, Yorkshire, and wife of Leonard Calvert, the father of George, first Lord Baltimore. This coat is quarterly, *argent and gules, a cross bottony counterchanged.* Above the shield was placed an earl's coronet; above that a helmet set full faced; and over that the Calvert crest, *two pennons, the dexter or, the other sable, staves gules, issuing from a ducal coronet.* The supporters upon this seal were a *plowman* and a *fisherman,* designated respectively by a spade and a fish held in the hand. The motto was that adopted by the Calvert family—Fatti maschi parole femine. Behind and surrounding both shield and supporters was depicted an ermine-lined mantle; and on the circle about this side of the seal were the words 'Scuto bonae voluntatis tuae coronasti nos.' The arms thus described have become the historic Arms of Maryland. . .' " [27]

MASSACHUSETTS

The seal of the Commonwealth of Massachusetts was adopted by an act of the General Court of the State approved June 4, 1885. [28]

This seal is circular in form and bears "upon its face a representation of the arms of the Commonwealth, with an inscription around about such representation, consisting of the words 'Sigilium Reipublicae Massachusettensis.' "

The act says:

"Section 2. The arms of the Commonwealth shall consist of a shield, wherof the field or surface is blue, and thereon an Indian dressed in his shirt and moccasins, holding in his right hand a bow, in his left hand an arrow, point downward, all of gold; and in the upper corner above

---

[27] *Heraldry in America,* Eugene Zieber (Published by the Department of Heraldry of The Bailey, Banks and Biddle Company, Philadelphia, Pennsylvania, 1895) p. 137.

[28] *Massachusetts Acts and Resolves, 1885: Acts and Resolves Passed by the General Court of Massachusetts, in the Year 1885, . . .* published by the Secretary of the Commonwealth (Wright and Potter Printing Company, State Printers, Boston, Massachusetts, 1885) p. 730.

his right arm a silver star with five points. The crest shall be a wreath of blue and gold, whereon is a right arm bent at the elbow, and clothed and ruffled, the hand grasping a broadsword, all of gold. The motto shall be 'Ense petit placidam sub libertate quietem.' "

MICHIGAN

General Lewis Cass is said to have presented the Great Seal now in use by the State of Michigan to the convention which framed the first Constitution for the State, in session at the City of Detroit, on June 2, 1835. [29]

This seal is circular in form. The requirements say that, "a shield shall be represented on which shall be exhibited a peninsula, extending into a Lake, with the sun rising, and [a] man standing on the peninsula with a gun in his hand. On the top of the shield will be the words TUEBOR and underneath in a scroll will be the words, SI QUAERIS PENINSULAM AMOENAM CIRCUMSPICE. There will be a supporter on each side of the shield, one of which will represent a Moose and the other an Elk.

"Over the whole, on a crest, will be the EAGLE of the United States with the motto E PLURIBUS UNUM.

"Around will be the words, GREAT SEAL OF THE STATE OF MICHIGAN A.D. MDCCCXXXV." [30]

MINNESOTA

Minnesota by a joint resolution of the State legislature, approved on July 16, 1858, adopted the Great Seal of the State. [31] This seal consists of a circular disk upon which

[29] *Heraldry in America,* Eugene Zieber (Published by the Department of Heraldry of The Bailey, Banks and Biddle Company, Philadelphia, Pennsylvania, 1895) p. 144.

See also *The Compiled Laws of the State of Michigan, 1915, Compiled, Arranged, and Annotated under Act 247 of 1913 and Act 232 of 1915,* by Edmund C. Shields, Lansing, Michigan, Cyrenius P. Black, Lansing, Michigan, Archibald Bloomfield, Big Rapids, Michigan, Commissioners (Wynkoop Hallenbeck Crawford Company, State Printers, Lansing, Michigan, 1916) p. 620.

[30] *Michigan Pioneer and Historical Collections: Collections and Researches Made by the Michigan Pioneer and Historical Society* (Wynkoop Hallenbeck Crawford Company, State Printers, Lansing, Michigan, 1906) vol. 30, p. 332.

[31] *The Legislative Manual of the State of Minnesota, 1927,* compiled by Mike Holm, Secretary of State (Press of Harrison and Smith Company, Minneapolis, Minnesota, 1927) p. 8.

is depicted "a white man plowing eastward, an Indian riding on horseback toward the West, and as a background the setting sun and the Falls of St. Anthony. *L'Etoile du Nord*, which means 'The Star of the North,' is above, and around the edge 'The Great Seal of the State of Minnesota,' with '1858' below." [32]

MISSISSIPPI

Zieber quotes a letter from Governor Stone, which says that Mississippi has never officially adopted a coat of arms, but that the present seal has been in use since Mississippi became a state [33] [in 1817]. Preble describes this seal as follows: "The seal and arms of Mississippi are simply an American eagle with outspread wings, occupying the entire surface of a silver circular field. In the right talon of the eagle is a bundle of four arrows, [should be one arrow] and the left talon holds an olive branch fruited. Around the outer circle of the seal is the legend, 'THE GREAT SEAL OF THE STATE OF MISSISSIPPI,' in Roman capitals; a silver six-pointed star in the base. The diameter of the seal is two inches." [34]

The Mississippi Code of 1930 says: "The great seal of the state now in use shall be the seal of the state until altered by the legislature, and all official acts of the governor, his approval or disapproval of bills and resolutions passed by the legislature excepted, shall be authenticated by the great seal of the state." [34a]

[32] *Our Minnesota, A History for Children,* Hester McLean Pollock (E. P. Dutton and Company, New York, 1917) p. 190.

[33] *Heraldry in America,* Eugene Zieber (Published by the Department of Heraldry of The Bailey, Banks and Biddle Company, Philadelphia, Pennsylvania, 1895) p. 147.

[34] *Origin and History of the American Flag,* George Henry Preble (Nicholas L. Brown, Philadelphia, Pennsylvania, 1917) vol. 2, p. 634.

[34a] *Mississippi Code of 1930 of the Public Statute Laws of the State of Mississippi, Revised and Annotated by the Code Commission under the Provisions of an Act of the Legislature, Approved April 26th, 1928, and Reported to and Revised, Amended and Adopted by the Legislature at Its Regular Session in 1930.* Published by Authority of the Legislature in Two Volumes (The Harrison Company, Law Book Publishers, Atlanta, Georgia, 1930) vol. II, p. 2064.

MISSOURI

The legislature of Missouri by an act approved on January 11, 1822, [35] adopted the seal of the state.

The law prescribes that "the device for an armorial achievement for the state of Missouri, shall be as follows, to wit: *Arms,* parter per pale, on the dexter side *gules,* the white or grizzly bear of Missouri, *passant guardant,* proper: on a chief engrailed *azure,* a crescent *argent;* on the sinister side *argent,* the arms of the United States; the whole within a band inscribed with the words *"United We Stand Divided We Fall."* For the crest, over a helmet full faced, grated with six bars, *or,* a cloud *proper,* from which ascends a star *argent,* and above it a constellation of twenty-three smaller stars *argent* on an azure field, surrounded by a cloud *proper. Supporters* on each side, a white or grizzly bear of Missouri, rampant, guardant *proper,* standing on a scroll, inscribed with the motto, *'Salus populi suprema lex esto,'* and under the scroll the numerical letters MDCCCXX [1820]. And the great seal of the state shall be so engraved as to present by its impression, the device of the armorial achievement aforesaid, surrounded by a scroll inscribed with the words, 'THE GREAT SEAL OF THE STATE OF MISSOURI,' in Roman capitals, which seal shall be in a circular form and not more than two and a half inches in diameter." [35]

MONTANA

The Great Seal of Montana was officially adopted by an act of the State legislative assembly approved on March 2, 1893.

This seal is circular in form, two and one-half inches in diameter, surmounted by the words, "The Great Seal of the State of Montana." Upon the obverse side of the seal is depicted, "a central group representing a plow, a miner's

[35] *Laws of Missouri, 1825: Laws of the State of Missouri, Revised and Digested by Authority of the General Assembly, in Two Volumes with an appendix. . .* (Printed by E. Charles for the State, St. Louis, Missouri, 1825) vol. 2, p. 721.

pick and shovel; upon the right a representation of the great falls of the Missouri River; upon the left mountain scenery, and underneath, the words 'Oro-Y-Plata.' " [37]

NEBRASKA

Nebraska by an act of her legislative bodies, approved June 15, 1867, designated the State seal, circular in form, having the following design: "The eastern part of the circle to be represented by a steamboat ascending the Missouri river; the mechanic arts to be represented by a smith with hammer and anvil; in the foreground, agriculture to be represented by a settler's cabin, sheaves of wheat and stalks of growing corn; in the background a train of cars heading towards the Rocky Mountains, and on the extreme west, the Rocky Mountains to be plainly in view; around the top of this circle to be in capital letters, the motto, 'EQUALITY BEFORE THE LAW,' and the circle to be surrounded with the words, 'Great Seal of the State of Nebraska, March 1st, 1867.' " [38]

NEVADA

The legislature of Nevada by an act, approved February 24, 1866, [39] selected the seal of the State, which depicts the designs and devices as follows: "In the foreground, two large mountains, at the base of which, on the right, there shall be located a quartz mill, and on the left a tunnel,

[36] *Laws of Montana, Third Session, 1893*: Laws, Resolutions and Memorials of the State of Montana Passed at the Third Regular Session of the Legislative Assembly, Held at Helena, the Seat of Government of Said State, Commencing January 2nd, 1893, and Ending March 2nd, 1893, published by authority (Inter Mountain Publishing Company, State Printers, Butte City, Montana, 1893) p. 42-3.

[37] *Nebraska Statutes, 1867*: The Statutes of Nebraska Embracing All of the General Laws of the State in Force August 1st, 1867, with Marginal Notes, . . . compiled by E. Estabrook (Culver, Page and Hoyne, Printers and Binders, Chicago, Illinois, 1867) p. 863.

[38] *Nevada Laws, 1866*: Statutes of the State of Nevada Passed at the Second Session of the Legislature, 1866, Begun on Monday, the First Day of January, and Ended on Thursday, the First Day of March (John Church, State Printer, Carson City, Nevada, 1866) p. 94-5.

penetrating the silver leads of the mountain, with a miner running out a carload of ore, and a team loaded with ore for the mill. Immediately in the foreground, there shall be emblems indicative of the agricultural resources of the State, as follows: A plow, a sheaf, and a sickle. In the middle ground, a train of railroad cars, passing a mountain gorge; also a telegraph line extending along the line of the railroad. In the extreme back-ground, a range of snow clad mountains, with the rising sun in the east. Thirty-six stars to encircle the whole groupe. In an outer circle, the words, 'The Great Seal of the State of Nevada,' to be engraven with these words, for the motto of our State, 'All for Our Country.' " [40]

NEW HAMPSHIRE

The seal of New Hampshire, devised by a committee appointed by the General Court was received and accepted by a senate concurrent resolution on November 4, 1784, and adopted by the State legislature on February 12, 1785, is two inches in diameter. It is inscribed with " 'a field encompassed with Laurels, round the field in capital Letters, SIGILLUM, REIPUBLICAE NEO HANTONIENSIS, on the field a rising Sun, and a Ship on the 'Stocks, with American Banners displayed.' " [41]

The present seal of New Hampshire was adopted by an act of the State legislature approved on April 29, 1931, [42] to take effect on January 1, 1932. The act reads as follows:

"Section 4 of chapter 8 of the Public Laws is hereby amended by striking out the whole thereof and substituting therefore the following: 4. Seal. The seal of the state

[39] *Nevada Laws, 1866: Statutes of the State of Nevada Passed at the Second Session of the Legislature, 1866, Begun on Monday, the First Day of January, and Ended on Thursday, the First Day of March* (John Church, State Printer, Carson City, Nevada, 1866) p. 95.

[40] *Laws of New Hampshire, Volume 5, First Constitutional Period 1784-1792: Laws of New Hampshire Including Public and Private Acts, Resolves, Votes, Etc.,* edited by Henry Harrison Metcalf, LL.B., A.M. (Rumford Press, Concord, New Hampshire, 1916) First Constitutional Period, 1784-1792, vol. 5, p. 40.

[41] *New Hampshire Laws 1931 and Special Session 1930: New Hampshire Public Acts and Joint Resolutions of the Legislature of 1931 and Special Session of 1930,* . . . published by the Secretary of State (The Clarke Press, Manchester, New Hampshire, 1931) p 44.

shall be two inches in diameter, circular, with the following detail and no other: A field crossed by a straight horizon line of the sea, above the center of the field; concentric with the field the rising sun, exposed above the horizon about one-third of its diameter; the field encompassed with laurel; across the field for the full width within the laurel a broadside view of the frigate Raleigh, on the stocks; the ship's bow dexter and higher than the stern; the three lower masts shown in place, together with the fore, main and mizzen tops, shrouds and mainstays; an ensign staff at the stern flies the United States flag authorized by act of Congress June 14, 1777; a jury staff on the mainmast and another on the foremast each flies a penant; flags and penants are streaming to the dexter side; the hull is shown without a rudder; below the ship the field is divided into land and water by a double diagonal line whose highest point is sinister; no detail is shown anywhere on the water, nor any on the land between the water and the stocks except a granite boulder on the dexter side; encircling the field is the inscription, SEAL . OF . THE . STATE . OF . NEW HAMPSHIRE, the words separated by round periods, except between the parts of New Hampshire; at the lowest point of the inscription is the date 1776, flanked on either side by a five-pointed star, which group separates the beginning and end of the inscription; . . ."

NEW JERSEY

The Senate and General Assembly of New Jersey by an act, approved March 26, 1928, [43] designated the Great Seal of the State as follows: "The Great Seal of this State be amended in description, and engraved as amended, on silver of the size and dimensions as heretofore; and that the arms be three ploughs in an escutcheon, azure; supporters, Liberty and Ceres. The Goddess Liberty to carry in her dexter hand a pole, proper, surmounted by a cap gules, with band azure at the bottom, displaying on the band six stars, argent; tresses falling on shoulders,

[42] New Jersey Laws, 1928: Acts of the One Hundred and Fifty-second Legislature of the State of New Jersey and Eighty-fourth under the New Constitution, 1928 (MacCrellish and Quigley Company, Printers, Trenton, New Jersey, 1928) p. 803.

proper; head bearing over all a chaplet of laurel leaves, vert; overdress, tenné; underskirt, argent; feet sandaled, standing on scroll. Ceres: Same as Liberty, save over-dress, gules; holding in left hand a cornucopia, or, bearing apples, plums and grapes surrounded by leaves, all proper; head bearing over all a chaplet of wheat spears, vert. Shield surmounted by sovereign's helmet, six bars, or; wreath and mantling, argent and azure. Crest: A horse's head, proper. Underneath the shield and supporting the goddess, a scroll azure, bordered with tenné, in three waves or folds; on the upper folds the words 'Liberty and Pros-perity'; on the under fold in Arabic numerals, the figures '1776.' These words to be engraved round the arms, viz., 'The Great Seal of the State of New Jersey.' " [43]

NEW MEXICO

The legislature of New Mexico by an act, approved March 13, 1913, [44] changed the word Territory on the Territorial seal to the word State. The law prescribes that the design of the seal be as follows:

"The coat of arms of the State shall be the Mexican eagle grasping a serpent in its beak, the cactus in its talons, shielded by the American eagle with outspread wings, and grasping arrows in its talons; the date 1912 under the eagles and, on a scroll, the motto: *Crescit Eundo.* The great seal of the State shall be a disc bearing the coat of arms and having around the edge the words 'Great Seal of the State of New Mexico.' " [45]

[43] *New Jersey Laws, 1928: Acts of the One Hundred and Fifty-second Legislature of the State of New Jersey and Eighty-fourth under the New Constitution, 1928* (MacCrellish and Quigley Company, Printers, Trenton, New Jersey, 1928) p. 802.

[44] *Laws of New Mexico, 1913: Laws of the State of New Mexico Passed at the Second Regular Session of the First Legislature of the State of New Mexico Which Convened at the City of Santa Fe, at the Capital, January 14, 1913, and Adjourned March 14, 1913,* prepared for publication by Antonio Lucero, Secretary of State, published by authority (New Mexican Printing Company, Sante Fe, New Mexico, 1913) p. 172.

[45] *New Mexico Statutes Annotated Codification, 1915: Containing the Codification Passed at the Second Session of the Legislature of the State of New Mexico, in Effect June 11, 1915, with the 1915 Session Laws as an Appendix,* compiled and annotated by Stephen B. Davis, Jr. and Mer-ritt C. Mechem, published by authority (The W. H. Courtright Publishing Company, Denver, Colorado, 1915) p. 1539.

NEW YORK

The Great Seal of New York has been modified five times since it was originally devised in 1777 by the committee appointed by the Provincial Congress on April 15, 1777. [46] The device prepared by this committee was adopted on March 6, 1778. [46a]

The dates for the modification of the Great Seal of New York are as follows: 1778, 1798, 1799, 1809, and 1882. [47]

Repeated attempts to find a "description in writing of the Arms and of the Great and Privy Seal of this State recorded and deposited in the office of the Secretary of this State," [48] proved unsuccessful.

In order to reëstablish the original Arms of the State of New York and to provide for the use thereof on public seals, the State legislature, by an act passed on May 20, 1882, [49] adopted the Great Seal of the State now in use.

The act reads as follows:

"Section 1. The device of arms of this state as adopted March sixteenth, seventeen hundred and seventy-eight, is hereby declared to be correctly described as follows:

"Charge. Azure, in a landscape, the sun in fess, rising in splendor, or, behind a range of three mountains, the middle one the highest, in base, a ship and sloop under sail, passing and about to meet on a river, bordered below by a grassy shore fringed with shrubs, all proper.

[46] *Report of the Commissioners on the Correct Arms of the State of New York, Transmitted to the Senate April 13, 1881* (Weed, Parsons and Company, Printers, Albany, New York, 1811) p. 10.

[46a] *The Correct Arms of the State of New York, as Established by Law Since March 16, 1778, A Historical Essay read before the Albany Institute, December 2, 1879*, by Henry A. Homes of the State Library (Weed, Parsons and Company, Printers, Albany, New York, 1880) p. 11.

[47] *Legislative Manual, New York, 1932: Manual for the Use of the Legislature of the State of New York, 1932*, prepared pursuant to the provisions of chapter 23, Laws of 1909, by Edward J. Flynn (J. B. Lyon Company, Albany, New York, 1932) p. 316 inset.

[48] *Report of the Commissioners on the Correct Arms of the State of New York, Transmitted to the Senate April 13, 1881* (Weed, Parsons and Company, Printers, Albany, New York, 1811) p. 8.

[49] *New York Laws, 1882: Laws of the State of New York, Passed at the One Hundred and Fifth Session of the Legislature, Begun January Third and Ended June Second, 1882, in the City of Albany*, Joseph B. Carr, Secretary of State (Weed, Parsons and Company, Printers, Albany, New York, 1882) vol. I, p. 227-8.

"Crest. On a wreath, azure and or, an American eagle, proper rising to the dexter, from a two-thirds of a globe terrestrial showing the North Atlantic ocean with the outlines of its shores.

"Supporters. On a quasi compartment formed by the extension of the scroll.

"Dexter. The figure of Liberty proper, her hair disheveled and decorated with pearls, vested azure, sandaled gules, about the waist a cincture or, fringed gules, a mantle of the last depending from the shoulders behind to the feet, in the dexter hand a staff ensigned with a Phrygian cap or, the sinister arm embowed, the hand supporting the shield at the dexter chief point, a royal crown by her sinister foot dejected.

"Sinister. The figure of Justice proper, her hair disheveled and decorated with pearls, vested or, sandaled, cinctured and mantled as Liberty, bound about the eyes with a fillet proper, in the dexter hand, a straight sword hilted or, erect, resting on the sinister chief point of the shield, the sinister arm embowed, holding before her her scales proper.

"Motto. On a scroll below the shield argent, in sable, EXCELSIOR."

NORTH CAROLINA

North Carolina's seal, adopted February 21, 1893, [50] has been described thus: " 'The Great Seal of the State of North Carolina is two and one-quarter inches in diameter, and its design is a representation of the figures of Liberty and Plenty, looking towards each other, but not more than half fronting each other, and otherwise disposed as follows: Liberty, the first figure standing, her pole with cap on it in her left hand and a scroll with the word "Constitution" inscribed thereon in her right hand. Plenty, the second figure, sitting down, her right arm half extended toward Liberty, three heads of wheat in her right hand, and in her left, the small end of her horn, the mouth of which is resting at her feet, and the contents of horn rolling out. In

---

[50] *Laws of North Carolina Session, 1893: Public Laws and Resolutions of the State of North Carolina Passed by the General Assembly at Its Session 1893, etc.*, published by authority (Joseph Daniels, State Printer and Binder, Raleigh, North Carolina, 1893) p. 109-10.

the exergue is inserted the words May 20, 1775, above the coat of arms. Around the circumference is the legend, 'The Great Seal of the State of North Carolina,' and the motto, "Esse Quam Videri." ' " [51]

NORTH DAKOTA

The seal of the State of North Dakota was provided for by the Constitution of 1889. This seal is two and one-half inches in diameter and depicts "a tree in the open field, the trunk of which is surrounded by three bundles of wheat; on the right a plow, anvil and sledge; on the left a bow crossed with three arrows, and an Indian on horseback pursuing a buffalo toward the setting sun; the foliage of the tree arched by a half circle of forty-two stars, surrounded by the motto 'Liberty and Union Now and Forever, One and Inseparable'; the words, 'Great Seal' at the top, the words 'State of North Dakota' at the bottom; 'October 1st' on the left and '1889' on the right." [52]

OHIO

On May 9, 1868, [53] the legislature of Ohio adopted the present Great Seal and Coat of Arms of the State, thus repealing the act of April 6, 1866, and also the act of April 16, 1867, amendatory thereto. The act says:

"Section 1. *Be it enacted by the General Assembly of the State of Ohio,* That the coat of arms of the State of Ohio shall consist of the following device: A shield, in form, a circle. On it, in the foreground, on the right, a sheaf of wheat; on the left, a bundle of seventeen arrows,

[51] *North Carolina Manual, 1927: North Carolina Manual, 1927,* compiled and edited by A. R. Newsome, Secretary of the North Carolina Historical Commission (Edwards and Broughton Company, State Printers, Raleigh, North Carolina, 1927) p. 314-15.
[52] *Revised Codes of North Dakota, 1895: The Revised Codes of the State of North Dakota, 1895, together with the Constitution of the United States and of the State of North Dakota with the Amendments Thereto,* by authority of the Legislative Assembly (Tribune Company, Printers and Binders, Bismarck, North Dakota, 1895) Constitution of North Dakota, article 17, section 207, p. 45.
[53] *Ohio Laws, 1868: General and Local Laws and Joint Resolutions, Passed by the Fifty-Eighth General Assembly of the State of Ohio, at Its First Session Begun and Held in the City of Columbus, January 6, 1868, and in the Sixty-Sixth Year of Said State* (L. D. Myers and Brother, State Printers, 1868) vol. 65, p. 175.

both standing erect; in the background, and rising above the sheaf and arrows, a mountain range, over which shall appear a rising sun.

"Section 2. The great seal of the state shall be two and one-half inches in diameter, on which shall be engraved the device as described in the preceding section, and it shall be surrounded with these words: 'The Great Seal of the State of Ohio.'. . .'"

OKLAHOMA

Oklahoma's Constitution of 1906 specifies that the State seal shall be designed as follows:

"In the center shall be a five pointed star, with one ray directed upward. The center of the star shall contain the central device of the seal of the Territory of Oklahoma, including the words, 'Labor Omnia Vincit.' The upper left hand ray shall contain the symbol of the ancient seal of the Cherokee Nation, namely: A seven pointed star partially surrounded by a wreath of oak leaves. The ray directed upward shall contain the symbol of the ancient seal of the Chickasaw Nation, namely: An Indian warrior standing upright with bow and shield. The lower left hand ray shall contain the symbol of the ancient seal of the Creek Nation, namely: A sheaf of wheat and a plow. The upper right hand ray shall contain the symbol of the ancient seal of the Choctaw Nation, namely: A tomahawk, bow, and three crossed arrows. The lower right hand ray shall contain the symbol of the ancient seal of the Seminole Nation, namely: A village with houses and a factory beside a lake upon which an Indian is paddling a canoe. Surrounding the central star and grouped between its rays shall be forty-five small stars, divided into five clusters of nine stars each, representing the forty-five states of the Union, to which the forty-sixth is now added. In a circular band surrounding the whole device shall be inscribed, 'GREAT SEAL OF THE STATE OF OKLAHOMA 1907.' " [54] The impression of the seal shows no insignia on the lower right hand ray.

[54] *General Statutes of Oklahoma, 1908, A Compilation of All the Laws of a General Nature, Including the Session Laws of 1907; Annotated to Volume 18 Oklahoma Reports, 96 Pacific Reports, 76 Kansas Reports and 150 California Reports*, Benedict Elder, published by authority (Pipes-Reed Book Company, Kansas City, Missouri, 1908) Constitution of 1906, article 7, section 35, p. 101.

OREGON

The State seal of Oregon, adopted by legislative action, was approved on February 24, 1903. [55]

The law specified that:

"The description of the seal of the State of Oregon shall be an escutcheon, supported by thirty-three stars, and divided by an ordinary, with the inscription, 'The Union.' In chief—mountains, an elk with branching antlers, a wagon, the Pacific Ocean, on which a British man-of-war departing, an American steamer arriving. The second—quartering with a sheaf, a plow, and a pickax. Crest—the American eagle. Legend—State of Oregon, 1859." [56]

PENNSYLVANIA

The Pennsylvania State seal was adopted on March 2, 1809. The Executive Minutes of July 1, 1809, say:

" 'In obedience to the directions of an Act of General Assembly, passed the second day of March, one thousand eight hundred and nine, the following description of the Great Seal is recorded, that is to say:

" 'The shield shall be parted PER FESS, OR, charged with a plough, PROPER, in chief; on a sea WAVY; PROPER, a ship under full sail, surmounted with a sky, Azure; and in BASE, on a field VERT, three GARBS, OR. On the SINISTER a stock of maize, and DEXTER an olive branch. And on the wreath of its colours a bald eagle—PROPER, PERCHED, wings extended, for the CREST. MOTTO: VIRTUE, LIBERTY, and INDEPENDENCE. Round the margin of the seal, COMMON-WEALTH OF PENNSYLVANIA. The reverse, Liberty, trampling on a Lyon, Gules, the emblem of Tyranny. MOTTO—'BOTH CAN'T SURVIVE.' " [57]

[55] *General Laws of Oregon, 1903: State of Oregon, the General Laws and Joint Resolutions and Memorials, Enacted and Adopted by the Twenty-second Regular Session of the Legislative Assembly, 1903, Begun on the Twelfth Day of January and Ended on the Twentieth Day of February, 1903* (J. R. Whitney, State Printer, Salem, Oregon, 1903) p. 172.
[56] *Ibidem*, p. 172.
[57] "The Arms of Pennsylvania and the Great Seal of the Commonwealth," by William H. Egle, State Librarian, in *Commonwealth of Pennsylvania, 1893, Official Documents, Comprising the Department and Other Reports, made to the Governor, Senate and House of Representatives of Pennsylvania* (Clarence M. Busch, State Printer of Pennsylvania, 1894) vol. iv. p. 215-16.

James Evelyn Pilcher, in his article on the seal and coat of arms of the Commonwealth of Pennsylvania, says:

"In 1868, however, the seal was again modified by the introduction of the scroll-work design in the lower segment of the circumferential band.

"In 1893, although the previous design continued occasionally to be used during that and the following year,—the seal now in use—was adopted, differing from the immediately preceding form in the omission of the wreath or festoon about the upper part of the shield, and, as in the seal of 1876, facing the plough and ship from right to left." [58]

RHODE ISLAND

The present Great Seal of Rhode Island consists of a circular disk upon which is depicted a golden anchor on a blue field, and the motto thereof is the word Hope. This seal was adopted on February 24, 1875:

The law says:

"There shall continue to be one seal for the public use of the state; the form of an anchor shall be engraven thereon; the motto thereof shall be the word Hope; and in a circle around the same shall be engraven the words, SEAL OF THE STATE OF RHODE ISLAND AND PROVIDENCE PLANTATIONS, 1636." [58a]

Arnold says that "a new seal 'being the anchor, with the motto Hope,' [59] was procured by the Assembly, in place of the one broken by Andros," but he does not give the date

---

[58] *The Seal and Arms of Pennsylvania,* James Evelyn Pilcher, Carlisle, Pennsylvania (William Stanley Ray, State Printer, Harrisburg, Pennsylvania, 1902) p. 10.

For a more recent statement of these facts, see *The Pennsylvania Manual 1931,* compiled under the Department of Property and Supplies, published by the Commonwealth of Pennsylvania (Bureau of Publications, Harrisburg, Pennsylvania, 1931) p. 273.

[58a] *Acts, Resolves and Reports of the General Assembly of the State of Rhode Island and Providence Plantations, 1875* (Providence Press Company, Printers to the State, Providence, Rhode Island, 1875) p. 166-7.

[59] *History of the State of Rhode Island and Providence Plantations* (1636-1700) Samuel Green Arnold (D. Appleton and Company, New York, 1859) vol. I, p. 519.

when this took place. The seal of the Province was ordered to be an anchor in 1647. [60]

SOUTH CAROLINA

The South Carolina Constitution of 1895 says that "the seal of the State now in use shall be used by the Governor officially, and shall be called 'The Great Seal of the State of South Carolina.'" [61]

The General Assembly of the Provincial Congress of South Carolina on April 2, 1776, authorized the designing and making of the Great Seal of South Carolina. [62] The designing of this seal is as follows:

"ARMS: A Palmetto-tree growing on the sea-shore, erect; at its base, a torn up Oak-tree, its branches lopped off, prostrate; *both proper*. Just below the branches of the Palmetto, two shields, pendent; one of them on the dexter side is inscribed March 26—the other on the sinister side July 4. Twelve Spears, *proper*, are bound crosswise to the stem of the Palmetto, their points raised; the band uniting them together, bearing the inscription QUIS SEPARABIT. Under the prostrate Oak, is inscribed MELIOREM LAPSA LOCAVIT; below which appears in large figures 1776. At the Summit of the Exergue, are the words SOUTH CAROLINA, and at the bottom of the same, ANIMIS OPIBUSQUE PARATI.

"REVERSE: A Woman walking on the Sea-shore, over swords and daggers; she holds in her dexter hand, a laurel branch—and in her sinister, the folds of her robe: she looks towards the sun, just rising above the sea; *all proper*. On the upper part, is the sky azure. At the summit of the Exergue, are the words DUM SPIRO SPERO: and within the field below the figure, is inscribed the word SPES. The

[60] *Heraldry in America, Eugene Zieber* (Published by the Department of Heraldry of The Bailey, Banks and Biddle Company, Philadelphia, Pennsylvania, 1895) p. 181.

[61] *Code of Laws of South Carolina, 1902: Code of Laws of South Carolina, 1902, in Two Volumes, State Constitution of 1895* (The State Company, State Printers, Columbia, South Carolina, 1902) Article IV, section 18, vol. 2, p. 70.

[62] *Handbook of South Carolina, Resources, Institutions and Industries of the State,* Second Edition, 1908, E. J. Watson, Commissioner, The State Department of Agriculture, Commerce and Immigration (The State Company, Columbia, South Carolina, 1908) p. 38.

Seal is in the form of a circle, four inches in diameter; and four-tenths of an inch thick." [63]

SOUTH DAKOTA

The Constitution of South Dakota, adopted on October 1, 1889, provides for the State seal. This document says:

"The design of the great seal of South Dakota shall be as follows: A circle within which shall appear in the left foreground a smelting furnace and other features of mining work. In the left background a range of hills. In the right foreground a farmer at his plow. In the right background a herd of cattle and a field of corn. Between the two parts thus described shall appear a river bearing a steamboat. Properly divided between the upper and lower edges of the circle shall appear the legend, 'Under God the People Rule' which shall be the motto of the State of South Dakota. Exterior to this circle and within a circumscribed circle shall appear, in the upper part, the words, 'State of South Dakota,' in the lower part the words, 'Great Seal,' and the date in Arabic numerals of the year in which the State shall be admitted to the Union." [64]

TENNESSEE

Each of the three constitutions of Tennessee says that "there shall be a seal of this state, which shall be kept by the governor, and used by him officially, and shall be called the 'Great Seal of the State of Tennessee.' " [65]

John Trotwood Moore, the late State Librarian and Archivist, says that "there is no evidence that any action

---

[63] *Handbook of South Carolina, Resources, Institutions and Industries of the State,* Second Edition, 1908, E. J. Watson, Commissioner, The State Department of Agriculture, Commerce and Immigration (The State Company, Columbia, South Carolina, 1908) p. 40.

[64] *South Dakota Revised Codes, 1903: The Revised Codes, 1903, State of South Dakota, Comprising the Political Code, Civil Code, Code of Civil Procedure, Probate Code, Justices Code, Penal Code and Code of Criminal Procedure, Official State Edition, State Constitution of 1889,* compiled and revised by G. C. Moody, Bartlett Tripp, and James M. Brown, printed Pursuant to Act of the Legislature of 1903 (State Publishing Company, Pierre, South Dakota, 1903) Article 21, section 1, p. 23.

[65] *Constitution of 1796,* article 2, section 15; *Constitution of 1834,* article 3, section 15; and *Constitution of 1870,* article 3, section 15.

was taken relative to procuring a great seal until April 29, 1796, when the General Assembly passed an act authorizing the governor to procure a seal for the use of the state." [66]

A committee was appointed by the legislative bodies of Tennessee to devise and report on a suitable State seal on September 26, 1801. [67] The report of this committee was made and adopted on November 14, 1801, which provided that " 'the said seal be a circle, two inches and a quarter in diameter, that the circumference of the circle contain the words THE GREAT SEAL OF TENNESSEE, that in the lower part of said circumference be inserted Feb. 6th, 1796, the date of the constitution of this state; that in the inside of the upper part of said circle be set in numerical letters xvi, the number of the state in chronological order; that under the base of the upper semicircle, there be the word AGRICULTURE; that above said base, there be the figure of a plough, sheaf of wheat and cotton plant; that in the lower part of the lower semicircle, there be the word COMMERCE, and said lower semicircle, shall also contain the figure of a boat and boatman.' " [68]

TEXAS

The act approved January 25, 1839, [69] amending an act approved December 10, 1836, adopting a National Seal and Standard for the Republic of Texas, reads as follows:

"Section 1. Be it enacted by the Senate and House of Representatives of the Republic of Texas in Congress assembled, That from and after the passage of this act the

[66] *Tennessee, The Volunteer State, 1769-1923: Tennessee, The Volunteer State, 1769-1923,* John Trotwood Moore and Austin P. Foster (The S. J. Clarke Publishing Company, Chicago, Illinois and Nashville, Tennessee, 1923) vol. 1, p. 297.

[67] *Ibidem,* p. 297.

[68] *Tennessee, The Volunteer State, 1769-1923: Tennessee, The Volunteer State, 1769-1923, John* Trotwood Moore and Austin P. Foster ('The S. J. Clarke Publishing Company, Chicago, Illinois and Nashville, Tennessee, 1923) vol. 1, p. 297-8.

[69] *Texas Laws, 1838-1846: The Laws of Texas 1822-1897, . . . Laws of the Republic of Texas, 1839, . . .* compiled and arranged by H. P. N. Gammel, with an introduction by C. W. Raines (The Gammel Book Company, Austin, Texas, 1898) vol. 2, p. 88.

national arms of the Republic of Texas be and the same is hereby declared to be a white star of five points, on an azure ground, encircled by an olive and live oak branches.

"Section 2. Be it enacted, That the national great seal of this Republic shall, from and after the passage of this act, bear the arms of this nation as declared by the first section of this act and the letters 'Republic of Texas.' "

The Texas Constitution of 1876 [69a] provides for the State seal, which one observes is the same in design as the seal of the Republic of Texas. The Constitution says that "the seal of the State shall be a star of five points, encircled by olive and live oak branches, and the words, 'The State of Texas.' "

UTAH

The legislature of Utah by an act, approved April 3, 1896, provides for the State seal and specifies:

"That 'The Great Seal of the State of Utah' shall be 2½ inches in diameter, with the following device inscribed thereon:

"In the center thereof a shield, with the American eagle with outstretched wings perched thereon; the top portion of said shield thereof pierced by six arrows; across the shield, below the arrows, the word 'Industry' appears, and beneath the word 'Industry' a bee-hive, on either side of which are growing sego lilies. Directly below the bee-hive are the figures '1847,' and on either side of said shield is our National flag.

"Encircling all, near the outer edge of said Seal, beginning at the lower left hand portion and ending at the lower right hand portion thereof, are the words, 'The Great Seal of the State of Utah,' at the base are the figures '1896.' " [70]

[69a] *McEachin's Civil Statutes Annotated: McEachin's Annotated Civil Statutes of the State of Texas,* James Somerville McEachin (T. H. Flood and Company, Chicago, Illinois, 1913) State Constitution of 1876, article 4, section 19, vol. 1, p. 26.

[70] *Laws of Utah, 1896: Laws of the State of Utah Passed at the Special and First Regular Sessions of the Legislature of the State of Utah, Held at Salt Lake City, the State Capital, in January, February, March and April, 1896, also the Enabling Act, Passed by Congress, and the State Constitution, etc. . . . .* published by authority (Deseret News Publishing Company, Salt Lake City, Utah, 1896) chap. 86, section 1, p. 297, 298.

VERMONT

Vermont by an act of her legislative assembly, approved on April 9, 1937, adopted the present Seal of the State.

The act reads as follows:

"It is hereby enacted by the General Assembly of the State of Vermont:

"Section 1. Section forty-eight of the Public Laws is hereby amended so as to read as follows:

"Section 48. *State Seal.* The state seal shall be the great seal of the state, a faithful reproduction, cut larger and deeper, of the original seal, designed by Ira Allen, cut by Reuben Dean of Windsor, and accepted by resolution of the general assembly, dated February 20, 1779. The seal shall be kept by the secretary of civil and military affairs.

"Section 2. *New reproduction.* The secretary of civil and military affairs is hereby directed to cause such reproduction of the original seal to be made and placed in a suitable press.

"Section 3. *Old seal damasked.* When the new reproduction of the original seal is ready to be brought into commission, the secretary of civil and military affairs shall present it to the governor, in the presence of the lieutenant governor, the speaker of the house of representatives, and the secretary of state, and shall submit the die and counter of the former seal to the governor, who shall in their presence, damask both die and counter

"Section 4. *Proclamation.* The governor shall, forthwith, by proclamation over his signature, with the counter signature of the lieutenant governor, the speaker of the house of representatives, and the secretary of state, and the attestation of the secretary of civil and military affairs, announce that the reproduction of the original seal has been brought into commission, and that he has damasked the former seal, and he shall cause the great seal to be thereto affixed. Copies of this proclamation, thus signed and sealed, shall be sent to the president of the United

States, the secretary of state of the United States, and to the governors of every state and territory of the United States.

"Section 5. *Appropriation.* The sum of three hundred dollars or as much thereof as may be necessary is hereby appropriated to provide for the making of this seal, and the mounting of it in a suitable press; for an accurate drawing of the seal; and for a line cut thereof, the use of which shall be restricted to the reproduction of documents requiring the signature of the governor, and the affixing of the great seal.

"Section 6. This act shall take effect from its passage." [71]

The Vermont Legislative Directory of 1915 describes this seal as follows:

"The principal figure is a pine tree, rising from the center of a thick growth of evergreens with conical tops. Above these tops start the limbs of the pine, and the bases of the evergreens extend in a horizontal line quite across the Seal. A sheaf of grain stands on each side of the pine, far in the background, and for want of proper perspective close up under high strata of clouds that occupy the upper edge of the Seal. And below the sheaf on the right of the observer, and above the tops of the evergreens, stands a cow. Below the line of evergreens, and in the form in which they are here printed, are the words:

| VERMONT |

FREEDOM
& UNITY

"A sheaf of grain stands at each end of the word freedom. All is encircled by a narrow border of consecutive arrow heads, the point of each inserted in the socket of the next." [72]

---

[71] *Laws of Vermont, 1937: Acts and Resolves Passed by the General Assembly of the State of Vermont at the Thirty-fourth Biennial Session 1937, Session Commenced January 6, 1937, Adjourned April 10, 1937,* published by authority (Vermont Printing Company, Brattleboro, Vermont, 1937) p. 3-4.
[72] *Vermont Legislative Directory, Biennial Session, 1915,* prepared pursuant to law by Guy W. Bailey, Secretary of State (St. Albans Messenger Print, St. Albans, Vermont, 1915) p. 368-9.

VIRGINIA

The present seals of the Commonwealth of Virginia were adopted by an act of the General Assembly of the State of Virginia, approved March 24, 1930. [73]

The act reads:

"Be it enacted by the general assembly of Virginia, That sections twenty-seven and thirty-one of the Code of Virginia, be amended and re-enacted so as to read as follows:

"Section 27. The great seal of the Commonwealth of Virginia shall consist of two metallic discs, two inches and one-fourth in diameter, with an ornamental border one-fourth of an inch wide, with such words and figures engraved thereon as will, when used, produce impressions to be described as follows: On the obverse, Virtus, the genius of the Commonwealth, dressed as an Amazon, resting on a spear in her right hand, point downward, touching the earth; and holding in her left hand, a sheathed sword, or parazonium, pointing upward; her head erect and face upturned; her left foot on the form of Tyranny represented by the prostrate body of a man, with his head to her left, his fallen crown near by, a broken chain in his left hand, and a scourge in his right. Above the group, and within the border conforming therewith, shall be the word Virginia, and in the space below, on a curved line, shall be the motto, sic semper tyrannis. On the reverse, shall be placed a group consisting of Libertas, holding a wand and pileus in her right hand; on her right, Aeternitas, with a globe and phoenix in her right hand; and on the left of Libertas, Ceres, with a cornucopia in her left hand, and an ear of wheat in her right; over this device in a curved line, the word perseverando.

"(a) The governor is hereby authorized and directed to cause a new great seal of the Commonwealth to be constructed and engraved, with all reasonable dispatch, in strict conformity with the foregoing description, by artists and engravers of high rank in their profession and under the supervision of the art commission of Virginia, and when completed, to also have constructed and engraved a

[73] *Acts of the General Assembly of the State of Virginia, Session Which Commenced at the State Capitol on Wednesday, January 8, 1930, Adjourned on March 18, 1930* (Division of Purchase and Printing, Richmond, Virginia, 1930) chap. 386, section 27, p. 820-2.

new lesser seal of the Commonwealth in accordance with section twenty-eight of the Code of Virginia. The governor shall, after said seals shall have been completed, and approved by him, proclaim the same, by such means as he may deem sufficient, to be the true great seal and lesser seal of the Commonwealth.

"(b)   The great and lesser seals now in use in the office of the secretary of the Commonwealth are hereby declared to be the true great and lesser seals of the Commonwealth for the time being, and to so continue and be used as such, until the new seals shall be completed and proclaimed as herein provided for, and all official acts done thereunder, in the name of the Commonwealth, are hereby declared to be valid in so far as the affixing of the seal of the State thereto, may have been, or may be, a necessary part of the due execution, or performance thereof.

"(c)   Any and all seals now under the care of the secretary of the Commonwealth shall, after the completion and proclamation of the new seals herein provided for, be cancelled by quartering the same with two straight lines crossing at right angles at the center of the discs, and cut at least as deep as the figures thereon, which seals so cancelled shall be safely kept in the office of the secretary of the Commonwealth and at least three clear impressions thereof filed with the State librarian to be by him duly indexed and safely kept in a suitable place.

"(d)   The new, and permanent, seals of the Commonwealth, herein provided for shall, when completed, be kept and used as provided by law, and at least three clear impressions thereof shall be made and filed with the State librarian to be by him kept and displayed in some suitable place in the State library, for public inspection.

"(e)   A sum sufficient, not to exceed fifteen hundred dollars, is hereby appropriated, out of any money in the treasury not otherwise appropriated, to meet the necessary expenses of carrying out the provisions of this act."

The *Proclamation by the Governor*, proclaiming the new seal of the Commonwealth of Virginia says:

. . . .

"Whereas it is provided by section twenty-eight of the Code of Virginia that 'The lesser seal of the Commonwealth shall be one and nine-sixteenths inches in diameter, and have engraved thereon the device and inscriptions contained in the obverse of the great seal,' "

. . . .

"Now, therefore, in conformity with the provisions of section twenty-seven of the Code of Virginia, I do hereby proclaim the first of the said seals, hereinabove described, to be the great seal of the Commonwealth, and the second of the said seals, to be the lesser seal of the Commonwealth.

"Given under my hand and under the lesser seal of the Commonwealth, at Richmond, this 2nd day of December, in the year of our Lord one thousand, nine hundred and thirty-one, and in the one hundred and fifty-sixth year of the Commonwealth."

By the Governor: "Jno. Garland Pollard, Governor, Peter Saunders, Secretary of the Commonwealth."

WASHINGTON

The State Constitution, adopted November 11, 1889, says that "the seal of the state of Washington shall be a seal encircled with the words: 'The seal of the State of Washington,' with the vignette of Gen. George Washington as the central figure, and beneath the vignette the figures '1889.' " [74]

WEST VIRGINIA

The report of the Joint Committee on Seals adopted by an act of the State legislature on September 26, 1863, describes the seal of the State as follows:

"The disc of the great seal to be two and one-half inches in diameter.

"The *obverse* to bear the legend, *'State of West Virginia,'* the constitutional designation of our republic, which, with the motto *'Montani semper liberi,'* (in English, 'Mountaineers always free,') is to be inserted in the circumference. In the centre, a rock with ivy, emblematic of stability and continuance, and on the face of the rock the

[74] *Pierce's Washington Code, Annotated, 1912: Pierce's Code, A Compilation of All the Laws in Force in the State of Washington Including the Session of 1911, Annotated,* compiled by Frank Pierce of the Seattle Bar, indexed by William Baxter France, Seattle, Washington (National Law Book Company, Publishers, Seattle, Washington, 1912) State Constitution of 1889, article 18, section 214, p. 53.

inscription 'June 20, 1863,' the date of our foundation, as if 'graved with a pen of iron in the rock forever.' On the right of the rock a farmer clothed in the traditional hunting shirt peculiar to this region, his right arm resting on the plow-handles, and his left supporting a woodman's axe, indicating that while our territory is partially cultivated, it is still in process of being cleared of the original forest. At his right, a sheaf of wheat and a cornstalk. On the left of the rock, a miner, indicated by a pickax on his shoulder, with barrels and lumps of mineral at his feet. On his left, an anvil, partly seen, on which rests a sledge hammer, typical of the mechanic arts, the whole indicating the principal pursuits and resources of the State. In front of the rock and figures, as if just laid down by the latter and ready to be resumed at a moment's notice, two hunter's rifles, crossed, and surmounted at the place of contact by the Phrygian cap, or cap of liberty, indicating that our freedom and independence were won and will be defended and maintained by arms.

"The above to be also the legend, motto and device of the less seal, the disc of which should have a diameter of an inch and a half.

"The reverse of the great seal to be encircled by a wreath composed of laurel and oak leaves, emblematic of valor and strength, with fruits and cereals, productions of our State. For device, a landscape. In the distance, on the left of the disc, wooded mountains, and on the right, a cultivated slope with the log frame house peculiar to this region. On the side of the mountain a representation of the viaduct on the line of the Baltimore and Ohio Railroad, in Preston county, one of the great engineering triumphs of the age, with a train of cars about to pass over it. Near the centre, a factory, in front of which a river with boats on the bank, and to the right of it nearer the foreground a derrick and shed appertaining to the production of salt and petroleum. In the foreground a meadow with cattle and sheep feeding and reposing, the whole indicating the leading characteristics, productions and pursuits of the State of this time. Above the mountains, &c., the sun emerging from the clouds, indicating that former obstacles to our prosperity are disappearing. In the rays of the sun, the motto *Libertas e Fidelitate,* (in English, 'liberty from loyalty,') indicating that our freedom and independence are the result of faithfulness to the principles of the Declaration of Independence and the National Constitution." [75]

WISCONSIN

The present seal of the State of Wisconsin was adopted by an act of the legislature approved on April 1, 1881. The law says:

"Section 1. The coat of arms of the state of Wisconsin is hereby declared to be as follows, viz:

"ARMS. Or, quartered, the quarters bearing respectively a plow, a crossed shovel and pick, an arm and held hammer, and an anchor, all proper; the base of shield resting upon a horn of plenty and pyramid of pig lead, all proper; over all, on fesse point, the arms and motto of the United States, viz.: *Arms*, palewise of thirteen pieces argent and gules; a chief azure; *motto* (on garter surrounding in escutcheon), 'E pluribus unum.'

"CREST. A badger, passant, proper.

"SUPPORTERS. Dexter, a sailor holding a coil of rope, proper; sinister, a yeoman resting on a pick, proper.

"MOTTO. Over crest, 'Forward.'

"Section 2. The great seal of the state shall consist of a metallic disc, two and three-eighths inches in diameter, containing, within an ornamental border, the following devices and legend, viz: The coat of arms of the state, as in this act described; above the arms, in a line parallel with the border, the words, 'Great Seal of the State of Wisconsin;' in the exergue, in a curved line, thirteen stars.

"Section 3. As the present great seal of the state has become so worn as to be incapable of making a fair impression, the governor is hereby authorized and directed to procure a new great seal, as hereinabove described, to be engraved in the best manner, with a suitable press for taking impressions therefrom; and thereafter to cause the great seal now in the keeping of the secretary of state to be defaced by filing two marks at right angles across the face of the same. The great seal now kept by the secretary of state shall continue to be used until the fourth day of

---

[75] *Laws of West Virginia, 1863: Acts of the Legislature of West Virginia at Its First Session, Commencing June 20th, 1863* (John F. M'Dermot, Public Printer, Wheeling, West Virginia, 1863) p. 274-5.

July, 1881, and thereafter the new seal, herein provided for, shall be used as the great seal of the state." [76]

WYOMING

The Great Seal of the State of Wyoming was adopted by an act of the Wyoming legislature, approved February 15, 1921, amending and re-enacting an act of 1920.

The act reads:

"Section 1. That Section 1, Wyoming Compiled Statutes 1920, be amended and re-enacted to read as follows:

" 'Section 1. There shall be a great seal of the State of Wyoming, which shall be of the following design, viz: A circle one and one-half inches in diameter, on the outer edge or rim of which shall be engraven the words 'Great Seal of the State of Wyoming,' and the design shall conform substantially to the following description: A pedestal, showing on the front thereof an eagle resting upon a shield, said shield to have engraven thereon a star and the figures, '44', being the number of Wyoming in the order of admission to statehood. Standing upon the pedestal shall be a draped figure of a woman modeled after the statue of the 'Victory of the Louvre,' from whose wrists shall hang links of a broken chain, and holding in her right hand a staff from the top of which shall float a banner with the words 'Equal Rights' thereon, all suggesting the political position of woman in this state. On either side of the pedestal, and standing at the base thereof, shall be male figures typifying the live stock and mining industries of Wyoming. Behind the pedestal, and in the background, shall be two pillars, each supporting a lighted lamp, signifying the light of knowledge. Around each pillar shall be a scroll with the following words thereon: On the right of the central figure the words 'Live Stock,' and 'Grain,' and on the left the words 'Mines' and 'Oil.' At the base of the pedestal, and in front, shall appear the figures '1869-1890' the former date signifying the organization of the territory of Wyoming, and the latter the date of its admission to statehood.' "

[76] *Laws of Wisconsin, 1881: The Laws of Wisconsin Passed at the Annual Session of the Legislature of 1881, together with Joint Resolutions,* published by authority (David Atwood, State Printer, Madison, Wisconsin, 1881) chap. 280, sec. 2 and 3, p. 353.

"Section 2. This act shall take effect and be in force from and after April 1, 1921." [77]

[77] *Session Laws of Wyoming, 1921: Session Laws of the State of Wyoming Passed by the Sixteenth State Legislature Convened at Cheyenne, January 11, 1921, Adjourned February 19, 1921,* W. E. Chaplin, compiled and published under Statutory Authority (The Laramie Printing Company, Printers, Laramie, Wyoming, 1921) chap. 49, p. 38, 39.

CHAPTER V

INTERPRETATION OF THE INSIGNIA ON THE STATE SEALS

People generally know that each state has a Great Seal, that there is a keeper of this seal, and that an impression of it is attached to important state documents; but perhaps comparatively few people have had the opportunity of studying in detail the coats of arms, the crests, the supporters, and other insignia depicted on the state seals.

It will probably be of interest to those reading this chapter to know that some of the facts which it contains were obtained from the impressions of the Great Seals of the various states by carefully studying them under a high-powered magnifying glass.

Those who have never made a systematic study of the symbolical messages on the Great Seals of the various states have yet a store of information open to them which is almost as fascinating as the contents of the cave in the *Arabian Nights,* which could be opened only by the magic command of Ali Baba or his forty thieves, "Open Sesame."

Since all of the states combined constitute the Union, perhaps it would not be amiss to describe, first, the Great Seal of the United States.

A design for the shield of this seal was suggested to John Adams, a member of the Committee on Seals, by a noted English antiquarian and friend of America, Sir John Prestwick. His suggestion was " 'A Norman shield, party per pale of thirteen stripes, white and red; the chief of the escutcheon blue, and spangled with thirteen stars, thus signifying the. protection of Heaven over the States.' " [1] This is very similar to the first design submitted by Wil-

---

[1] *Story of the Great Seal of the United States or History of American Emblems,* B. J. Cigrand (Cameron, Amberg Company, Chicago, Illinois, 1903) p. 211-12.

liam Barton, "'differing only in the spangling of the
stars; the English aristocrat places the stars on the shield,
while Will Barton placed them in the blue heavens above
the shield, a more real and significant manner by far than
our friend across the sea proposes.' " [1]

The seal adopted is based on Barton's first design, very
slightly modified by the suggestions of Prestwick. The
stars are placed above the shield in a crest as in Barton's
design.

The Great Seal of the United States, three inches in
diameter, having both obverse and reverse sides, was
adopted on June 20, 1782.

Before describing any of the seals, it will be well to get
clearly in mind what a seal really is, and if necessary, to
disabuse our minds of the impression that a seal is a die, or
stamp, by which an impress, or a seal, is made. Pilcher
says: "It should be observed that the seal is the impression
made upon a plastic material by compression between the
plates of a seal-press. The error of referring to the seal-
press as a seal, is not uncommon, and has crept into some
of the dictionaries, but strict accuracy dictates the rejec-
tion of its employment in that sense. A seal, then, is an
impressed device attached to a paper for purposes of
authentication, and the instrument, by which it is made is
a seal-press or stamp." [2]

The obverse side of the Great Seal of the United States
is all that has been cut up to the present time. The technical description, or blazon of this part of the seal is as
follows:

"ARMS: Paleways stripes of thirteen pieces, argent and
gules; a chief, azure; the escutcheon on the breast of the
American eagle displayed proper, holding in his dexter
[right] talon an olive branch, and in his sinister [left] a
bundle of thirteen arrows, all proper, and in his beak a
scroll, inscribed with this motto, 'E Pluribus Unum.' " [3]

[2] *The Seal and Arms of Pennsylvania*, James Evelyn Pilcher (William Stanley Ray, State Printer, Harrisburg, Pennsylvania, 1902) p. 3.

[3] *Story of the Great Seal of the United States or History of American Emblems*, B. J. Cigrand (Cameron, Amberg Company, Chicago, Illinois, 1903) p. 253.

The technical blazon of the circular figure, or crest, above the eagle's head is as follows:

" 'Over the head of the eagle, which appears above the escutcheon, a glory, or, breaking through a cloud, proper, and surrounding thirteen stars, forming a constellation, argent, on an azure field.' "

So far the reverse side of the seal has never been cut. As adopted, it contains:

"A pyramid unfinished. In the zenith, an eye in a triangle, surrounded with a glory proper. Over the eye these words, 'Annuit Coeptis.' On the base of the pyramid the numerical letters, MDCCLXXVI, And underneath the following motto, 'Novas Ordo Seclorum.' "

The technical descriptions given above are taken from the report of the secretary to whom the several reports on the device for a Great Seal were referred, and who gives the coat of arms and insignia of the Great Seal of the United States which were adopted June 20, 1782. [4]

The chief, or top part of the shield, represents the Congress of the United States, and the pales or stripes below it typify the states of the Union. The chief is always considered the place of honor on a shield; and this place is given to the central government on the United States seal, in token of its preeminent position. The blue color of the chief stands for the protection of Heaven to the new union of states. [5] In blazonry, blue signifies vigilance, perseverance and justice. [6]

The individual states are held together by the chief, or the central union, and each in turn helps hold the others together and thus to support the Union. The shield as a whole stands for military strength and protection. The fact that the escutcheon has no other supporters than the eagle signifies that the American government is self-supporting.

---

[4] *The Seal of the United States—How It Was Developed and Adopted,* Gaillard Hunt (Department of State, Washington, D. C. 1892) p. 23-4.
[5] *The Coat of Arms, Crest and Great Seal of the United States of America: The Emblem of the Independent Sovereignty of the Nation: History and Meaning Illustrated,* Leonard Wilson (Leonard Wilson, San Deigo, California, 1928) p. 40.
[6] *The Seal of the United States—How It Was Developed and Adopted,* Gaillard Hunt (Department of State, Washington, D. C. 1892) p. 22

The white color of the pales denotes "purity and in-nocence" [7]; and the red, "hardiness and valor." [7]

The eagle, often called the *King of Birds,* has been con-sidered throughout the ages the symbol of supreme author-ity and power, and of strength and nobility. On the United States Seal it signifies the power and authority of Congress. It was used as a symbol by the Persians, the Assyrians, the Egyptians, and finally it became the symbol of the Roman legions. During the following centuries, Germany, Austria, Prussia, and the French Empire adopted the eagle as a heraldic device. The double-headed eagle is used as a bearing on Russian, Austrian, and German arms.

Thirteen, the number of olives and of leaves on the branch, and the number of arrows held by the eagle, alludes to the thirteen original states.

The arrows stand for military protection, readiness for war, and preparedness for military service. The olive branch in his right talon justifies the inference that the United States Government prefers peace to war.

The arrows are feathered and turned point upward, in flying position, further signifying readiness in war.

The scroll or ribbon held in the beak of the eagle is an appropriate place for the motto, *E Pluribus Unum.*

In natural symbolism the stars stand for immensity of space and for an overseeing power; the sun is the source of life, and, together with the rain-cloud, it is the sus-tainer of all earthly life. The rayed sun has come to be the symbol of glory and of hope.

In heraldic symbolism the stars denote divine protec-tion; the rays of the sun, absolute power; and the clouds, sublimity and stateliness.

The stars, or mullets in the crest, are thirteen in num-ber, and again refer to the thirteen original states. The constellation denotes " 'a new State [Nation] taking its place and rank among the sovereign powers.' "

[7] *The Seal of the United States—How It Was Developed and Adopted,* Gaillard Hunt (Department of State, Washington, D.C. 1892) p. 24-5.

The pyramid on the reverse side of the seal symbolizes the strength and lasting qualities of the new Union, and the fact that it was built with care and patience. It was left unfinished to show that there was room for expansion by the addition of new states. The fact that the pyramid is unfinished signifies also that the complete development of the United States Government had not, at the time of the cutting of the seal, been realized.

The mystic triangle above the pyramid with the eye and the fringe of sun's rays signifies the Creator of the Universe, and that He is the supreme builder. The triangle itself stands for perfection and is the symbol of the Deity. The all-seeing eye denotes "the ever-watchful providence" and power of God. His eternal glory is set forth in the rays of the sun. The Holy Trinity, Father, Son, and Holy Spirit, are represented by the form of the equilateral triangle. [8]

The date at the bottom of the pyramid, 1776, is that of the signing of the Declaration of Independence or of the birth of the new nation.

As to the origin of the motto on the obverse side of the seal, *E Pluribus Unum*, some scholars are of the opinion that it came from the identical expression found on the title page of the *Gentlemen's Magazine*, an English publication which had a wide circulation in the American colonies from the appearance of its first number in 1731. On the title page of the first volume of the magazine named above was the device, a hand holding a bunch of flowers, and the epigraph, *E Pluribus Unum*.

Another possible origin is this:

Essay Number 148 in *The Spectator* of August 20, 1711, opens with a Latin phrase: *Exempta juvat spiris e pluribus una*, translated freely: *Better one thorn plucked out than all remain.* This particular essay was written by Richard

---

[*] For a noteworthy discussion of the symbolism of the devices shown on the obverse side of the Great Seal, see *The Coat of Arms, Crest and Great Seal of the United States of America: The Emblems of the Independent Sovereignty of the Nation: History and Meaning Illustrated.* Leonard Wilson (Leonard Wilson, San Diego, California, 1928) p. 25-33.

Steele. The Latin expression given above is found in Horace's *Second Book of Epistles.*

A Virgilian origin is quite commonly ascribed to the motto. In line 103 of the *Moretum,* a poem written by Virgil, appears the phrase *Color est e pluribus unus.* The poem deals with the making of a salad. It is thought to be the first known use of this phrase in any form.

In 1776 the Continental Congress ordered the President to have a seal, and *E Pluribus Unum* appeared on this seal. It was also used on some of the early American coins, and is still employed on the coins of the United States today. Congress adopted this motto in 1781.

There are a few unauthenticated sources given for this quotation, and several suggested ones have proved to be of much later origin than its first use on the Great Seal. [9]

The motto, *E Pluribus Unum,* though capable of many different interpretations, is generally taken to mean *From many, one,* and to refer to the separate colonies being combined into one nation.

The motto over the eye, *Annuit Coeptis,* is found in Virgil's *Aeneid,* Book IX, line 625, where it appears in the form: *Audacibus annue coeptis,* meaning *Favor the bold attempts.* It is also found in Virgil's *Georgics,* Book I, line 40. In the exact form used on the shield, it means *He* [God] *has favored our undertakings.* William Barton changed and curtailed this motto to its present form.

Virgil's phrase, *Magnus ab integro saeclorum nascitur ordo,* which means *A great series of ages begins anew,* as found in Eclogue I, line 5, was likewise shortened and changed by William Barton, when he submitted his design for a seal, to *Novus Ordo Seclorum,* signifying *A new series of ages.*

In discussing the state seals, they will be grouped together and treated according to certain common symbols or characteristics instead of discussing them separately.

[9] For further discussion of various theories of the origin of this phrase, see *Story of the Great Seal of the United States,* B. J. Cigrand (Cameron, Amberg and Company, Chicago, Illinois, 1903) p. 343-61.

DATES

A wealth of historical information can be gathered from the dates found on the Great Seals of the states. These record the dates of settlements, of the formation of territories, and of the admission of states into the Union; dates of the ratification of constitutions, of the reports of committees, and of the adoption of state seals; important dates in history; dates of significant political issues, and that of the signing of the *Declaration of Independence.*

Three state seals, those of Michigan, Missouri, and New Jersey, have their dates in Roman numerals.

Michigan's seal has MDCCCXXXV (1835), which is the date when Honorable Lewis Cass presented to the members of the first State Constitutional Convention the design for the State seal.

Missouri has on her seal the date MDCCCXX (1820), in which year, on March 6, the *Missouri Compromise* was passed.

The Roman numerals, MDCCLXXVI (1776), on New Jersey's seal, represent the date of the signing of the *Declaration of Independence,* and also that of the report of the committee to prepare the Great Seal of New Jersey.

The following twenty-five states have the dates on their seals in Arabic numerals:

Arizona, Colorado, Delaware, the District of Columbia, Georgia, Illinois, Indiana, Kansas, Maryland, Minnesota, Nebraska, New Hampshire, New Mexico, North Carolina, North Dakota, Oklahoma, Oregon, Rhode Island, South Carolina, South Dakota, Tennessee, Utah, Washington, West Virginia, and Wyoming.

The seal of Arizona has 1912, the date of her admission into the Union.

Colorado has on her seal 1876, the date of her admission to statehood.

Neither of the dates on the seal of Delaware is that of her admission into the Union. The first one, 1793, is that of the ordering of the third Great Seal of the State. The second, 1847, marks the date of the ordering of the fourth and last Great Seal of the State.

The seal of the District of Columbia displays the figures, 1871, the date on which the design of the seal was approved.

The seal of Georgia carries the date 1776, the year in which she elected five delegates to represent her at the Continental Congress, and in which, on July 4, the *Declaration of Independence* was signed. Georgia also adopted her first Constitution in 1776. She also has on the reverse side of her seal the date 1799, the year in which the cutting of the seal, after the formation of the third Constitution in 1798, was made.

Various dates appear on the State seal of Illinois. The inscription on the edge, below the seal proper, is August 26, 1818, the date of the adoption of the first State Constitution by the State Constitutional Convention which convened at Kaskaska on August 26, 1818. It has also two dates on the face of the seal, one of which is 1818, the date of its admission into the Union on December 3. The other date on the seal of Illinois, 1868, seems to be the date of the year in which the seal giving the present arrangement of the State motto was cut and first used.

The date, 1816, on Indiana's seal is both that of her admission to statehood and that of the act providing for a State seal.

The seal of Kansas gives the exact date of her admission into the Union, January 29, 1861.

Maryland's seal shows the figures, 1632, as the date of the year in which the Charter of Maryland was signed. The present seal of Maryland was adopted by the joint resolutions of her governing bodies in the year 1876.

The seal of Minnesota gives the date 1858, the year of her admission to statehood; and Nebraska's seal, March 1, 1867, the full date of her admission.

New Hampshire shows on her seal the figures, 1776, the date of the signing of the *Declaration of Independence*.

The seal of New Mexico shows the date, 1912, the year in which her legislature first met after she had been granted statehood by the Senate in 1910.

North Carolina proudly records on her State seal the date May 20, 1775, that of the *Mecklenburg Declaration of Independence*. This was the first declaration of its kind in America and was made by the citizens of Mecklenburg County as a declaration of their independence from Great Britain. According to tradition, it was sent to the Continental Congress.

Both North and South Dakota have on their seals the same figures 1889, the date of the year in which they were admitted into the Union.

The people of Oklahoma having adopted their State Constitution in 1907, the State was admitted into the Union that same year; so the date on the State seal commemorates these facts.

Oregon's seal displays one date 1859, that of her admission into the Union; but the seal of Rhode Island records the date 1636, that of her first settlement.

South Carolina's seal has the date 1776, which is that of the *Declaration of Independence,* also that on which an independent government was set up by the Provincial Congress of South Carolina, March 26, 1776.

Tennessee being admitted into the Union on June 1, 1796, records the year of her admission on her seal.

Utah's seal records two dates: 1847, the date of her first settlement; and 1896, the year of her admission into the Union on January the fourth.

The State of Washington shows on her seal the year of her admission into the Union, 1889 (November 11), while West Virginia's seal records the full date of the founding of the State, June 20, 1863.

Wyoming, in one date on her seal, 1869, commemorates the organization of the Territorial government. This seal also displays the figures 1890, which is the date of Wyoming's admission into the Union.

The names of the twenty-one states which do not have any dates on their seals are as follows: Alabama, Arkansas, California, Connecticut, Florida, Idaho, Iowa, Kentucky, Louisiana, Maine, Massachusetts, Mississippi, Montana, Nevada, New York, Ohio, Pennsylvania, Texas, Vermont, Virginia, and Wisconsin.

Tennessee and Wyoming are unique in the fact that they are the only states whose seals record dates showing the order of their admission into the Union. Tennessee gives the Roman numerals XVI at the top of her seal, showing that she was the sixteenth state to enter the Union. On the small shield at the bottom of the seal of the State of Wyoming, her order of admission is shown in Arabic numerals, 44, signifying that (counting the District of Columbia) she was the forty-fourth state to be admitted into the Union.

Most of the seals are circular, ranging from one and one-half to four inches in diameter. The seal of Connecticut alone, being elliptical, varies in form from those of the other states.

LANDSCAPES

The landscapes depicted on the Great Seals of the states represent a very high type of art. They show a considerable variety of scenery, including mountains, plains, rivers, oceans, lakes, and other scenes. Much of the scenery depicted on the landscapes is native to the states upon whose seals they are pictured.

Several of the states have seals on which landscapes do not figure prominently but merely furnish the base upon which other insignia rest. These are: Arkansas; Kentucky, whose seal has the picture of a landscape with two men standing on a precipice in the foreground; Maine, the seal of which sketches a landscape outside of the shield, on which two men are standing, but the landscape depicted inside the shield is prominent; New Jersey, whose seal delineates a small landscape supporting two figures; New York, the design of the landscape on the main seal being scant, but that on the inside of the shield being very prominently pictured; and North Carolina, the seal of which sketches a landscape as a base upon which classical figures are placed.

Besides the seals which use landscapes for purely utilitarian purposes, there are many which use plains. Idaho on the main part of her shield shows plains with vegetation growing on the right. Illinois represents on her seal prairie lands which are so typical of this State. The seal of Indiana pictures a forest and a prairie with the surface somewhat undulated.

Montana's seal represents plains with trees, and North Dakota's pictures a plain with a tree and the sun setting behind the plain. Ohio delineates a plain in the foreground on her seal; but in the center of hers, Oklahoma sketches a plain upon which men are standing. At the top of Tennessee's seal there is shown a plain with a stalk of cotton, a sheaf of wheat, and a plow.

West Virginia has landscapes on both sides of the State seal. On the obverse side, a landscape displaying a boulder, growing corn, a bundle of wheat, and two men in the foreground.

WATER AND STREAMS

Of the seals picturing water and streams, three have seashores. Georgia has a seashore on the reverse side of her seal; Oregon pictures the shore of the Pacific Ocean on her shield; and South Carolina, in the right panel of her seal, sketches the seashore on which the figure, *Hope,* stands, and on the left panel, a seashore on which is growing a palmetto tree.

Waterfalls are depicted to the right on the state seals of Minnesota and Montana.

Two state seals picture oceans. On the top of her shield Pennsylvania represents a ship on the ocean. Oregon's seal displays a picture of the Pacific Ocean with a steamship, and a brig flying the American colors.

New Hampshire's seal sketches a body of water with a ship on the stocks.

In addition to the Pacific Ocean, some of the other
bodies of water sketched on the state seals are native to
the states picturing them. On the seal of the District of
Columbia the river represented is the Potomac with the
Virginia shore in the background. The river pictured on
the shield of Idaho's seal is the Snake river with the Owy-
hee Mountains on one side and the Pannock and Bannock
Mountains on the other. The Mississippi river is depicted
in the background of the landscape of Iowa's seal.

Michigan is the only state that represents a peninsula
on her seal.

The body of water pictured on California's seal is
designated as a "bay or river which winds its course
among the majestic mountains on either side." [10]

Tennessee delineates a river in the lower part of her
seal on which is a boat.

Florida's seal depicts a body of water on which is a
paddle-wheeled steamboat with sail rigging on its front.
The seal of Oregon delineates the Pacific Ocean bearing
a steamship displaying sails.

Kansas pictures a river on her seal; Montana, the
Missouri river with waterfalls; and Nebraska, the Missouri river in the background.

The lower right-hand ray of the five pointed star composing the seal of Oklahoma pictures a canoe.

There is a river with boats on it pictured in the center
of the reverse side of the seal of West Virginia.

TREES

Trees are imaged on many of the state seals. Florida
depicts on her seal the cocoa tree; and Vermont, on her
shield, the pine tree. Maine's seal delineates the pine tree
also; and South Carolina, the palmetto which has been
used for building fortifications.

North Dakota pictures on her seal one tree on a plain;
the seals of Nebraska, Nevada, and Oregon depict trees

[10] *The Origin and History of the American Flag,* George Henry Preble
(Nicholas L. Brown, Philadelphia, Pennsylvania, 1917) vol. 2, p. 649.

on mountain-sides, probably representing the snowline. On the reverse side of her seal, Georgia represents a tree shading a flock of sheep.

Indiana's seal shows two trees standing, the larger one being in front, and a third one having been cut down.

FIELDS

Fields, both cultivated and primitive, are depicted on various state seals. Kansas pictures a man plowing in a field in the foreground of her seal. South Dakota's seal represents a field of corn in the right background. The seal of Arizona displays an irrigated field; and that of Delaware, a level field around the escutcheon. On the reverse side of Georgia's seal there is a sketch of a farmer plowing a field.

Arizona's seal depicts irrigated fields and orchards. The seal of the State of Iowa shows the picture of a landscape upon which a field of wheat is standing. Nebraska's seal delineates a field with wheat shocks and stalks of growing corn.

In the front of her seal, South Dakota shows a man plowing and cattle and a field of corn. Utah pictures on her seal sego lilies growing in a field.

ROCKS

As to rocks, West Virginia depicts one on her seal; Minnesota, several which surround waterfalls; and Illinois has the image of a rock on her seal.

THE RISING SUN

In order to comprehend the significance of the rising sun pictured on the state seals, one must turn to ancient symbolism. In the Egyptian, Phoenician, and Syrian mysteries, as well as elsewhere in ancient symbolism, the rising sun stands for eternal life, for the regeneration of the soul, or for its resurrection after death. Mountains have always stood for strength and grandeur. On these seals, where the sun is pictured as rising from behind the mountains, it signifies the dawn of a new day or the rise of a state.

The sun rising from behind mountains is depicted on the seals of Arizona, Florida, Idaho, Kansas, Nevada, New York, and Ohio. Illinois on her seal represents the sun rising over a prairie, and Michigan on her shield depicts the sun rising over a lake. Nevada's seal depicts two mountains in the foreground with a range of mountains in the far background over which the sun is rising. The seal of New Hampshire sketches the sun rising over a ship on the stocks. The District of Columbia pictures the rising sun. On the reverse side of her seal, West Virginia delineates the risen sun emerging from behind clouds which indicates that the State is going forward, the former obstacles of her progress having been removed.

MOUNTAINS

Mountains are pictured on the state seals other than in connection with a rising sun as follows: California's seal represents snow-capped mountains. The seal of Colorado sketches on its shield three mountains which are snow-capped. Nevada's seal depicts two mountains in the foreground with a range of mountains in the background. Idaho pictures a range of mountains. The seal of Montana depicts mountains, and Nebraska's seal represents the Rocky Mountains in the distance. South Dakota displays on her seal a sketch of four hills in the left background. The seal of Vermont depicts mountains on its shield in the background. Virginia has mountains on the obverse side of her seal, and West Virginia's seal represents them on the reverse side.

IMMIGRATION AND SETTLEMENT

Immigration and settlement have a comparatively small representation on the state seals, only six out of the forty-nine states picturing them.

The seal of Indiana delineates a woodman or pioneer chopping down a tree, by which act the westward trend of civilization is indicated.

Kansas sketches on her seal a settler's cabin and a train of covered wagons with their teams heading toward the West.

Minnesota pictures on her seal a settler's gun leaning against a stump with a powder horn suspended from its muzzle and a settler plowing, all of which are indicative of a transitional period. The gun is depicted to denote that defense against the Indians was at that time necessary, and also that the settlers could not depend entirely upon agricultural products for sustenance without the aid of game.

The seal of Nebraska delineates a settler's cabin; and that of Oregon, a four-horse covered wagon such as was used by immigrants. West Virginia pictures to the right on the obverse side of her seal, a farmer in hunting-shirt with a woodman's ax on his left arm. The image of the ax indicates that some of the land has still to be cleared of the primeval forests.

INDIANS

Indians are fairly well represented on the great seals of the states.

Florida depicts in the foreground of her seal an Indian woman scattering flowers. The seal of Kansas pictures two mounted Indians pursuing retreating buffaloes.

The seal of Massachusetts shows the image of an Indian chief in shirt and moccasins with an arrow in his left hand, and a bow in his right. He is pictured not as a hostile Indian, but as one who is friendly to the settlers.

North Dakota pictures on the left side of her seal a bow crossed with three arrows, and an Indian on horseback chasing and about to spear a buffalo.

The fact that Oklahoma is now the center of Indian civilization is shown by the fact that her State seal is composed of the seals of five Indian nations, and by its having an Indian sketched in the center. In the ray directed upward, stands the image of an Indian warrior upright with bow and shield; in the upper right-hand ray, a tomahawk, a bow, and three crossed arrows are pictured. In the lower right-hand ray is represented a village with houses and a factory beside a lake upon which an Indian paddling a canoe is depicted.

As civilization advanced, the Indian receded farther towards the West. On Minnesota's seal the red man is pictured as retreating before the advance of the white man. On that of Kansas, there are two mounted Indians who are pursuing buffaloes toward the West.

Agricultural Implements and Products

That agriculture is recognized as a basic industry by the inhabitants of the majority of the states of the Union is evidenced by the fact that twenty-eight states delineate on their coats of arms or on their seals insignia representative of agricultural implements or agricultural products.

The plow is pictured on the state seals more frequently than any of the other farming tools or implements. The seals of sixteen states depict plows; namely, Arkansas, Georgia, Iowa, Kansas, Minnesota, Montana, New Jersey, Nevada, North Dakota, Oklahoma, Oregon, Pennsylvania, South Dakota, Tennessee, West Virginia, Wisconsin. New Jersey on her shield delineates three plows, the only farming tools she depicts.

Georgia's seal pictures a man plowing. The seal of Kansas depicts a farmer with a span of horses hitched to a plow.

Minnesota on her seal represents a farmer holding a plow; and South Dakota, a farmer and a span of horses hitched to a plow.

The ax is delineated on two state seals, that of Indiana which has no other agricultural insignia, and that of West Virginia. The latter state pictures on her seal a plow, a farmer in hunting-shirt, a woodman's ax, an anvil, and a sledge hammer.

Scythes are represented on only one state seal, that of Maine which depicts a farmer and a scythe. The state seals of Iowa and Nevada depict sickles in combination with other farming tools.

The anvil is represented on three state seals; namely, Nebraska, which depicts a man working at an anvil; North Dakota, which images an anvil, plow and sledge; and West Virginia, which pictures an anvil and sledge hammer.

Iowa's seal sketches a plow, a sickle, and a rake.

Of the state seals depicting agricultural insignia, twenty sketch agricultural implements; and twenty-one delineate agricultural products. Of the state seals delineating agricultural products or implements, fourteen of each show both implements and products, leaving six which have implements only, and seven which depict products only.

Of the agricultural products depicted on the state seals, the single sheaf of wheat appears most often. The seals of five states picture it; namely, Arkansas, Nevada, Ohio, Oklahoma, and Oregon. Six states sketch on their seals a sheaf of wheat and one other agricultural product as follows: Iowa: a sheaf of wheat and standing wheat Nebraska, three sheaves of wheat and stalks of growing corn; North Dakota, three bundles of wheat surrounding a tree; Tennessee delineating in the upper central part of her seal a sheaf of wheat, and to the right, a stalk of cotton; Vermont, three sheaves of wheat; and West Virginia depicting a sheaf of wheat lying down and a stalk of corn.

The seal of Connecticut pictures three fruited grape vines supported by stakes. Delaware's seal sketches a sheaf of wheat, an ear of maize, and a cow. The District of Columbia depicts on her seal a sheaf of wheat and other agricultural products. On the reverse of her seal representing the exports of her state, Georgia pictures bales of cotton and hogsheads of tobacco. Idaho's seal has the images of a sheaf of wheat and two cornucopias containing fruits.

The figure of the *Goddess Ceres* on New Jersey's seal holds in her hand a cornucopia containing apples, plums, and grapes surrounded by leaves. She has a chaplet of wheat spears. The seal of North Carolina pictures the *Goddess Ceres* holding three heads or ears of wheat in one hand, and in the other, a cornucopia pouring out farm products.

Pennsylvania's seal depicts as emblems of agriculture or husbandry a stalk of maize, three sheaves of wheat, and an olive branch.

South Dakota pictures on her seal a herd of cattle and a field of corn, these representing her dairying and farming interests.

Virginia on the reverse side of her seal displays the image of the *Goddess Ceres* with ears of wheat in one hand, and in the other, a cornucopia, the symbol of plenty or abundance.

Wisconsin's seal depicts a cornucopia pouring out farm products.

Ceres, the Goddess of Agriculture

Three of the state seals show the image of the *Goddess Ceres, the Goddess of Agriculture.* She was the goddess of growing things, of sprouting seeds, and of the fruiting of trees and plants. "She is always represented as fully draped, with ears of corn and poppies in her hands, and on her head a corn-measure." [11]

New Jersey's seal pictures the *Goddess Ceres* with the cornucopia filled with apples, grapes, plums, and other fruits.

North Carolina depicts on her seal the *Goddess of Liberty* and the *Goddess of Plenty,* or *Ceres.* The latter has three ears of wheat in her right hand; and in her left, the small end of her cornucopia which is pouring out its contents at her feet.

On the reverse of her seal Virginia represents the *Goddess Ceres* holding the cornucopia and ears of wheat.

[11] *The Encyclopedia Americana* (Americana Corporation, New York, 1929) vol. 6, p. 225.

Since the days of the Greeks and the Romans, the cornucopia has been very extensively used as the symbol of abundance. It is the usual emblem of plenty employed by the *Goddess Ceres*.

Idaho and Wisconsin each picture, at the bottom of their seals, cornucopias pouring out fruits on the ground, Idaho depicting two and Wisconsin displaying one. On the reverse side of her seal Virginia displays the image of the *Goddess Ceres* with the cornucopia, and New Jersey likewise displays the image of the *Goddess Ceres* on the obverse side of her seal. North Carolina's seal depicts the *Goddess of Liberty* and the *Goddess of Plenty*, the latter having in her left hand a cornucopia with its mouth pointing downward.

THE FISHING INDUSTRIES

Fishing is one of the prominent resources of the United States, the value of the annual products amounting to about $77,800,000. The fishing industry is very scantily represented on the state seals, Maryland being the only state that pictures it, she having as one of the supporters of her shield the image of a fisherman holding a fish in his left hand.

THE MINING INDUSTRIES

The value of the mining products in the United States is tremendous. This industry is well represented; twelve state seals depict miners, mines, or mining implements.

The seal of Arizona pictures a miner standing with a pick and a shovel; near him is depicted a quartz mill at his left. California's seal shows the image of a miner and his pick with which he is digging for gold in the rocks. On the ground beside him is pictured a miner's cradle.

On the lower part of her shield, Colorado images a miner's pick and a mallet crossed while Idaho sketches a miner with a pick on his shoulder and a shovel in his hand. Iowa pictures on her seal a lead furnace with a pile of piglead. Montana in the foreground of her seal delineates a miner's pick and shovel crossed in front of a plow.

Nevada's seal depicts a quartz-mill, and a tunnel entering the silver leads of a mountain. On this seal a miner is also pictured running out a carload of ore, and a team is sketched pulling a wagon loaded with ore towards the mill.

Oregon on the bottom of her shield represents a pick lying across a plow. South Dakota pictures a miner, a smelting furnace, and other features of mining work in the left foreground of her seal. West Virginia's seal shows the image of a miner with a pickax on his shoulder and lumps and barrels of mineral at his feet. Wisconsin in the top righthand corner of her seal pictures a miner's pick and shovel crossed.

At the base of the pedestal on her State seal Wyoming depicts figures typifying the live stock and mining industries of the State. The miner imaged has a pick. The word *Mines* is inscribed on the seal at the left of the central figure.

THE OIL INDUSTRY

Two states on their seals have representations of oil interests. West Virginia's seal on the reverse side pictures an oil shed and a derrick, and Wyoming on the pillars on her seal has inscribed the words *Grain, Mines, and Oil.*

COMMERCE AND TRANSPORTATION

Commerce and transportation are represented on seventeen state seals by boats, trains, and covered wagons.

Arkansas on her seal pictures a steamboat on a river; and California, a body of water with two clipper ships and one small ship. Delaware sketches a ship above the shield at the top of her seal. Florida's seal delineates a ship sailing on a body of water. Iowa on her seal represents the Steamer Iowa under weigh; and Kansas, a river and a steamboat symbolizing commerce.

The seal of Nebraska pictures a sidewheeler on a river, and that of New York images two sail ships approaching each other on a river. Oregon depicts on her seal a combination of a steam and a sailing vessel on a body of water; and Pennsylvania, a body of water on which is a sailing vessel.

South Dakota's seal pictures a steamboat on a river; and the seal of Tennessee, a body of water on which is a boat with the word *Commerce* inscribed below. On the ship pictured on Oregon's seal the sails are not being used.

The seals of four states depict trains or railroads. The District of Columbia delineates on her seal a railway train; and Nebraska, "a train of cars leading towards the Rocky Mountains." Nevada's seal sketches a train of cars passing a mountain gorge and a telegraph line following the railroad. The seal of West Virginia shows on its reverse the picture of a train of cars crossing the viaduct on the Baltimore and Ohio Railroad in Preston County. West Virginia is proud of this viaduct because it is "one of the great engineering triumphs of the age."

Two of the state seals depict wagons such as the immigrants used. These were discussed under the topic *Immigration and Settlement* above. The seal of Oregon sketches one covered wagon, and that of Kansas pictures a train of them.

FIGURES OF MEN

Twenty-five of the state seals delineate figures of men. The male figures imaged on the seals of five states, Kansas, Massachusetts, North Dakota, Oklahoma, and Minnesota, were discussed under the subject *Indians*. The seal of Kansas depicts a man plowing and two Indian men on horseback.

The male figures pictured on the seals of three states, Indiana, Minnesota, and West Virginia, were discussed under the heading of *Immigration and Settlement*. West Virginia also depicts a miner as one of the supporters of her shield.

The male figures imaged on the seals of Arizona, California, Idaho, Nevada, and Wyoming were discussed under the topic *Mining*.

South Dakota depicts both a miner, and a farmer at his plow. Delaware has the picture of a husbandman and a

hunter as supporters of the shield. The statue depicted
on the pedestal of the Great Seal of the District of Columbia represents George Washington. On the obverse
side of Georgia's seal there is depicted a man standing
with a drawn sword; and on the reverse, a man plowing.

Iowa pictures on her seal a citizen soldier; and Kentucky, two men shaking hands, one using his right hand
and the other his left.

The seal of Maine delineates a seaman leaning on an
anchor and a farmer resting on a scythe. For supporters
Maryland's seal sketches a plowman and a fisherman, the
former leaning on a spade.

Nebraska on her seal pictures a smith with his hammer
and anvil; Nevada, a miner running a carload of ore out
of a mine; and Oregon, a male figure standing on a man-
of-war.

Tennessee shows on her seal the image of a boatman
sitting at the end of a boat; the seal of Virginia depicts
a man prostrate under the foot of *Virtus,* the genius of
the Commonwealth; and Washington's seal sketches a
bust figure of General George Washington.

FIGURES OF WOMEN

Besides the *Goddess Ceres,* who has been considered
above, there are on the state seals the images of many
female figures, most of which represent classical or symbolical characters.

The *Goddess of Justice* is pictured on three state seals.
The seal of the District of Columbia sketches the *Goddess
of Justice* with a tablet in her left hand on which is inscribed the word *Constitution* in three lines, and a wreath
in her right hand. New York's seal has the image of the
Goddess of Justice, robed and blindfolded, holding a pair
of scales. The seal of Oklahoma also depicts the *Goddess
of Justice* holding her scales.

Arkansas on her seal delineates the figure of an angel,
on which is inscribed the word *Mercy.* Florida has on her
seal an Indian woman scattering flowers. The seal of

South Carolina sketches *Hope* advancing over swords and daggers.

The *Goddess of Liberty* is represented on various seals. Arkansas pictures at the top of her seal the *Goddess of Liberty,* holding in her right hand a liberty pole surmounted by a liberty cap, and in her left hand a wreath. New Jersey's seal depicts her standing sandalled with the pole and liberty cap in her left hand.

To the right of the shield on New York State's seal, stands the image of the *Goddess of Liberty* robed with the liberty cap and pole in her right hand, and her left hand supporting the shield.

The *Goddess of Liberty* depicted on North Carolina's seal bears in her right hand a scroll inscribed with the word *Constitution,* and in her left hand she has the liberty cap and pole.

On the reverse side of her seal Virginia delineates the *Goddess Libertas* with her riband and pileus, and in addition the *Goddess Aeternitas.*

Idaho's seal pictures the *Goddess of Justice* holding the liberty pole and a pair of balances, which symbol is generally associated with the *Goddess of Justice.*

The liberty cap originated among the Phrygians in their homeland in Asia Minor. They wore it during classical times to distinguish them from the primitive peoples of the land. As early as 750 B. C. they stamped the image of the cap on their coins and seals.

It was adopted by the Romans to designate the slaves who had been emancipated from those yet in servitude and was called the pileus. The liberty cap placed upon the spear was a part of the official insignia of Salturnius in use about 263 B. C.

The *Goddess of Liberty* with the cap on a staff was used in Du Simitere's design for the *Great Seal of the United States,* and this is the form in which it appears now on the state seals.

This cap has stood for liberty for at least twenty-seven centuries, and the spear or staff has been in use for nearly twenty-two centuries. The cap is pointed and was worn with the point forward.

The six state seals picturing the *Goddess of Liberty* depict the liberty pole and cap as her symbols. The seal of West Virginia delineates the liberty cap without the image of the goddess or of the liberty pole. Here the cap is pictured on top of two guns crossed to show that liberty was won through arms and that it will be maintained and defended by force of arms if necessary.

North Carolina's seal sketches the *Goddess of Liberty* and the *Goddess of Plenty*.

BOTH MEN AND WOMEN

California's seal represents a miner with a pick, and the *Goddess Minerva* dressed in her corselet and helmet, holding her spear and buckler. She is not chanting her war song, but is peacefully sitting. On her Aegis or shield is a Gorgon's head.

The seal of the District of Columbia depicts the *Goddess of Justice* dressed in the national colors and holding a scroll in her left hand. On the pedestal is represented a statue of George Washington.

Idaho delineates the *Goddess of Liberty* dressed as she is described above. Idaho's seal also pictures a miner with a pick.

In addition to the image of the *Goddess of Justice* with her scales, the seal of Oklahoma depicts a white man shaking hands with an Indian, and Indians on two of the seals of the Indian nations which seals help to make up the rays of the star on Oklahoma's State seal.

Virtus, the genius of the Commonwealth, is pictured on the State seal of Virginia. She is represented as an Amazon, and has under her foot the image of a prostrate man from whose head a crown has fallen. He holds a piece of broken chain in his left hand and in his right, a scourge. The male figure depicted represents *Tyranny,* which has been overcome by *Virtus.* She rests one hand upon a spear and holds in the other a sword.

Wyoming's seal delineates along with male figures the figure of a woman, draped and modeled after the statue of the *Victory of the Louvre*. At her head is pictured a scroll bearing the words *Equal Rights,* which refer particularly to the fact that Wyoming came into the Union as a pioneer in the equal suffrage movement.

THE LICTORS AND FASCES

The lictors and fasces were the symbol of power in Imperial Rome. The lictors were public servants, usually twelve in number, who attended the chief magistrates to fulfill their commands. Each bore upon his shoulder a bundle of reeds with an ax tied up in it, which together were called the fasces. The lictors preceded the chief magistrates in single file.

Colorado pictures on her State seal fasces, which denote governmental power and authority.

THE ALL-SEEING EYE

Colorado is the only state representing on her seal the all-seeing eye, which symbol was described and interpreted under the discussion of the Great Seal of the United States.

SWORDS AND OTHER IMPLEMENTS OF WARFARE

Five states delineate swords on their seals. The seal of Arkansas depicts a sword on the right-hand side with the word *Justice* inscribed on it. At the right of the last pillar on Georgia's seal stands the image of a man with a drawn sword, which represents the aid of the military forces in the defense of the Constitution.

Massachusetts, besides the bow and arrow, pictures on her seal an arm, clothed and ruffled, bent at the elbow, the hand of which is grasping a broadsword. New York's seal images the *Goddess of Justice* with a sword in her right hand.

On the obverse side of her seal Virginia depicts *Virtus* with a sword in one hand and a spear in the other. This is the only state except South Carolina with pictures of spears on its seal. The latter state has the images of two bundles of them supporting a palmetto tree.

Five state seals sketch guns. On Delaware's seal the hunter depicted has a gun in his left hand, and Iowa on her seal represents a citizen soldier supporting the American flag and liberty cap in one hand and a gun in the other. Michigan on her seal images a man standing on a peninsula with a gun in his hand. The seal of Minnesota has, resting against a stump, a gun with a powder horn hanging from its muzzle. The obverse side of the seal of West Virginia depicts two guns crossed, upon which is placed a liberty cap.

Nine states image bows, arrows, or both bows and arrows on their seals.

The seal of Massachusetts pictures an Indian chief with a bow and arrow. Several state seals delineate the eagle with arrows in his talons. On the seals of Mississippi and Oregon the eagles depicted on the shields each hold three arrows. New Mexico shows an eagle with three arrows held in both talons. On the left of North Dakota's seal there is pictured a bow crossed with three arrows.

Seventeen arrows are imaged on the left foreground of the seal of Ohio. Utah's seal depicts six arrows passed through a hole at the top of the shield.

The seal of Oklahoma delineates the greatest number of Indian symbols. In the center of the star, which represents the arms of the State, is pictured an Indian with his bow. In the upper right-hand ray the ancient seal of the Choctaw nation depicts a tomahawk, a bow, and three arrows crossed. In the ray directed upward, which contains the ancient seal of the Chickasaw nation, is imaged an Indian warrior standing upright with a bow and shield.

South Carolina's seal depicts *Hope* walking on the sea-shore, with the way around her littered with the swords and daggers of her conquered enemies.

EAGLES

The Indians were probably the first in America to use the eagle in an emblematic manner. They used him with his wings outspread, and to them he stood for speed and wisdom. They also used his feathers to decorate their head-dresses.

The Hessian soldiers were the first in America to use the eagle as an armorial bearing. They displayed the picture of this bird as a device on their flag at the battle of Trenton in 1776. [12]

Washington's life guard in 1777 was the second to use the image of the eagle as an armorial device. They employed that of the American eagle.

In 1781 the New York soldiers bore a colonial standard, the crest of which was the image of the American eagle.

Thirteen states represent the eagle on their seals in one form or another.

Arkansas on her seal delineates the eagle. The seal of New Mexico pictures both the American and the Mexican eagles, the American overshadowing the Mexican one.

Illinois designates the eagle depicted on her seal as the American spread eagle, which is the one used on several of the state seals as well as the one used on the Great Seal of the United States.

The State seal of New York depicts the heraldic eagle, not the American eagle of today.

The other states picturing the eagle on their seals are Alabama, Iowa, Michigan, Mississippi, Missouri, Oregon, Pennsylvania, Utah, and Wyoming.

OTHER ANIMALS AND BIRDS

One bird other than the eagle is depicted on the state seals. The pelican with her young is sketched as the sole device on the State seal of Louisiana.

---

[12] For a discussion of the various uses of the eagle as an armorial device, see *Story of the Great Seal of the United States or History of American Emblems*, B. J. Cigrand (Cameron, Amberg and Company, Chicago, Illinois, 1903) p. 374-6.

The image of ten different animals are displayed on state seals; namely, the bear, beaver, buffalo, bull, cow, elk, horse, lion, moose, and the sheep.

The grizzly bear is pictured on California's seal, and two grizzlies are delineated on that of Missouri. The beaver is imaged on the crest of Wisconsin's seal.

Indiana, Kansas, and North Dakota depict the buffalo on their seals. The seal of Kansas represents buffaloes and horses—a man plowing with a horse, four horses to each of the immigrants' covered wagons, and two Indians on horseback pursuing buffaloes. The seal of North Dakota pictures an Indian on horseback, pursuing a buffalo.

Besides Kansas and North Dakota, Minnesota depicts on her seal one horse; Oregon, four horses hitched to a settler's wagon; and South Dakota, two farm horses.

Delaware's seal shows the image of a bull, and Vermont's, that of a red cow.

Idaho delineates on her seal a moose's head; Maine, a moose deer; and Michigan, a moose and an elk; while the seal of Oregon displays an elk with branching antlers.

The reverse of Pennsylvania's seal depicts the *Goddess of Liberty* trampling upon a lion, the emblem of *Tyranny*.

A flock of sheep is pictured in the background on the reverse side of Georgia's seal; and cattle and sheep, on the reverse of West Virginia's.

At the top of her seal, New Jersey displays as a crest a heraldic horse's head.

BEEHIVES

Two seals, those of Arkansas and Utah, represent bee-hives, symbols of industry.

Arkansas's seal depicts a beehive and a plow in the middle of the shield; and Utah images on her seal, as the sole device, a beehive on a stand with the word *Industry* inscribed above it

SHIELDS

Besides Minerva's Aegis pictured on the seal of California, twenty-one states sketch shields on their seals.

Alabama and Wyoming on their seals delineate the shield of the United States, Wyoming's being a small one, and Alabama's a large shield. The seal of Illinois pictures an eagle grasping a United States shield with both talons; both Arkansas and the District of Columbia have their shield displayed on the eagle's breast.

Other state seals picturing the designs of shields are Arizona, Colorado, Delaware, Idaho, Maine, Maryland, Massachusetts, Michigan, Missouri, New Jersey, New York, Oregon, Pennsylvania, Utah, and Vermont.

FLAGS

Iowa pictures on her seal the United States flag, and Utah sketches two of them. Maryland depicts two flags at the top of her crest, floating free; and New Hampshire images one floating from the stern of a ship.

RIBBON SCROLLS

Twenty-four states display their mottoes or legends on ribbon scrolls.

The following states picture scrolls at the bottom of their seals: Connecticut, Delaware, the District of Columbia, Maine, Maryland, Missouri, Montana, Nevada, New Mexico, and New York. The pictured shield rests on the image of a scroll at the bottom of Colorado's seal. Kentucky's scroll is depicted as starting at the bottom and running up each side more than half-way to the top. Massachusetts's imaged scroll has a similar arrangement.

The seal both of Alabama and of Illinois have their scrolls pictured as streaming from the eagle's beak, and Arkansas also depicts a scroll as extending from the beak of the eagle. The sketched scroll on Iowa's seal is very long, coming from the eagle's beak and arranging itself into four folds.

Michigan pictures her scrolls one at the top and one at the bottom of her seal. The following states have their scrolls depicted at the top of the seal: Idaho, Minnesota, Nebraska, Wisconsin, and Wyoming, which drapes the imaged scroll around the two pictured columns.

Georgia depicts a ribbon scroll wrapped around the pillars pictured on her seal and draped from pillar to pillar.

New Hampshire's ribbon bow is delineated under the wreaths on her seal.

CROWNS

Maryland's seal pictures a ducal crown, which belongs to the arms of the Calverts. The seal of Virginia depicts a crown fallen from the head of *Tyranny* on whom *Virtus,* the genius of the Commonwealth, has set her foot in token of triumph.

WREATHS

Only six state seals display the images of wreaths. Arkansas depicts one grasped in the hand of the angel pictured at the top of the seal; the District of Columbia, one held in the hands of the *Goddess of Justice.*

New Hampshire encircles the inside circle of her seal with the sketch of a wreath tied with a bow of ribbon at the bottom. Oklahoma pictures a wreath inside the center of the star imaged on her seal.

Pennsylvania and Texas both have large wreaths delineated on their seals.

STARS

Twenty-three of the state seals picture stars either in groups or singly. Those which sketch stars only to separate the legend from the date, etc. are as follows: Alabama, Idaho, Mississippi, New Mexico, New York, North Carolina, Ohio, South Dakota, and Tennessee. Thus it becomes evident that more than half of the state seals depicting stars employ them for utilitarian purposes.

Texas pictures one big star in the center of her seal. Oklahoma delineates one big five-pointed star with the seal of an Indian tribe in each of the five points.

Alabama depicts seven stars on her shield as well as two sketched on her seal to separate the legend from the other inscriptions.

Wisconsin pictures thirteen stars at the bottom of the seal in a circular row. These evidently represent the original thirteen colonies.

Massachusetts delineates one star to the left and at the top of the Indian's head on her shield. Illinois on her seal shows the image of two stars, separating the legend from the date.

Maine depicts one big star at the top of her seal above the motto.

Those state seals picturing the flag and the shield of the United States sketch stars on these devices.

Some of the stars pictured denote the order in which the states were admitted into the Union. The State seals imaging stars for this purpose are those of California, Kansas, Missouri, North Dakota, Oklahoma, and Oregon.

MOTTOES

Many mottoes and legends containing single words only appear on the seals of the states. These are for the most part the mottoes of the states.

These mottoes may be classified under religious ideals, conceptions of freedom and justice, military sentiments, and expressions denoting union.

Mottoes Containing Religious Ideals

The following mottoes refer to God or His care: Arizona: *Ditat Deus;* Colorado: *Nil Sine Numine;* Connecticut: *Qui Transtulit Sustinet;* Michigan: *Tuebor;* Rhode Island: *Hope;* South Carolina: *Dum Spiro, Spero;* South Dakota: *Under God the People Rule;* and Florida: *In God We Trust.* All of these are state mottoes except that of Michigan.

Mottoes Embodying Conceptions of Freedom

The state mottoes denoting freedom are as follows:

Arkansas: *Regnat Populus;* Delaware: *Liberty and Independence*; Iowa: *Our Liberties We Prize and Our Rights We Will Maintain;* Massachusetts: *Ense Petit Placidam Sub Libertate Quietam;* Missouri: *Salus Populi Supreme Lex Esto;* Nebraska: *Equality Before the Law;* New Jersey: *Liberty and Prosperity;* North Dakota: *Liberty and Union, Now and Forever, One and Inseparable;* Pennsylvania: *Virtue, Liberty, and Independence;* South Dakota: *Under God the People Rule;* Vermont: *Freedom and Unity;* Virginia: *Sic Semper Tyrannis;* West Virginia: *Montani Semper Liberi;* and Wyoming: *Equal Rights.*

Mottoes Denoting Conceptions of Justice

Four states express conceptions of justice in the wording of their mottoes. They are: the District of Columbia: *Justitia Omnibus;* Georgia: *Wisdom, Justice, Moderation;* Louisiana: *Union, Justice and Confidence;* and Nebraska: *Equality Before the Law.*

Mottoes Disclosing Military Sentiments

Three states have mottoes expressing military sentiments. Iowa has *Our Liberties We Prize and Our Rights We Will Maintain;* Maryland, *Scuto Bonae Voluntatis Tuae Coronasti Nos;* Massachusetts, *Ense Petit Placidam Sub Libertate Quietam.*

Mottoes Signifying Union

Eight state mottoes convey the idea of union or unity on their state seals. Of the expressions signifying such ideas, those on the seals of Colorado, Michigan, and Missouri are not state mottoes.

The states whose seals have mottoes specifically denoting union are: Colorado: *Union, Constit[ution];* Illinois: *State Sovereignty, National Union;* Kentucky:

United We Stand, Divided We Fall; Louisiana: *Union, Justice and Confidence;* Michigan: *E Pluribus Unum;* Missouri: *United We Stand, Divided We Fall;* North Dakota: *Liberty and Union, Now and Forever, One and Inseparable;* and Oregon: *The Union.*

It will be noted that both Kentucky and Missouri have on their seals the expression *United We Stand, Divided We Fall.*

State Seals Having Insignia on Their Reverse Sides

Four states, Georgia, Pennsylvania, Virginia, and West Virginia, have insignia on the reverse sides of their seals.

The reverse of the State seal of Georgia has the words *Agriculture and Commerce* and the date 1799.

The reverse of the seal of Pennsylvania has the image of the *Goddess of Liberty* trampling on a lion, the symbol of *Tyranny,* with the motto *Both Can't Survive.*

The reverse of the State seal of Virginia has the image of the three goddesses *Libertas, Aeternitas,* and *Ceres,* with their accustomed symbols and the Latin motto *Perseverando.*

The motto *Libertas Et Fidelitate* on the reverse side of the seal of West Virginia is also discussed under the *Latin Mottoes.*

CHAPTER VI

THE FLAGS OF THE STATES

A flag may be defined as a strip of bunting or other lightly woven cloth, varying in color and in form, and usually displaying some emblematic design.

Flags are usually attached by one end to a rope, pole, or staff so that the other end flies free. "The length of a flag from the part near the staff to the free end is called the fly, and the measurement at right angles to this is known as the hoist, height, or depth." Flags are commonly used by nations, countries, states, corporations, companies, and private individuals. They are used as military insignia, civic emblems, nautical tokens, quarantine signs, and weather signals. The use of flags dates back to ancient times. Biblical records show accounts of standard bearers. The Greeks and the Romans as well as other ancient nations employed flags. The custom of using flags was transported from Europe to America by the colonists.

Since the flag of the United States belongs to the states collectively, it seems advisable to discuss it before considering the flags of the various states.

THE FLAG OF THE UNITED STATES

The War Department "prescribes rules and regulations governing the use of the flag" within its jurisdiction;[1] but it does not attempt to make rules and regulations governing the use of the flag by civilians. On June 14, 1923, at Washington, D. C. "representatives of over

[1] *Flag Circular, War Department,* The Adjutant General's Office (Government Printing Office, Washington, D C. 1925) p. 1.

sixty-eight patriotic organizations" convened "under the auspices of the National Americanism Commission of the American Legion and drafted a code of flag etiquette" recommended for civilian usage. [2]   The conference flag code practically agrees with the rules and regulations in use by the War Department.

The War Department publishes official pamphlets giving information about the flag and its usage.   Most of the facts about the flag of the United States given below are taken from these pamphlets as the footnotes will show.

There is no one fixed standard size for the National flag of the United States prescribed in feet and inches; but whatever size it may take, with the exception of the colors and the standards carried by the United States troops, it must have the following relative proportions: hoist (width) of the flag, one; fly (length) of the flag, one and nine-tenths times the width; hoist (width) of the union, seven-thirteenths of the width of the flag; fly (length) of the union, seventy-six one-hundredths of the length of the flag; width of each stripe, one-thirteenth of the width of the flag; and the diameter of each star, six hundred and sixteen ten-thousandths of the width of the flag. [3]

The flag of the United States has thirteen horizontal stripes, seven red and six white, the red and white stripes alternating, and a canton or union which consists of white stars of five points on a blue field placed in the upper corner next to the staff and extending to the lower edge of the fourth red stripe from the top.   The number of stars is the same as the number of states in the Union. The canton or union now contains forty-eight stars arranged in six horizontal and eight vertical rows, each star with one point upward.   If a new state should be added to the Union, a new star would be added to the union of

[2] *Flag Circular, War Department,* The Adjutant General's Office (Government Printing Office, Washington, D.C. 1925) p. 1.

[3] *Army Regulations Number 260-10, Flags, Colors, Standards and Guidons,* by Order of the Secretary of War (Government Printing Office, Washington, D. C. 1026) p. 5.

the flag, and this addition would take place on the fourth of July succeeding the admission of the state. [4]

There are four names used by the War Department to designate the National flag, or the Stars and Stripes; namely, the flag, the color, the standard, and the ensign. The term flag is used in general to designate the Stars and Stripes "regardless of size, relative proportions, or manner of display." "A color is a flag carried by unmounted units." "A standard is a flag carried by mounted or motorized units," and "an ensign is a flag flown on ships, tenders, launches, and small boats." [5]

All official flags must be manufactured by the authority of the Secretary of War. [6] United States flags are made both of silk and of wool bunting. Silk national and regimental colors or standards may be carried by an authorized unit or organization "at the headquarters of that unit in battle or campaign, and on all occasions of ceremony in which two or more companies of the unit participate and represent the unit." Silk flags may be bordered with a knotted silk fringe two and one-half inches wide. They may also have attached to their staffs a cord made of red, white, and blue strands of silk thread with tassel made of the same material attached to each of the ends of the cord. The cord including the tassels is usually eight feet and six inches long.

"For a number of years there has been prescribed in Army Regulations a knotted fringe of yellow silk on the national standards of mounted regiments and on the national colors of unmounted regiments. The War Department, however, knows of no law which either requires or prohibits the placing of a fringe on the flag of the United States. No act of Congress or Executive order has been found bearing on the question. In flag manufacture

[4] *Army Regulations Number 260-10, Flags, Colors, Standards, and Guidons,* by Order of the Secretary of War (Government Printing Office, Washington, D. C. 1926) p. 4-5.

[5] *Army Regulations Number 260-10, Flags, Colors, Standards, and Guidons,* by Order of the Secretary of War (Government Printing Office, Washington, D. C. 1926) p. 1.

[6] *Ibidem,* p. 2.

a fringe is not considered to be a part of the flag, and it is without heraldic significance."[7]

National flags made of wool bunting are of the following sizes:[8]

1. The garrison flag is twenty feet hoist and thirty-eight feet fly. It is flown only on holidays and important occasions at the permanent headquarters of the "army, army corps, corps area, department, division, brigade, regiment, Coast Artillery district, harbor defense command, United States Military Academy, a general service school, a special service school, or an arsenal."

2. The post flag is ten feet hoist and nineteen feet fly. This flag is flown during pleasant weather at garrisoned posts and national cemeteries.

3. The storm flag is five feet hoist, and nine feet and six inches fly. It is flown during stormy and windy weather at garrisoned posts and national cemeteries. Semipermanent camps display this flag in any weather during such hours as the commanding officer may designate.

4. Recruiting station flags are of two dimensions; namely, five feet hoist and nine feet and six inches fly, and two and thirty-seven one hundredths feet hoist and four and five-tenths feet fly.

5. There are four sizes of ensigns; namely, the dress ensign, ten feet hoist by nineteen feet fly, is used on special occasions. The standard ensign, five feet hoist by nine feet and six inches fly, is ordinarily used in fair weather; the launch ensign or storm size, three and fifty-two hundredths feet hoist by six and sixty-nine hundredths feet fly; and the small launch ensign, two and thirty-seven hundredths feet hoist by four and five-tenths feet fly.

The following flags are flown over the United States Capitol building: The flag flown over the central portion

[7] *Flag Circular, War Department,* The Adjutant General's Office, (Government Printing Office, Washington, D. C. 1925) p. 2.

[8] *Army Regulations Number 260-10, Flags, Colors, Standards, and Guidons,* by Order of the Secretary of War (Government Printing Office, Washington, D. C. 1926) p. 5.

of the Capitol and that flown over the wing designated as the House of Representatives are seven feet and six inches wide by fourteen feet long. The blue field of each is seventy-one inches wide by fifty-four inches long; each of the stripes is seven inches wide; and each of the stars from the center to the points is two inches wide. The flag flown over the wing known as the Senate Chamber is ten feet wide by fifteen feet long. The size of the blue field of this flag is sixty-three inches wide by seventy-one inches long. The width of each of the stripes is nine and one-fourth inches wide, and each star from the center to the points is two and one-half inches wide. The flag on the central portion of the Capitol building is flown continuously. [9]

In the rotunda of the building of the Post Office Department at Washington, D. C. are displayed the flags of the various states of the Union. There is also suspended in the center of the rotunda a mammoth United States flag, thirty-seven feet wide, and seventy-one feet and four inches long. Its blue field is twenty feet wide and twenty-eight feet long. Each stripe of this flag is two and eleven-thirteenths feet wide, and each star is thirty inches across. The weight of this flag, which was bought in 1920 at a cost of three hundred dollars, is ninety pounds. In addition to the flags named above are also to be found there flags of several foreign countries.

"Old or worn-out flags should not be used either for banners or for any secondary purpose. When a flag is in such a condition that it is no longer a fitting emblem for display, it should not be cast aside nor used in any way that might be viewed as disrespectful. If not preserved, it should be destroyed as a whole, privately, preferably by burning or by some other method lacking in any suggestion of irreverence or disrespect to it as a military emblem." [10]

[9] This information was furnished in a communication from the Architect of the Capitol, Washington, D. C. in August 1931.

[10] *Army Regulations Number 260-10, Flags, Colors, Standards, and Guidons,* by Order of the Secretary of War (Government Printing Office, Washington D. C. 1926) p. 23.

It is interesting to note the length and the size of the various flagstaffs. At forts the flagstaffs are permanently constructed and vary in height from seventy-five to one hundred feet. At camps they are made of any suitable construction and are usually about fifty feet in height. The flagstaff of any other unmounted unit is called a pike. The flagstaff of a mounted or motorized unit is called a lance. Both the pike and the lance are made of wood, and inclusive of the nickel-plated spearhead and ferrule, each is nine feet and six inches in length. The staff of the flag of the President of the United States "made of wood, single screw jointed," including the gold-plated head and the ferrule, is ten feet and three inches long. The staffs of automobile flags are made of wood and inclusive of the acorn shaped head and the ferrule are four feet and nine inches in length. The War Department authorizes the following designs of staff designs of staff heads; the eagle, the acorn, the gilt lance, the ball, the gilt star, the spear, and the flag truck. [11]

The following facts about the use of the flag are valuable to each American citizen: [12]

1. It is proper to display the flag only from sunrise to sunset unless other hours are designated by the proper authorities.

2. When a flag is flown to indicate mourning, it should be raised briskly to the top of the flagstaff, remain there a moment, then it should be lowered slowly to half mast. On such occasions flags are usually flown at half mast from sunrise until noon and at full mast from noon until sunset.

3. In raising or lowering a flag or when it is used on burial occasions, it should never be allowed to touch the ground.

4. In lowering the flag, before it is detached from its fastening, it should be folded into the shape of a cocked hat.

---

[11] *Army Regulations Number 260-10, Flags, Colors, Standards, and Guidons,* by Order of the Secretary of War (Government Printing Office, Washington, D. C.   July 2, 1927) p. 2.

[12] *Flag Circular, War Department,* The Adjutant General's Office (Government Printing Office, Washington, D. C. 1925) p. 3-6.

5. If decorations are desired on patriotic occasions, red, white, and blue bunting should be used. The flag should never be draped over speakers' stands, or over the front of stages or rostrums. When bunting is used, it should be placed so that the blue will be above.

6. The flag should never be used to make garments or costumes.

7. No emblem should ever be placed above the flag, nor should any advertising sign ever be fastened to a pole from which it is flown.

8. The flag should neither be displayed nor stored in such a manner as to permit its being torn or soiled.

9. Whenever the United States flag is used on a speaker's platform, if it is displayed flat, it should be located above and behind the speaker; if displayed from a staff, it should be at the speaker's right.

10. If the flag is displayed in a church, it should be to the congregation's right as they face the speaker.

11. If the flag is used in connection with an unveiling service, it should never be employed as a covering for the statue; but its appearance should be a distinctive feature of the ceremony.

12. When the United States flag is carried in a procession with other flags, it should be either on the marching right or in front of the center of the line of flags.

13. When the United States flag is displayed with other flags either official or non-official, it should be at the center or at the highest point of the group.

14. When the United States flag is flown from an adjacent staff with other flags, it should always be hoisted first and lowered last.

15. When the flag is being hoisted or lowered, or whenever the flag is passing in parade or in review, "all persons should face the flag, stand at attention, and salute." Those in uniform should render the right-hand salute. The men "not in uniform should remove their headdresses with

the right hand and hold them at the left shoulder," with the hand over the heart. Women should place their right hands over their hearts. When the National Anthem, the Star-Spangled Banner, is being played or sung, those present "should stand and face toward the music"; civilian men "should stand at attention" removing their hats. Those men "in uniform should salute at the first note of the Anthem, retaining this position until the last note" is sounded.

The red, white, and blue of the flag are the national American colors. However, they have been used in combination many times throughout the ages. Charles W. Stewart, Superintendent of the Naval records and library of the United States Navy Department, traces their use back to the Ark of the Covenant within the Tabernacle, the curtains of which employed the colors blue, purple, and scarlet. "Red is for courage, zeal, fervency; white is for purity, cleanness of life, and rectitude of conduct; blue is for loyalty, devotion, friendship, justice, and truth." [13]

The thirteen stripes represent the thirteen original states, which are also represented by the first thirteen of the stars.

ALABAMA

The State flag of Alabama is rectangular. It has a red St. Andrew's Cross on a field of white. On February 16, 1895, this flag was made official by legislative action which provided that the crimson bars forming the cross should not be less than six inches broad and that they should extend diagonally across the flag. [14] The design of this flag was adopted out of affection for the battle flag of the Confederacy.

---

[13] *Flags of the World*, Byron McCandless and Gilbert Grosvenor (Published by the National Geographic Society, Press of Judd and Detweiler, Incorporated, Washington, D. C. 1917) p. 303.

[14] *Alabama Acts, 1895: Acts of the General Assembly of Alabama Passed at the Session 1894-95, Held in the City of Montgomery, Commencing Tuesday, November 13th, 1894, with a Separate Index to the General and Local Laws* (Roemer Printing Company, Montgomery, Alabama, 1895) p. 719.

ARIZONA

The flag of Arizona is one of the most colorful of the state flags. It was adopted by legislative action on February 27, 1917.

The law prescribes that "the lower half of the flag shall be a blue field; the upper half shall be divided into thirteen equal segments or rays, which shall start at the center, on the lower line and continue to the edges of the flag, colored alternately light yellow and red, consisting of six yellow and seven red rays; in the center of the flag, super-imposed, a copper colored five-pointed star, so placed that the upper points shall be one foot from the top of the flag and the lower points, one foot from the bottom of the flag. The red and blue shall be of the same shade as the colors in the flag of the United States; the flag to have a four foot hoist and a six foot fly, with a two foot star; the same proportions to be observed for flags of other sizes. The flag represents the copper star of Arizona rising from a blue field in the face of a setting sun." [15]

ARKANSAS

The State flag of Arkansas was adopted by legislative action on April 4, 1924. It consists of a red field upon whose center is pictured a blue-colored diamond with twenty-five white stars arranged around its outside edge, showing thereby that Arkansas was the twenty-fifth state to enter the Union. Depicted within this blue-colored diamond again is a white diamond with the State name inscribed across it in blue. Above the smaller diamond is pictured one star, and below it, three blue stars, signifying "the three nations of Spain, France and the United States to which the state successively belonged. They also indicate that it was the third state carved out of the Louisiana Purchase." The twin stars at the bottom "parallel with each other typify that Arkansas and

<hr>

[15] *Session Laws of Arizona, 1917: Acts, Resolutions and Memorials of the Regular Session of the Third Legislature of the State of Arizona, . . . Session Begun January 8, 1917, Session Adjourned March 8, 1917* (The McNeil Company, Phoenix, Arizona, 1917) chap. 7, p. 7.

Michigan are twin States, having been admitted to the Union together on June 15, 1836. The star above [the word] '*Arkansas*' is to commemorate the Confederacy, and the diamond signifies that this state is the only diamond bearing State in the Union." [16]

CALIFORNIA

The State flag of California, known as the bear flag, was approved by legislative action on February 3, 1911. Its length equals one and one-half times its width. The upper five-sixths of the width of the flag is a white field and the lower one-sixth of the width is a red stripe. Upon the "white field in the upper left-hand corner" is pictured a single red star. "In the center of the white field" is depicted "a California grizzly bear upon a grass plat, in the position of walking toward the left of" the field. The bear thus depicted is brown in color, and its length equals one-third of the length of the flag. At the bottom of the white field are inscribed the words *California Republic*. [17]

COLORADO

The flag of Colorado, approved by legislative action [18] on February 28, 1929, is two-thirds as wide as it is long. It consists of a blue field with a white stripe across its center. Imaged upon this blue field is a red capital letter *C* with a golden disc completely filling its center. The *C* has a diameter equal to one-sixth of the width of the flag

[16] *Acts of Arkansas, 1924, Special Session: Acts and Joint and Concurrent resolutions and Memorials of the Forty-fourth General Assembly of the State of Arkansas* (The Democrat Printing and Lithographing Company, Little Rock, Arkansas, 1924) part I, house current resolutions number 11, section 3, p. 27-8.

[17] *Statutes and Amendments to the Codes of California, 1911, Extra Session, 1910: The Statutes of California and Amendments to the Constitution, Passed at the Extra Session of the Thirty-eighth Legislature, 1910* (W. W. Shannon, Superintendent of State Printing, Sacramento, California, 1911) chap. 9, section 2, p. 6.

[18] *Session Laws of Colorado, 1929: Laws Passed at the Twenty-seventh Session of the General Assembly of the State of Colorado . . . 1929*, published by authority of Charles M. Armstrong, Secretary of State (The Smith-Brooks Press, Denver, Colorado, 1929) chap. 176, section 489, p. 621.

and is placed at a distance from the staff equal to one thirty-sixth of the length of the flag. The color of the *C* is the same as the red used in the American flag.

CONNECTICUT

The present State flag of Connecticut was made official by an act of the legislature in 1918, [19] to become effective on July 1st. The law reads as follows:

"The following-described flag is the official flag of the State. The dimensions of the flag shall be five feet and six inches in length; four feet and four inches in width. The flag shall be of azure blue silk, charged with a shield of roroco design of argent white silk, having embroidered in the center three grape vines, supported and bearing fruit in natural colors. The bordure to the shield shall be embroidered in two colors, gold and silver. Below the shield shall be a white streamer, cleft at each end, bordered by gold and browns in fine lines, and upon the streamer shall be embroidered in dark blue letters the motto "QUI TRANSTULIT SUSTINET"; the whole design being the arms of the state."

DELAWARE

While the flag of Delaware is official, it has never been formally adopted by legislative action. [20] It is composed of a colonial blue field upon which is imaged a buff diamond in the center of which is pictured the State coat of arms. Below the diamond in yellow letters is inscribed

---

[19] *The General Statutes of Connecticut, Revision of 1918, in force July 1st, 1908, with the Constitution of the United States and the Constitution of the State of Connecticut,* Published by Authority of the State (Press of The Case Lockwood, and Brainard Company, Hartford, Conneticut, 1918) chap. 118, section 2006, p. 680.

[20] On February 20, 1913, the House Joint Resolutions empowered the Secretary of State, President pro tempore of the Senate, and the Speaker of the House to decide upon a uniform and standard flag for the State of Delaware with respect to design, size, and color, with the instructions that the colors decided upon by the above-named committee should be recognized as the official flag and colors of the State of Delaware. See *Delaware Laws, 1913: Laws of the State of Delaware Passed at the Ninety-fourth Session of the General Assembly Commenced and Held at Dover on Tuesday, January 7th, A. D. 1913, . . .* (The Delaware Leader, Laurel, Delaware, 1913) vol. XXVII, chap. 306, sections 1, 2, and 3, p. 848.

December 7, 1787, [21] the date of the entry of Delaware
into the Union.

The District of Columbia

The District of Columbia has no flag that is designated
as a District flag; but the one which is carried by the
National Guard consists of a blue field, upon the center
of which is depicted an ax or hatchet. Below this device
is imaged a scroll upon which is inscribed the expression
District of Columbia Militia. [22]

Florida

The Florida State Constitution of 1885 provides for
the State flag as described below. It is three-fourths as
wide as it is long and consists of a white field upon which
is delineated the seal of the State with a diameter equal
to one-third the length of the flag. Red bars in width
one-eighth of the length of the flag are imaged as extending from each corner toward the center to the outer rim
of the seal. [23]

Georgia

The present State flag of Georgia was officially sanctioned by an act of the legislature on May 21, 1916. [24]

The act describes the flag as follows:

"The flag of the State of Georgia shall be a vertical
band of blue next to the flagstaff, and occupying one-third
of the entire flag; the remainder of the space shall be
equally divided into three horizontal bands, the upper and
lower of which shall be scarlet in color, and the middle

[21] *A History of Delaware,* Walter A. Powell (The Christopher Publishing House, Boston, Massachusetts, 1928) p. 339.
[22] *The Encyclopedia Americana* (Americana Corporation, New York,
1929) vol. xi, p. 320.
[23] *Florida Revised General Statutes, 1920: The Revised General
Statutes of Florida . . . Adopted by the Legislature of the State of Florida, June 9, 1919,* James Calkins (The E. O. Painter Printing Company,
Deland, Florida, 1920) Constitution of Florida, article xvi, section 12,
vol. 1, p. 112.
[24] *Acts and Resolutions of the General Assembly of the State of
Georgia, 1916,* compiled and published by Authority of the State (Charles
P. Byrd, State Printer, Atlanta, Georgia, 1916) p. 177-8.

band white. On the blue field shall be stamped, painted or embroidered the coat-of-arms of the State. . ."

IDAHO

The State flag of Idaho came into official existence on March 12, 1907, by legislative action which gave the Adjutant General supervision over the construction of it. [25]

He prescribed that it be made of copenhagen blue silk, five feet and six inches long, and four feet and four inches wide, bordered by gilt fringe two and one-half inches in width, with the State seal of Idaho twenty-one inches in diameter embroidered in colors in the center of the blue field. He further prescribed that the words *State of Idaho* be embroidered in block letters two inches in height, on a red band three inches in width and twenty-nine inches in length, the band being embroidered in gold and placed about eight and one-half inches above the lower border of the fringe and parallel to it. [26]

ILLINOIS

The flag of Illinois, which consists of a white field upon which is a reproduction of the emblem of the Great Seal of the State of Illinois in black or in national colors, was adopted by action of the legislature July 6, 1915. [27]

[25] *Session Laws of Idaho, 1907: General Laws of the State of Idaho, Passed at the Ninth Session of the State Legislature*, published by authority of the Secretary of State (Sims-York Company, Printers and Binders, Boise, Idaho, 1907) section 1, p. 304.

[26] This information is taken from a folder entitled *Idaho State Flag*, furnished by Clay Kollsch, Librarian of the Idaho State Law Library, Boise, Idaho, in a letter dated July 20, 1930.

See also, *The Compiled Statutes of Idaho, Volume I, Political Code*, Prepared by B. W. Oppenheim, Code Commissioner, and adopted at the 1919 session of the legislature under the title of Compiled Laws. Revised by I. W. Hart, Clerk of the Supreme Court, to incorporate the permanent laws of the 1919 session under the authorized title of Compiled Statutes (Syms-York Company, Printers and Binders, Boise, Idaho, 1919) chap. 40, section 701, p. 205.

[27] *Illinois Revised Statutes, 1917: The Revised Statutes of the State of Illinois, 1917, Containing all the General Statutes of the State in Force January 1, 1918, . . .* compiled and edited by Harvey B. Hurd (Chicago Legal News Company, Chicago, Illinois, 1918) chap. 56a, section 12. p. 1570.

INDIANA

The dimensions of Indiana's State flag are five feet and six inches by four feet and four inches. The design on this flag was made by Paul Hadley and was chosen by the Daughters of the American Revolution after examining two hundred competitive designs.[28] The act adopting the State flag by the General Assembly of Indiana went in force on May 31, 1917.[29] The flag consists of a blue field with a yellow border. The device depicted upon the center of the flag is a torch with six rays extending out from the flame. Around the outside of this device are pictured thirteen stars, six of which are at the ends of the rays, and one in the center above the tip of the flame. Three stars are delineated on each side between the lowest rays and the bottom of the torch. One large star with the word *Indiana* inscribed above it is imaged between the tip of the flame and the central star above. Within the circle of stars below the rays, five other stars are represented, arranged two on each side, and the lower one cutting through the handle of the torch. All of the stars depicted have five points. Both the torch and the stars are pictured in gold. "The torch represents liberty and enlightenment, the thirteen stars in the outer circle represent the thirteen original states (the six rays from the flame to the upper stars are merely decorative), the five stars in the inner half of the circle below the torch represent the states admitted prior to Indiana; the large star above the flaming torch represents Indiana, the nineteenth state of the Union."[30]

[28] A sheet containing a picture of the Indiana State Banner furnished by Miss Louise J. Bailey, Librarian, Indiana State Library, Indianapolis, Indiana, July 22, 1930.

[29] *Burns' Annotated Indiana Statutes, Supplement of 1921, Sessions Laws 1915, 1917, 1920, 1921, Annotations of Constitutions and Statutes: Burns' Annotated Indiana Statutes Supplement of 1921, Containing all the General Statutes* . . . Harrison Burns and Samuel Grant Gifford (The Bobbs-Merrill Company, Indianapolis, Indiana, 1921) vol. 2, chap. 126, section 10135b, p. 2021.

[30] This information is taken from a folder entitled *Indiana State Banner*, furnished by Miss Louise J. Bailey, Librarian, Indiana State Library, Indianapolis, Indiana, in a letter dated July 22, 1930.

IOWA

When the United States entered the World War, Iowa had no State flag. "It was expected that the Iowa men would fight in State regiments as they had in former wars and this emphasized the desirability of a State flag to designate the Iowa units. The organization most interested in this matter was the Iowa Society of the Daughters of the American Revolution which had already prepared two designs. On May 11, 1917, Mrs. Lue B. Prentiss, chairman of the Society's flag committee, Mrs. Dixie Gebhardt, and a number of other interested persons appeared before the State Council of National Defense, presented a flag design submitted by Mrs. Gebhardt, and asked that it be adopted as the State flag for use by the Iowa soldiers. The Council approved the plan without much discussion. Thereupon the Daughters of the American Revolution had a number of flags manufactured and presented one to each of the Iowa National Guard regiments, one of which—as the 168th United States Infantry—was already in France. The use of State flags, however, was soon rendered almost impossible by the policy adopted by the War Department of assigning men to military units without regard to the State from which they came." [31]

The Iowa State flag "consists of three vertical stripes of blue, white and red, the blue stripe being nearest the staff and the white stripe being in the center, and upon the central white stripe being depicted a spreading eagle bearing in its beak blue streamers on which is inscribed, in white letters, the state motto, 'Our liberties we prize and our rights we will maintain,' and with the word 'Iowa' in red letters below such streamers. . . ." [32]

[31] *The Palimpsest,* edited by John Ely Briggs (Published monthly at Iowa City by the State Historical Society of Iowa) October, 1924, vol. 5, p. 396-7.
[32] *Acts and Joint Resolutions Passed at the Regular Session of the Thirty-ninth General Assembly of the State of Iowa, Begun January 10, and Ended April 8, A. D. 1921,* prepared and published by and under the direction of U. G. Whitney, Reporter of the Supreme Court and Code Editor (Published by the State of Iowa, Des Moines, Iowa, 1921) chap. 76, section 1, p. 73.

This flag was authorized by legislative action on March 29, 1921.

KANSAS

The official flag of Kansas was ratified by legislative action approved on March 21, 1927. [33] The act reads:

"Be it enacted by the Legislature of the State of Kansas:

"Section 1. That a state flag be and the same is hereby adopted to be used on every and all occasions, when the state is officially represented, with the privilege of the use by all citizens on all fitting and appropriate occasions which shall be authorized by state authorities.

"Section 2. That the official state flag of the state of Kansas shall be a rectangle of dark-blue silk or bunting, three and six-tenths feet on the staff by five and sixty-five one-hundredths feet fly. The great seal of the state of Kansas, without its surrounding band of lettering, shall be located in the center of the rectangle and surmounted by a crest. The seal shall be two and thirty-one hundredths feet in diameter. The crest to be on a wreath or and azure, a sunflower slipped proper, which divested of its heraldic language is a sunflower as torn from its stalk in its natural colors on a bar of twisted gold and blue. The crest shall be six-tenths of one foot in diameter; the wreath shall be seventy-eight one-hundredths of one foot in length. Larger or smaller flags will be of the same proportional dimensions. The colors in the seal shall be as follows: Stars, silver; hills, purple; sun, deep yellow; glory, light yellow; sky, yellow and orange from hills half way to motto, upper half, azure; grass, green; river, light blue; boat, white; house, dark brown; ground, brown; wagons, white; near horse, white; off horse, bay; buffalo, dark, almost black; motto, white; scroll, light brown.

---

[33] *State of Kansas Session Laws, 1927, Passed at the Forty-second Regular Session—the same being the Twenty-Fifth Biennial Session—of the Legislature of the State of Kansas,* date of publication of this volume, June 1, 1927 (Printed by Kansas State Printing Plant, B. P. Walker, State Printer, Topeka, Kansas, 1927) chap. 281, sections 1, 2, 3, p. 487-8.

ALABAMA

ARIZONA

ARKANSAS

CALIFORNIA

COLORADO

CONNECTICUT

DELAWARE

DISTRICT OF COLUMBIA

FLORIDA

GEORGIA

IDAHO

ILLINOIS

STATE FLAGS

INDIANA

IOWA

KANSAS

KENTUCKY

LOUISIANA

MAINE

MARYLAND

MASSACHUSETTS

MICHIGAN

MINNESOTA

MISSISSIPPI

MISSOURI

STATE FLAGS

MONTANA

NEBRASKA

NEVADA

NEW HAMPSHIRE

NEW JERSEY

NEW MEXICO

NEW YORK

NORTH CAROLINA

NORTH DAKOTA

OHIO

OKLAHOMA

OREGON

STATE FLAGS

PENNSYLVANIA

RHODE ISLAND

SOUTH CAROLINA

SOUTH DAKOTA

TENNESSEE

TEXAS

UTAH

VERMONT

VIRGINIA

WASHINGTON

WEST VIRGINIA

WISCONSIN

WYOMING

STATE FLAGS

"Section 3. That this act shall take effect and be in force from and after its publication in the official state paper."

KENTUCKY

The State flag of Kentucky varying in dimensions, was approved by legislative action on March 26, 1918. It is made of "navy blue silk or bunting, with the seal of the Commonwealth of Kentucky encircled by a wreath of goldenrod, embroidered, printed or stamped on the center thereof." [34]

LOUISIANA

According to the Louisiana legislative act of July 1, 1912, the Louisiana State flag consists of "a solid blue field with the Coat-of-Arms of the State, the pelican feeding its young, in white in the center, with a ribbon beneath, also in white, containing in blue the motto of the state, 'Union, Justice and Confidence.' " [35]

MAINE

The State flag of Maine is five feet and six inches in length, and four feet and four inches in breadth. It has a knotted yellow silk fringe two and one-half inches wide bordering the fly sides and end of the flag, and a cord eight feet and six inches in length, composed of white and blue silk strands interwoven, with tassels. The field is blue of the same color as the blue field in the flag of the United States, upon the center of which on both sides of the flag the State coat of arms is embroidered in colored silk in proportionate size. The length of the staff is nine feet including the brass spearhead and ferrule. This flag was

[34] *Acts 1918, Kentucky: Acts of the General Assembly of the Commonwealth of Kentucky,* . . . *1918* (The State Journal Company, Frankfort, Kentucky, 1918) chap. 40, p. 126.
[35] *Acts of the State of Louisiana, Regular and Extra Sessions, 1912: Acts Passed by the General Assembly of the State of Louisiana at the Regular Session* . . . *1912,* published by authority of the State (Ramires-Jones Printing Company, Baton Rouge, Louisiana, 1912) p. 47.

officially authorized by action of the legislature on February 24, 1909. [36]

MARYLAND

According to legislative action on March 9, 1904, [37] the coloring and arrangement of the State flag of Maryland were designed as follows: "Quartered—the first and fourth quarters being paly of six pieces, or and sable, a bend dexter counterchanged; the second and third, quarterly, argent and gules, a cross bottony countersigned; that is to say, the first and fourth quarters consist of six vertical bars alternately gold and black with a diagonal band on which the colors are reversed, the second and third consisting of a quartered field of red and white, charged with a Greek Cross, its arms terminating in trefoils, with the coloring transposed, red being on the white ground and white on the red, and all being as represented upon the escutcheon of the present Great Seal of Maryland."

MASSACHUSETTS

The law prescribes that the flag of the Commonwealth of Massachusetts "shall bear on one side a representation of the coat-of-arms of the Commonwealth, . . . upon a white field, and on the other side a blue shield bearing a representation of a green pine tree, upon a white field." [38] There are no dimensions for the flag of Massachusetts prescribed by law, but the one carried by the State troops is five feet and six inches by four feet and four inches. [39]

[36] *Laws of Maine, 1909: Acts and Resolves of the Seventy-fourth Legislature of the State of Maine, 1909,* . . . (Kennebec Journal Print, Augusta, Maine, 1909) chap. 19, section 1, p. 18.

[37] *Maryland Laws, 1904: Laws of the State of Maryland, Made and Passed at the Session of the General Assembly, Made and Held at the City of Annapolis, on the Sixth Day of January, 1904, and Ended on the Fourth Day of April, 1904,* published by authority (William J. C. Dulany Company, State Printers, Baltimore, Maryland, 1904) chap. 48, section 1, p. 68.

[38] *General Acts of Massachusetts, 1915: General Acts Passed by the General Court of Massachusetts in the Year 1915,* . . . (Wright and Potter Printing Company, State Printers, Boston, Massachusetts, 1915) chap. 37, p. 35.

[39] A letter from Edward H. Redstone, Librarian, State Library of Massachusetts, Boston, Massachusetts, dated July 18, 1930.

The legislative act, approving this flag, was passed on March 6, 1915.

MICHIGAN

The State flag of Michigan consists of a blue field upon which is delineated the State coat of arms. It was sanctioned by legislative action on April 29, 1911. [40]

MINNESOTA

Minnesota's flag consists of a white background upon which is placed a blue circular design in the center of which is depicted the State seal of Minnesota, leaving an outer circular plot upon which is placed around the outer edge of the seal pictures of the white moccasin flower with its deep green leaves. A red ribbon scroll is depicted across the top of the seal which contains the State motto. The scroll is interwoven with the flowers and extends to the bottom of the seal. It is here tied in a knot and the ends are left floating in waves on either side of the flag. Just below the knot of the ribbon scroll is inscribed in gold letters the word *Minnesota*. Outside of the circle are nineteen stars representing the order of the admission of *Minnesota* into the Union, after the original thirteen states. The stars are arranged in five groups each, equidistant from the other groups and all except the top group containing four stars each. The three stars in this group are larger than the stars in the others. Above the motto is the date 1858 which is that of the admission of Minnesota into the Union. The date 1819 inscribed in gold on the ribbon scroll is that of the settlement of Minnesota; the date, April 4, 1893, [41] is that of the adoption of the State flag. The reverse side of the flag is dark

---

[40] *Public Acts of Michigan, Session of 1911: Public Acts of the Legislature of the State of Michigan, Passed at the Regular Session of 1911,* . . . compiled by Frederick C. Martindale, Secretary of State (Wynkoop, Hallenbeck, Crawford Company, State Printers, Lansing, Michigan, 1911) act no. 209, section 3, p. 363.

[41] *Laws of Minnesota, 1893: General Laws of the State of Minnesota, Passed During the Twenty-eighth Session of the State Legislature, 1893,* official publication by the Secretary of State (The Pioneer Press Company, St. Paul, Minnesota, . . . 1893) chap. 16, section 2, p. 112.

blue. At the top of the flag staff is the golden image of a gopher from which hangs a gold colored cord and tassels. [42] Three sides of the fly of the flag are bound with a golden colored cord.

MISSISSIPPI

The committee to design a flag and State seal was appointed by legislative action on February 7, 1894, and the same provided that the report of the committee should become the official flag. [43] The committee recommended for the flag "one with width two-thirds of its length; with a union square, in width two-thirds of the width of the flag; the ground of the union to be red and a broak blue saltier thereon, bordered with white and emblazoned with thirteen (13) mullets or five-pointed stars, corresponding with the number of original States of the Union; the field to be divided into three bars of equal width, the upper one blue, the center one white, and the lower one, extending the whole length of the flag, red—the national colors; the staff surmounted with a spear-head, and a battle-axe below; the flag to be fringed with gold, and the staff gilded with gold." [44]

MISSOURI

The law prescribes that the State flag of Missouri, approved by the legislature on March 13, 1913, "shall be rectangular in shape, the vertical width of which shall be to the horizontal length as seven (7) is to twelve (12). It shall have one red, one white and one blue horizontal stripe of equal width; the red shall be at the top and the blue at the bottom. In the center of the flag there shall

[42] This description is taken from a picture of the flag sent by Lois M. Fawcett, Head of the Reference Department, Minnesota Historical Society, St. Paul, Minnesota, July 23, 1930.

[43] *Mississippi Laws, 1894: Laws of the State of Mississippi, Passed at a Special Session of the Mississippi Legislature Held in the City of Jackson, Commencing January 2, 1894 and Ending February 10, 1894* (The Clarion-Ledger Publishing Company, Jackson, Mississippi, 1894) p. 33.

[44] *Ibidem,* p. 154.

be a band of blue in the form of a circle inclosing the coat-of-arms in the colors as now established by law on a white ground. The width of the blue band shall be one-fourteenth (1-14) of the vertical width of the flag and the diameter of the circle shall be one-third (1-3) the horizontal length of the flag. In the blue band there shall be, set at equal distance from each other, twenty-four (24) five (5) pointed stars." [45]

MONTANA

The State flag of Montana, sanctioned by legislative action on February 27, 1905, consists of a "blue field, with a representation of the Great Seal of the State in the center, and with golden fringe along the upper and lower borders of the flag; the same being the flag borne by the First Montana Infantry, U. S. V., in the Spanish American War with the exception of the device '1st Montana Infantry, U. S. V.'" [46]

NEBRASKA

The Nebraska State flag consists of a field of national blue upon the center of which is depicted in gold and silver the Great Seal of the State. This banner was designed by Mrs. B. G. Miller of Crete, Nebraska.

The act of the legislature authorizing this flag was passed on March 28, 1925. [47]

NEVADA

The flag of Nevada was made official by legislative action on March 26, 1929. The law specifies that "the

[45] *Laws of Missouri, 1913: Laws of Missouri, Passed at the Session of the Forty-seventh General Assembly Which Convened at the City of Jefferson January 8, 1913,* by authority (The Hugh Stephens Printing Company, Jefferson City, Missouri, 1913) p. 349-50.

[46] *Laws of Montana, Ninth Session, 1905: Laws, Resolutions and Memorials of the State of Montana, Passed at the Ninth Regular Session of the General Assembly,* . . . published by authority (State Publishing Company, Stationers, Printers and Binders, Helena, Montana, 1905) chap. 42, section 2, p. 79.

[47] *Session Laws of Nebraska, 1925: Session Laws Passed by the Legislature of the State of Nebraska at the Forty-third Session, 1925,* . . . compiled and published by Charles W. Pool, Secretary of State (The Kline Publishing Company, Lincoln, Nebraska, 1925) chap. 151, house roll no. 62, section 1, p. 387-8.

body of the flag shall be of solid cobalt blue. On the field in the upper left quarter thereof shall be two sprays of sagebrush with the stems crossed at the bottom to form a half-wreath. Within the sprays a five-pointed silver star with one point up. The word 'Nevada' shall also be inscribed within the sprays and shall be inscribed in the same style of letters as the words 'Battle Born' and shall be inscribed in the following manner: Beginning at the upper point shall appear the letter 'N,' the other letters shall appear equally spaced between the points of the star. Above the wreath, and touching the tips thereof, a scroll bearing the words 'Battle Born'; the scroll to be golden yellow, and the lettering thereon black-colored Roman capital letters." [48]

NEW HAMPSHIRE

The State flag of New Hampshire officially adopted by the State legislature on February 24, 1909, had been in use since 1784. The present flag of New Hampshire was adopted by an act of the legislature approved on May 1, 1931, to take effect on January 1, 1932.

The act says:

"*Be it enacted by the Senate and House of Representatives in General Court convened:*

"1. *Flag Altered.* Section 1 of chapter 8 of the Public Laws is hereby amended by striking therefrom the words, 'the motto shall include the date 1784': so that said section shall read as follows: 1. *Flag.* The state flag shall be of the following color and design: The body or field shall be blue and shall bear upon its center in suitable proportion and colors a representation of the state seal; the seal shall be surrounded by a wreath of laurel leaves with nine stars interspersed. When used for military

[48] *Statutes of the State of Nevada, 1928-29: Statutes of the State of Nevada, Passed at the Special Session of the Legislature, 1928,* . . . (State Printing Office, Carson City, Nevada, 1928) chap. 147, section 1, p. 193.

purposes the flag shall conform to the regulations of the United States." [49]

NEW JERSEY

By legislative action the State flag of New Jersey was approved March 26, 1896. The law provides that it "shall be of buff color, having in the center thereof the arms of the state properly emblazoned thereon." [50]

NEW MEXICO

In 1915 the legislature of New Mexico adopted a flag; but the seventh regular session of that body on March 19, 1925, repealed this act and confirmed the present State flag which the law states "shall be the ancient Zia Sun Symbol of red in the center of a field of yellow. The colors shall be the red and yellow of old Spain. The proportions of the flag shall be a width of two-thirds its length. The sun symbol shall be one-third the length of the flag. Said symbol shall have four groups of rays set at right angles; each group shall consist of four rays. The two inner rays of the group shall be one-fifth longer than the outer rays of the group. The diameter of the circle in the center of the symbol shall be one-third of the width of the symbol." [51]

NEW YORK

The State flag of New York is composed of a blue field. Upon the center of this field is imaged the State coat of arms with the motto *Excelsior* inscribed on a white ribbon

[49] *New Hampshire Laws, 1931, and Special Session 1930: New Hampshire Public Acts and Joint Resolutions of the Legislature of 1931 and Special Session of 1930,* Published and distributed under direction of Governor John G. Winant and Executive Council, Charles B. Hoyt, Sandwich, William S. Davis, Barrington, James J. Powers, Manchester, Fred T. Wadleigh, Milford, William B. McInnis, Concord, published by the Secretary of State (The Clarke Press, Manchester, New Hampshire, 1931) p. 44.
[50] *New Jersey Laws, 1896: Acts of the One Hundred and Twentieth Legislature of the State of New Jersey and Fifty-second under the New Constitution* (MacCrellish and Quigley, Current Printers, Trenton, New Jersey, 1896) chap. 120, joint resolution 2, section 1, p. 176.
[51] *Laws of New Mexico, 1925: Laws of the State of New Mexico, Passed by the Seventh Regular Session of the State Legislature of the State of New Mexico, . . . 1925,* Soledad C. Chacon, Secretary of State (Valliant Printing Company, Albuquerque, New Mexico, 1925) chap. 115, section 1, p. 223.

scroll depicted beneath. This flag was adopted April 2, 1901. [52]

NORTH CAROLINA

North Carolina's State flag was ratified by the General Assembly on March 9, 1885. The act establishing the State flag provides for the following:

"That the flag of North Carolina shall consist of a blue union, containing in the center thereof a white star with the letter N. in gilt on the left and the letter C. in gilt on the right of said star, the circle containing the same to be one-third the width of the said union.

"That the fly of the flag shall consist of two equally proportioned bars; the upper bar to be red, the lower bar to be white; that the length of the bars horizontally shall be equal to the perpendicular length of the union, and the total length of the flag shall be one-third more than its width.

"That above the star in the center of the union there shall be a gilt scroll in semi-circular form, containing in black letters this inscription: 'May 20th, 1775', and that below the star there shall be a similar scroll containing in black letters the inscription: 'April 12th, 1775.' " [53]

NORTH DAKOTA

The flag of North Dakota is made up of a blue silk field "four feet [and] four inches on the pike and five feet [and] six inches on the fly, with a border of knotted yellow fringe two and one-half inches wide. On each side of said flag in the center thereof, shall be embroidered an eagle with outspread wings and with opened beak, the eagle to be three feet [and] four inches from tip to tip of wing, and one foot [and] ten inches from top of head to bottom of olive branch hereinafter described; the right foot of the eagle shall grasp a sheaf of arrows, the left

[52] *Laws of New York One Hundred Twenty-fourth Session, 1901: Laws of the State of New York, Passed at the One Hundred Twenty-fourth Session of the Legislature, Begun January 2, 1901, and Ended April 23, 1901, in the City of Albany* (J. B. Lyon Company, Printers, Albany, New York, 1901) vol. 1, chap. 299, p. 669-70.

[53] *Laws of North Carolina, Session of 1885; Laws and Resolutions of the State of North Carolina, Passed by the General Assembly at Its Session of 1885, ...* published by authority (P. M. Hale, State Printer and Binder, Raleigh, North Carolina, 1885) chap. 291, sections 1, 2, 3, p. 539.

foot shall grasp an olive branch showing three red berries; on the breast of the eagle shall be displayed a shield, the lower part showing seven red and six white stripes placed alternately; through the opened beak of the eagle shall pass a scroll bearing the words *'E Pluribus Unum,'* beneath the eagle a scroll on which shall be borne the words 'North Dakota'; over the scroll carried through the eagle's beak shall be shown thirteen (13) five-pointed stars, the whole device being surmounted by a sunburst." [54] The State legislature approved this flag on March 3, 1911.

OHIO

Ohio's State flag, eight-thirteenths as wide as it is long, was adopted by legislative action on May 9, 1902. The law says that it "shall have three red and two white horizontal stripes; the union of the flag shall be seventeen five-pointed stars, white, in a blue triangular field, the base of which shall be the staff end or verticle edge of the flag, and the apex of which shall be the center of the middle red stripe. The stars shall be grouped around a red disc superimposed over a white circular 'O.' " [55]

OKLAHOMA

Oklahoma by senate joint resolution, number fifty-two, approved on April 2, 1925, adopted the present State flag.

The resolution states that the flag shall be:

"a sky blue field with a circular rawhide shield of an American Indian Warrior, decorated with six (6) painted crosses on the face thereof, the lower half of the shield to be fringed with seven (7) pendant eagle feathers and superimposed upon the face of the shield a calumet or peace pipe, crossed at right angles by an olive branch, as illustrated by the design accompanying

[54] *Laws of North Dakota, 1911: Laws Passed at the Twelfth Session of the Legislative Assembly of the State of North Dakota,* . . . (Knight Printing Company, Fargo, North Dakota, 1911) chap. 238, p. 519.

[55] *Laws of Ohio, 1902: General and Local Acts Passed and Joint Resolutions, Adopted by the Seventy-fifth General Assembly At Its Regular Session, Begun and Held in the City of Columbus, January 6, 1902,* published by State authority (Fred J. Heer, State Printer, Columbus, Ohio, 1902) house bill no. 213, section 1, p. 445.

this resolution, and the same is hereby adopted as the official flag and banner of the State of Oklahoma." [56]

OREGON

The date of the adoption of Oregon's State flag is February 26, 1925.

The law prescribes that this flag "shall bear on one side on a navy blue field the State escutcheon in gold, supported by thirty-three gold stars and bearing above said escutcheon the words 'State of Oregon' in gold and below such escutcheon the figures '1859' in gold, and on the other side on a navy blue field a representation of the beaver in gold." [57]

PENNSYLVANIA

The law requires that the State flag of Pennsylvania "shall be of blue, [the] same color as the blue field in the flag of the United States, and of the following dimensions and design; to wit, The length, or height, of the staff to be nine feet, including brass spear-head and ferrule, the fly of the said flag to be six feet [and] two inches, and to be four feet [and] six inches on the staff; in the center of the flag there shall be embroidered in silk the same on both sides of the flag the coat of arms of the Commonwealth of Pennsylvania, in proportionate size; the edges to be trimmed with knotted fringe of yellow silk, two and one-half inches wide; a cord, with tassels, to be attached to the staff at the spear-head, to be eight feet [and] six inches long, and composed of white and blue silk strands." [58]

This State flag was approved by legislative action on June 13, 1907.

[56] *State of Oklahoma Session Laws of 1925* (Harlow Publishing Company, Oklahoma City, Oklahoma, 1925) p. 340.

[57] *General Laws of Oregon, 1925: State of Oregon, Constitutional Amendments Adopted and Laws Enacted by the People at the General Election November 4, 1924, together with the General Laws and Joint Resolutions, Concurrent Resolutions and Memorials Adopted by the Thirty-third Regular Session of the Legislative Assembly* . . . compiled by Sam A. Kozer, Secretary of State (State Printing Department, Salem, Oregon, 1925) chap. 227, section 1, p. 410.

[58] *Laws of Pennsylvania, 1907: Laws of the General Assembly of the Commonwealth of Pennsylvania, Passed at the General Session of 1907,* . . . by authority (Harrisburg Publishing Company, State Printer, Harrisburg, Pennsylvania, 1907) no. 373, section 1, p. 560-1.

RHODE ISLAND

The law, adopting the State flag of Rhode Island, passed on May 19, 1897, provides that it "shall be white, five feet and six inches fly and four feet and ten inches deep on the pike, bearing on each side in the center a golden anchor, twenty-two inches high, and underneath it a blue ribbon twenty-four inches long and five inches wide, or in these proportions, with the motto 'Hope' in golden letters thereon, the whole surrounded by thirteen golden stars in a circle: The flag to be edged with a yellow fringe. The pike shall be surmounted by a spearhead, and the length of the pike shall be nine feet, not including the spear-head." [59]

SOUTH CAROLINA

The flag of South Carolina consists of a blue field upon the center of which is imaged a palmetto tree. Near the upper corner, next to the staff, is pictured a crescent pointing toward the center. [60] This, the flag of the State as a member of the Southern Confederacy, was adopted by action of the State legislature on January 28, 1861.

SOUTH DAKOTA

The act of the legislature, approving the flag of South Dakota on March 8, 1909, requires that it "shall consist of a field of blue one and two-thirds as long as it is wide, in the center of which shall be a blazing sun in gold two-fifths as wide in diameter as the width of the flag. Above this sun shall be arranged in the arc of a circle, in gold letters, the words 'South Dakota' and below the sun in the arc of a circle shall be arranged the words, in gold letters, 'The Sunshine State,' and on the reverse of the blazing sun shall be printed in dark blue the great seal of the state of South Dakota. The edges of the flag shall be

[59] *Rhode Island Acts and Resolves, January 1897: Acts and Resolves, Passed by the General Assembly of the State of Rhode Island and Providence Plantations at the General Session, 1897* (E. L. Freeman and Sons, State Printers, Providence, Rhode Island, 1897) chap. 460, p. 33.
[60] *South Carolina Laws, 1910: Acts and Joint Resolutions of the General Assembly of the State of South Carolina, Passed at the Regular Session of 1910,* . . . (Gonzales and Bryan, State Publisher, Columbia, South Carolina, 1910) p. 753.

trimmed with a fringe of gold to be in proportion to the width of the flag. The staff shall be surmounted with a spear-head to which shall be attached cord and tassels of suitable length and size." [61]

TENNESSEE

The State flag of Tennessee as approved by an act of the legislature on April 17, 1905, [62] consists of a red field upon the center of which is depicted a blue circle edged with white, which contains three white five-pointed stars. At the fly end of the flag is a blue stripe separated from the red field by a narrow white stripe. The flag is one and two-thirds times as long as it is wide. The blue circle is three-fifths of the entire width of the flag. "The three white stars represent the three political divisions of the state, organized at different periods in its history. They are bound together by the circular blue field; the symbol represents three making one." [63]

TEXAS

The flag of the State of Texas was approved by the Republic of Texas on January 25, 1839. The State Constitution of 1876 ratified this act which requires that the "national flag of Texas shall consist of a blue perpendicular stripe of the width of one-third of the whole length of the flag, with a white star of five points in the center thereof, and two horizontal stripes of equal breadth, the upper stripe white, the lower red, of the length of two-thirds of the whole length of the flag." [64]

[61] Session Laws of South Dakota, 1909: Enabling Act and Constitution and the Laws Passed at the Eleventh Session of the Legislature of the State of South Dakota . . . Official Edition (Hipple Printing Company, Pierre, South Dakota, 1909) chap. 230, section 1, p. 361.

[62] Acts of Tennessee, 1905: Acts of the State of Tennessee Passed by the Fifty-fourth General Assembly, 1905, published by authority (Brandon Printing Company, Nashville, Tennessee, 1905) p. 1098-9.

[63] Tennessee: State Flag, Flower, Song, Seal and Capitol (Published by the Division of Library and Archives in the Department of Education, John Trotwood Moore, Librarian and Archivist, Nashville, Tennessee, 1923) p. 1.

[64] Texas Laws, 1838-1846: the Laws of Texas 1822-1897 . . . Laws of the Republic of Texas. 1839 . . . , compiled and arranged by H. P. Gammel, with an introduction by C. W. Raines (The Gammel Book Company, Austin, Texas, 1898) vol. 2, p. 88.

In March, 1933, [65] the Legislature of the State of Texas passed "an act for the purpose of making plain the salute to the Texas Flag and giving uniformity to the salute; providing a clear description of the Flag to the end that pupils in the lower grades of the elementary school will be able to draw or make the Flag; providing for the standardization of the star in the blue stripe in the dimensions used and its position in the stripe so that uniformity shall be the result hereafter in the making of Texas Flags; describing the method of construction of the star in language that is definite and clear; and outlining rules for correct use and display of the Texas Flag and declaring an emergency."

The act reads:

"Be it enacted by the Legislature of the State of Texas:

"Section 1. This act of the Legislature is not a substitute for any previous legislation pertaining to the Lone Star Flag of Texas which may have been passed by either the Republic of Texas or the Legislature of this State, but the sole purpose of this act is to clarify the description of the Texas Flag, to standardize the star in the blue field, and to outline some important rules to govern the correct use of the Texas Flag.

"Section 2. A drawing of the Texas Flag to illustrate the general outline of the three stripes, and the star in the blue stripe:

The Texas Flag

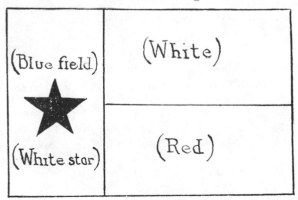

[65] House Bill Number 575 of the Legislature of the State of Texas, sent to the printer on March 3, 1933.

"Section 3. Salute to the Texas Flag
'Honor the Texas Flag of 1836;
I pledge allegiance to thee,
Texas, one and indivisible.'

"Section 4. Description of the Texas Flag

"The Texas Flag is an emblem of four sides, and four angles of 90 degrees each. It is a rectangle having its width equal to two-thirds of its length. The flag is divided into three equivalent parts, called bars or stripes, one stripe being blood red, one white, and the other azure blue. These stripes are rectangles, also, and they are exact duplicates of one another in every respect. The width of each stripe is equal to one-half of its length, or one-third of the length of the Flag, while the length of each stripe is equal to the width of the Flag, or two-thirds of the length of the Emblem.

"One end of the Flag is blue, and it is called the Flag's 'right'. This stripe is a perpendicular bar next to the staff or the halyard, and it is attached by means of a heading made of strong and very durable material. The remaining two-thirds of the Flag is made up of two horizontal bars of equal width, one being white and the other red, and this end of the Emblem is called the Flag's 'left'. Each one of the stripes is perpendicular to the blue stripe, and when the Flag is displayed on a flagpole or staff, or flat on a plane surface, the white stripe should always be at the top of the Flag, with the red stripe directly underneath it. Thus, each stripe of the Texas Flag touches each of the other stripes, which signifies that the three colors are mutually dependent upon one another in imparting the lessons of the Flag; bravery, loyalty, and purity.

"Section 5. Description of the Star

"In the center of the blue stripe is a white star of five points. One point of this star is always at the top, and in vertical line drawn from one end of the blue stripe to the other, and midway between its sides. This line is the vertical axis of the blue stripe, and it is perpendicular to the horizontal axis at the central point of the stripe. The two lowest points of the star are in a line parallel to the horizontal axis, and the distance from the topmost point of the star to the line through these two points is equal to approximately one-third of the length of the blue stripe, or one-third of the width of the Flag. The center of the star is at the point of intersection of the horizontal axis with the vertical axis, or at the central point of the blue stripe. The other two points of the star are above the horizontal axis, and near the sides of the blue stripe.

"A few fundamental facts concerning the dimensions of the star and its position in the blue stripe are outlined here for the assistance of makers of the Texas Flag: It is a white star of five points. The center of the star is at the central point of the blue stripe. The five points of the star are on a circle whose center is at the central point of the blue stripe. The length of the diameter of the circle which passes through the five points of the star is always equal to three-fourths of the width of the blue stripe, or three-eighths of the Flag. The radius of the circle which passes through the five points of the star, then, is equal to three-eighths of the width of the blue stripe. The topmost point of the star is at the point of intersection of this circle with the vertical axis of the blue stripe. The two lowest points of the star are in a line parallel to the horizontal axis of the blue stripe, and the distance from the topmost point of the star to this line is equal to approximately one-third of the length of the blue stripe, or it is equal to approximately one-third of the width of the Flag. The other two points of the star are above the horizontal axis, and near the sides of the blue stripe, and these two points are in a line parallel to the horizontal axis. The five angles of the points of the star are equal to one another, and each angle contains 36 degrees. The geometrical figure in the center of the star is a regular pentagon, or polygon of five sides and five equal angles, and each angle of the pentagon contains 108 degrees. With the use of a ruler and a compass, this star is very easily constructed. First, draw the line through the middle points of the ends of the blue stripe, or draw the vertical axis; then, draw the line through the middle points of the sides of the blue stripe, or draw the horizontal axis. These two axes intersect in the central point of the blue stripe, and they bisect each other. Now, divide the horizontal axis into eight equal parts, and draw a circle with its center at the central point of the blue stripe and its radius equal to three-eighths of the length of the horizontal axis. The point in which this circle intersects the vertical axis above the central point of the blue stripe is the topmost point of the star.

"Next, find the middle point of the radius of this circle which coincides with one end of the horizontal axis. Using this point as a center, and with a radius equal to the distance to the topmost point of the star, describe an arc intersecting the opposite end of the horizontal axis. The distance from the last point found to the topmost point of the star is equal to one-fifth of the circumference of the circle. Then, beginning at the topmost point of the star, and using the measure just found as a unit of length, divide the circumference of the circle into five equal parts. The four additional points found on the circle in this way are the remaining points of the star. Two of these points are above the horizontal axis and two of them are below it, while two of the points are at the left of the vertical axis and two are at the right of it. Now, connect the topmost point of the star with the two points below the horizontal axis. Then, connect the point which is below the horizontal axis and at the left of the vertical axis with the point which is above the horizontal axis and at the right of the vertical axis. Likewise, connect the point which is below the horizontal axis and at the right of the vertical axis with the point which is above the horizontal axis and at the left of the vertical axis. Finally, connect the two points which are above the horizontal axis and on the opposite side of the vertical axis, and the symmetrical figure thus completed is the beautiful Lone Star of the Texas Flag.

"Section 6. Rules Governing the Use of the Texas Flag.

"When the Texas flag is displayed out-of-doors, it must be on either a flagpole or staff, and the staff should be at least two and one-half times as long as the Flag. The Flag is always attached at the spearhead end of the staff, and the heading must be made of material strong enough to protect the Colors. The Texas Flag should not be unfurled out-of-doors earlier than sunrise, and it should be taken down, or furled, not later than sunset. Of course the Flag may be flown for any length of time between sunrise and sunset, as may be directed by proper authority.

It is disrespectful to the Texas Flag to leave it unfurled in inclement weather, such as rain, sleet, snow, hail, or storm, and it should never be left out-of-doors at night. "The Texas Flag shall be displayed on all State Memorial Days, and on special occasions of historical significance. Every school in Texas should fly the Texas Flag on all regular school days. This courtesy is due to the Lone Star Flag of Texas. The Texas Flag should always be hoisted briskly, and furled slowly with appropriate ceremonies.

"The Texas Flag should not be fastened in such a manner that it can be torn easily. When the Texas Flag is flown from a flagpole or staff, the white stripe should always be at the top of the Flag, except in cases of distress, and the red stripe should be directly underneath the white.

"The Texas Flag should be on the marching left when it is carried in a procession in which the Flag of the United States of America is unfurled. The Texas Flag should be on the left of the Flag of the United States of America, and its staff should be behind the staff of the National Colors, when the two are displayed against a wall from crossed staffs.

"When the Texas Flag is flown from the same halyard as the Flag of the United States of America is flown, it must be underneath our National Colors. When the Texas Flag is flown on a flagpole adjacent to the flagpole on which the Flag of the United States of America is flown, it must be unfurled after our National Colors, and it must be displayed at the left of the Flag of the United States of America. When the Texas Flag and the Flag of the United States of America are displayed at the same time, they should be flown on separate flagpoles of equal length, and the Flags should be approximately the same size. When the Texas Flag is flown from a window sill, balcony, or front of a building, and flat against the wall, it should be on a staff, and the blue field should be at the observer's left. When the Texas Flag and the Flag of the United States of America are displayed on a speaker's platform at the same time, the Texas Flag should be on the left side of the speaker, while our National Colors are on the right side of the speaker. The Texas Flag should never be used to cover a platform or speaker's desk, nor to drape over the front of a speaker's platform. When the Texas Flag is displayed flat on the wall of a platform, it should be above the speaker, and the blue field must always be at the Flag's right.

"When the Texas Flag is displayed on a motor car, the staff should be fastened firmly to the chassis of the car, or clamped firmly to the radiator cap. When the Texas Flag is displayed on a float in a parade, it should always be attached securely to a staff. The Texas Flag should not be allowed to touch the ground or the floor, nor to trail in water. The Texas Flag should not be draped over the hood, top, sides, or back of any vehicle, or of a railroad train, boat, or aeroplane. The Texas Flag should not be used as a covering for a ceiling. The Texas Flag should not be used as any portion of a costume or athletic uniform.

"The Texas Flag should not be embroidered upon cushions or handkerchiefs, nor printed on paper napkins or boxes. The Texas Flag must not be treated disrespectfully by having printing or lettering of any kind placed upon it. The Texas Flag should not be used in any form of advertising, and, under no circumstances, may advertisements of any kind be attached to the flagpole or staff. It is disrespectful to the Texas Flag to use it for purposes of decoration, either over the middle of streets, or as a covering for automobiles or floats in a parade, or for draping speaker's platforms or stands or for any other similar purpose of decoration. For such purposes of decoration the colors of the Flag may be used in bunting or other cloth.

"The Texas Flag should not be carried flat or horizontally, but always aloft and free, as it is carried in a parade. The Texas Flag is flown at half-mast by first raising it to the top of the flagpole, and then slowly lowering it to a position one-fourth of the distance down the flagpole, and there leaving it during the time it is to be displayed, observing the rule, of course, that it must not be raised before sunrise, and it must be taken down each day before sunset. In taking the Flag down, it should first be raised to the top of the flagpole, and then slowly lowered with appropriate ceremony.

"The Texas Flag should not be displayed, used, nor stored in such a manner that it can be easily soiled or otherwise damaged. When the Texas Flag is in such condition of repair that it is no longer a suitable Emblem for displaying, it should be totally destroyed, preferably by burning, and that privately; or this should be done by some other method in keeping with the spirit of respect and reverence which all Texans owe the Emblem which represents the Lone Star State of Texas.

"Section 7. The fact that the Texas Flag represents all the people of this State, and stands for the Alamo and Goliad and San Jacinto and all the glorious history of the past, as well as the living present and the matchless future possibilities; and, in view of the fact that there is much confusion and doubt in the minds of the citizenry concerning the description, meaning, and use of the Texas Flag, and that all minds should be clear in this matter creates an emergency and an imperative need requiring that the constitutional rules that bills be read on three separate days shall be suspended and that this law shall go into effect from and after its passage, and such rule is hereby suspended, and this law shall take effect from and after its passage, and it is so enacted."

UTAH

The State flag of Utah is composed of a "blue field fringed with gold borders with the following devices worked in natural colors on the center of the blue field:

'The center a shield above the shield and thereon an American eagle with outstretched wings; the top of the shield pierced with six arrows crosswise; upon the shield under the arrows the word "Industry," and below the word "Industry" on the center of the shield a bee-hive; on each side of the bee-hive, growing sego lilies below the bee-hive and near the bottom of the shield the word "Utah," and below the word "Utah" and on the bottom of the shield the figures "1847." With the appearance of being back of the shield there shall be two American flags on flagstaffs placed crosswise with the flags so draped that they will project beyond each side of the shield, the heads of the flag staffs appearing in front of the eagle's wings and the bottom of each staff appearing over the face of the draped flag below the shield; below the shield and flags and upon the blue field the figures "1896." Around the entire design a narrow circle in gold.' " [66] The eagle has outstretched wings.

This Utah State flag was approved by legislative action on March 11, 1913.

VERMONT

The present State flag of Vermont was adopted by an act of the State legislature approved on March 26, 1923. [67] The act reads as follows:

"It is hereby enacted by the General Assembly of the State of Vermont:

"Section 1. Section 304 of the General Laws, as amended by No. 8 of the acts of 1919, is hereby amended so as to read as follows:

"Section 304. *State Flag.* The flag of the State shall be blue with the coat of arms of the state thereon."

VIRGINIA

An act of the legislature of Virginia, approved March 24, 1930, [68] says:

"The flag of the Commonwealth shall hereafter be made of bunting or merino. It shall be a deep blue field, with a circular white centre of the same material. Upon this circle shall be painted or embroidered, to show on both sides alike, the coat-of-arms of the State, as described in section twenty-seven of the Code of Virginia, as

[66] *Laws of Utah, 1913: Laws of the State of Utah Passed at the Tenth Regular Session of the Legislature of the State of Utah . . .* published by authority (Century Printing Company, Salt Lake City, Utah, 1913) House joint resolution number 1, p. 232-3.

[67] *Laws of Vermont, 1923: The Acts and Resolves Passed by the General Assembly of the State of Vermont at the Twenty-Seventh Biennial Session, 1923, Session Commenced January 3, 1923, Adjourned March 31, 1923,* published by authority (P. H. Gobie Press, Incorporated, Bellows Falls, Vermont) p. 4.

[68] *Acts of the General Assembly of the State of Virginia, Session Which Commenced at the State Capitol on Wednesday, January 8, 1930, Adjourned March 18, 1930* (Division of Purchase and Printing, Richmond, Virginia, 1930) chap. 386, section 31, p. 822.

amended by this act, for the obverse of the great seal of
the State; and there shall be a white silk fringe on the
outer edge, furthest from the flag-staff. This shall be
known and respected as the flag of Virginia."

WASHINGTON

The flag of the State of Washington was officially
adopted March 5, 1923. The law requires that this flag
shall be composed of "dark green silk or bunting and
shall bear in its center a reproduction of the Seal of the
State of Washington embroidered, printed, painted or
stamped thereon. The edges of the flag may, or may
not, be fringed. If a fringe is used the same shall be dark
green of the same shade as the flag. The dimensions of
the flag may vary." [69]

WEST VIRGINIA

West Virginia by Senate joint resolution number
eighteen, approved March 7, 1929, adopted the present
State Flag. The resolution says:

WHEREAS, The legislature of West Virginia, by joint
resolution passed on the twenty-fourth day of February,
one thousand nine hundred and five, adopted a state flag,
prescribing the design thereof; and

WHEREAS, The design so adopted is impractical of manufacture, making the cost of purchase thereof prohibitive
to the schools of the state and others desiring to purchase
said flag; and

WHEREAS, There has been worked out a design embodying all of the features of the first West Virginia state flag
so adopted, but so designed as to be practical of manufacture at a reasonable cost to those desiring to purchase the
same; and

WHEREAS, It seems desirable to change the design of
the West Virginia state flag; therefore, be it

RESOLVED BY THE LEGISLATURE OF WEST VIRGINIA :

[69] *Laws of Washington, 1923: Session Laws of the State of Washington, Eighteenth Session . . . 1923,* compiled by J. Grant Hinkle, Secretary
of State, published by authority (Frank M. Lamborn, Public Printer,
Olympia, Washington, 1923) chap. 174, section 1, p. 573-4.

That the legislature of West Virginia hereby adopts a state flag of the following design and proportions to-wit: The proportions of the flag of the state of West Virginia shall be the same as those of the United States ensign; the field shall be pure white, upon the center of which shall be emblazoned in proper colors, the coat-of-arms of the state of West Virginia, upon which appears the date of the admission of the state into the Union, also with the motto "Montani Semper Liberi" (Mountaineers Always Freeman) above the coat-of-arms of the state of West Virginia there shall be a ribbon lettered, state of West Virginia, and arranged appropriately around the lower part of the coat-of-arms of the state of West Virginia a wreath of rhododendron maximum in proper colors. The field of pure white shall be bordered by a strip of blue on four sides. The flag of the state of West Virginia when used for parade purposes shall be trimmed with gold colored fringe on three sides and when used on ceremonial occasions with the United States ensign, shall be trimmed and mounted in similar fashion to the United States flag as regards fringe cord, tassels and mounting." [70]

WISCONSIN

The Wisconsin State flag is made of "dark blue silk, five feet [and] six inches fly and four feet [and] four inches on the pike; the State coat of arms embroidered on each side with silk of approriate colors . . . the edges trimmed with knotted fringe of yellow silk two and one-half inches wide; the pike nine feet long including spear head and ferrule; the cord eight feet [and] six inches long with two tassels, and composed of blue and white silk strands intermixed." [71]

This flag was officially approved by legislative action on April 26, 1913.

[70] *Acts of the West Virginia Legislature, Regular and Extended Sessions, 1929.* (Neither the publisher nor the place of publication is given) p. 495.

[71] *Laws of Wisconsin, 1913: Wisconsin Session Laws, Acts, Resolutions and Memorials, Passed at the Biennial Session of the Legislature, 1913,* published by authority (Democrat Printing Company, State Printer, Madison, Wisconsin, 1913) p. 107-8.

WYOMING

The flag of Wyoming is unusual in the respect that it images a native animal of the State. The act of January 31, 1917, requires that the flag shall be in width "seven-tenths of its length; the outside border to be in red, the width of which shall be one-twentieth of the length of the flag; next to said border shall be a stripe of white on the four sides of the field, which shall be in width one-fortieth of the length of said flag. The remainder of said flag to be a blue field, in the center of which shall be a white silhouetted buffalo, the length of which shall be one-half of the length of the said blue field; the other measurement of said buffalo to be in proportion to its length. On the ribs of said buffalo shall be the great seal of the State of Wyoming in blue. Said seal shall be in diameter one-fifth the length of said flag. Attached to the flag shall be a cord of gold with gold tassels. The colors to be used in said flag as red, white and blue shall be the same colors used in the flag of the United States of America." [72]

This State flag was "designed by Miss Vera Keays, of Buffalo, Wyoming, and was selected from thirty-seven designs submitted in a contest conducted by the Daughters of the American Revolution, and the following legend was written by Miss Keays:

'The Great Seal of the State of Wyoming is the heart of the flag.

'The seal on the bison represents the truly western custom of branding. The bison was once "monarch of the plains."

'The red border represents the Red Men, who knew and loved our country long before any of us were here; also, the blood of the pioneers who gave their lives reclaiming the soil.

'White is an emblem of purity and uprightness over Wyoming.

[72] *Session Laws of Wyoming, 1917: Session Laws of the State of Wyoming, Passed by the Fourteenth State Legislature, . . .* compiled and published under statutory authority by Frank L. Houx, Secretary of State (Wyoming Labor Journal Company, Cheyenne, Wyoming, 1917) chap. 8, section 1, p. 7.

'Blue, which is found in the bluest of blue Wyoming skies and the distant mountains, has through the ages been significant of fidelity, justice, and virility.

'And finally, the red, the white, and the blue of the flag of the State of Wyoming are the colors of the greatest flag in all the world, the Stars and Stripes of the United States of America.' " [73]

[73] *Wyoming—Its Symbols—Its Capitol—Its Historical Department*, issued by the State Historian, Cheyenne, Wyoming, September, 1922.

CHAPTER VII

THE STATE CAPITOL BUILDINGS

The capitol buildings of the various states are creations of architectural beauty and splendor. It is a noteworthy fact that forty out of the forty-eight of these buildings have domes. In no "type of architecture does modern American taste adopt itself to classical architecture more pronouncedly" than in these monumental edifices. It has been said that the domed structure in civic architecture has become so popularized that "the average American has come to feel that one can scarcely govern correctly unless from under a dome." [1] The writer quoted above in speaking of the domed capitols, says that "all such designs go back in inspiration to the Capitol at Washington and thence to the great European examples of domed architecture from Bramante's time." [1]

It is the purpose of this chapter, so far as it is possible, to give the following facts about each State capitol building: its location, its dimensions, the architect who designed it, the style of architecture it represents, the material out of which it is constructed, and its cost.

ALABAMA

The capitol building of the State of Alabama is located at Montgomery. The capitol was located at Montgomery, the fourth capital city, by an act of the State legislature in 1847. The first building, designed by Stephen D. Button, was destroyed by fire on December 14, 1849. The central section of the present capitol was built on the foundation of the old one with a few variations in dimensions. It, being two hundred feet long, and one hundred and fifty

[1] *American Architecture of To-Day*, G. H. Edgell (Charles Scribner's Sons, New York, 1928) p. 226.

feet wide, was completed in 1851 at a cost of sixty thousand dollars. The rear extension, being seventy feet long and fifty feet wide, was added in 1885, the cost amounting to twenty-five thousand dollars. The south wing, being one hundred and thirty feet long, and one hundred and thirty feet wide, was constructed in 1906 out of its proportional part of the one hundred fifty thousand dollars appropriated by the legislature to pay for it and the south end of the capitol square. In 1911 the north wing, being one hundred and fifty feet long, and one hundred and thirty feet wide, was built at an expense of one hundred thousand dollars.

Frank Lockwood of Montgomery designed the south and the north wings. The *Official Guide to the City of Montgomery for 1920* states that "every effort was made to keep these additions in harmony with the original Greek type of architecture." [2]

This building was constructed out of brick with plaster finish. [3] It has the rectangular form of the early period of Greek architecture with the Ionic columns. There is a low, flat, box tower covering the clock built on top of the many-columned Grecian portico over the front entrance.

Rising from the central portion of the building is a dome, which is so characteristic of the American capitol buildings, and which goes back for its origin to Byzantine architecture.

ARIZONA

The location of the Arizona capitol building is at Phoenix. The architect who designed it was J. Reilly Gordon. This structure as a whole has marked characteristics of modern Classical Renaissance architecture modified by Spanish influence.

The ground story has the Roman arched windows and the arched apertures through which passageways lead.

---

[2] *Official Guide to the City of Montgomery*, The Tintigil Club (The Paragon Press, Montgomery, Alabama, 1920) p. 11.

[3] A letter from Mrs. Marie B. Owen, Director of the State Department of Archives and History, Montgomery, Alabama, August 14, 1931.

The windows in the second story are rectangular. The front of the second story consists of a Grecian columned portico. The half story on the top resembles that of the Cabildo in New Orleans, Louisiana. The low central dome, shaped as is the half of an egg shell, has balanced opposite it on each side a low flat rectangular turret. The dome is crowned with a figure which resembles that of the *Goddess of Liberty*.

The west wing, designed by A. J. Gilford, was begun in 1918 and finished in 1919 at a cost of one hundred fifty-five thousand dollars.

The foundation of this structure is built out of granite taken from the hills near Phoenix. The walls are constructed of "tufa [rock], a loosely-compacted volcanic ash, brought from Kirkland Valley, a hundred miles" [4] to the north of Phoenix.

ARKANSAS

The capitol of Arkansas is situated at Little Rock. The architects who designed this edifice were George R. Mann and Cass Gilbert. Its style of architecture is Grecian. This structure closely resembles in design and exterior appearance the United States Capitol at Washington, D. C. Section seven of the act providing for the erection of this Statehouse says that "the State Penitentiary Board shall turn over to the Board of State Capitol commissioners, such a number of convicts as can be advantageously worked upon the construction of the Capitol building and the manufacture of brick and the quarrying and cutting of stone therefor, not exceeding two hundred (200) in number." [5]

It is built out of Batesville marble and Indiana oölitic limestone. The interior is finished with Alabama marble.

[4] *Arizona, The Youngest State: Arizona, Prehistoric—Aboriginal—Pioneer—Modern,* James H. McClintock (The S. J. Clarke Publishing Company, Chicago, Illinois, 1916) vol. 2, p. 349.

[5] *Acts of Arkansas, 1899: Acts and Resolutions of the General Assembly of the State of Arkansas . . .* by authority (Neither the name of the publisher nor the place of publication is given.) p. 210-11.

This structure was completed in 1912, the approximate cost being two million, five hundred thousand dollars.

CALIFORNIA

Sacramento contains the site of the capitol building of California. The area of the capitol grounds is forty and two-tenths acres. This building, completed in 1874, is two hundred and forty-seven feet long, one hundred and sixty-four feet wide, and two hundred and thirty-seven feet high to the top of the dome. The wings, built one at the north end and one at the south end of the east side, are each eighty-one feet long, fifty-eight feet wide, and ninety-four feet high. The semicircular wing in the middle of the east side is sixty-nine feet wide across and is "built out for a distance of fifty-four feet." The dome, fifty-three and one-half feet in diameter at its base, and one hundred and twenty-five feet high, closely resembles in appearance the one on the United States Capitol.

F. M. Butler was the architect who drew the original plan or design for this structure. The superintending architects were Reuben Clark, who having resigned on account of ill health in 1865, was succeeded the following year by G. P. Cummings, who was also succeeded later by A. A. Bennett, under whose supervision the building was completed.

The cost, including the changes made from 1906 to 1908, was approximately two million, nine hundred seventy-two thousand, nine hundred and twenty-five dollars. George G. Radcliff, Chairman of the State Board of Control, says that "the architecture of the building is of the florid Roman-Corinthian type, reminiscent of the Forum in Rome, [and that] the exterior walls of the basement and the first story are constructed of California granite and the three upper stories are of hard burned brick covered with mastic and white paint." [6]

⁶ *California Blue Book, Legislative Manual or State Roster, April, 1924*, compiled by and under the supervision of and published and distributed by Frank C. Jordan, Secretary of State (State Printing Office, Sacramento, California, 1924) p. 123-5.

COLORADO

The Colorado Statehouse is built at Denver, its site containing ten acres of land. Its cornerstone was laid in 1890, but the building was not completed until 1900.

This structure is three hundred and eighty-four feet long, three hundred and thirteen feet wide, and one hundred and two feet high to the cornices. The top of the dome, which is inlaid with fourteen carat gold, is two hundred and seventy-six feet from the plane of the ground beneath.

The architects who designed this building were E. E. Myers and Son of Detroit, Michigan; but F. E. Edbrook of Denver was the architect who supervised its construction.

This capitol building represents the Doric type of Grecian architecture, "with Corinthian ornamentations." [7] It is constructed out of Gunnison granite and native onyx at an approximate cost of two million, five hundred thousand dollars.

CONNECTICUT

The capitol building of Connecticut is located on the Capitol grounds adjacent to Bushnell Park at Hartford. It was designed by R. M. Upjohn of New York City.

It has the following dimensions: "extreme length, two hundred [and] ninety-five feet [and] eight inches; width of central part, one hundred [and] eighty-nine feet [and] four inches; of wings, one hundred [and] eleven feet [and] eight inches; height from ground to top of roof, ninety-two feet [and] eight inches; to top of crowning figure, two hundred [and] fifty-seven feet [and] two inches." [8]

This building is patterned after the secular Gothic type of Grecian architecture. Its length is "broken by

[7] "The History of Colorado," in *Colorado Civil Government and History,* Dorus R. Hatch and Eugene Parsons (Herrick Book and Stationery Company, Denver, Colorado, 1930) p. 65.

[8] *The Connecticut State Register and Manual, 1928,* Francis A. Pallotti, Secretary of State (Press of the Wilson H. Lee Company, New Haven, Connecticut, 1928) p. 5.

columns, arches, galleries, arcades, and commemorative sculptures and statuary." [9]

Its dome, consisting of twelve sides and rising to a height of two hundred and seventy-five feet, "is crowned by a bronze statue of 'The Genius of Connecticut.'" [9]

The Connecticut capitol building, constructed out of East-Canaan white marble, cost approximately two million, five hundred thirty-two thousand, five hundred and twenty-four dollars and forty-three cents, "including heating and ventilating apparatus and such statuary as was placed at the time of erection." [10]

The Connecticut State Library and Supreme Court Building is located on Capitol Avenue due south of the State Capitol, to which it forms a suitable companion. The style of the architecture of this building belongs to the Italian Renaissance type of Classical architecture. This beautiful granite structure is built in the shape of a capital *T*, the front of which is two hundred ninety-four feet and eight inches long, with a north and south depth of one hundred thirty-seven feet and six inches, the ends of the *T* being eighty-four feet wide. The stem of the *T* which forms the south wing of this building is seventy-six feet long and sixty feet wide. Three main floors and a basement compose the interior of this building. The basement, located under the central portion of the building, contains the machinery used to heat and ventilate the structure, and from which a proposed subway will lead to the Capitol. The main floor houses the main reading room, Memorial Hall, and the Supreme Court Room.

DELAWARE

Dover is the site of the Delaware Statehouse. The original structure was built in 1722 to be used as the

[9] *King's Handbook of the United States,* planned and edited by Moses King, text by M. F. Sweetser (Moses King Corporation, Publishers, Buffalo, New York, 1891) p. 123.

[10] *The Connecticut State Register and Manual, 1928,* Francis A. Pallotti, Secretary of State (Press of the Wilson H. Lee Company, New Haven, Connecticut, 1928) p. 5.

court house of Kent County. It became the home of the state governing officials in 1777.

The present building, which was begun in 1783 and completed in 1792, was built on the site of the original building. The Statehouse has been remodeled twice and built to the same number of times, the remodeling having been done from 1788 to 1891, and in 1870. An addition consisting of two stories and a basement, to be used as the Senate chamber and State library, was added in 1836, the size being forty by fifty feet, and the cost amounting to about three thousand dollars. [11] A library wing was added in 1909, and a rear annex was constructed in 1926, the architects for the annex being Brown and Whiteside of Wilmington, Delaware.

This Statehouse, built on the order of the New England town hall, may be classified as the Colonial or the modern Georgian type of architecture. The building is constructed out of brick with stone trimmings. From the central portion of this structure rises a three storied hexagonal tower, the top of which is crowned with a dome supported by Grecian columns.

In 1795 the State paid one thousand sixty-six dollars and seventy-seven cents for putting a new roof on this structure, for adding stone steps to it, for completing the battlements, and for painting. This building was purchased by the State in 1873, at a cost of fifteen thousand dollars.

FLORIDA

The location of the capitol building of Florida is at Tallahassee. The corner stone of this structure was laid in 1826, [12] but the edifice was not completed until 1842. However, J. H. Reese says that the "dates on the cornerstone . . . show [that] the main body of the building was erected in 1839-42." [13]

[11] *History of Delaware, 1609-1888,* John Thomas Scharf (L. J. Richards and Company, Philadelphia, Pennsylvania, 1888) vol. 2, p. 1033.
[12] *History of Florida, Past and Present, Historical and Biographical,* Henry Gardner Cutler (The Lewis Publishing Company, Chicago and New York, 1923) vol. 1, p. 113.
[13] *Florida Flashlights,* J. H. Reese (The Hefty Press, Miami, Florida, 1917) p. 60.

During the interval of time from 1901 to 1902, "the dome, the north and south wings, and the stone steps were added." [14] The legislature of 1901 appropriated seventy-five thousand dollars to pay for these additions. [15] During the time intervening between the years 1921 and 1922, "initiatory steps were taken" to remodel and to extend the Statehouse by adding to it eastern and western extensions at a cost of two hundred fifty thousand dollars. The additions, designed by H. J. Klutho of Jacksonville, give the building the general shape of a cross.

This structure, built out of brick, is patterned after the Grecian type of architecture. The dome, supported by Grecian columns, crowns a rectangular tower. There is a smaller dome, supported by columns, built on top of the larger one.

GEORGIA

The Georgia Statehouse, built at Atlanta, was begun in 1884 and completed in 1899. The architects who designed this building were Edbrooke and Burnham of Chicago, Illinois. It represents the Classical Renaissance style of architecture, having Corinthian columns on the front of the second story, Roman arched windows to the ground story, and the Byzantine dome.

This structure is built of Indiana oölitic limestone. [16] The foundation and basement are constructed out of Georgia granite, [17] and the interior is finished in Georgia marble.

This building, three hundred and forty-seven feet and five inches long from north to south, two hundred and seventy-two feet and four and one-half inches wide from

---

[14] *A History of Florida,* Caroline Mays Brevard (American Book Company, New York, Cincinnati, and Chicago, 1919) p. 200.

[15] *Florida Laws, 1901: Acts and Resolutions Adopted by the Legislature of Florida at Its Eighth Regular Session, April 2 to May 31, 1901, under the Constitution of A. D. 1885,* . . . published by authority of Law under the direction of the Attorney-General (The Tallahasseean Book and Job Print, Tallahassee, Florida, 1901) p. 31.

[16] *King's Handbook of the United States,* planned and edited by Moses King, text by M. F. Sweetser (Moses King Corporation, Publishers, Buffalo, New York, 1891) p. 185.

[17] *First Lessons in Georgia History,* Lawton B. Evans (American Book Company, New York, Cincinnati, and Chicago, 1929) p. 310.

east to west, and one hundred and seventy-two feet high to the top of the dome, cost nine hundred ninety-nine thousand, eight hundred and eighty-one dollars and fifty-seven cents. [18]

IDAHO

The site of the Idaho Statehouse is at Boise. The main structure, begun in 1906, was completed in 1912. During the years 1919 and 1920 the east and the west wings were added. Tourtellette and Hummell of Boise were the architects who designed this edifice. The dimensions of the completed building are three hundred and ninety-eight feet long, two hundred and twenty-four feet wide, and one hundred and ninety-five feet to the top of the dome.

This Statehouse, built out of Boise sandstone and finished in Vermont marble, representing the Grecian type of architecture, was patterned after the United States capitol building in the respect that it has the conventional dome and wings. Over the center of each wing is a mushroom shaped circular covering with skylights, in which respect it resembles in structure the central dome of the Library of Congress. The total cost of the building was two million, two hundred ninety thousand dollars.

ILLINOIS

The Illinois capitol building is situated at Springfield. The cornerstone was laid on October 5, 1868; but the structure was not completed until 1888.

This Statehouse, constructed in the form of a huge Latin cross, is three hundred and seventy-nine feet long from north to south, and two hundred and sixty-eight feet deep from east to west. "The tip of the flagstaff which surmounts the dome is 405 feet above the ground." [19]

[18] A letter from John B. Wilson, Secretary of the State of Georgia, Atlanta, Georgia, July 25, 1931.
[19] *Blue Book of the State of Illinois, 1915-1916,* edited by Lewis G. Stevenson, Secretary of State (Illinois Printing Company, Danville, Illinois, 1916) p. 343.

John C. Cochrane of Chicago, Illinois, designed the building. It represents a combination of the Grecian and of the Roman type of architecture, having in the first and third stories the Roman arched windows, a columned portico over the entrances, and a dome rising from the center of the structure. The dome rests on its own basic foundation twenty-five and one-half feet below the surface of the earth beneath. The foundation of this dome is circular, ninety-two and one-half feet in diameter.

The walls of the foundation are built out of granular magnesian limestone, transported from the Sonora quarries in Hancock County, Illinois. The walls of the superstructure are constructed out of Niagara limestone. The interior is finished in blue limestone and in Missouri red granite.

This Statehouse cost approximately four million, five hundred thousand dollars. [20]

INDIANA

The capitol of Indiana is located at Indianapolis. The campus on which it is situated contains about nine acres of land.

This structure, in the form of a huge Latin cross, is four hundred and ninety-six feet long from north to south, and two hundred and eighty-three feet wide from east to west. The top of the dome rises to a height of two hundred and thirty-five feet. The skylights over the north and south corridors are each one hundred and fifteen feet long, and thirty-five feet wide. [21]

Edwin May of Indianapolis was the architect who designed this building, which represents a combination of the Grecian and of the Roman types of architecture.

[20] For a full description of this State capitol building, see the *Blue Book of the State of Illinois for 1915-1916*, edited by Lewis G. Stevenson, Secretary of State (Illinois Printing Company, Danville, Illinois, 1916) p. 343-5.

[21] *Year Book of the State of Indiana for the Year 1919*, compiled and published under the direction of James P. Goodrich, Governor, by Charles Kettleborough, Director of the Legislative Reference Bureau (Fort Wayne Printing Company, Fort Wayne, Indiana, 1920) p. 950-1.

"The exterior walls of the building are of oölitic and [of] blue limestone, and domestic marble and granite is used in the interior finish of the corridors." [22] The cost of this structure was approximately two million, ninety-nine thousand, seven hundred and ninety-four dollars.

IOWA

The site of the Iowa Statehouse is at Des Moines. The cornerstone of this building was laid on November 23, 1871; but the structure was not completed until July 4, 1886.

The firm of Cochrane and Pinquenard were the architects who designed this State capitol building, which represents a combination of the Grecian and of the Roman types of architecture. It is constructed in the form of a Greek cross and has the Grecian columns, the Roman arched windows, and a central dome, balanced opposite which are two pairs of domes situated on the opposite ends of the wings.

The length of this Statehouse from north to south is three hundred and sixty-three feet and eight inches, the width from east to west is two hundred and forty-six feet and eleven inches. The "top of the finial above the dome" is two hundred and seventy-five feet. The diameter of the dome at its base is sixty-six feet and eight inches.

The area of the capitol grounds is ninety-three and one-quarter acres. "The foundation and basement [is] built out of Iowa stone." The walls of the main edifice are constructed out of stone obtained both from Carroll County, Iowa, and from St. Genevieve, Missouri. In the finishing work "twenty-nine kinds of domestic and imported marble" were used. The woodwork consists mainly of "Iowa black walnut, butternut, cherry, oak, and catalpa."

[22] *Year Book of the State of Indiana for the Year 1919,* compiled and published under the direction of James P. Goodrich, Governor, by Charles Kettleborough, Director of the Legislative Reference Bureau (Fort Wayne Printing Company, Fort Wayne, Indiana, 1920) p. 951.

The total cost of this building was three million, two hundred ninety-six thousand, two hundred and fifty-six dollars. [23]

KANSAS

The capitol of Kansas is located at Topeka. It was started in 1866 and completed in 1903. This structure, built in the shape of a cross, is three hundred and eighty-six feet from east to west, and three hundred and ninety-nine feet from north to south. [24] The top of the dome surmounted by the statue of the *Goddess Ceres*, is three hundred and four feet from the plane of the ground beneath.

McDonald Brothers of Louisville designed the building. Haskell and Wood of Topeka, Kansas, were the superintending architects. The architecture represents the Greek Classical type.

The foundation is constructed out of Kansas stone. The walls of the superstructure are built of yellow and gray native stone. It cost three million, two hundred thousand, five hundred and eighty-eight dollars and ninety-two cents to erect this structure.

KENTUCKY

The capitol building of Kentucky is situated at Frankfort. This Statehouse, begun in 1905, was not completed until 1909. It is four hundred and two feet and ten inches long from east to west, and one hundred and eighty feet wide through the central portion from north to south. The lantern on the top of the dome is two hundred and ten feet from the level of the ground beneath. F. M. Andrews and Company of New York City designed this structure.

[23] For a full description of the Iowa State capitol building, see *Iowa Official Register, 1929-1930*, H. N. Whitney, compiled under the direction of Robert Henderson, Superintendent of Printing (Published by the State of Iowa, Des Moines, Iowa, 1929) p. 91.

[24] "The Capitols of Kansas" by Franklin G. Adams in *Kansas Historical Collections: Transactions of the Kansas State Historical Society, 1903-1904; Together with Addresses at Annual Meetings, Miscellaneous Papers, and a Roster of Kansas for Fifty Years*, edited by George W. Martin, Secretary (George A. Clark, State Printer, Topeka, Kansas, 1904) vol. 8, p. 331-51.

C. M. Fleenor was the superintending architect. "The building is of the French Renaissance [type of] architecture with the neo-classic feature of the dome." [25] The total cost of the structure was one million, two hundred fifty thousand dollars.

LOUISIANA

Baton Rouge is the site of the Louisiana capitol building. The original Statehouse was erected in 1847, J. H. Dakin being the architect who designed it. The next Statehouse, designed by W. A. Freret, was built during the years from 1880 to 1882. This building was "a fine Gothic structure, with circular turrets which rise from the ground and crown the extremities of the building, and smaller turrets which top the larger ones." [26] King describes it as "a picturesque Elizabethan building . . . with battlemented towers and [with] Gothic windows." [27]

The present Louisiana capitol building, being constructed of Indiana oölitic limestone, will be three hundred and twenty-two feet long, one hundred and twenty feet wide, and four hundred and thirty-three feet high to the top of the tower, which is seventy feet square inside. [28]

MAINE

The location of the Maine capitol building is at Augusta. The length of the building is three hundred feet, including the north and south wings. The dome is one hundred and eighty-five feet high. [29]

[25] *Press Reference Book of Prominent Kentuckians*, Editor-in-chief, Colonel Ben. LaBree (The Standard Printing Company, Incorporated, Louisville, Kentucky, 1916) p. 5.

[26] *Louisiana: Comprising Sketches of Counties, Towns, Events, Institutions, and Persons, Arranged in Cyclopedic Form,* edited by Alcée Fortier (Southern Historical Association, Atlanta, Georgia, 1909) vol. 1, p. 159.

[27] *King's Handbook of the United States,* planned and edited by Moses King, text by M. F. Sweetser (Moses King Corporation, Publishers, Buffalo, New York) p. 306-7.

[28] A letter from James A. McMillen, Librarian, Louisiana State University and Agricultural and Mechanical College Library, Baton Rouge, Louisiana, July 30, 1931.

[29] *The Maine Book,* Henry E. Dunnack (Henry E. Dunnack, Augusta, Maine, 1920) p. 90.

The statue of *Augusta* surmounting the cupola, designed and executed by W. Clark Noble, is "made of copper covered with gold." The original building, completed in 1832, was designed by Charles Bulfinch; the Statehouse was completely remodeled in 1909 and 1910 according to the designs made by G. Henri Desmond.

The white granite used for the original building and for the additions was taken from the quarry at Hallowell, Maine.

The original cost of the structure, which represents the Greek Renaissance type of architecture, was one hundred twenty-five thousand dollars, and of the remodeling, three hundred fifty thousand dollars. [30]

MARYLAND

The Statehouse of Maryland at Annapolis was in the process of building from 1772-1775. It has been built to several times, the last addition having been built in 1905. It is a brick structure with stone trimmings crowned with a four storied hexagonal dome made of wood. Joseph Clarke was the architect who designed it; but William Buckland, an architect-builder, was the interior decorator.

The legislature of 1769 appropriated £7,500 sterling to build the original structure. Elihu S. Riley says that "the building committee was Daniel Dulany, Thomas Johnson, John Hall, William Paca, Charles Carroll, Barrister, Launcelot Jacques, and Charles Wallace, [and that] the majority were empowered to contract with workmen, and to purchase materials, and were authorized to draw on the dual treasurers of the State for whatever further sums might be required to complete the building." [31]

The original structure was about one hundred and twenty feet long, eight-two feet wide, and two hundred

---

[30] *Maine: Its History, Resources, and Government*, Revised Edition, Glenn Wendell Starkey (Silver, Burdett and Company, New York, Boston, and Chicago, 1930) p. 47-8.
[31] *"The Ancient City": A History of Annapolis, in Maryland, 1649-1887*, Elihu S. Riley (Record Printing Office, Annapolis, Maryland, 1887) p. 161.

feet high. It was patterned after the Colonial type of architecture. "The dome was not added" until after the close of "the Revolutionary war." The library building, an octagonal room, was added to the west side of this building in 1859. This was removed and replaced by a square building in 1905.

MASSACHUSETTS

The Massachusetts Statehouse at Boston is one of the best known and one of the most beautiful of the capitol buildings. The original cornerstone was laid on July 4, 1795, and the erecting of the "forward projection of the west wing" was legally sanctioned on May 13, 1915, thus it may be seen that one hundred and twenty years elapsed from the starting of this structure to the beginning of its last addition.

The original capitol, designed by Charles Bulfinch, was constructed out of red brick at a cost of one hundred thirty-five thousand dollars. This capitol building was one hundred and seventy-two feet long, sixty-five feet wide, and one hundred and fifty-five feet high to the top of the dome. [32] It has the columned portico at the front of the second story, the arched apertures through which front entrance is made, the Roman arched windows to the second story, and a dome surmounted by a cupola.

During the interval of time from 1798 to 1866, additions were built on the north front and on the north side. In 1866 a movement was launched to remodel the State-house. In 1889 the remodeling program was authorized, and the money was appropriated by the legislature of the commonwealth to meet the expense of the undertaking.

The Bulfinch Statehouse was altered, enlarged, and additions were built to it; but the original front was preserved. William Chapmen, R. Clipston Sturgis, and Robert D. Andrews were the architects. The architecture

[32] *The State House, Boston, Massachusetts,* Ninth Edition, Ellen Mudge Burrill (Wright and Potter Printing Company, Boston, Massachusetts, 1927) p. 9.

is a combination of the Classical and of the American Academic type. The entire structure was to be kept in harmony with the Bulfinch front. Lateral projections were constructed on the east and the west sides of the Bulfinch house, and then east and west wings were added.

The dimensions of this Statehouse are four hundred and fifty-four feet and four inches long from east to west, four hundred and sixty-two feet broad from north to south, and fifty-nine feet high to the top of the cupola on the dome.

The total cost of the buildings and the improvements amounted to about nine million, five hundred seventy-five thousand, two hundred and fifty-three dollars and fifty cents.

The foundations are of granite, part of the walls of the superstructure is of English buff brick, and part is of Vermont marble. Part of the marble was brought from Lee, Massachusetts, and part of the granite came from Augusta, Maine. The dome of this building is covered with twenty-three carat leaf gold.

MICHIGAN

The capitol building at Michigan is located at Lansing. Its campus contains ten acres of land. This edifice is four hundred and twenty feet long, two hundred and seventy-four feet wide, and two hundred and sixty-seven feet high. [33] Elijah E. Myers of Springfield, Illinois, was the architect who designed it. The cornerstone was laid in 1873, and the building was completed in 1878.

The architecture of this structure may be classified as the Academic-Roman type of later Classical Renaissance architecture.

New Hampshire granite was used in constructing this building. The total cost was one million, five hundred ten

[33] For a discussion of the Michigan Capitol building, see *Michigan's Official Directory and Legislative Manual for the Years 1921 and 1922,* compiled by Charles J. DeLand, Secretary of State (Neither the name of the publisher, the place, nor the date of publication is given.) p. 1-2.

thousand, one hundred and thirty dollars and fifty-nine cents.

MINNESOTA

St. Paul is the site of the capitol building of Minnesota. The cornerstone of this structure was laid July 27, 1898; but it was not completed until 1905. Cass Gilbert of New York City designed this edifice. It belongs to the Italian Renaissance type of architecture.

This Statehouse, constructed of grayish white Georgia marble and of St. Cloud granite, is four hundred and thirty-three feet in length, two hundred and twenty-eight feet through its central portion, and two hundred and twenty feet high to the top of the dome. [34] The dome is constructed of marble and crowned with a golden ball. The total cost of this capitol was three million, nine hundred and seventy-five dollars. [34]

MISSISSIPPI

The capitol building of Mississippi is located at Jackson. This building, designed by Theodore C. Link of St. Louis, Missouri, was completed in 1903. It is constructed out of bright gray Indiana oölitic stone. This Statehouse, one hundred and thirty-five feet high, represents the French Renaissance type of architecture and cost one million, ninety-three thousand, six hundred and forty-one dollars. [35]

MISSOURI

The Statehouse of Missouri is situated at Jefferson City. It was in the process of construction from 1912 to 1917. Tracy and Swartwout of New York City designed this building. This edifice is four hundred and thirty-seven feet long, three hundred feet through the central portion, and two hundred and sixty-two feet high from

[34] *Minnesota and Its People,* edited by Joseph A. A. Burnquist (The S. J. Clarke Publishing Company, Chicago, Illinois, 1924) p. 380.

[35] A letter from Dunbar Rowland, State Historian and Director of the State Department of Archives and History, Jackson, Mississippi, August 3, 1931.

the basement floor to the top of the dome. "The building stands upon 285 concrete piers of varying sizes, which extend to solid rock at depths ranging from twenty to fifty feet." [36]

Dr. John Pickard says that "the beautiful fluted columns, free and engaged, entirely surrounding the structure, give the appearance of a Grecian temple erected in the halcyon days of ancient architecture." [37]

The superstructure is built out of a pure white limestone marble from Carthage and from Phoenix, Missouri. The interior is finished in Missouri gray marble. The total cost of this capitol was three million, seven hundred and seventy-five thousand dollars.

MONTANA

Helena contains the location of the capitol building of Montana. The construction of this edifice extended over a period of sixteen years from 1896 to 1912. George R. Mann of St. Louis, Missouri, designed the original building. Mann, whose plan had been adopted, was discharged in 1897 by an act of the legislature which provided that " 'all architects, superintendents and contractors shall be citizens of the State of Montana.' " [38] Bell and Kent of Helena, Montana, were selected in 1898 to draw the plans for the building.

The finished structure represents the Ionic pattern of Greek architecture and was built out of Montana sandstone taken from the quarries at Columbus, Montana. This Statehouse is "two hundred [and] fifty feet long and one hundred [and] thirty feet wide." The building, furnishings, and decorations cost four hundred ninety thousand, four hundred and sixty-four dollars.

[36] *The Missouri State Capitol: Report of the Capitol Decoration Commission, 1917-1928,* John Pickard (The Hugh Stephens Press, Jefferson City, Missouri, 1928) p. 19.

[37] *Ibidem,* p. 23.

[38] *Montana, The Land and The People,* Robert George Raymer (The Lewis Publishing Company, Chicago and New York, 1930) vol. I, p. 376.

NEBRASKA

The capitol of Nebraska, located at Lincoln, is most unique and original in design and in structure. It was built out of oölitic limestone from Bedford, Indiana, during the period of time from 1922 to 1932. Bertram Goodhue of New York City designed this edifice. It consists of a square group of two story buildings from the center of which rises a square tower crowned with a dome. This edifice is in the form of a rectangle four hundred and thirty-seven feet square, and the central tower is four hundred feet high.

Dr. Edgell says that the design is "frankly modern and closely related to the trend of modernistic architectural expression in the Scandinavian countries." [39]

He says that "Mr. Goodhue designed a low mass of buildings, telling as one story, with an immense and severe portico in the centre and an enormous tower dominating the whole. . . . The windows are rectangular and unadorned with any enframements, classic or otherwise. The detail of the main portal is as original and simple as it is massive. The great tower, crowned with a cupola, is slashed with vertical openings which broadcast its steel construction." [40]

The approximate cost was about ten million dollars "for completing, decorating, furnishing, landscaping and construction of a heating and lighting plant for the capitol." [41]

NEVADA

The Nevada Statehouse is located at Carson City. It was completed in 1871. Joseph Goseling of San Francisco, California, designed this building, which represents the Classical type of Renaissance architecture. It is con-

[39] *The American Architecture of To-Day,* G. H. Edgell (Charles Scribner's Sons, New York, London, 1928) p. 231.

[40] *Ibidem,* p. 231.

[41] *The Nebraska Blue Book, 1930* (A Publication of the Nebraska Legislative Reference Bureau, Lincoln, Nebraska, December, 1930) p. 18.

structed out of native sandstone taken from the State prison yard about one mile east of Carson City. [42] The dimensions are one hundred and forty-four feet long, seventy-two feet wide, fifty-six feet to the top of the side walls, and one hundred and twenty feet to the top of the dome. In 1913 additions were added to each end, forty feet long, and eighty-four feet wide.

NEW HAMPSHIRE

Concord contains the site of the capitol of New Hampshire. Steward C. Park designed the original building. This structure represents the Classic type of architecture having Doric columns on the front and a Classic dome, the top of which is surmounted by the image of an American eagle. This building, constructed out of New Hampshire stone, is one hundred and twenty-six feet in length, and forty-nine feet in width. The total cost was eighty-one thousand, eight hundred and twenty-seven dollars and sixty cents. [43]

It was remodeled during the period of time from 1864 to 1866 at a cost of one hundred fifty thousand dollars. At this time there was added to the central part a structure fifty feet long, and twenty-eight feet wide; and on each wing, a building thirty-eight feet by twenty-eight feet. The entire structure was remodeled and enlarged again in 1919.

NEW JERSEY

The New Jersey capitol at Trenton, completed in 1889, has been several times enlarged by additional buildings. The original structure is one hundred and sixty feet long, sixty-seven feet wide, and one hundred and forty-five feet high to the top of the dome. L. H. Broome of Jersey City

[42] A letter from V. M. Henderson, Librarian, Nevada State Library, Carson City, Nevada, August 4, 1931.

[43] For a discussion of the New Hampshire Statehouse, see *State of New Hampshire Manual for the General Court, 1901,* prepared and published under section 14, chap. 15, of the Public Statutes, no. seven (Arthur E. Clarke, Public Printer, Manchester, New Hampshire, 1901) p. 291-5.

was the designer. It represents the Classical style of Renaissance architecture. "The walls are constructed of solid, fire-proof, brick masonry, faced with a light-colored stone from Indiana, known as Salem oölitic, with foundations and trimmings of New Jersey free stone, from the Prallsville quarries, in Hunterdon county." [44] The cost of this original capitol was two hundred seventy-five thousand dollars.

In 1891 an assembly chamber was added to this structure. James Moylan of Jersey City designed this new part, which is one hundred and twenty feet long, and seventy-five feet wide. The foundation is built of "brown stone, from the Stockton quarries, and the trimmings of light Indiana stone." The cost of this addition was one hundred forty thousand, five hundred dollars.

A senate chamber was erected in 1903 at a cost of one hundred eighty-two thousand dollars, Arnold H. Moses of Merchantville being the architect.

In 1907 another building, representing the Classical style of architecture, was added. George E. Poole, the State architect, designed this structure which is built of brick. In 1911 and 1912, one hundred thirty thousand dollars was appropriated for constructing the east and west wings. The completed edifice stands upon a nineteen-acre tract of land, the total cost of all the buildings and improvements amounting to about four hundred thousand dollars. [45]

NEW MEXICO

The site of the capitol of New Mexico is at Santa Fe. It was completed in 1900, at a cost of one hundred and twenty-five thousand dollars. However, additions have been added to it twice since. The architects who designed it were I. H. and W. M. Rapp. This structure represents the Grecian type of classic architecture. It was con-

---

[44] *State of New Jersey, Manual of the Legislature of New Jersey, One Hundred and Fifty-fifth Session, 1931,* by authority of the Legislature, Josephine A. Fitzgerald, Publisher, John P. Dullard, Compiler (MacCrellish and Quigley Company, Trenton, New Jersey, 1931) p. 79.

[45] *Ibidem,* p. 80.

structed out of brick and of buff sandstone. Above the basement, it is three stories high and is surmounted by a circular dome.

NEW YORK

The capitol of New York is located at Albany. The cornerstone was laid on June 24, 1871; and the original edifice was completed in 1879. The part of the capitol destroyed by fire in 1911 has been rebuilt. This structure was designed by Thomas Fuller. Other architects who have helped to shape it into its present form were Frederick Law Olmstead, Leopold Eidlitz, Henry H. Richardson, Isaac G. Perry, and Louis F. Pilcher. This building may be said to belong to the French-Academic type of architecture. It is four hundred feet long, three hundred feet wide, and one hundred and eight feet high. It is constructed of granite and cost approximately twenty-five million dollars. The interior is finished in Knoxville (Tennessee) marble, in Mexican onyx, and in Sienna (Italian) marble. It is one of the most picturesque and elaborate of statehouses.

NORTH CAROLINA

The site of North Carolina Statehouse is at Raleigh. This building, completed in 1840, was designed by David Patton of New York City; and the construction was superintended by David Patton. The length from north to south is one hundred and sixty feet, the width from east to west, one hundred and forty feet, and the height, ninety-seven and one-half feet.

This edifice, built of granite, represents the Greek type of architecture. It has been said that "the columns and entablature are Grecian Doric, and copied from the Temple of Minerva, commonly called the Parthenon, which was erected in Athens about 500 years before Christ. An octagon tower surrounds the rotunda, which is ornamented with Grecian cornices, etc., and its dome is decorated at top with a similar ornament to that of the Choragic

Monument of Lysicrates, commonly called the Lanthorn of Demosthenes." [46]

The approximate cost of the structure was five hundred thirty-one thousand, six hundred and seventy-four dollars and forty-six cents.

There was a State administration building constructed in 1911, at a cost of one hundred eighty-eight thousand dollars.

NORTH DAKOTA

The location of the capitol building of North Dakota is at Bismarck. This "State Capitol is built of three kinds of brick, having been built in three parts; first the center, built in 1883, then the front with portico in 1893, and lastly the large addition at the rear in 1902." [47]

.There was available for this building about one million, two hundred thousand dollars. [48]

L. S. Buffington of Minneapolis, Minnesota, was the architect for the central portion; George Hancock of Fargo, North Dakota, was the architect for the front section; and Butler Brothers and Ryan of Saint Paul, Minnesota, were the architects of the back portion. This building was completely destroyed by fire in December, 1930.

The new capitol is about three hundred and ninety feet long, "the greatest dimension being about 160 feet. It is an 'L' shaped building. The round dimension has a height of about 60 feet. The one end of this building rises to 236 feet and the dimensions are 95 by 95 feet. The building is a steel skeleton building, fire-proofed with tile and brick,

[46] *Publications of the North Carolina Historical Commission, North Carolina Manual, 1927,* compiled and edited by A. R. Newsome, Secretary of the North Carolina Historical Commission (Edwards and Broughton Company, State Printers, Raleigh, North Carolina, 1927) p. 300.

[47] *North Dakota of Today,* Zena Irma Trinka (Bismarck Tribune Publishing Company, Bismarck, North Dakota, 1919) p. 193.

[48] *History of North Dakota,* Lewis F. Crawford (The American Historical Society, Inc. Chicago and New York, 1931) vol. 1, p. 467.

faced on the outside with Indiana limestone and the type of architecture represented is modern American." [49]

The architects who designed this building are "De Remer, Kurke, Holabird and Root, altho the responsibility for the design lies with Holabird and Root, 333 North Michigan Avenue, Chicago, Illinois." [49] The cost of this Statehouse will be about one million, seven hundred fifty thousand dollars. [49]

OHIO

The Ohio capitol building at Columbus, begun in 1838 and completed in 1861, cost one million six hundred forty-four thousand, six hundred and seventy-seven dollars. The architects who designed it were Henry Walter of Cincinnati, Martin E. Thompson of New York City, and Thomas Cole of Catskill, New York. From 1848 to 1861 the supervising architects were William Russell West and J. O. Sawyer. West resigned in 1854 and N. B. Kelly was appointed to take his place. This Statehouse is "built of limestone taken from the State owned quarry, five miles northwest of the city. The labor was done by convicts from the State penitentiary." [50] The style of architecture is Doric Greek, of which it is a splendid specimen. This State capitol is three hundred and four feet long, one hundred and eighty-four feet wide, and one hundred and fifty-eight feet high. An annex or judicial building was constructed on the east front of this structure, begun in 1898 and dedicated in 1901. This addition, two hundred and twenty feet long, and ninety-nine feet wide, constructed of the same material as the building proper, cost four hundred thousand dollars.

OKLAHOMA

Oklahoma City is the site of the capitol of Oklahoma. It was completed in 1917. S. A. Layton and S. Wemyss-

[49] A letter from Frank L. Anders, Secretary of the Board of State Capitol Commissioners, Bismarck, North Dakota, May 18, 1932.

[50] A letter from Alice Boardman, Reference Librarian, Ohio State Library, Columbus, Ohio, August 12, 1931.

Smith of Oklahoma City were the architects who designed it. The type of architecture is a combination of the Greek and of the Roman Classical. The outside walls are built of Georgia pink granite and of limestone. This State-house, in the form of a huge cross, is four hundred and eighty feet long from east to west, three hundred and forty feet deep from north to south, and is five stories high above the basement. The total cost was one million, five hundred thousand dollars.

OREGON

The Statehouse of Oregon at Salem was completed in 1876. Justus F. Krumbein of Portland, Oregon, was the architect who designed it. The structure is built of brick with limestone and with sandstone trimmings, taken from the Douglas County quarries. It has been said that "the general plan of the building is that of a cross, the length being from north to south, and the width from east to west. The main fronts are on the east and west wings, which are 60 feet in width, and the wings extending north and south are 100 feet in length and 80 feet in width. The east and west main fronts project 40 feet from the main walls, and there are porticoes 50 feet wide and 16 feet deep across each, with steps full width. The porticoes are supported on large Corinthian columns with heavy pedestals. These columns extend in one length the height of two stories." [51] The cost of this structure was approximately three hundred twenty-five thousand dollars. The copper dome and porticoes have been added since the completion of this structure, the cost of which is not included in that of the original statehouse.

PENNSYLVANIA

The Pennsylvania capitol building at Harrisburg was begun in 1904 and completed in 1906. Joseph M. Huston was the architect who designed it. This edifice is con-

[51] *The Oregon Blue Book, 1929-1930: State of Oregon, Blue Book and Official Directory, 1929-1930*, compiled by Hal E. Hoss, Secretary of State (State Printing Department, Salem, Oregon, 1929) p. 25.

structed out of Vermont granite and represents the Classical type of Renaissance architecture. This Statehouse is five hundred and twenty feet long, two hundred and fifty-four feet wide, and two hundred and seventy-two feet high. The cost of the building, furniture, and equipment was eleven million, thirty-three thousand, four hundred dollars and eighty-nine cents. [52]

RHODE ISLAND

The Rhode Island Statehouse is located at Providence. McKim, Mead, and White of New York City were the architects who designed it. This building, representing the Greek type of Renaissance architecture, is constructed out of brick, iron, and Georgia marble. It is three hundred and thirty-three feet long through the wings, one hundred and eighty feet wide through the central portion, and two hundred and thirty-five feet to the top of the statue on the dome.

The cost of the grounds, buildings, furnishings, and decorations was three million, eighteen thousand, four hundred and sixteen dollars and thirty-three cents. [53]

SOUTH CAROLINA

The Statehouse of South Carolina, located at Columbia, was begun in 1851 and completed in 1904. The original architect was Major John R. Niernsee who died before the building was completed. The succeeding architects were J. Crawford Neilson, J. Frank Niernsee, Frank P. Milburn, and Charles C. Wilson. This structure was built of local granite. It represents a rather free style of the Corinthian type of Roman architecture. The building

[52] For a detailed discussion of this building, see *The Pennsylvania Manual,* compiled under the direction of the Department of Property and Supplies, published by the Commonwealth of Pennsylvania (Bureau of Publications, Harrisburg, Pennsylvania, 1929) p. 241.

[53] *Rhode Island Manual, 1929-1930: Manual with Rules and Orders for the Use of the General Assembly of the State of Rhode Island, 1929-1930,* prepared in accordance with the provision of section 9, chapter 28, of the General Laws, Ernest L. Sprague, Secretary of State (Press of E. L. Freeman Company, Printers and Binders, Providence, Rhode Island, 1929) p. iv.

from start to finish cost more than three million, five hundred forty thousand dollars.

South Dakota

The capitol of South Dakota is located at **Pierre**. This structure, begun in 1908, was completed in 1910. C. E. Bell of Minneapolis, Minnesota, designed this building. It represents the Classical Renaissance type of architecture. The foundations were built of "granite boulders native to the vicinity of Pierre." The superstructure was constructed of "mahogany granite taken from the Hunter Quarries in Grant County, South Dakota and in Lac Qui Prairie County, Minnesota." [54] This Statehouse is two hundred and ninety-seven feet long, one hundred and forty-two feet wide, and one hundred and sixty-five feet high from the plain of the "ground to the top of the lantern of the dome." This edifice cost approximately eight hundred thousand dollars. An annex was added to this structure in 1932 at a cost of three hundred thousand dollars.

Tennessee

Nashville is the site of the Tennessee Statehouse. The cornerstone was laid on July 4, 1845; but the structure was not completed until 1855. William Strickland of Philadelphia, Pennsylvania, was the architect who designed it. This building "follows the lines of a Greek Ionic Temple with the tower rising two hundred and five feet from the ground, patterned after 'Demosthenes' Lantern' of Athens." [55] This structure built in the form of a parallelogram is two hundred and thirty-nine feet and three inches long, one hundred and twelve feet and five inches wide, and one hundred and ninety-one feet and seven inches high from the ground to the top of the tower.

[54] *South Dakota Legislative Manual, 1931*, compiled according to provisions of law by the Division of Purchasing and Printing, John P. Baer, Director (State Publishing Company, Pierre, South Dakota, 1931) p. 527.

[55] *The Capitols of the South*, Henry D. Boynton (The Edgell Company, Philadelphia, Pennsylvania, 1917) p. 15.

It is built of stratified limestone embedded with fossils, quarried about a half mile west of the building. The cost of this capitol building was about one million dollars. [56]

TEXAS

The capitol of Texas, built at Austin, was started in 1885 and completed in 1888. Colonel E. E. Myers of Detroit, Michigan, was the architect who designed it. This structure represents the Classical Renaissance type of architecture with freedom in variations.

This Statehouse is five hundred and sixty-six feet and six inches long, two hundred and twenty-eight feet and ten inches wide, and three hundred and eleven feet high to the top of the five pointed star held by the Goddess of Liberty, which surmounts the dome "patterned after that of St. Peter's at Rome." [57] This building was constructed out of Texas red granite at a cost of approximately three million, seven hundred forty-four thousand, six hundred and sixty dollars and sixty cents for material and labor.

UTAH

The Utah Statehouse is located at Salt Lake City. It is situated on Capitol Hill, a tract of land containing about twenty acres, one part of which was donated by the city and the other part was bought from the original owners. The cornerstone was laid April 4, 1914; but the structure was not completed until 1916.

Ten of the twenty-one qualifying architects and architectural firms submitted plans for the capitol. When the ballot was taken, the designs by Richard K. A. Kletting of Salt Lake City were selected by the Capitol Commission. This building represents the pure Corinthian type of Classical architecture.

[56] *King's Handbook of the United States,* planned and edited by Moses King, text by M. F. Sweetser (Moses King Corporation, Publishers, Buffalo, New York, 1892) p. 803.

[57] *History of Texas, Fort Worth and the Texas Northwest Edition,* Captain B. B. Paddock (Lewis Publishing Company, Chicago, and New York, 1922) vol. 2, p. 478.

The provision in the original plans for "fifty-two columns, each thirty-two feet in height and three and one-half feet in diameter, to be placed along the South front and East and West ends of the building," [58] caused much discussion as to whether or not an extra expenditure of about two hundred thousand dollars for monolithic columns of polished Vermont marble would be justified. It was decided to use sectional columns made of Utah granite.

The superstructure was built out of Little Cottonwood Canyon granite taken from the Birdseye Marble Company's quarries near Thistle, Utah. The interior of the building was finished in Georgia marble and in Utah onyx or travertine. This edifice is four hundred and four feet long, two hundred and forty feet wide, and two hundred and eighty-five feet high. The cost of this Statehouse was two million, seven hundred thirty-nine thousand, five hundred and twenty-eight dollars and fifty-four cents.

VERMONT

The Vermont capitol, located at Montpelier, was built in 1838 and remodeled in 1858. Ammi B. Young designed the original building. J. R. Richards of Boston, Massachusetts, designed the addition which was added in 1857-1858. It represents the Classical type of Greek architecture with liberal variations. This edifice is constructed in the shape of a Greek cross having a dome.

It is built out of white Vermont granite quarried at Barre. The central building is one hundred and seventy-six feet and eight inches wide, and sixty feet high to the apex of the roof. This building is surmounted by a dome with a cupola, the dome being forty-four feet in diameter at its base, and fifty-six feet and nine inches high, the cupola of the dome being capped by a statue of the *Goddess Ceres*. The wings added to the central building are each

[58] *Utah Since Statehood, Historical and Biographical,* Noble Warrum, Editor (The S. J. Clarke Publishing Company, Chicago and Salt Lake City, 1919) vol. I, p. 216.

fifty-two feet long, fifty feet and eight inches wide, and about forty-seven feet and eight inches high to the apex of the roof. This structure cost approximately two hundred twenty thousand dollars.

VIRGINIA

The site of the Virginia capitol is at Richmond. The central building, begun in 1785, was completed in 1792. The wings were added in 1902. Thomas Jefferson designed this building. It represents the Classical type of architecture, which Thomas Jefferson designated as cubic architecture. [59] Jefferson patterned this structure after the Maison Quarree of Nismes, an ancient Roman temple. This structure is one hundred and forty-six feet long, eighty-four and one-half feet wide, and fifty-three feet high, [60] not including the wings added in 1906. The cost of the original building was about one hundred and twelve thousand dollars.

WASHINGTON

The capitol of Washington is located at Olympia. This building, designed by Wilder and White of New York City, represents the Classical type of Renaissance architecture. It is constructed of native sandstone known as Wilkeson stone and was completed in 1928. This structure is three hundred and thirty-nine feet long, two hundred and thirty-five feet wide through the central portion, ninety feet high in the central portion, and two hundred and seventy-eight feet high to the top of the lantern on the top of the dome. The cost was six million, five hundred fifty-four thousand, three hundred and ninety-six dollars and forty cents. This description, dimensions, and cost apply only to the legislative building. This Statehouse is built on the group plan including six buildings; namely, the old capitol building, the Governor's mansion, the temple of justice, the

[59] The *Old Dominion Magazine,* July 15, 1871.

[60] A letter from H. J. Eckenrode, Director of the Division of History and Archeology, of the State Commission on Conservation and Development, Richmond, Virginia, August 13, 1931.

insurance building, the power house and heating plant, and the legislative building. [61]

WEST VIRGINIA

Charleston contains the site of the West Virginia capitol, which was designed by Cass Gilbert of New York City. This building represents the Classical type of Renaissance architecture. It has the Grecian portico on the front, wings, and a dome. The west wing is three hundred feet long, sixty feet wide, and sixty-seven feet high. It has an ell seventy-three feet long. This wing is built of steel and of Indiana limestone. The east wing duplicates the west wing in size and in structure. The cost of the west wing was a little more than a million dollars. [62]

WISCONSIN

The Statehouse of Wisconsin, situated at Madison, was begun in 1906 and completed in 1917. George B. Post and Sons of New York City designed this building. It belongs to the Classical type of Renaissance architecture. This structure, built in the form of a Greek cross, is four hundred and thirty-eight and eight-tenths feet long from east to west, four hundred and thirty-eight and fifty-two hundredths feet wide from north to south, and eighty-four and two-tenths feet high to the end of the gable roof. The top of the statue on the dome is two hundred and eighty-five and nine-tenths feet above the ground beneath. The area of the park upon which the capitol is located is thirteen and four-tenths acres. [63]

The total cost of this building including decorations, furnishings, and equipment was seven million, two hundred three thousand, eight hundred and twenty-six dollars and thirty-five cents.

[61] *Brief Outline of the History of Washington's State Capitol Group,* Clark V. Savidge, Secretary, State Capitol Committee (Jay Thomas, Public Printer, Olympia, Washington, 1927) p. 12-15.
[62] *West Virginia in History, Life, Literature and Industry,* Morris Purdy Shawkey (The Lewis Publishing Company, Chicago and New York, 1928) vol. 2, p. 169.
[63] *The Wisconsin Blue Book, 1923* (compiled and published under the direction of the State Printing Board, 1923) p. 48.

WYOMING

The site of the Wyoming capitol is at Cheyenne. This building, begun in 1888, was completed in 1917. D. W. Gibbs and Company of Toledo, Ohio, designed this structure. It represents the Classical type of Renaissance architecture with liberty in variations. The structure is two hundred feet long, one hundred and twenty feet wide, and one hundred and forty-six feet high to the top of the dome.

The total cost of this Statehouse was approximately four hundred two thousand, five hundred and sixty-nine dollars and thirteen cents. [64]

[64] *Wyoming—Its Symbols—Its Capitol—Its Historical Department,* issued by the State Historian, Cheyenne, Wyoming, September, 1922.

CHAPTER VIII

THE STATE FLOWERS

The use of flowers to express certain sentiments and ideals may be traced back to the dawn of history. Perhaps the flower language of the Orientals is capable of expressing more varieties of sentiment than that of any other group of peoples.

The symbolic messages of the language of flowers are arbitrary with each country, state, or nation using them. Yet in spite of this there are certain flowers around which gradually sentiments have crystallized in the minds of all people. The white of the lily always stands for purity; the rose means, first of all, beauty, then love and majesty. "There's rosemary, that's for remembrance; . . . and there is pansies, that's for thoughts,"[1] Ophelia said. The narcissus recalls to our minds the hapless youth who pined away for the love of his own image seen in a pool; and the hyacinth, the flower on the petals of which the Greeks thought they discerned the letters *Ai! Ai!* or Woe! Woe!, stands for grief. The very name forget-me-not suggests the "loving, utter faithfulness in love" enjoined on the Knights of King Arthur's Round Table. The shy modesty of youth is symbolized by the violet, and the innocence which we associate with that period of life by the white violet. The daisy foretells the future by methods known to the peoples of many lands. The poppy has come to stand for sleep or oblivion because for ages, in many countries, people have known and used the narcotic properties of this plant. The daffodil has come to stand for unrequited love. The orange blossom always betokens marriage.

[1] *The Tragedy of Hamlet, Prince of Denmark*, William Shakespeare. Act IV, scene V.

Leaves, as well as flowers, have been used to carry symbolical messages; bay leaves for the poet, oak for the patriot, and laurel for the victor.

Various nations have floral emblems. Each national flower has some legendary, traditional, or historical significance, which usually accounts for its having been chosen.

The rose is the national emblem of England; the fleur-de-lis, of France; the corn flower, of Germany; the shamrock, of Ireland; the nopal cactus, of Mexico; the thistle, of Scotland; the pomegranate, of Spain; and the leek, of Wales.

The United States has as yet no national flower; but the goldenrod, according to the expression of public preference in 1889, was generally favored for the national flower.

In the contest of the American Nature Association, which ended on December 31, 1929, the citizens of the United States, (that is those who voted, there being only 1,067,676 votes cast), selected the wild rose for the American national flower, and the columbine was given second choice. "The wild rose won in every state, but Colorado, Florida, Illinois, Minnesota, Massachusetts, Vermont, and Washington." [2]

No less interesting and significant than those of the nations are the state flowers, which were selected by the state legislatures, school children, women's clubs, or by other organizations or persons.

ALABAMA

The goldenrod [genus *Solidago*] was adopted as the State flower of Alabama by an act of the legislature on September 6, 1927. [3] Many years prior to this act, however, the school children of the State had selected this

---

[2] *My Weekly Reader Number One,* March 14, 1930.
[3] *General Acts of Alabama, Regular Session, 1927, Special Session, 1926-1927: General Laws and Joint Resolutions of the Legislature of Alabama, Passed at the Session of 1927, Held in the Capitol, in the City of Montgomery, Commencing Tuesday, January, 11, 1927,* John Brandon, Secretary of State (The Brown Printing Company, State Printers and Binders, Montgomery, Alabama, 1927) p. 627.

flower as the State floral emblem. The goldenrod was chosen because "it blooms everywhere [throughout the State] and brightens the fall months with its liberal plume-like flowers." [4]

ARIZONA

The State flower of Arizona is the Sahuara cactus (*Cereus giganteus*) also known as the giant cactus. [5] It is said to have been adopted as the flower of the Territory of Arizona in 1901, and to have been retained as the floral emblem of the State. [6]

Arizona by legislative action, approved on March 16, 1931, officially adopted the Sahuara cactus as the State flower.

The act says:

Section 2. The pure white waxy flower of the Cereus Giganteus (Giant Cactus) or Sahuara, shall be the state flower of Arizona. [7]

ARKANSAS

The apple blossom [*Pyrus malus*] was adopted as the State floral emblem of Arkansas by an act of the legislature on January 30, 1901. As to why the apple blossom was chosen as the State flower, the law says:

"*Whereas,* Most of the states have by resolution declared what should be their state floral emblem; and,

"*Whereas,* Arkansas has not by resolution of the General Assembly declared what is her floral emblem; be it therefore

---

[4] A letter from Mrs. Marie Bankhead Owen, Director of the State Department of Archives and History, Montgomery, Alabama, March 18, 1930.

[5] *Arizona Blue Book, 1929-1930,* compiled by I. P. Fraizer, Secretary of State (Republican Print Shop, Phoenix, Arizona, 1929) p. 4.

[6] *Our Arizona,* Ida Flood Dodge (Charles Scribner's Sons, New York and Boston, 1929) p. 134.

[7] *1931 Session Laws, Arizona, Tenth Legislature, Regular Session, Initiative and Referendum Measures Voted on at General Election, November 4, 1930: Acts, Resolutions and Memorials of the Regular Session, Tenth Legislature of the State of Arizona, 1931, Regular Session Convened January 12, 1931, Regular Session Adjourned Sine Die March 14, 1931,* Scott White, Secretary of State (The Arizona Printers, Inc., Phoenix, Arizona, 1931) p. 149.

"Resolved by both Houses of the General Assembly, That the 'Apple Blossom' be declared the state floral emblem of Arkansas." [8]

CALIFORNIA

The golden poppy, *Eschscholtzia,* generally called the California poppy [*Eschscholtzia californica*], was selected as the State flower of California by an act of the legislature on March 2, 1903. [9] There are several traditions and legends about this flower, few of which seem to be authentic. The best one perhaps is that of the great cold which destroyed all of the Indians save one brave and his squaw. They wandered about in search of food and shelter until finally in answer to their prayers, the Great Spirit sent the fire flower or golden poppy to drive away the evil spirit of the cold and frost, and to bring warmth and plenty to the land. [10]

COLORADO

The Colorado legislature on April 4, 1899, [11] officially declared the State flower to be the white and lavender Columbine [*Aquilegia caerulea*], commonly known as the Rocky Mountain Columbine.

On April 4, 1925, the State legislature passed a law

[8] *Arkansas Laws, 1901: Acts and Resolutions of the General Assembly of the State of Arkansas, Passed at the Session Held at the Capital, Which Began on Monday, January 14, and Adjourned on Saturday, May 4, 1901,* by authority (Democrat Printing and Lithographing Company, Little Rock, Arkansas, 1901) p. 408.

[9] *The Statutes of California and Amendments to the Codes, Passed at the Thirty-fifth Session of the Legislature, 1903, Begun on Monday, January Fifth, and Ended on Saturday, March Fourteenth, Nineteen Hundred and Three* (W. W. Shannon, Superintendent State Printing, Sacramento, California, 1903) p. 78.

[10] *California Blue Book or State Roster, 1909,* compiled by and under the supervision of, published and distributed by, Charles Forrest Curry, Secretary of State (State Printing Office, Sacramento, California, 1909) p. 276.

[11] *Colorado Laws, 1899: Laws Passed at the Twelfth Session of the General Assembly of the State of Colorado, Convened at Denver, on the Fourth Day of January, A. D. 1899,* published by authority (The Smith-Brooks Printing Company, State Printers, Denver, Colorado, 1899) chap. 139, p. 349.

restricting and regulating the gathering, possession, display and sale of the State flower. [12]

Section one of this act says:

"It is hereby declared to be the duty of all citizens of this State to protect the white and lavender Columbine, Aquilegia Caerulea (the State Flower), from needless destruction or waste."

Section two reads:

"It shall be unlawful for any person to tear the said flower up by the roots when grown or growing upon any State, school, or other public lands, or in any public highway or other public place, or to pick or gather upon any such public lands or in any such public highway or place more than twenty-five stems, buds or blossoms of such flower in any one day, and it shall also be unlawful for any person to pick or gather such flower upon private lands without the consent of the owner thereof first had or obtained."

The penalty for violating this law is not less than five nor more than fifty dollars.

The columbine was chosen as the State flower, says Albert B. Sanford, because its colors have significance to the people of Colorado. The blue signifies the hue of the skies, "the white represents the snowy ranges of the mountains, and the yellow, the gold that first attracted people here in 1858." [13]

CONNECTICUT

The mountain laurel (*Kalmia latifolia*) was declared to be the floral emblem of the State of Connecticut by an act of the legislature approved on April 17, 1907. [14] It was

[12] *Session Laws of Colorado, 1925: Laws Passed at the Twenty-fifth Session of the General Assembly of the State of Colorado, Convened at Denver at 12 O'clock Noon on Wednesday, January 7, A. D. 1925, and Adjourned Sine Die at 6 O'clock P. M. on Thursday, April 16, A. D. 1925,* published by authority of Carl S. Milliken, Secretary of State (Eames Brothers, Printers, Denver, Colorado, 1925) chap. 81, p. 221.

[13] A letter from Albert B. Sanford, Assistant Curator of History, State Historical Society, Denver, Colorado, March 24, 1930.

[14] *Connecticut Public Acts, 1907: Public Acts Passed by the General Assembly of the State of Connecticut, in the Year 1907,* published by authority (The Case, Lockwood and Brainard Company, The Hartford Press, Hartford, Connecticut, 1907) chap. 38, p. 612.

selected because of the "beauty of its blossom and foliage, the latter remaining a glossy green throughout the year, its sturdy and abundant growth in the state, and its general popularity." [15]

DELAWARE

The peach blossom [*Prunus persica* or *Amygdalus persica*] is regarded by common consent as the flower of the State of Delaware. It was chosen because of the supremacy of the state in peach growing. Mrs. Agnes G. Willey says that "one must see Delaware in the spring time to appreciate its fertility and beauty . . . One may ride from the northern to the southern boundaries of the state over an avenue of cement through groves of pine and flowering pear, apple and peach orchards—'a riot of white and delicate pink blossoms.' " [16]

THE DISTRICT OF COLUMBIA

The official flower of the District of Columbia is the American beauty rose [genus *Rosa*]. After considering the suitableness of a number of flowers to become the District flower, the Board of Commissions of the District, on June 6, 1925, adopted the American beauty rose. [17]

FLORIDA

The orange blossom [*Citrus trifoliata* or *Citrus sinensis*] was adopted by the State legislature sometime between April 6, and June 4, 1909, the date of the adoption not being recorded in the resolution designating the State flower. As to why the orange blossom was adopted as Florida's State flower, the resolution says:

"Whereas, the State of Florida is universally known as the 'Land of Flowers'; therefore,

[15] A letter from George S. Godard, Librarian, Connecticut State Library, Hartford, Connecticut, March 20, 1930.

[16] A letter from Mrs. Agnes G. Willey, Librarian, Delaware State Library, Dover, Delaware, March 18, 1930.

[17] These facts were obtained by telephone from the office of Daniel E. Garges, Secretary of the Board of Commissioners of the District of Columbia, Washington, D. C. February 21, 1931.

"Be it Resolved by the House of Representatives, the Senate Concurring:

"That the Orange Blossom be, and the same is hereby chosen and designated as the State Flower in and for the State of Florida." [18]

GEORGIA

The House of Representatives of the State of Georgia, the Senate concurring, carrying out the suggestion and the request of the State Federation of Women's Clubs, declared the floral emblem of the State of Georgia to be the Cherokee rose (*Rosa sinica*). This adoption took place on August 18, 1916. [19]

This flower was selected according to the wording of the act, because it, "having its origin among the aborigines of the northern portion of the State of Georgia, is indigenous to its soil, and grows with equal luxuriance in every county of the State." [20]

It is the opinion of those connected with the National Department of Agriculture "that the rose was introduced into the State perhaps directly from China or from China by way of England," [21] that it was brought to England probably about 1757, and that it reached the United States shortly after that time.

Some authorities say that "the name, Cherokee Rose, is a local appellation derived from the Cherokee Indians who widely distributed the plant, which elsewhere is known by the botanical name of *rosa sinica*." [21]   The

[18] *Laws of Florida, 1909: Regular Session, 1909, Acts and Resolutions Adopted by the Legislature of Florida at Its Twelfth Regular Session (April 6 to June 4, 1909) under the Constition of A. D. 1885, . . .* published by authority under the direction of the Attorney General (Capital Publishing Company, State Printer, Tallahassee, Florida, 1909) resolution no. 15, p. 688.

[19] *Georgia Laws, 1916: Acts and Resolutions of the General Assembly of the State of Georgia, 1916,* compiled and published by authority of the State (Charles P. Byrd, State Printer, Atlanta, Georgia, 1916) p. 1046-7.

[20] *Georgia Laws, 1916: Acts and Resolutions of the General Assembly of the State of Georgia, 1916,* compiled and published by authority of the State (Charles P. Byred, State Printer, Atlanta, Georgia, 1916) p. 1046-7.

[21] *Georgia Official and Statistical Register: State of Georgia, Department of Archives and History, Georgia's Official Register, 1927,* compiled by Ruth Blair, State Historian and Director (Stein Printing Company, State Printers, Atlanta, Georgia, 1927) p. 410.

Cherokee rose, being a climbing shrub, is frequently used to form hedges. It blooms in the spring regularly, and frequently in the fall. It has "a waxy white [flower] with [a] large golden center" and with petals of magnificent "velvety texture."

IDAHO

The legislature of Idaho on March 2, 1931, adopted the syringa (*Philadelphus lewisii*) to be the floral emblem of the State. [22]

Cornelius J. Brosnan states that the syringa was originally selected by "a committee of Boise women, known as the Columbian Committee," organized in 1893 to assist in furnishing the Idaho building at the World's Exposition at Chicago. [23] He further states that "by common consent, Idahoans have for a quarter of a century conferred upon it [the syringa] the affectionate title 'State Flower'. . ." [23]

ILLINOIS

The State legislature on February 21, 1903, declared the native violet [probably the wood violet, or the Bird'-foot violet, *Viola pedate*] to be the State flower of Illinois. This law went into effect on July 1, 1908. [24]

INDIANA

The carnation was adopted as the State flower of Indiana by house concurrent resolution number six, approved on March 15, 1913. [25]

[22] *Session Laws of Idaho, Regular 1931 and Extraordinary: General Laws of the State of Idaho, Passed at the Twenty-first Session of the State Legislature 1931,* published by authority of the Secretary of State (Capital News Publishing Company, Boise, Idaho, 1931) p. 132.

[23] *History of the State of Idaho,* Cornelius J. Brosnan (Charles Scribner's Sons, New York and Chicago, 1926) p. 176.

[24] *Illinois Revised Statutes, Keyed to Annotate Statutes, 1921: Revised Statutes of the State of Illinois, Embracing all the General Laws of the State of Illinois in Force up to January 1, 1922,* compiled and edited by James C. Cahill (Callaghan and Company, Chicago, Illinois, 1922) chap. 130a, p. 3297.

[25] *Laws of the State of Indiana, Passed at the Sixty-eighth Regular Session of the General Assembly, Begun on the Ninth Day of January, A. D. 1913,* by authority, L. G. Ellingham, Secretary of State (William B. Burford, Contractor for State Printing and Binding, Indianapolis, Indiana, 1913) chap. 363, p. 967.

The flower of the tulip tree (*Liriodendron tulipifera*) was officially designated as the State flower of Indiana by an act of the State legislature approved on March 1, 1923, [26] this act repealing the house concurrent resolution adopting the carnation mentioned above.

The General Assembly of the State of Indiana, on March 3, 1931, [27] adopted as the State flower the zinnia (*Zinnia elegans*). This act repealed the act of March 1, 1923, adopting the flower of the tulip tree (*Liriodendron tulipifera*) as the State floral emblem.

IOWA

Iowa selected the wild rose [*Rosa virginiana* or *Rosa acicularis*] both of which grow in the State, as her State flower. It was adopted by an act of the General Assembly of Iowa on May 7, 1897. [28] The Iowa Federation of Women's Clubs at Dubuque, Iowa, had previously voted to select the wild rose as the official floral emblem of the State.

KANSAS

The wild native sunflower [*Helianthus annuus*] was designated as the State flower and floral emblem of the State of Kansas by an act of the State legislature approved on March 12, 1903. [29]

[26] *Acts, 1923, Indiana, Seventy-third Session, Including the Special Session of 1921: Laws of the State of Indiana, Passed at the Special Session of the General Assembly, Begun on the Fourteenth Day of December, 1921,* by authority of Ed Jackson, Secretary of the State (William B. Burford, Contractor for State Printing and Binding, Indianapolis, Indiana, 1923) p. 105.

[27] *Acts, 1931, Indiana, 77th Session: Laws of the State of Indiana, Passed at the Seventy-seventh Regular Session of the General Assembly, Begun on the Eighth Day of January, A. D., 1931,* by authority, Frank Mayr, Jr. Secretary of State (Fort Wayne Printing Company, Contractors for State Printing and Binding, Fort Wayne, Indiana, 1931) p. 113.

[28] *Journal of the Senate, Extra Session, Twenty-sixth General Assembly of the State of Iowa, Which Convened at the Capitol at Des Moines, January 19, 1897* (F. R. Conaway, State Printer, Des Moines, Iowa, 1897) p. 1164.

[29] *Kansas Laws, 1903: State of Kansas, Session Laws, 1903, Passed at the Thirtieth Regular Session—the Same Being the Thirteenth Biennial Session—of the Legislature of the State of Kansas, Date of Publication of this Volume, June 1, 1903* (W. Y. Morgan, State Printer, Topeka, Kansas, 1903) chap. 479, p. 725-6.

The legislative act adopting the flower gives two reasons for choosing it, stated as follows:

"*Whereas,* Kansas has a native wild flower common throughout her borders, hardy and conspicuous, of definite, unvarying and striking shape, easily sketched, molded, and carved, having armorial capacities, ideally adapted for artistic reproduction, with its strong, distinct disk and its golden circle of clear glowing rays—a flower that a child can draw on a slate, a woman can work in silk, or a man can carve on stone or fashion in clay; and

"*Whereas,* This flower has to all Kansans a historic symbolism which speaks of frontier days, winding trails, pathless prairies, and is full of the life and glory of the past, the pride of the present, and richly emblematic of the majesty of a golden future, and is a flower which has given Kansas the world-wide name, 'the Sunflower State'"; [30] therefore it is designated and declared to be the State flower and floral emblem.

KENTUCKY

The General Assembly of the Commonwealth of Kentucky selected the goldenrod [probably *Solidago patula*] as the official State flower, sometime in March, 1926, the exact date of the adoption not being given in the acts. [31] The resolution of the Senate, the House concurring, was neither approved nor disapproved. The goldenrod is one of the most common and widespread of American wild flowers.

LOUISIANA

Louisiana by legislative action, approved July 12, 1900, designated the magnolia [*Magnolia foetida* or *Mag-*

[30] *Kansas Laws, 1903: State of Kansas, Session Laws, 1903, Passed at the Thirtieth Regular Session—the Same, Being the Thirteenth Biennial Session—*of the *Legislature of the State of Kansas, Date of Publication of this Volume, June 1, 1903* (W. Y. Morgan, State Printer, Topeka, Kansas, 1903) chap. 479, p. 725-6.

[31] *Kentucky Acts, 1926: Acts of the General Assembly of the Commonwealth of Kentucky, Passed at the Regular Session of the General Assembly, Which Was Begun in the City of Frankfort, Kentucky, on Tuesday, January Fifth, 1926, and Ended Wednesday, March Seventeenth, 1926* (This volume does not record the name of the publisher, the place, nor the date of publication.) p. 1025-6.

[32] *Acts of Louisiana, 1900: Acts Passed by the General Assembly of the State of Louisiana at the Regular Session, Begun and Held in the City of Baton Rouge, on the 14th Day of May, 1900,* published by authority (The Advocate, Official Journal of the State of Louisiana, Baton Rouge, Louisiana, 1900) act no. 156, house bill no. 280, p. 239.

nolia grandiflora] as the State flower. [32] It was chosen probably because there is such an abundant growth of this tree throughout the State.

MAINE

The State flower of Maine is the pine cone and tassel (*Pinus strobus*). The pine cone was chosen under the direction of the Maine Floral Emblem Society during the months of November and December, 1894, during which time "everyone was urged to register his choice," [33] and the ballots were published in the newspapers.

The sixty-seventh legislature on February 1, 1925, declared that the pine cone and tassel should be the floral emblem for Maine, "in the National Garland of Flowers." [34]

The Women's Congress at the World's Fair at Chicago in 1893 conceived the idea of having a National Garland of Flowers. The idea grew out of the facts that the United States is one nation composed of different states, that in America there is one language containing "the vestiges of all the languages of the world," and that the flag of the United States has "thirteen stripes and forty-eight stars"; consequently they felt that there should be a National Garland of Flowers composed of the various state flowers, selected by the different state legislatures. [35]

MARYLAND

By an act of her legislature approved on April 18, 1918, the State of Maryland designated and adopted the Black-eyed Susan (*Rudbeckia hirta*) as the floral emblem of the State. [36]

[33] *The Maine Book,* Henry E. Dunnack (Henry E. Dunnack, Augusta, Maine, 1920) p. 91.
[34] *Laws of Maine, 1895: Acts and Resolves of the Sixty-seventh Legislature of the State of Maine, 1895,* published by the Secretary of State, agreeably to Resolves of June 28, 1820, February 18, 1840, and March 16, 1842 (Burleigh and Flynt, Printers to the State, Augusta, Maine. 1895) chap. 3, p. 5.
[35] *The Maine Book,* Henry E. Dunnack (Henry E. Dunnack, Augusta, Maine, 1920) p. 91.
[36] *Laws of Maryland, 1918: Laws of the State of Maryland, Made and Passed at the Session of the General Assembly, Made and Held at the City of Annapolis on the Second Day of January, 1918, and Ending on the First Day of April, 1918,* published by authority (King Brothers, State Printers, Baltimore, Maryland, 1918) chap. 458, p. 949.

MASSACHUSETTS

The General Court of the Commonwealth of Massachusetts on May 1, 1918, adopted the mayflower (*Epigaea repens*) also commonly known as the trailing arbutus, or the ground-laurel, as the flower or floral emblem of the Commonwealth. [37]

On May 17, 1925, this law was amended by adding a paragraph for the protection of the flower. The amendment states that "any person who pulls up or digs up the plant of the mayflower or any part thereof, or injures such plant or any part thereof except in so far as is reasonably necessary in procuring the flower therefrom, within the limits of any state highway or any other public way or place, or upon the land of another person without written authority from him, shall be punished by a fine of not more than fifty dollars; but if a person does any of the aforesaid acts while in disguise or secretly in the night time he shall be punished by a fine of not more than one hundred dollars." [38]

MICHIGAN

Michigan by an act of the State legislature, approved on April 28, 1897, designated as her State flower, the apple blossom (*Pyrus coronaria*). [39] The act adopting this State flower states that it was selected because the "blossoming apple trees add much to the beauty of" Michigan's landscape, because "Michigan apples have gained world wide reputation," and because the tree of this apple is one of the most "beautiful flowered species" of native apple trees.

---

[37] *Acts and Resolves of Massachusetts, 1925: Acts and Resolves, together with Returns of Votes upon Constitutional Amendments and Questions to Voters, Tables Showing Changes in the Statutes, etc. Passed by the General Court of Massachusetts in the Year 1925*, published by the Secretary of the Commonwealth (Wright and Potter Printing Company, Boston, Massachusetts, 1925) chap. 112, p. 91-2.

[38] *Ibidem*.

[39] *Michigan Acts, 1897, Public Acts: Public Acts of the Legislature of the State of Michigan, Passed at the Regular Session of 1897, With an Appendix Containing Joint and Concurrent Resolutions, and the State Treasurer's Report for the Year Ending June 30, 1897*, printed by authority (Robert Smith Printing Company, State Printers and Binders, Lansing, Michigan, 1897) p. 429.

MINNESOTA

The official State flower of Minnesota is the pink and white moccasin flower (*Cypripedium reginae*). This floral emblem was adopted by an act of the State legislature on February 19, 1902. [40] This flower is also known as the lady slipper and as the Indian shoe, from the fact that the most conspicuous petal of the flower somewhat resembles a shoe. [41] It belongs to the orchid family and is quite commonly called the wild orchid.

The State legislature, by an act of February 3, 1893, [42] selected for the State flower, the wild lady's slipper or moccasin flower (*Cypripedium calceolus*). After the women of the Saint Anthony Study Circle of Minneapolis announced that the Cypripedium calceolus was not found in Minnesota, the State legislature on February 19, 1902, changed the designation of the State flower from the Cypripedium calceolus to the Cypripedium reginae. [43]

On April 25, 1925, the State legislature passed a law saying that "no person within the State of Minnesota knowingly shall buy, sell, offer or expose for sale, the state flower (Cypripedium reginae) or any species of lady slipper (Cypripedae) or any member of the orchid family trillium of any species, lotus (Nelumbo lutea), a gentian (Gentiana), arbutus (Epigaea repens), or any species of lilies (Lilium), or any thereof, dug, pulled or gathered from any public land, or from the land of any private

[40] *Minnesota Senate Journal, Extra Session, February 1902: Journal of the Senate of the Extra Session of the Legislature of the State of Minnesota* (McGill-Warner Company, State Printers, St. Paul, Minnesota, 1902) p. 56, 68.

[41] *The Legislative Manual of the State of Minnesota,* compiled for the Legislature of 1929 by Mike Holm, Secretary of State (Press of Harrison and Smith Company, Minneapolis, Minnesota, 1929) p. 49.

[42] *Journal of the Senate, 1893: Journal of the Senate of the Twenty-eighth Session of the Legislature of the State of Minnesota* (J. W. Cunningham, State Printer, St. Paul, Minnesota, 1893) p. 167-8.

[43] *The Legislative Manual of the State of Minnesota,* compiled for the Legislature of 1929 by Mike Holm, Secretary of State (Press of Harrison and Smith Company, Minneapolis, Minnesota, 1929) p. 49.
Minnesota Senate Journal, Extra Session, February, 1902: Journal of the Senate of the Extra Session of the Legislature of the State of Minnesota (McGill-Warner Company, State Printers, St. Paul, Minnesota, 1902) p. 56, 68.

owner without the written consent of such owner or other occupant of such land." [44]

MISSISSIPPI

Sydnor and Bennett say that "the school children of the state selected the state flower, and no one else was permitted to vote. The election was held in November, 1900, and the children sent in 23,278 votes. The magnolia received 12,745 votes, the cotton blossom 4,171, and the cape jasmine 2,484. There were a few votes for other flowers. The magnolia won, and has since been our state flower." [45]

MISSOURI

The General Assembly of Missouri, by an act approved on March 16, 1923, declared the floral emblem of the State to be "the hawthorne, the blossom of the tree commonly called the 'red haw' or 'wild haw' " [46] [genus *Crataegus*] and stated that it should "be the duty of the state boards of agriculture and horticulture to recognize it as such and [to] encourage the cultivation of said tree on account of the beauty of its flower, fruit and foliage." [46]

MONTANA

The bitter root (*Lewisia rediviva*) was adopted by an act of the Montana legislature as the State flower, the law taking effect on February 27, 1895. [47]

[44] *Minnesota Laws, 1925: Session Laws of the State of Minnesota, Passed During the Forty-fourth Session of the State Legislature at the Session Commencing January 6, 1925,* published by Mike Holm, Secretary of State (Louis F. Dow Company, Saint Paul, Minnesota, 1925) p. 580-1.

[45] *Mississippi History,* Charles Sackett Sydnor and Claude Bennett (Rand McNally and Company, New York, Chicago, and San Francisco, 1930) p. 251.

[46] *Laws of Missouri, 1923: Laws of Missouri, Passed at the Session of the Fifty-second General Assembly Which Convened at the City of Jefferson, Wednesday, January 3, 1923,* published by authority, compiled by Charles U. Becker, Secretary of State (The Hugh Stephens Press, Jefferson City, Missouri, 1923) p. 293-4.

[47] *Montana Code, 1895, Political Code, Civil Code: The Codes and Statutes of Montana in Force July 1st, 1895, Including the Political Code, Civil Code, Code of Civil Procedure and Penal Code . . .* compiled by D. S. Wade, Commissioner (Inter Mountain Publishing Company, Printers, Butte, Montana, 1895) vol. 1, p. 425.

NEBRASKA

Nebraska adopted the goldenrod (*Solidago serotina*) as the floral emblem of the State, by an act of her legislative bodies on April 4, 1895. [48]

Since there are forty or fifty distinct species of the goldenrod growing in the northern part of the United States east of the Rocky Mountains, it is helpful here to note that the particular species, *Solidago serotina,* selected as the State flower of Nebraska, often called the late goldenrod, "has a stout smooth stem [from] two to seven feet high, bearing many leaves which are about three to six inches long, from half an inch wide in the widest part, and tapering to each end. The flower cluster at the top of the stem is a somewhat compact mass of small yellow heads, which is generally bent over and inclined to be nodding." [49]

NEVADA

The sagebrush [*Artemisia tridentata* or *Artemisia trifida*] was adopted as the State flower of Nevada by the Senate, the Assembly concurring, on March 20, 1917. [50]

NEW HAMPSHIRE

New Hampshire, by legislative action on March 28, 1919, selected as her State floral emblem the purple lilac (*Syringa vulgaris*). [51] The State Reference Librarian

---

[48] *Laws of Nebraska, 1895: Laws, Joint Resolutions, and Memorials, Passed by the Legislative Assembly of the State of Nebraska at the Twenty-fourth Session, Begun and Held at the City of Lincoln, January 1, 1895,* published by authority (Omaha Printing Company, State Printers, Omaha, Nebraska, 1895) chap. 120, p. 441.

[49] *Cobbey's Annotated Statutes of Nebraska, Volumes I and II, 1909: Cobbey's Annotated Statutes of Nebraska, Edition 1909, . . .* (Published and sold by J. E. Cobbey, Beatrice, Nebraska, 1909) section 2801, p. 1103-4.

[50] *Statutes of Nevada, 1917: Statutes of the State of Nevada, Passed at the Twenty-eighth Session of the Legislature, 1917, Begun on Monday, the Fifteenth Day of January, and Ended on Thursday, the Fifteenth Day of March* (State Printing Office, Joe Farnsworth, Superintendent, Carson City, Nevada, 1917) p. 490.

[51] *New Hampshire Laws, 1919: Laws of the State of New Hampshire, Passed in 1919, Legislature Convened January 1, 1919, Adjourned March 28, 1919, Special Session Convened September 9, 1919, Adjourned September 11, 1919* (Edson C. Eastman Company, Publishers, Concord, New Hampshire, 1919) chap. 148, p. 212.

says that this flower was chosen because "it is a fair representative of the flowers that grow in abundance" [52] throughout the State. It is an old English flower which was brought to America by the early settlers.

NEW JERSEY

New Jersey, by a concurrent resolution of her legislative bodies in 1913, [53] adopted as her State floral emblem the violet [genus *Viola*] of which there are many varieties growing wild in the State. It was chosen partly because of its hopeful blue color, and partly because it is so very common in the State of New Jersey.

NEW MEXICO

By an act of the State legislature on March 14, 1927, New Mexico adopted as her State flower the Yucca flower [genus *Yucca*]. It was recommended by the First State Federation of Women's Clubs, and previous to its legal adoption, it was selected as the State flower by the Mexican school children. [54]

NEW YORK

New York State has never adopted a floral emblem by legislative action; but her "school children on Arbor Day in 1891, selected the rose as the State flower, the goldenrod being accorded second choice. No particular variety or color of the rose was specified when the vote was taken." [55]

[52] A letter from Jeanie F. Hardy, Reference Librarian, New Hampshire State Library, Concord, New Hampshire, March 20, 1930.
[53] *Minutes of Assembly, New Jersey, 1913: Minutes of Votes and Proceedings of the One Hundred and Thirty-seventh General Assembly of the State of New Jersey* (MacCrellish and Quigley, State Printers, Trenton, New Jersey, 1913) p. 1741.
[54] *New Mexico Laws, 1927: Laws of the State of New Mexico, Passed by the Eighth Regular Session of the Legislature of the State of New Mexico,* . . . prepared for publication by Jennie Fortune, Secretary of State (Valliant Printing Company, Albuquerque, New Mexico, 1927) chap. 102, p. 301.
[55] *Legislative Manual, New York, 1929: Manual for the Use of the Legislature of the State of New York, 1929,* prepared pursuant to the provisions of chapter 23, Laws, 1909, by Edward J. Flynn (J. B. Lyon Company, Albany, New York, 1929) p. 289.

North Carolina

The State Librarian of North Carolina says that the State has not yet selected a floral emblem, that the goldenrod is always spoken of as the State flower, but that it has never been adopted by legislative enactment. [56]

North Dakota

North Dakota, by an act of her legislature approved on March 7, 1907, adopted as her State floral emblem, the wild prairie rose [*Rosa blanda* or *Rosa arkansana*.] [57] "Contributing something to the choice was the fact that the State University of North Dakota had selected the colors, pink and green, chosen directly from the wild prairie rose growing on the campus." [58]

Ohio

The legislature of Ohio on February 3, 1904, chose the scarlet carnation [genus *Dianthus*] as the State flower.[59]

The law reads:

"WHEREAS, It is fitting and proper that a state should honor and perpetuate the memory of its illustrious sons, in order that our citizens of the future may emulate their example of patriotic devotion and sacrifice to the welfare of the republic; and

"WHEREAS, William McKinley was a beloved and devoted citizen of Ohio, and one of the loftiest characters

[56] A letter from Carrie L. Broughton, Librarian, North Carolina State Library, Raleigh, North Carolina, March 18, 1930.

[57] *Laws of North Dakota, 1907: Laws Passed at the Tenth Session of the Legislative Assembly of the State of North Dakota, Begun and Held at Bismarck, the Capitol of Said State on Tuesday, the Eighth Day. of January, A. D. 1907, and Concluding March Eighth, 1907* (Tribune, State Printers and Binders, Bismarck, North Dakota, 1907) chap. 231, p. 365.

[58] A letter from Mrs. Florence H. Davis, Librarian, Library of the State Historical Society of North Dakota, Bismarck, North Dakota, March 20, 1930.

[59] *Laws of Ohio, 1904: The State of Ohio, General and Local Acts Passed and Joint Resolutions Adopted by the Seventy-sixth General Assembly at Its Regular Session, Begun and Held in the City of Columbus, January 4, 1904* (The Springfield Publishing Company, State Printers, Springfield, Ohio, 1904) vol. 97, p. 631.

ever given by any state to the history of the nation and the world; and

"WHEREAS, The scarlet carnation, because of his love for it, is closely associated with his memory, and the state of Ohio having no floral emblem; Therefore,

"*Be it resolved by the General Assembly of the State of Ohio, the Governor approving*: That the scarlet carnation be adopted as the state flower of Ohio, as a token of love and reverence for the memory of William McKinley."

OKLAHOMA

The State floral emblem of Oklahoma is the mistletoe [probably *Phoradendron flavescens*]. It was adopted by the Territorial Legislature on February 11, 1893. [60]

The *Compiled Oklahoma Statutes* for 1921 says, "The mistletoe shall be the floral emblem of the State." [61]

OREGON

According to senate concurrent resolution number four of the Oregon Legislative Assembly, the State of Oregon on January 30-31, 1899, adopted as her State flower, the Oregon grape (*Berberis aquifolium*). [62]

[60] *The Statutes of Oklahoma, 1893, Being a Compilation of all the Laws now in force in the Territory of Oklahoma, compiled under the Direction and Supervision of Robert Martin, Secretary of the Territory* by W. A. McCartney, John H. Beatty and J. Malcolm Johnston, a committee elected by the Legislative Assembly (State Capital Printing Company, Guthrie, Oklahoma, 1893) chap. LXXVII, p. 1129.

[61] *Compiled Statutes of Oklahoma, 1921, annotated* by Clinton Orrin Bunn, of the Ardmore Bar, under the provisions of chapter 125, Session Laws of Oklahoma, 1921. Supervised and approved by the code commission, . . . *In Two Volumes, Embracing the Constitution of the United States and of the State of Oklahoma, with the Amendments thereto; together with the Revised Laws of Oklahoma, 1910, and all Session Laws Enacted Subsequent thereto, Including* Session Laws, 1921. *Volume I Embracing Constitutions and Codes. Volume II Embracing General Laws* (Bunn Publishing Company, Ardmore, Oklahoma, 1922) vol. I, chap. 17, p. 1455.

[62] *Laws of Oregon, 1899: The State of Oregon, General and Special Laws and Joint Resolutions and Memorials, Enacted and Adopted by the Twentieth Regular Session of the Legislative Assembly, 1899, Begun on the Ninth Day of January and Ended on the Eighteenth Day of February, 1899* (W. H. Leeds, State Printer, Salem, Oregon, 1899) p. 1131.

PENNSYLVANIA

Pennsylvania by an act of the General Assembly, approved on May 5, 1933, [63] adopted the mountain laurel [*Kalmia latifolia*] as the State flower.

The act says:

"Section 1. Be it enacted by the Senate and House of Representatives of the Commonwealth of Pennsylvania in General Assembly met and it is hereby enacted by the authority of the same That the mountain laurel (Kalmia latifolia) is hereby adopted as the State flower of Pennsylvania."

RHODE ISLAND

The violet [genus *Viola*] was selected by the public school children of the State of Rhode Island as the State flower, in May, 1897. [64]

SOUTH CAROLINA

The State legislature of South Carolina passed a concurrent resolution on March 14, 1923, to appoint a commission to select a suitable State flower. This commission was to consist of "two members from the House of Representatives, to be appointed by the Speaker, and one member from the Senate, to be appointed by the President of the Senate." [65]

The Legislative Manual of South Carolina, 1927, says that upon "the report of a select legislative commission

[63] *Act Number 107 of the General Assembly of the Commonwealth of Pennsylvania,* sent in a communication from Miss Gertrude MacKinney, Director of the State Library, Harrisburg, Pennsylvania, June 29, 1933.

[64] *Rhode Island Manual, 1931-1932: Manual with Rules and Orders for the Use of the General Assembly of the State of Rhode Island, 1931-1932,* prepared in accordance with the provisions of section 9, chapter 28, of the General Laws, by Ernest L. Sprague, Secretary of State (E. L. Freeman Company, Printers and Binders, Providence, Rhode Island, 1931) p. x.

[65] *Acts of South Carolina, 1923: Acts and Joint Resolutions of the General Assembly of the State of South Carolina, Passed at the Regular Session of 1923, Printed by Order of the General Assembly and Designed to Form a Part of the Thirty-third Volume of the Statutes at Large, Commencing with the Acts of the Regular Session of 1923* (Gonzales and Bryan, State Printers, Columbia, South Carolina, 1923) p. 892-3.

consisting of Senator T. B. Butler, of Gaffney, and Representatives G. B. Ellison, of Columbia, and T. S. Heyward, of Buffton," the General Assembly on February 1, 1924, adopted as the State flower the yellow jessamine, [66] called also the Carolina jessamine [*Gelsemium sempervirens*].

SOUTH DAKOTA

The American pasque flower (*Pulsatilla hirsutissima*) was adopted as the State flower of South Dakota in 1903. [67] Willis E. Johnson says that "it received its name in France because it blossoms there at about Easter time, the word pasque (in modern French it is 'pâque') meaning Easter. As it is the first flower to blossom on our prairies, the motto accompanying the flower is 'I Lead.' " [68]

TENNESSEE

The General Assembly of the State of Tennessee by senate joint resolution number thirteen, on January 23, 1919, resolved:

"That the Governor of the State be authorized and requested to name a commission of five distinguished citizens of the State, who shall serve without compensation, which commission shall be headed by the State Superintendent of Public Instruction, to name a date on which the school children of the State may have the right and opportunity of voting on a State flower for the State of Tennessee," [69] also

"That the flower which shall be named by the school children and certified by said commission shall be the recognized State flower." [69]

[66] *Legislative Manual, 1927: Legislative Manual of the Seventy-seventh General Assembly of South Carolina, at Columbia, First Session Commencing January 11, 1927*, . . . J. Wilson Gibbs, Clerk of the House of Representatives (The State Company, Columbia, South Carolina, 1927) p. 168.

[67] *The South Dakota Revised Code, 1919*, published by authority (Hipple Printing Company, Pierre, South Dakota, 1919) vol. 2, p. 1198.

[68] *South Dakota, A Republic of Friends*, Willis E. Johnson (Capital Supply Company, Pierre, South Dakota, 1915) p. 25.

[69] *Public Acts of Tennessee, 1919: Public Acts of the State of Tennessee, Passed by the Sixty-first General Assembly, 1919*, published by authority (McCowat-Mercer, Jackson, Tennessee, 1919) p. 830-1.

The flower selected was the passion flower, [genus *Passiflora*] also called the wild apricot, the may-pop, and the ocoee. From this flower the Indians took the names of the Ocoee valley and river, and they prized it as the most abundant and beautiful of all their flowers. [70]

Tennessee, by Senate joint resolution number fifty-three approved on April 19, 1933, [71] adopted the Iris [genus Iridaceae] as the State flower.

The resolution says:

"Whereas: The State of Tennessee has never adopted a State Flower; and,

"Whereas, the Iris is one of the most beautiful and one of the most popular flowers in the State, its profusion and beauty attracting many visitors to the State, now, therefore,

"Be it resolved by the Sixty-eighth General Assembly of the State of Tennessee, the Senate and House concurring, that the Iris be adopted as the State flower of Tennessee."

The law adopting the iris as the State flower of Tennessee does not abolish the act of 1919 adopting the flower to be selected by the school children of the state which was the passion flower named above. As to whether or not Tennessee now has two official state flowers, Mrs. John Trotwood Moore, Tennessee State Librarian and Archivist, says, "The people have been so interested, and at the same time confused, as to which really is the flower or whether or not both are now the State Flower, that I requested the Attorney General's opinion on the subject that I might be able to give an intelligent answer to the many questions which were coming to my desk from the school children, teachers, women's garden clubs, etc.   His

[70] *Tennessee: State Flag, Flower, Song, Seal, and Capitol* (Published by the Division of Library and Archives in the Department of Education, John Trotwood Moore, Librarian and Archivist, Nashville, Tennessee, 1923) p. 2.

[71] A copy of *Senate Joint Resolution Number Fifty-three,* sent in a communication from Mrs. John Trotwood Moore, State Librarian and Archivist of the Division of Library and Archives, Nashville, Tennessee, June 28, 1933.

decision is that the new law repeals the former law and that the Iris is now the State Flower." [71a]

TEXAS

Texas by an act of her legislature, approved on March 7, 1901, adopted as her State flower the blue bonnet or buffalo clover (*Lupinus subcarnosus*). [71b]

UTAH

By an act of her legislature, approved on March 18, 1911, [72] Utah declared the sego lily (*Calochortus nuttallii*) to be the State floral emblem. Kate C. Snow, President of the Daughters of Utah Pioneers, in a letter to the writer, written from Salt Lake City, dated April 17, 1930, says that "between 1840 and 1851" food became very scarce in Utah due to a crop-devouring plague of crickets, and that "the families were put on rations, and during this time they learned to dig for and to eat the soft, bulbous root of the sego lily. The memory of this use, quite as much as the natural beauty of the flower, caused it to be selected in after years by the Legislature as the floral emblem of the State."

VERMONT

The State flower of Vermont is the red clover [*Trifolium pratense*]. It was adopted by an act of the General Assembly of the State of Vermont on November 9, 1894. [73]

[71a] A letter, Mrs. John Trotwood Moore, State Librarian and Archivist of the Division of Library and Archives, Nashville, Tennessee, December, 4, 1933.
[71b] *Laws of Texas, 1901: General Laws of the State of Texas, Passed at the Regular Session of the Twenty-seventh Legislature, Convened at the City of Austin, January 8, 1901, and Adjourned April 9, 1901* (Von Boeckmann, Schutze and Company, Austin, Texas, 1901) p. 323-4.
[72] *Laws of Utah, 1911: Laws of the State of Utah, Passed at the Ninth Regular Session of the Legislature of the State of Utah Which Convened at Salt Lake City, the State Capitol, January 9th, 1911, and Adjourned March 9th, 1911,* published by authority (Press and Bindery of the Skeleton Publishing Company, Salt Lake City, Utah, 1911) p. 137.
[73] *Laws of Vermont, 1894: Acts and Resolves, Passed by the General Assembly of the State of Vermont at the Thirteenth Biennial Session, 1894,* published by authority (The Free Press Association, Printers and Binders, Burlington, Vermont, 1894) p. 133.

The red clover was designated the State flower because of the value of this plant to the farming industry of the State. [74]

VIRGINIA

Virginia, by an act of her General Assembly on March 6, 1918, declared the American dogwood, (*Cornus florida*), to be the floral emblem of the State. [75] It was selected as the State flower because it is so prevalent in the State and because it adds beauty to the Virginia landscape, especially in the spring. [76] The blossom of the American dogwood, (*Cornus florida*), varies in color from white to rose-red, and both the white and the pink varieties are found growing in the State. The act adopting the Virginia floral emblem does not specify what the color shall be, but the dogwood with white flowers is more generally found throughout the State.

WASHINGTON

The rhododendron, the western variety, [*Rhododendron californicum* or *Rhododendron machrophyllum*], is the State flower of Washington. *The World Almanac* states that this flower was selected by the people, but it does not say when. [77] It was selected "because it blooms in all its beauty here . . . It does not grow everywhere in the State, however," [78] says the Reference Librarian of the Washington State Library. Again another says of it "hiding within the shade of these [wild fruits and berries], playing hide and seek with nature lovers who enjoy

[74] A letter from Harrison J. Conant, Librarian, State Library, Montpelier, Vermont, March 18, 1930.
[75] *Acts of Assembly, Virginia, 1918: Acts and Joint Resolutions (Amending the Constitution) of the General Assembly of the State of Virginia, Session Which Commenced at the State Capitol on Wednesday, January 9, 1918* (Davis Bottom, Superintendent of Public Printing, Richmond, Virginia, 1918) chap. 435, p. 788.
[76] A letter from H. R. McIlwaine, Librarian, Virginia State Library, Richmond, Virginia, March 19, 1930.
[77] *The World Almanac and Book of Facts for 1931*, edited by Robert Hunt Lyman (Published by *The New York World*, New York, 1931). p. 524.
[78] A letter from Ida A. Hitt, Reference Librarian, Washington State Library, Olympia, Washington, March 21, 1930.

threading the romantic trails for which this section of the world is noted, is many a modest flower which in some sections blooms nearly the whole year round, so soft is the climate; while the ping petaled rhododendron, of bolder nature, Washington's state flower, is prominent in June tossing its beautiful head among the dry logs and lining the course of many a pretty driveway." [79]

WEST VIRGINIA

On January 23, 1903, West Virginia by an act of her legislative bodies designated the big laurel or rhododendron [*Rhododendron maximum*] as her State flower. [80] It was selected as the State flower by the school children of West Virginia on November 26, 1902. [81]

WISCONSIN

The violet [genus *Viola*] was selected as the State flower of Wisconsin by a vote of the school children in 1908. [82]

WYOMING

The State of Wyoming, by an act of the legislature on January 31, 1917, adopted the Indian paint brush (*Castillija linariaefolia*) as her State floral emblem. [83]

[79] *The Beauties of the State of Washington, A Book for Tourists,* Harry F. Giles, Deputy Commissioner, Department of State, Bureau of Statistics and Immigration (Frank M. Lamborn, Public Printer, Olympia, Washington, 1915) p. 17.

[80] *Acts of West Virginia, Regular Session, 1903: Acts of the Legislature of West Virginia at Its Twenty-sixth Regular Session Commencing January 14, 1903* (The Tribune Printing Company, Charleston, West Virginia, 1903) p. 303-4.

[81] *West Virginia School Journal* (J. H. Hickman, Editor, Charleston, West Virginia, November, 1929) vol. 58, no. 3, p. 87.

[82] *The Wisconsin Blue Book, 1929,* compiled and published under the direction of the State Printing Board, William J. Anderson and William A. Anderson, Editors (The Democrat Printing Company, State Printer, Madison, Wisconsin, 1929) p. 876.

[83] *Session Laws of Wyoming, 1917: Session Laws of the State of Wyoming, Passed by the Fourteenth State Legislature, Convened at Cheyenne, January 9, 1917, Adjourned February 17, 1917,* compiled and published under Statutory authority by Frank L. Houx, Secretary of State (Wyoming Labor Journal Company, Cheyenne, Wyoming, 1917) chap. 9, p. 7.

FLOWERS SELECTED BY TWO OR MORE STATES

Three states have selected the violet as their floral emblems; namely, Illinois, New Jersey, and Rhode Island. Both Michigan and Arkansas designated the apple blossom as their State flowers.

The goldenrod, officially chosen or otherwise, is the State flower of Alabama, Kentucky, Nebraska, and North Carolina.

Two southern states have chosen the magnolia as their state flowers; namely, Louisiana and Mississippi.

Washington and West Virginia adopted the rhododendron as their state floral emblems.

The rose seems to have been a special favorite with the states, the District of Columbia, Iowa, New York, and North Dakota having chosen it as their state flowers.

CHAPTER IX

THE STATE TREES

Trees add indescribable beauty to the scenery of nature. They furnish cool and inviting shade to weary man and beast. It is from trees that luscious fruits hang with alluring grace and charm, or drop to supply both men and animals with nourishing food. How tiresome would be the dull gray stretches of landscape were it not for trees to add color to the vast expanse of bare earth and blue sky! The service that trees render to living creatures can scarcely be estimated for one could mention blessing after blessing that they bring for the comfort and enjoyment of man and beast without exhausting the supply. Trees frequently grow in such proximity that they furnish shade, as soft and shadowy as twilight. It is evident that not all people share with Joyce Kilmer the feeling of admiration that must have thrilled him when he said:

> "I think that I shall never see
> A poem lovely as a tree."

In recent years people have learned to realize the true worth of trees to the extent that much is being done in the way of planting and protecting them. Seven states have adopted trees, officially or otherwise.

IDAHO

Idaho by an act of her legislative bodies, approved on February 13, 1935, designated the white pine to be the State tree. [1] This act says:

WHEREAS, the members of Ellen Wright Camp, Franklin County Chapter, Daughters of Pioneers, by resolution,

[1] *General Laws of the State of Idaho, Passed at the Twenty-third Session of the State Legislature, 1935,* published by authority of the Secretary of State (Capital News Publishing Company, Boise, Idaho, 1935) 35.

have asked that the White Pine be designated as the state tree of the State of Idaho.

NOW THEREFORE:

Be It Enacted by the Legislature of the State of Idaho: SECTION 1. The White Pine (Pinus Monticolae) is hereby designated and declared to be the state tree of the State of Idaho."

ILLINOIS

Illinois, by an act of her legislative bodies approved on February 21, 1908, declared the native oak tree to be the State tree.[1a] This law went into effect on July 1, 1908.

INDIANA

The tulip tree (*Liriodendron tulipifera*) was adopted as the official State tree of Indiana by an act of the State legislature approved on March 3, 1931.[2]

OKLAHOMA

Oklahoma by senate joint resolution, number five, approved on March 30, 1937, adopted the redbud (*Cercis canadensis* or *cercis reniformis*) as the official State tree.

The resolution [2a] says:

Be it Resolved by the Senate and the House of Representatives of the Sixteenth Legislature of the State of Oklahoma:

WHEREAS, In the beginning of this great commonwealth, when the sturdy and hardy pioneers thereof trekked across its rolling hills and plains, one of the first sights to greet them, spread out in a glorious panorama, was the redbud

---

[1a] *Illinois Revised Statutes, 1921, Keyed to Annotated Statutes: Revised Statutes of the State of Illinois, Embracing all General Laws of the State of Illinois in Force January 1, 1922,* compiled and edited by James C. Cahill (Callaghan and Company, Chicago, Illinois, 1922) p. 3297.

[2] *Acts 1913, 68th Session: Laws of the State of Indiana, Passed at the Sixty-eighth Regular Session of the General Assembly Begun on the 9th Day of January, A. D. 1913,* by authority, L. G. Ellingham, Secretary of State (Wm. B. Burford, Contractor for State Printing and Binding, Indianapolis, Indiana, 1913) p. 693.

[2a] *Oklahoma Session Laws of 1936-1937,* Edited by C. W. Van Eaton (Harlow Publishing Corporation, Oklahoma City, Oklahoma, 1937) senate joint resolution no. 5, p. 562-3.

tree—a tree, that as it arose in the Spring from the verdant fields, was emblematic of the eternal renewal of all life; a tree that in its beauty renewed the worn spirit and gave hope to the tired heart of a people seeking homes in a new land, and;

WHEREAS, It is the will of this Legislature that the adoption of the redbud tree as the official State Tree of the State of Oklahoma would be small, but fitting tribute, to the part it has played in, and the beauty it has lent to, the lives of the people of this State.

Now, Therefore, be it Resolved by the Senate of the State of Oklahoma and the House of Representatives of the State of Oklahoma:

That the redbud tree be adopted and the same be made the official tree of this State.

PENNSYLVANIA

The hemlock is the official State tree of Pennsylvania, adopted by an act of the legislature approved on June 22, 1931. [3] The act says:

"Whereas, The hemlock (Tsuga Canadensis Linnaeus) is still today, as it was of old the tree most typical of the forests of Pennsylvania; and

"Whereas, The hemlock yielded to our pioneers the wood from which they wrought their cabin homes; and

"Whereas, The hemlock gave its bark to found a mighty industry; and

"Whereas, The hemlock everywhere lends kindly shelter and sure haven to the wild things of forests; and

"Whereas, The lighted hemlock at Christmas time dazzles the bright eyes of the child with an unguessed hope, and bears to the aged, in its leaves of evergreen, a sign and symbol of faith in immortality; now therefore,

"Section 1. Be it enacted, &c., That the hemlock tree (Tsuga Canadensis Linnaeus) be adopted as the State tree of Pennsylvania."

[3] *Laws of Pennsylvania, 1931, Regular and Special Sessions: Laws of the General Assembly of the Commonwealth of Pennsylvania, Passed at the Session of 1931 in the One Hundred and Fifty-fifth Year of Independence, Together with a Proclamation by the Governor, Declaring That He Has Filed Certain Bills in the Office of the Secretary of the Commonwealth, with His Objections Thereto,* by authority (Harrisburg, Pennsylvania, 1931) p. 661.

RHODE ISLAND

Rhode Island has the maple for her State tree. It was selected by a vote of the public school children during April, 1894. [4]

TEXAS

The thirty-sixth legislature of the State of Texas on March 20, 1919, [5] adopted the pecan as the State tree. On March 25, 1927, the Texas State Legislature passed a law saying that "it shall be the duty of the State Board of Control and the State Park Board to give due consideration to the Pecan Tree when planning beautification of State Parks or other public property belonging to the State." [6]

[4] *Manual with Rules and Orders for the Use of the General Assembly of the State of Rhode Island, 1931-1932, prepared in accordance* with the provisions of section 9, Chapter 28 of the General Laws, by Ernest L. Sprague, Secretary of State (E. L. Freeman Company, Printers and Binders. Providence, Rhode Island, 1931) p. x.

[5] *General Laws of Texas, Thirty-sixth Legislature 1919: General Laws of the State of Texas, Passed by the Thirty-sixth Legislature at Its Regular Session, Convened January 12, 1919, and Adjourned March 19, 1919,* George F. Howard, Secretary of the State (A. C. Baldwin and Sons, Austin, Texas, 1919) p. 155.

[6] *Texas General and Special Laws, 1927: General and Special Laws of the State of Texas, Passed by the Fortieth Legislature at the Regular Session, Convened at the City of Austin, January 11, 1927, and Adjourned March 16. 1927,* printed under the authority of the State of Texas, Jane Y. McCallum, Secretary of State (Neither the name of the publisher, the place, nor the date of publication is given) p. 234-5.

CHAPTER X

THE STATE BIRDS

Probably no aspect of the nature movement, so noticeable today, is more prominent than that pertaining to birds. Economic Ornithology has taught mankind that certain birds are destructive to his interests and that others are "so valuable to him that every measure should be taken to preserve and increase them." It seems strange that the American colonists should have passed laws providing for the destruction of certain birds and that they should have offered liberal rewards for the heads of these when today there is so much stress put on the importance of birds and their worth to mankind.

It has been shown that birds eat "countless millions of larvae, plant lice, ants, canker worms, leaf-hoppers, flies," [1] and tent caterpillars. It has been asserted also that if all of the birds should be exterminated, within ten years the insects, unchecked, would have completely devoured all vegetation. In addition to destroying numberless eggs and larvae of insects, birds devour countless millions of seeds each year which would produce weeds or other plants troublesome to mankind.

STATES HAVING OFFICIALLY ADOPTED BIRDS

Twenty-two states have adopted birds; namely, Alabama, Arizona, Arkansas, California, Colorado, Florida, Idaho, Illinois, Indiana, Iowa, Kentucky, Maine, Michigan, Missouri, Montana, Nebraska, Ohio, Oregon, Pennsylvania, Tennessee, Texas, and Wyoming. Fourteen birds have been selected by these states as follows: the

[1] *Birds: Selected from the Writings of Neltje Blanchan, The Nature Library,* Neltje Blanchan (Published for Nelson Doubleday, Incorporated, by Doubleday Page and Company, Garden City, New York, 1926) p. 7.

bluebird, the cactus wren, the California valley quail, the cardinal, the chickadee, the goldfinch, the lark bunting, the ruffed grouse, the meadow lark, the mocking bird, the mountain bluebird, the robin, the western meadow lark, and the yellowhammer.

ALABAMA

Alabama by an act of her legislature, approved on September 6, 1927, [2] adopted the yellowhammer as the official State bird. The members of the above-named legislative body officially selected this bird as the avian emblem of Alabama because the cavalrymen of the Confederate Army wore gray uniforms trimmed with yellow, the colors of the yellowhammer having suggested these gray and yellow uniforms.

The name yellowhammer is said to be "erroneously given in some parts of the United States to the common flicker." [3] The name flicker is derived by the process of onomatopoeia from the call of the bird. Technically the flicker is known as the *Colaptes auratus lateus.* This bird, belonging to the woodpecker family, is called by about thirty-six different names, some of which are: the golden-winged woodpecker, clape, pigeon woodpecker, yellow-hammer, high hole or high-holder, yarup, wake up, and yellow-shafted woodpecker.

This bird is both beneficial and destructive to the interests of the farmer. It often pecks holes in trees, including those that bear fruit. It feeds both on the ground and on trees. Its favorite food on the ground is ants and acorns. It is affirmed that for a single meal the flicker has been known to eat as many as three thousand ants. From beneath the bark of trees, the flicker picks out and eats the eggs and the grubs of beetles, spiders, and numerous other insects.

[2] *General Acts of Alabama, Regular Session, 1927, Special Session, 1926-1927; General Laws (and Joint Resolutions) of the Legislature of Alabama, Passed at the Session of 1927, Held at the Capitol, in the City of Montgomery, Commencing Tuesday, January 11, 1927,* John Brandon, Secretary of State (The Brown Printing Company, State Printers and Binders, Montgomery, Alabama, 1927) p. 628.
[3] *The New International Encyclopaedia,* Second Edition (Dodd, Mead, and Company, New York, 1930) vol. 23, p. 797.

The yellowhammer is usually about eleven inches in length, his long slender bill is about one and one-half inches long, his brownish gray back is striped with black; but his rump and some of the tail feathers are white. The top of the head and the lateral portions of the neck are ash colored, having a scarlet band around the nape of the neck; the under parts of the body are lilac-brown in front and creamy yellow in the posterior parts which have circular black spots. The underneath of the wings and tail are a bright golden yellow.

ARIZONA

The cactus wren, technically known as *Coues' Cactus Wren* or *Heleodytes brunneicapillus couesi,* was designated as the State bird of Arizona by an act of the State legislature approved on March 16, 1931. [4] Its adoption was urged by the State Federation of Women's Clubs.

The law says:

"The cactus wren, otherwise known as Coues' Cactus Wren or Heleodytes brunneicapillus couesi (Sharpe) shall be the State bird of Arizona." [4]

The cactus wren is one of the largest species of the wren family, being about eight and one-half inches long. This bird is a resident of the desert sections of the southwestern part of the United States, its chief habitat being along the Mexican border. It may be found, however, in any locality from Texas westward to the border of lower eastern California and to the north as far as "southern Nevada and Utah." The color of this bird is grayish brown and yellow varying in shade to a creamy white. *The Encyclopedia Americana* describes it as being "grayish brown above, darker on the head, nearly pure white beneath, with a spotted breast, and a white line over the

---

[4] *1931 Session Laws of Arizona Tenth Legislature, Regular Session: Initiative and Referendum Measures Voted on at the General Election, November 4, 1930: Acts, Resolutions and Memorials of the Regular Session, Tenth Legislature of the State of Arizona, 1931, Regular Session Convened January 12, 1931, Regular Session Adjourned Sine Die, March 14, 1931,* Scott White, Secretary of State (The Arizona Printers, Inc. Phoenix, Arizona, 1931) p. 148-9.

eye." [5] However, as one looks at this bird, its neck, back, wings, and tail seem to be blackish brown streaked with creamy yellow; and its breast and under parts, including the tail, appear to be creamy yellow dotted with a blackish brown. The cactus wren feeds on insects, seeds, and the scanty fruits common to its desert abode.

ARKANSAS

Arkansas by house concurrent resolution number twenty-two, passed by the Senate on March 5, 1929, [6] adopted the mocking bird as the State bird.

The resolution reads:

"Whereas, most of the States of the American Union have by resolution declared what should be their State Bird; and,

"Whereas, the State of Arkansas has not by Resolution of the General Assembly declared what shall be regarded as the State Bird; and,

"Whereas, the Arkansas Federation of Women's Clubs have done much for the protection of the birds of the State;

"Now, therefore be it resolved, by the House of the Forty-seventh General Assembly of the State of Arkansas, the Senate concurring therein, the 'Mocking Bird', be declared and everywhere recognized as the State Bird of the State of Arkansas."

The mocking bird [*Mimus polyglottus* or *Orpheus polyglottus*] inhabits chiefly the southern part of the United States, but it is found also to a limited extent in practically all parts of this country in such localities as are suited to its manner of living.

Mocking birds eat wild and cultivated fruits, insects, and worms; but they feed their young chiefly upon insects.

The length of the mocking bird varies from ten to eleven inches. In describing it, one would say that the

[5] *The Encyclopedia Americana* (Americana Corporation, New York, 1921) vol. 5, p. 131.
[6] *Journal of the Senate of Arkansas, Forty-seventh General Assembly, Regular Session, Convened at the Capitol in the City of Little Rock, at Noon on Monday, January 14, 1929,* by authority (Russellville Printing Company, Russellville, Arkansas, 1929) p. 785.

back of this bird is an ashy gray, the wings and tail are of a darker shade of gray; and the back under parts are a dingy white. The feathers in the under parts of the wings and some of the tail feathers are tipped with white. The plumage of the male is more colorful than that of the female.

The mocking bird is unable to refrain from singing either night or day; and he is generally in motion, flitting from perch to perch, or flying short distances from one tree to another. He often hops half flying over the ground or sustains himself in flight, pouring out a ripple of song as he flies. The mocking bird seems to enjoy imitating every sound about him, made by man, bird, or beast.

CALIFORNIA

California by an act of her legislative bodies, approved on June 12, 1931, to go into effect August 14, 1931, [7] adopted as her State bird the California valley quail. The Audubon Society, having selected this bird, recommended its official adoption.

The law says:

"The California valley quail (Lophortyx californica) is hereby designated and adopted as the official bird and avifaunal emblem of the State of California."

The California valley quail is found along the coastal regions "of California, Oregon, Washington, and British Columbia." It is about ten inches long. The back, wings, breast, and tail of this bird vary in color from light grays and olive-browns to slate-colored blues streaked with white and black. The belly is chestnut colored, streaked with white and black. The part of the head between the bill and the top is white with a white lateral streak extending over and beyond the eyes. The throat is black, edged around with a white outer streak.

[7] *Statutes and Amendments to the Codes of California, 1931: Statutes of California, 1931, Constitution of 1879 as Amended, Measures Submitted to Vote of Electors 1930: General Laws, Amendments to Codes, Resolutions and Constitutional Amendments Passed at the Regular Session of the Forty-ninth Legislature 1931* (California State Printing Office, Harry Hammond, State Printer, Sacramento, California, 1931) p. 1617.

The distinguishing characteristic is "a crest of several club-shaped [black] feathers, which are erect and extend forward."

This bird feeds on insects, grapes, vegetation, seeds, or grain. The California quail is often very tame and the coveys of it are frequently large, sometimes including as many as five hundred birds.

COLORADO

The lark bunting was designated as the State bird of Colorado by an act of the State legislature approved on April 29, 1931. [8]

The law reads:

"Section 1. The Lark Bunting, scientifically known as Calamospiza melanocorys Stejneger, is hereby made and declared to be the State bird of the State of Colorado."

The lark bunting, being about seven and three-fourths inches long, is a native of the western part of the United States east of the Rocky Mountains, ranging from Kansas to Utah. However, it is sometimes found in southern California, Idaho, Minnesota, and as far north as Assiniboi. It migrates to Mexico to spend the winter months.

The male bird, during the annual period of breeding, has a black plumage with a white spot near the butt or upper part of each wing. After the breeding season is past, the male takes on the coloring of the female, which is a gray streaked with brown with a small white patch on each wing. While the lark bunting is in flight, it sings a varied and pleasing song. Its food consists of insects and the seed of weeds.

FLORIDA

The mocking bird is the State bird of Florida. It was adopted by senate concurrent resolution number three,

[8] *Session Laws of Colorado, 1931: Laws Passed at the Twenty-eighth Session of the General Assembly of the State of Colorado, Convened at Denver at 12 O'clock Noon on Wednesday, January 7, A. D. 1931, and Adjourned Sine Die at 6 P. M. on Friday, April 24, A. D. 1931,* published by authority of Charles M. Armstrong, Secretary of State (Eames Brothers, Printers, Denver, Colorado, 1931) p. 735.

approved on April 23, 1907. As to why this bird was chosen, the resolution says:

"WHEREAS, The Legislature of the State of Florida has thrown the arm of its protecting care around the Mocking Bird by the enactment of suitable legislation and,

"WHEREAS, The melody of its music has delighted the heart of residents and visitors to Florida from the days of the rugged pioneer to the present comer, and

"WHEREAS, This bird of matchless charm is found throughout our State, therefore

"Be It Resolved by the Legislature of the State of Florida:

"Section 1. That the Mocking Bird be and it is hereby designated as the State Bird for the State of Florida." [9]

For a description of the mocking bird, see the discussion of it under the topic *Arkansas*.

IDAHO

An act of the State legislature approved on February 28, 1931, [10] designated the mountain bluebird as the State bird of Idaho.

The act says:

"Be It Enacted by the Legislature of the State of Idaho:

"Section 1. That the Mountain Bluebird (Sialia arctcia) is hereby designated and declared to be the state bird of the State of Idaho."

The mountain bluebird (*Sialia arctcia*) is about seven and one-half inches long. Its habitat is the Rocky Mountain regions, ranging from New Mexico to the Great Slave

[9] *Laws of Florida, 1927, General Laws: General Acts and Resolutions Adopted by the Legislature of Florida at Its Twenty-first Regular Session, April 5 to June 3, 1927, under the Constitution of A. D. 1885,* published by authority of Law under direction of the Attorney-General (T. J. Appleyard, Incorporated, Tallahassee, Florida, 1927) vol. I, p. 1612-13.

[10] *Session Laws of Idaho, Regular Session, 1931, and Extraordinary: General Laws of the State of Idaho, Passed at the Twenty-first Session of the State Legislature, 1931,* published by authority of the Secretary of State (Capital News Publishing Company, Boise, Idaho, 1931) p. 113.

Lake district. Its back and upper parts are a cerulean blue, shading into a paler color on the throat and breast. Its belly is a whitish color. The bluebird feeds chiefly on flies, gnats, and other small insects. It warbles a short musical song.

ILLINOIS

Illinois, by an act of her legislature, approved June 4, 1929, [11] designated the cardinal (*Cardinalis cardinalis*) as her State bird.

The cardinal is from seven and three-quarters to nine inches in length. This bird is generally found from the Middle States southward. However, it is occasionally seen in many other parts of the United States. The cardinals, except during the mating season, usually are gregarious in their habits. They eat insects, larvae, bugs, flies, fruits, and seeds. The throat and a narrow ring around the bill of the cardinal are black, the bill is red, and a crest of feathers crowns the head. Most of the plumage of the male is a deep rich red, the crest, wings, and tail being deeper in color, and the back having a greyish tinge. The female is duller in color than the male. Both the male and the female have a pleasing song, that of the female being even more charming in quality than her mate's. This bird is usually found in thickets or in undergrowth.

INDIANA

The red bird or cardinal was adopted as the State bird of Indiana by an act of the State legislature, approved on March 2, 1933. [11a]

[11] *Laws of Illinois, 1929, Fifty-sixth General Assembly: Laws of the State of Illinois, Enacted by the Fifty-sixth General Assembly at the Regular Biennial Session, Begun and Held at the Capitol, in the City of Springfield, on the Ninth Day of January, A. D. 1929, and Adjourned Sine Die on the Twentieth Day of June, A. D. 1929*, printed by authority of the State of Illinois (Schnepp and Barnes, Springfield, Illinois, 1929) p. 757.
[11a] *Engrossed Senate Bill No. 160, Approved March 9, 1933 by the General Assembly of the State of Indiana*. This bill was sent to the writer by Louis J. Bailey, Librarian, Indiana State Library, Indianapolis, Indiana, in a letter dated June 12, 1933.

The act reads as follows:

"Section 1. Be it enacted by the General Assembly of the State of Indiana, That the bird commonly known as the red bird or cardinal (Richmondena cardinalis cardinalis) is hereby adopted and designated as the official state bird of the State of Indiana."

For a description of the cardinal, see the discussion of it under the topic *Illinois*.

IOWA

Iowa by concurrent resolution number twenty-two, approved by the House on March 21, and by the Senate on March 22, 1933, adopted as the official State bird the Eastern goldfinch (*Spinus tristis tristia*).

The resolution says:

"Whereas, many states have not only adopted certain named flowers as their state flowers, but have also adopted certain named birds as their state birds, and

"Whereas, the Iowa Ornithological Union, an association comprising students and lovers of birds, residing within our state at their annual meeting held in Des Moines, Iowa, in May, 1922, by resolution and vote designated the Eastern Goldfinch as their choice for a state bird, and recommended that the Eastern Goldfinch be adopted as the official state bird of Iowa, therefore,

"Be it Resolved by the House of Representatives, the Senate concurring, that the Eastern Goldfinch, Spinus tristis tristia, is hereby designated and shall hereafter be officially known as the state bird of Iowa." [12]

This bird is about five inches long. The feathers of the crown, wings, and tail are black. The other plumage is a rich lemon yellow. The wings are striped with white, and the margins of the tail feathers are tipped with white. This goldfinch lives in the eastern part of the United States north of the Carolinas, ranging as far as the Rocky mountains. Its food consists chiefly of the seed of the pine and the hemlock trees, the goldenrod, mullein, rag-

[12] *Des Moines Register*, March 27, 1933, cols. 6 and 7, p. 2.

weed, and the thistle. This bird, as it flies, utters a note of song consisting of a rippling twitter.

KENTUCKY

The Kentucky cardinal (*Cardinalis cardinalis*) commonly known as the red bird, was officially selected as the State bird of Kentucky by a resolution of the Senate of Kentucky, the House of Representatives concurring, approved on February 26, 1926. [12a]

This bird was chosen because it is a native of the State of Kentucky.

For a description of the cardinal, see the discussion of it under the topic *Illinois*.

MAINE

A resolve of the Eighty-third Legislature of Maine, approved April 6, 1927, [13] declared the chickadee to be the State bird of Maine.

The chickadee or the blackcapped titmouse (*Penthestes artricapillus*) is about five and one-fourth inches long. This bird is common in the eastern part of the United States. It feeds on the twigs and the bark of evergreen trees during the winter season; but at other times of the year it eats insects, ants, canker worms, and beetles. The chickadee, however, will eat nuts, seeds of the pine, of the poison ivy, of weeds, and other kinds of food.

It is easily distinguished from other kinds of birds by its gray back, black cap and throat, and dingy-white under parts. This bird often feeds hanging upside down. Its call or song consists of the cry chicadee-dee-dee-dee.

[12a] *Kentucky Acts, 1926: Acts of the General Assembly of the Commonwealth of Kentucky, Passed at the Regular Session of the General Assembly, Which Was Begun in the City of Frankfort, Kentucky, on Tuesday, January the Fifth, 1926, and Ended Wednesday, March the Seventeenth, 1926* (The name of the publisher, the place, and the date of publication are not given on the title page of the acts.) p. 1021-2.

[13] *Laws of Maine, 1927: Acts and Resolves as Passed by the Eighty-third Legislature of the State of Maine, 1927,* published by the Secretary of State, in accordance with the Resolves of the Legislature, approved June 28, 1820, March 18, 1840, and March 16, 1842 (Kennebec Journal Print Shop, Augusta, Maine, 1927) p. 553.

MICHIGAN

The robin red breast was designated as the State bird of Michigan by house concurrent resolution number thirty, the Senate concurring, on April 8, 1931.[14]

The resolution reads:

"WHEREAS, A widely and generally conducted contest to choose a State bird, carried on by the Michigan Audubon Society, resulted in nearly 200,000 votes being cast, of which Robin Red Breast received many more votes than any other bird as the most popular bird in Michigan; and

"WHEREAS, The robin is the best known and best loved of all the birds in the State of Michigan; therefore be it

Resolved by the House of Representatives (The Senate concurring), That the robin be and the same is hereby designated and adopted as the official State bird of the State of Michigan."

The robin (*Merula migratoria*) is about ten inches long. Its back and wings are olive-gray; the top and sides of its head are black; its throat is white and black streaked; and its breast and under parts are cinnamon-rufous or a rust brown. Its back under parts are a dingy-white. This bird is found in all parts of the United States. Its food chiefly consists of earth worms, insects, berries, and other small fruits, especially ripe cherries.

MISSOURI

An act of the General Assembly of Missouri, approved on March 30, 1927, [15] adopted the bluebird, (*Sialia sialis*) as the State bird. The bluebird inhabits all parts of the United States. It is about six and one-half inches long.

---

[14] *Michigan House Journal, 1931: Journal of the House of Representatives of the State of Michigan, 1931,* Myles F. Gray, Clerk of the House of Representatives (Franklin DeKleine Company, Printers and Binders, Lansing, Michigan, 1931) vol. 1, p. 637-8.

[15] *Laws of Missouri, 1927: Laws of Missouri, Passed at the Session of the Fifty-fourth General Assembly, 1927, Which Convened at the City of Jefferson, Wednesday, January 5th, 1927, and Adjourned Monday, April 4th, 1927, . . .* compiled by Charles U. Becker, Secretary of State (The Hugh Stephens Press, Jefferson City, Missouri, 1927) p. 121.

Its head, neck, back, wings, and tail are bright blue. The throat, breast, and sides of this bird are cinnamon red. Its underparts are white. In autumn its color has a rusty wash. The color of the female is much duller than that of the male.

The bluebird eats moths, spiders, young grasshoppers and other insects, cutworms, the larvae of the soldier-beetle, ground beetles, soldier bugs, caterpillars, young crickets, winged ants, raspberries, gooseberries, and elder-berries.

MONTANA

The meadow lark was chosen as the State bird of Montana in 1930 by a vote of the school children of the State. Montana, by an act of her legislative body approved on March 14, 1931, [16] adopted the western meadow lark as the official State bird.

The act reads:

"Section 1. The bird known as the Western Meadow Lark, Sturnella-Neglecta (Audubon) as preferred by a referendum vote of Montana school children, shall be designated and declared to be the official bird of the State of Montana."

The western meadow lark (*Sturnella neglecta*) is about eleven inches long. It has a thick stout body with large legs and a long straight bill. The upper parts of this meadow lark are deep brown and black, varied with chestnut. Its crown is streaked with brown and black with a cream colored stripe on each side. The under-neath parts of this bird are yellow. The outer tail feathers show white when the bird is flying. The throat and breast are a canary yellow, the breast showing a black crescent. Its food consists of grain, insects, cater-pillars, cutworms, army worms, grasshoppers, beetles, and chinch bugs.

[16] *Laws of Montana, Twenty-second Session, 1931: Laws, Resolutions and Memorials of the State of Montana, Passed by the Twenty-second Legislative Assembly in Regular Session, Held at Helena, the Seat of Government of Said State, Commencing January 5th, 1931, and Ending March 5th, 1931, Including Referendum Measures Voted Upon by the People at the General Election Held November 4th, 1931*, published by authority (State Publishing Company, Helena, Montana, 1931) p. 389.

NEBRASKA

Nebraska by a joint and concurrent resolution of her legislative bodies, approved on March 22, 1929, [17] adopted the western meadow lark as the official State bird.

The resolution says:

"WHEREAS, the Nebraska Federation of Women's Clubs had its convention at Kearney, passed almost unanimously a resolution in favor of the adoption of a state bird, and

"WHEREAS, the Conservation Division of said Federation followed up the action taken by the resolution aforesaid by submitting a list of the five (5) birds receiving the highest vote, to the schools of the State of Nebraska, with a request that the pupils of such schools express their privilege of indicating their particular favorite bird, and

"WHEREAS, the Ornithologists Union of Nebraska in the spring of 1928, went on record as choosing the Western Meadowlark as a state bird, and

"WHEREAS, the Western Meadowlark was also the choice of the Convention of the Nebraska Federation of Women's Clubs, each organization a unit, and

"WHEREAS, an intensive study of birds in Nebraska ought to be encouraged, and recognized by this Legislature for the reason that it will stimulate the interest of present and prospective citizens of the State of Nebraska in the natural life of this state,

"NOW THEREFORE:

"BE IT RESOLVED BY THE HOUSE OF REPRESENTATIVES OF THE STATE OF NEBRASKA, THE SENATE CONCURRING:

"Section 1. That the 'Western Meadowlark,' be and hereby is declared the state bird of Nebraska."

For a description of the western meadow lark, see the discussion of it under the topic *Montana*.

[17] *Session Laws, Laws Passed by the Legislature of the State of Nebraska at the Forty-fifth Session, 1929, which Convened in the City of Lincoln, Nebraska, Tuesday, January 1st and Adjourned April 24th, 1929,* compiled and published by Frank Marsh, Secretary of State (York Blank Book Company, Law Publishers, Printers and Binders, York, Nebraska, 1929) chap. 139, p. 495.

NEW JERSEY

New Jersey by an act of her legislative assemblies, approved on June 27, 1935, adopted the Eastern goldfinch [17a] as the official State bird.

See the topic *Iowa* for a discussion of this bird.

OHIO

Ohio by an act of the General Assembly, passed on February 21, 1933, and approved on March 2, 1933, [18] adopted the cardinal (*Cardinalis cardinalis*) as the State bird.

For a description of the cardinal, see the discussion of it under the topic, *Illinois*.

OREGON

The western meadow lark is the State bird of Oregon. This bird was chosen "in the spring of 1927 by a popular vote of the school children, sponsored by the Oregon Audubon Society. In July, 1927, Governor I. L. Patterson issued a proclamation naming it the state bird. No legislative action has been taken." [19]

For a description of the meadow lark, see the discussion of it under the topic *Montana*.

PENNSYLVANIA

Pennsylvania by an act of her legislature, approved on June 22, 1931, chose the ruffed grouse (*Bonasa umbellus*) as her State game bird. [20]

[17a] *Acts of the One Hundred and Fifty-ninth Legislature of the State of New Jersey and Ninety-first under the New Constitution, 1935* (Mac-Crellish and Quigley Company, Printers, Trenton, New Jersey, 1935) p. 913.

[18] A copy of the act sent in a communication from C. B. Galbreath, Secretary of the Ohio State Archaeological and Historical Society, Columbus, Ohio, June 28, 1933.

[19] A letter from Harriet C. Long, Librarian, Oregon State Library, Salem, Oregon, June 19, 1931.

[20] *Laws of Pennsylvania, 1931, Regular and Special Session: Laws of the General Assembly of the Commonwealth of Pennsylvania, Passed at the Session of 1931, in the One Hundred and Fifty-fifth Year of Independence, . . .* by authority (Harrisburg, Pennsylvania, 1931) p. 662.

The act reads:

"Be it enacted by the Senate and House of Representatives of the Commonwealth of Pennsylvania in General Assembly met and it is hereby enacted by the authority of the same That the ruffed grouse (bonasa umbellus) is hereby selected, designated and adopted as the State game bird of Pennsylvania."

The ruffed grouse is about eighteen inches long. Its back, upper parts of the wings, and tail are a chestnut color, streaked with blackish brown and yellow. The head, breast, and neck are a yellowish brown color, striped or specked with a deeper shade of brown. The belly and back under parts are a lighter shade of brown, marked with heart-shaped spots running across the body from side to side, thus forming stripes. The tail is a "warm brown or grayish ash, crossed with six or seven narrow bands of blackish brown, the subterminal one [being] much wider, the feathers tipped with white." The tail feathers are "somewhat doubly notched, so that it is nearly half diamond shaped when spread." The head has a coronet-shaped topknot, the legs are heavily feathered, toes are slightly feathered, and the neck surrounded by a purplish black ruff, which is very thick on the sides. The range of the ruffed grouse is the eastern part of the United States, ranging from Minnesota and Michigan to Tennessee and Georgia.

The food of the ruffed grouse consists chiefly of fruits, grain, mast, grasshoppers, cutworms, beetles, ants, spiders, wasps, and caterpillars.

TENNESSEE

Tennessee by Senate joint resolution number fifty-one, on April 19, 1933, [21] adopted the mocking bird [*Mimus polyglottos*] as the official State bird.

---

[21] A copy of *Senate Joint Resolution No. 51,* sent to the writer by Ernest N. Haston, Secretary of State, from Nashville, Tennessee, May 18, 1933.

The resolution says:

"WHEREAS, forty-five of the forty-eight States of the Union have chosen an official bird for their commonwealth, and

"WHEREAS, the State of Tennessee did not, until this year, determine to choose the State Bird, and

"WHEREAS, The Tennessee Ornithological Society, aided by the Garden Clubs, the Parent Teacher Associations, the Superintendents of Schools, the State Department of Education, the State Department of Agriculture and the Division of Game and Fish, has just conducted a campaign of education in connection with the state-wide choice of an official bird, and

"WHEREAS, an election has just been concluded in which every person within the confines of the State has been afforded an opportunity of expressing a preference for a State bird, and

"WHEREAS, the Mocking bird received more votes, according to the official count of the ballots, made by the Department of Game and Fish, now

"THEREFORE, Be It Resolved, That the Mocking Bird is hereby declared the official State Bird of Tennessee."

The *Nashville Banner* [22] says that on April 11, 1933 the mocking bird was selected as the State bird of Tennessee by popular vote, that The Tennessee Ornithological Society planned a state-wide ballot for the selection of the official bird, and that there was a total of seventy-two thousand and thirty-one votes cast, distribu ted as follows: the mocking bird, 15,553, the robin, 15,073, the cardinal, 13,969, the bobwhite, 10,460, the bluebird, 9,125, and others, 8,751. Those serving on the committee with Dr. G. R. Mayfield were Miss Jacqueline Hall of Memphis, Tennessee, Mr. John Bamberg, of Knoxville, Tennessee, and Mr. Bruce P. Taylor, of Johnson City, Tennessee.

For a description of the mocking bird, see the discussion of it under the topic *Arkansas*.

[22] The *Nashville Banner*, April 16, 1933.

TEXAS

The mocking bird was selected as the State bird of Texas by an act of the legislature, approved on January 31, 1927. [23] The mocking bird was selected because: (1) "It is found in all parts of the State " [23a] of Texas; (2) Texas "ornithologists, musicians, educators and Texans in all walks of life unite in proclaiming the Mocking bird the most appropriate species for the state bird of Texas" [23b] ; (3) it "is a singer of distinctive type, a fighter for the protection of his home, falling if need be, in its defense, like any true Texan" [23b] ; (4) the Texas Federation of Women's Clubs named the mocking bird as the State bird of Texas, and asked the Fortieth Legislature to adopt it.

For information about the mocking bird, see the discussion of it under the topic *Arkansas*.

WYOMING

Wyoming by an act of her legislature, approved February 5, 1927, selected the meadow lark as the State bird of Wyoming. The law says: "An American icteroid bird (genus Sturnella), the bird commonly known as the Meadow lark, is hereby made and declared to be the State Bird of the State of Wyoming." [24]

A comprehensive discussion of the meadow lark may be found under the topic *Montana*.

[23] *Texas General and Special Laws, 1927: General and Special Laws of the State of Texas, Passed by the Fortieth Legislature at the Regular Session, Convened at the City of Austin, January 11, 1927, and Adjourned March 16, 1927,* printed under the authority of the State of Texas, Jane Y. McCallum, Secretary of State (A. C. Baldwin and Sons, State Printers, Austin, Texas, 1927) p. 466.

[23a] *Ibidem,* p. 486.

[23b] *Ibidem,* p. 486.

[24] *Session Laws of Wyoming, 1927: Session Laws of the State of Wyoming, Passed by the Nineteenth State Legislature, Convened at Cheyenne, January 11, 1927, Adjourned February 19, 1927,* compiled and published under Statutory authority by A. M. Clark, Secretary of State (The Casper Printing and Stationery Company, Casper, Wyoming, 1927) p. 8.

A List of the Birds and of the States Selecting Each

Since more than one state in several instances adopted the same bird, it is thought advisable here to list the birds and to name the states choosing each. They are: Alabama, the yellowhammer; Arizona, the cactus wren; Arkansas, Florida, Tennessee, and Texas, the mocking bird; California, the Californian valley quail; Colorado, the lark bunting; Idaho, the mountain bluebird; Illinois, Indiana, Kentucky, and Ohio, the cardinal; Iowa, the goldfinch; Maine, the chickadee; Michigan, the robin; Missouri, the bluebird; Montana, the meadow lark; Nebraska and Oregon, the western meadow lark; Pennsylvania, the ruffed grouse; and Wyoming, the meadow lark.

States Having No Officially Adopted Bird

The following states have not officially adopted birds, but in each of these states public sentiment has crystallized or is crystallizing about some bird to the extent that it will likely be selected as the State bird. In the case of many of these states, birds have been selected by common consent, by vote of the public school children, by Audubon Societies, or by the Federated Women's Clubs; but they have not yet been officially adopted by legislative action. The Federated Women's Clubs have been very active in this work, having in several instances been instrumental in getting the state legislatures to adopt the birds which they have selected; and in reference to other birds, they are planning to ask for legislative action in the future. The facts about what the various Federated Women's Clubs have done and are doing in this matter were obtained chiefly from answers to personal letters from the writer to the presidents or secretaries of these organizations. The footnotes throughout the remaining part of this chapter refer to these letters as well as to communications from other individuals or organizations giving facts about the selection of State birds.

Connecticut

A bird that has been suggested for the State bird of Connecticut is the ruby-crowned kinglet[25] (*Regulus calendula*). This bird is about four and two-fifths inches long. Its range is northward from the northern borders of the United States; in the Rocky mountain regions it ranges as far south as southern California or southern Arizona; and in the eastern part of the United States it is found as far south as Virginia. It spends its winter months in a range extending from South Carolina and Oregon to Central America. The upper parts of the head, neck, back, and tail of the kinglet are olive-green tinged with gray. The under parts are pale olive-green shading into a dingy-white tinged with buff. The top of the head is crowned with a bright red crest. The eyes are partly encircled with a narrow white ring, and the wings are striped with whitish bars. This bird feeds largely upon such insects, their eggs and larvae, as are found on fruit trees. These small birds, when the mating season is past, are gregarious. They fight hawks, crows, and jaybirds. The song of the kinglet is a soft, flute-like warble.

Delaware

The scarlet cardinal was selected because he spends and recommended by the State Federation of Women's Clubs of Delaware as their State bird, but so far no legislative action has been taken to make this selection official.

The cardinal (*Cardinalis cardinalis*) has been selected the entire year in Delaware. Other reasons for choosing this bird may be summed up by saying that "he is first of all, a good father and an excellent husband. . . . , [that] he is also one of the most beautiful birds in existence, [that] his carriage and bearing are aristocratic, [that] he is polite to his neighbors, and [that he] is a very great gentleman." Since Delaware has been and is the home

[25] *Nature Magazine*, April, 1932, vol. 19, no. 4, p. 231.

of so many aristocratic families, "it is a good idea to have the state represented by this crested prince of the bushes." [26]

For a description of the cardinal, see the discussion of it under the topic *Illinois*.

The District of Columbia

A communication from the Secretary of the Board of Commissioners of the District of Columbia reveals the fact that there is no officially adopted bird for the District. The District Federation of Women's Clubs, however, has selected as the club bird the woodthrush (*Hylocichla mustelina*). [27]

The woodthrush is about seven and one-half inches long. This bird is native to the eastern part of the United States. It is rarely found south of Kansas, Kentucky, Virginia, North Carolina, and Tennessee except during the winter months, during which time it sometimes migrates as far south as Central America. The back and upper parts of the woodthrush are reddish cinnamon-brown with the rump and tail feathers shading into an olive-brown. The under parts are white, shaded with buff and sprinkled with round black spots. The woodthrush eats spiders, worms, beetles, grasshoppers, caterpillars, potato bugs, mulberries, blackgum berries, dogwood and other berries that grow wild. Its song is low and flute or bell-like.

Georgia

In 1928 the school children of Georgia selected as the State bird the brown thrasher (*Toxostoma rufum*). "The campaign was inaugurated by the Fifth District of the State Federation of Women's Clubs and was sponsored by the Atlanta Bird Club and kindred groups." [28] Proposals

[26] *A State Bird For Delaware*, a copy of some material taken from *The Source Research Bureau* and sent to the writer by Mrs. Lillie V. Atkins in a letter from Lewes, Delaware, May 24, 1932.
[27] *Nature Magazine*, April, 1932, vol. 19, no. 4, p. 230.
[28] *Ibidem*, p. 234.

have been made to the Legislature and bills to adopt this bird officially as the State avian emblem introduced bu no action has been taken thereupon.

The thrasher is a native of the eastern part of the United States, ranging from the Gulf States to Maine It spends the winter months in the extreme southern par of the United States. The thrasher is about eleven and one-half inches long, including the tail which is abou five inches in length. The upper parts of this bird are : rusty brown. The under parts are white, strongly marked with black or cinnamon-brown stripes. The wings have white bars near the butts. This bird eats grasshoppers worms, bugs, and fruits. It is shy and dislikes to be watched by human beings. Its varied song is clear musical, and rich in tone quality.

Kansas

In 1925 the Kansas Audubon Society conducted a con test in which the school children of the State chose by ballot the bird which they wished to become the State bird. The western meadow lark, the quail, the cardinal and the robin were the closest competitive candidates There were 121,191 votes cast. The western meadow lark received 48,395 votes which was about 10,000 votes more than its nearest competitor. [29]

The western meadow lark, being a native of the prairie states, is found in all parts of Kansas. Its custom of sitting on the fences makes it well known both to those touring through the State and to the natives; conse quently its beauty and its cheerful notes of song are familiar both to the adults and to the children of the State.

For a description of the western meadow lark, see the discussion of it under the topic Montana.

Louisiana

The American brown pelican (Pelecanus occidentalis has come to be considered the State bird of Louisiana by

[29] A letter from George A. Allen, Jr., State Superintendent of Publi Instruction, Topeka, Kansas, May 2, 1933.

common consent. It came to be so designated in all probability from the fact that the pelican is a conspicuous part of the coat of arms displayed on the State seal.

The pelican resides chiefly along the Gulf coast and the southern Atlantic coast of the United States. It breeds along the coastal region from South Carolina and Louisiana to the northern part of South America. However, it breeds on Pelican Island, a bird reservation consisting of about five and one-half acres, and located in the Indian river off the coast of Florida.

The brown Pelican is from four to six feet in length. The back and tail of this pelican are silverish gray. The under parts are a blackish brown. The wing coverts, head, chest, and sides of the neck are a straw-colored white. The pouch and throat are a dark greenish brown. The edges of the bill are pink. The pelican, being a maritime bird, feeds chiefly on fish.

Maryland

The State bird of Maryland is the Baltimore oriole (*Icterus galbula*). The writer is unable to find when, why, or by whom this bird was adopted as Maryland's official bird. An act approved on March 30, 1882, [30] says:

"Section 16. No person in the State of Maryland shall shoot or in any manner catch, kill or have in possession any bird of the species known as the 'Baltimore Oriole Icterus,' or molest or destroy the eggs or nests of the said birds in the said State.

"Section 17. Any person violating the preceding section shall, on conviction, pay a fine of not less than ten dollars or more than twenty dollars for each and every bird of the species known as the 'Baltimore Oriole Icterus' shot or in any manner caught, killed or in their possession, or for any eggs or nest of the said birds molested or destroyed contrary to the preceding section, said fines to be recovered before a justice of the peace of the county

[30] *Laws of the State of Maryland, Made and Passed at a Session of the General Assembly Begun and Held at the City of Annapolis on the Fourth Day of January, 1882, and Ended on the Third Day of April, 1882,* published by authority (Luther F. Colton, State Printer, Annapolis, Maryland, 1882) p. 208.

or city where the offence is committed, or by indictment in the court having criminal jurisdiction in the county or city where the offence is committed; and in default of payment of fine or fines imposed hereunder, together with the costs, the offender shall be committed to jail for not less than ten or more than sixty days for each offence, and the nonpayment of each and every fine shall be considered a separate offence within the meaning hereof; one-half of all fines imposed shall go to the informer."

The oriole eats garden peas, cherries, and grapes; but it also feeds on the tent caterpillar, canker worms, and various insects. The Baltimore oriole is found in the eastern part of the United States. The plumage of this bird with the exception of that on the head, throat, upper parts of the back, the middle tail feathers, and some of the wing feathers, is a rich orange color. The plumage of the head, throat, back, and central tail feathers are black. Some of the wing feathers have white tips.

Massachusetts

"The Executive Board of the State Federation of Women's Clubs adopted the veery for [their] State bird of Massachusetts in November 1931." [31] An unsuccessful bill was introduced into the legislature of the Commonwealth in 1931 to officially adopt the veery as the State bird.

The veery (*Hylocichla fuscescens*) is about seven and one-half inches long. This bird is found in the eastern part of the United States. Its range, however, varies from New Foundland south to the Carolinas. The head, back, upper wings, and tail of the veery are a cinnamon-brown. The throat, belly, and under tail parts are a buffish white, and the sides of the breast have wedge shaped spots of cinnamon-brown. The veery eats spiders, bugs, worms, snails, insects, and small fruits.

[31] A letter from R. B. Parmenter, Extension Forester, Boston, Massachusetts, May 17, 1932.

Minnesota

The Minnesota Federation of Women's Clubs adopted as the Club bird the American goldfinch [32] (*Astragalinus tristis*). "Minnesota, through Mrs. Willard Bayliss, then State President of the State Federation of Women's Clubs, put on a campaign to secure a state bird in 1926.

"The campaign was spirited and far-reaching in its influence, with much press publicity and many candidates, —in fact an embarrassment of fine candidates. The Ten Thousand Lakes residents wanted the blue heron; those near the woodlands, the veery; some thought the white-throated sparrow, the voice of the tamarack swamps, a fine choice, but the majority vote was for the 'goldfinch,' with his gay plumage and musical flight, 'per-chic-o-ree,' as he bounds through the air." [33]

For a description of the goldfinch see the discussion of it under the topic *Iowa*.

Mississippi

In 1929 the Mississippi Federation of Women's Clubs conducted a State bird campaign which resulted in the selection of the mocking bird as their State avian emblem. [34]

For a description of the mocking bird, see the discussion of it under the topic *Arkansas*.

Nevada

The Nevada Federation of Women's Clubs, during the years of 1930 and 1931, by vote of the citizens and the school children of the State, selected the mountain blue-bird as their choice for the State bird of Nevada. [35]

[32] A letter from Mrs. Irene C. Powell, Minneapolis, Minnesota, May 11, 1932.

[33] *The Minnesota Club Woman*, Biennial Convention Issue, the Official Publication of the Minnesota Federation of Women's Clubs, Incorporated, May-June, 1932, vol. xv, no. 5, p. 7.

[34] *Nature Magazine*, April, 1932, vol. 19, no. 4, p. 235.

[35] *Ibidem*, p. 235.

For a description of the mountain bluebird, see the discussion of it under the topic *Idaho*.

New Hampshire

The New Hampshire Federation of Women's Clubs, in 1927, by popular vote, selected the purple finch (*Carpodacus purpureus*) as their State bird. [36]

The purple finch is about six and one-fifth inches in length. The home of this bird is the eastern part of the United States, extending westward to Illinois and Minnesota. The plumage of the purple finch is a rose-colored purple with the back parts, the upper wing parts, and the tail shading into, or striped with a blackish brown. The belly is white. Its food consists largely of the seeds of weeds and of smaller plants.

New Mexico

The road-runner (*Geococcyx californianus*) is being advocated for adoption as the State bird of New Mexico. It lives in the western part of the United States, its range being from Central Mexico northward to Kansas, Oregon, and California. Its color is a glossy olive-brown. The separate feathers of its body and tail are tipped or edged with white. Its fan shaped tail is very conspicuous and adds to its speed in running. This bird is especially fond of feeding on mice, lizards, snakes, insects and cactus fruit. It utters a sound similar to the clucking of a hen.

New York

The campaign, conducted by Mrs. Charles Cyrus Marshall, President of the New York Federated Women's Clubs, in 1927-1928, [36] showed that the people favored the adoption of the bluebird as the State avian emblem.

[36] *Nature Magazine*, April, 1932, vol. 19, no. 4, p. 235.

For a description of the bluebird, see the discussion of it under the topic *Missouri*.

North Carolina

The Carolina chickadee (*Parus carolinensis*) was designated as the State bird of North Carolina by a popular vote of the people in 1931. [37] This contest was sponsored by Mrs. E. S. Paddison, President of the State Federated Women's Clubs. The chickadee and the red-winged blackbird were rivals for this honor because they both spend the entire year in North Carolina. [37]

The Carolina chickadee is about four and one-half inches long; the range of this bird is in the southeastern part of the United States, extending as far north as southern Illinois and southern New Jersey. The color of the chickadee is a grayish black tinged with brown, the feathers of the outer margins of the wing coverts being grayish white. The tail, the top of the head, and the throat are black. The sides of the throat have a rather wide white stripe. The flanks are colored a whitish buff. It feeds chiefly on moths, seeds, and small insects.

North Carolina by joint resolution number fifty-one, approved on May 8, 1933, [38] adopted the chickadee as the official State bird.

The act reads as follows:

"WHEREAS, in a State-wide contest conducted by the newspapers which was sponsored by the division of conservation of the civics department of the State Federation of Women's Clubs, the bird known as the 'Carolina Chickadee' was voted first choice as the official bird of the State; and

[37] A letter from Mrs. E. S. Paddison, Nashville, North Carolina, May 17, 1932.
[38] A copy of *joint resolution number 51, Adopting the Chickadee as the Official bird of North Carolina,* sent in a communication from Carrie L. Broughton, Librarian, North Carolina State Library, Raleigh, North Carolina, July 11, 1933.

"WHEREAS, the Carolina Chicadee has proved most beneficial to agriculture in that it lives on insects and bugs which are harmful to crops: Now therefore,

"Resolved by the House of Representatives, the Senate concurring:

"Section 1. That the bird known as the 'Carolina Chickadee' be and the same is hereby declared to be the official bird of North Carolina.

"Section 2. That all laws and clauses of laws in conflict with this resolution are hereby repealed.

"Section 3. That this resolution shall be in full force and effect from and after its ratification."

By joint resolution of her legislative bodies, ratified on May 15, 1933, [39] North Carolina repealed the act quoted above making the chickadee the official State bird.

The act reads as follows:

"The General Assembly of North Carolina do enact:

"Section 1. That House Bill 1560, a joint resolution making the chickadee the official bird of the State, ratified May 8, 1933, be and the same is hereby repealed."

North Dakota

Mrs. W. S. Parker, Corresponding Secretary of the North Dakota Federated Women's Clubs, says that a questionnaire was sent out to all the Women's Clubs of the State to select a State bird and that the replies favored the western meadow lark, but that it was not adopted as the club bird. [40]

For a description of the western meadow lark, see the discussion of it under the topic *Montana*.

Oklahoma

The people of Oklahoma expressed their preference for the bobwhite as the State bird, the contest being sponsored by the State Federation of Women's Clubs. [41]

---

[39] A copy of the *Act Repealing Joint Resolution number 51, Adopting The Chickadee as the Official bird of North Carolina,* sent in a communication from Carrie L. Broughton, Librarian, State Library, Raleigh, North Carolina, July 11, 1933.

[40] A letter from Mrs. W. S. Parker, Corresponding Secretary of the Federated Women's Clubs of North Dakota, Lisbon, North Dakota, May 14, 1932.

[41] *Nature Magazine,* April, 1932, vol. 19, no. 4, p. 235.

The bobwhite (*Colinus virginianus*) is about ten inches long. This bird is well-known in practically all parts of the United States. The upper parts are usually a chestnut brown, mottled with bars of black or white. The under parts are white speckled with bars of black. The throat is white. A broad white line extends from the bill over each eye. The bobwhite feeds upon insects, berries, small mast, seeds, and grain.

Rhode Island

The bobwhite was selected as the State bird of Rhode Island in a contest sponsored by the Division of Conservation of the Rhode Island Federated Women's Clubs in 1931. Those who voted in this contest were: the school children, the boy scouts, the campfire girls, the grangers, the golf clubs, the four-high clubs, and other patriotic organizations. [42]

The contesting birds were: the bobwhite, the osprey, the flicker, the tree swallow, the song sparrow, and the catbird. The bobwhite was chosen because he is widely distributed throughout the State, his plumage and song are attractive, he is a permanent resident, and he is the farmer's friend. [42]

For a description of the bobwhite, see the discussion of it under the topic *Oklahoma*.

South Carolina

In 1931 the South Carolina Federated Women's Clubs adopted as their State bird the Carolina wren. [43]

The Carolina wren (*Thryothorus ludovicianus*) is about five and one-half inches in length. Its habitation is the southern part of the United States, extending as far north as Connecticut. Its color is a bright rusty brown. It has a white throat and a white line extending from the

[42] A letter from Miss Alice A. Griffin, Chairman of the Department of Education, Providence, Rhode Island, May 4, 1932.

[43] A letter from Miss Claudia Phelps, Chairman of the Division of Conservation of the Federated Women's Clubs of South Carolina, Aiken, South Carolina, May 23, 1932.

bill through the eyes. Its food consists of bugs, worms, and small insects.

South Dakota

The South Dakota Federated Women's Clubs, on October 23, 1931, adopted as their State bird, the western meadow lark. [44]

For a description of the western meadow lark, see the discussion of it under the topic *Montana.*

Utah

The California gull (*Larus californicus*) is considered the State bird of Utah by common consent, probably in commemoration of the fact that these gulls saved the people of the State by eating up the Rocky mountain crickets which were destroying the crops in 1848.

Orson F. Whitney says that in the midst of the devastation of the crickets, "when it seemed that nothing could stay the devastation, great flocks of gulls appeared, filling the air with their white wings and plaintive cries, and settled down upon the half-ruined fields . . . All day long they gorged themselves, and when full, disgorged and feasted again, the white gulls upon the black crickets, like hosts of heaven and hell contending, until the pests were vanquished and the people were saved." [45] After devouring the crickets, the gulls returned "to the lake islands whence they came." [45]

The gull is about two feet long. The color of this bird is pearly-blue. It is sometimes barred or streaked with blackish gray. This gull is commonly found on and

[44] A letter from Mrs. C. E. Lange, President of the Second District of the South Dakota Federated Women's Clubs, Murdo, South Dakota, May 16, 1932.

[45] *History of Utah Comprising Preliminary Chapters on the Previous History of Her Founders, Accounts of Early Spanish and American Explorations in the Rocky Mountain Regions, the Establishment and Dissolution of the Provisional Government of the State of Deseret, and the Subsequent Creation and Development of the Territory,* Orson F. Whitney (George Q. Cannon and Sons Company, Salt Lake City, Utah, 1892) p. 378.

around the Great Salt Lake in Utah and along the western
coast of Lower California.

Vermont

The Vermont Federated Women's Clubs in 1927
adopted as their State bird the hermit thrush [46] (*Hylocichla gutta pallasi*).

The hermit thrush is about seven inches long. The
upper parts of this bird including the head, back, and
upper part of the wings, are an olive-brown, the tail being
a yellowish or a brownish red. The under parts are a
dingy-white tinged with buff marked with wedge shaped
or round spots of a darker buff. Its home is in the
northern part of the New England States. The food of the
hermit thrush consists of flies, weevils, ants, caterpillars,
moths, worms, berries, seeds and small fruits. The song
of this bird is remarkable for its exquisite quality.

Virginia

Virginia has never officially adopted a State bird, [47]
but in 1912 there was a law passed protecting the robin.

The act says:

"1. Be it enacted by the General Assembly of Virginia,
That it shall be unlawful for any person to shoot at, kill,
or capture robins at any time, or to take or destroy their
nests or eggs.

"2. Any person violating any of the provisions of this
act shall be deemed guilty of a misdemeanor, and shall
be punished by a fine of not less than five nor more than
fifty dollars." [48]

The robin is discussed under the topic *Michigan*.

[46] *Nature Magazine,* April, 1932, vol. 19, no. 4, p. 235.
[47] A letter from Peter Saunders, Secretary of the Commonwealth,
Richmond, Virginia, May 7, 1932.
[48] *Acts of the Assembly of Virginia, 1912: Acts and Joint Resolutions (Amending the Constitution) of the General Assembly of the State
of Virginia. . . .* (Davis Bottom, Superintendent of Public Printing,
Richmond, Virginia, 1912) p. 104.

Washington

A prospective candidate for the honor of State bird of Washington is the willow goldfinch [49] (*Astragalinus tristis salicamans*). This bird is found along the Pacific coast regions from southern California to Oregon. Its favorite habitat is clumps of willow bushes growing in marshy places or on the borders of streams. It feeds on sunflower seed, weed and thistle seeds, the buds of bushes, and sycamore and alder seeds. The color of the willow goldfinch is dark or a pale olive-green, shading into black on its sides and flanks with white or light colored wing and tail markings.

West Virginia

The tufted titmouse (*Baeolophus bicolor*) will probably be considered for official adoption as the State avian emblem of West Virginia. It has been selected as the club bird of the State Federated Women's Clubs. [49]

The titmouse is about six inches in length. It is found in the eastern part of the United States, ranging from Iowa and New Jersey to the Gulf of Mexico. The plumage of the upper parts of the body is gray. Its breast and under parts are a whitish gray. It has a gray topknot, a black spot above the bill, and a rusty brown patch beneath each wing. It eats seeds, small insects, and small fruits.

Wisconsin

The robin was selected as the State bird of Wisconsin by a vote of the school children of the State in 1926, [50] The campaign was conducted by Mrs. Walter Bowman, Conservation Chairman of the State Federated Women's Clubs. [51]

A discussion of the robin may be found under the topic *Michigan*.

[49] *Nature Magazine*, April, 1932, vol. 19, no. 4, p. 230.

[50] *The Wisconsin Blue Book, 1929*, compiled and published under the direction of the State Printing Board, William J. Anderson and William A. Anderson, Blue Book Editors (The Democrat Printing Company. State Printer, Madison, Wisconsin, 1929) p. 876.

[51] *Nature Magazine, April*, 1932, vol. 19, no. 4, p. 235.

CHAPTER XI

THE STATE SONGS

State songs are built out of emotions and sentiments often inspired by patriotism. Such productions are closely akin to those of a national or of a religious nature in the respect that both the words and the melody appeal to the masses. Not all state songs were written as such, but frequently they have been selected because of approximate wording which suited them to a particular occasion or to some significant use. Many of them were chosen because of their popular rather than because of their classical appeal, for in several instances neither the words nor the music can be classed as masterpieces of poetical or of musical invention.

STATES HAVING OFFICIALLY ADOPTED SONGS

Twenty-one states have officially adopted songs as follows: Alabama, Arizona, Arkansas, Colorado, Delaware, Florida, Georgia, Idaho, Illinois, Indiana, Iowa, Kentucky, Louisiana, Nevada, New Mexico, North Carolina, Oklahoma, Oregon, Tennessee, Texas, and Washington.

Alabama

Alabama by a house joint resolution of the State legislature, approved on March 9, 1931, [1] adopted as her official State song *Alabama*. Miss Julia S. Tutweiler wrote the words of, and Mrs. Edna Gockel-Gussen composed the music to, this composition.

[1] *General Acts of Alabama, Regular Session, 1931: General Laws (and Joint Resolutions) of the Legislature of Alabama, Passed at the Session of 1931, Held at the Capitol in the City of Montgomery, Commencing Tuesday, January 13, 1931*, Pete B. Jarman, Jr., Secretary of State (Birmingham Printing Company, State Printers and Binders, Birmingham, Alabama, 1931) p. 190.

The house joint resolution reads:

"WHEREAS, the beautiful and inspiring words of the poem 'Alabama', a gift to the people of the State from that distinguished citizen and educational leader, Julia S. Tutweiler, whose life was dedicated to unselfish service for humanity, has never been fittingly set to original music in keeping with its beauty; and,

"WHEREAS, Mrs. Edna Gockel-Gussen, another distinguished creative artist of Alabama has written an original composition fittingly adopted to the inspiring lines of this poem, which has been approved and adopted by the Alabama Federation of Music Clubs and was awarded its prize at their annual Convention at Gadsden in 1917, and for ten years has been sung and used as the State song of Alabama by musicians of the State; and,

"WHEREAS, the gift by Mrs. Gussen of this beautiful arrangement of music to the words of this poem is a service which is deeply appreciated by the people of our State and deserves recognition, and renders the poem much more beautiful and inspiring than with music not specially composed for it:

"NOW, THEREFORE, BE IT RESOLVED BY THE HOUSE OF REPRESENTATIVES OF THE STATE OF ALABAMA, THE SENATE CONCURRING, that this original music written by Mrs. Gussen for the poem 'Alabama' and as approved and adopted by the Federation of Music Clubs of Alabama be, and the same hereby is, adopted;

"BE IT FURTHER RESOLVED, That said poem as set to music by Mrs. Gussen be, and the same is hereby adopted as the State Song for the State of Alabama."

The oldest copy of the words of this musical composition in print "is found in the *Montgomery Advertiser* [for] Sunday, April 24, 1881." Miss Tutweiler composed the words about 1868 or 1869, during reconstruction days when people were much "concerned" about the future outcome. She with absolute trust in the ability of her fellow citizens prophesies in beautiful verse a successful reconstruction.

Arizona

Arizona, the State anthem, was selected by the State legislature of 1919, the act becoming a law on February

28, 1919. [2] The words of this march were written by Margaret Rowe Clifford and the music was composed by Maurice Blumenthal. It was published for the author by the Hatch Music Company, Philadelphia, Pennsylvania, in 1915. This composition was copyrighted in 1915 by Margaret Rowe Clifford, but the copyright is now State property "insofar as relates to the production of said composition for public purposes." The act adopting this song, *Arizona,* requires that all schools, all public institutions, and the Battleship Arizona be furnished with copies by the Commission of State Institutions.

In this song, reference is made to the sunshine, the rivers and valleys, the mountain scenery, gold and silver, and to the heroes and pioneers of the State. The appeal is to the past, the present, and the future; to nature, to religion, and to human aspiration.

Arkansas

The State song of Arkansas, entitled *Arkansas,* the words and the music of which were composed by Mrs. Eva Ware Barnett, was adopted by senate concurrent resolution number six on January 12, 1917. [3] This composition was published by the Central Music Company, Little Rock, Arkansas, in 1916. It was copyrighted by Eva Ware Barnett and Will M. Ramsey.

In the first stanza of the lyric, the composer tells how her thoughts return to the Southland—to the home of her childhood days; how she roamed through the woods and the meadows amidst roses, magnolias, jasmines, and violets; and how the State waits to welcome her wandering children.

[2] *Session Laws of Arizona, 1919, Initiative and Referendum Measures Passed in 1918: Acts, Resolutions and Memorials of the Regular Session, Fourth Legislature of the State of Arizona, Amendments to the Constitution, Referendum and Initiative Measures,* . . . *Session Begun January 13, 1919, Session Adjourned March 13, 1919* (The Manufacturing Stationers, Incorporated, Phoenix, Arizona, 1919) p. 26.

[3] *Arkansas, Senate Journal, 41st Session, 1917: Journal of the Senate of Arkansas, Forty-first Regular Session, Convened at the Capitol, in the City of Little Rock, at 12 M. Monday, January 8, 1917, and Adjourned Thursday, at 12 M. March 8, 1917,* by authority (Journal Printing Company, Newark, Arkansas, 1917) p. 76.

In the second stanza, she praises Arkansas's products, Arkansas—the land of joy and sunshine—rich in pearls and diamonds; tells how the Arkansans extend hope, faith, and love to strangers; and depicts the spacious fields abounding in rice, corn, cotton, hay, and fruits.

Colorado

Where the Columbines Grow is the official State song of Colorado. The words and the music were composed by Dr. Arthur J. Fynn of Denver.[4] This quartette was copyrighted by A. J. Fynn in 1918. The act, authorizing the use of these words as the State song, was approved on May 8, 1915.[5]

The columbine is the State flower of Colorado. The song refers to the mountainous character of the State, her plains which are watered by rivers, and the presence of the columbine from primitive days to the present.

Delaware

Our Delaware, with words by George B. Hynson and music by Will M. S. Brown, is the State song of Delaware. It was so designated by an act of the State legislature, approved on April 7, 1925.[6]

Three counties of Delaware are each described in one of the three stanzas: New Castle, the northern county, with its hills and valleys; Kent, the middle county, with its plains and myriad peach trees; and Sussex, the southern county, with its long ocean shore-line and the corresponding evergreen trees. Two other ideas stressed in the song are the sunniness of the State and the loyalty of its citizens.

[4] A reply to the questionnaire sent to Annie P. Hyder, Librarian, Colorado State Library, Denver, Colorado, by the writer from Fredericksburg, Virginia, July 15, 1930.

[5] *Session Laws of Colorado, 1915: Laws Passed at the Twentieth Session of the General Assembly of the State of Colorado, Convened at Denver, the Sixth Day of January, A. D. 1915,* published by the authority of John E. Ramer, Secretary of State, compiled under the direction of the Secretary of State by A. R. Morrison of the Denver Bar (Western Newspaper Union, State Printers, Denver, Colorado, 1915) p. 446.

[6] *Delaware Laws, 1925: Laws of the State of Delaware, Passed at the One Hundredth Session of the General Assembly, Commenced and Held at Dover, on Tuesday, January 6th, A. D., 1925, and in the Year of the Independence of the United States, the One Hundred and Forty-ninth* (Printed at the press of the Index Publishing Company, Dover, Delaware, 1925) vol. 34, p. 564-5.

This song was copyrighted in 1906 by the publishers, Brown and Edwards Music Company, Wilmington, Delaware. [7]

Florida

Florida by house concurrent resolution number twenty-two in 1935 adopted as the State Song *The Swanee River* also known as *Old Folks at Home,* written by Stephen Collins Foster in 1851 and published by Firth, Pond and Company of New York City in August of that year.

The house concurrent resolution [7a] adopting this song says:

"Be It Resolved by the House of Representatives of the State of Florida, the Senate Concurring:

"That, from and after the adoption of this amendment the official song of the State of Florida, to be sung in the schools and at all other public or official gatherings, shall be "The Swanee River (Old Folks at Home)", written by Stephen Foster and entered according to an act of Congress by Firth, Pond and Co., in 1851, in the Clerk's office of the District Court of the Southern District of New York. The following is the song* * * "

The Suwanee river, the small stream immortalized by Foster in this song, rises in the Okefinokee swamp in the southern part of Georgia, and flows down through Florida until it empties into the Gulf of Mexico.

This well-known Southern melody is a popular favorite with the American people today. E. P. Christy, a famous minstrel actor and singer of negro melodies aided in popularizing Foster's songs. Foster sent many of his negro melodies to Christy who sang them on his programs. Christy often assisted Foster in getting many of his songs published. The fact that Christy introduced Foster's negro

[7] *Catalogue of Copyright Entries,* published by authority of the Act of Congress of March 3, 1891, 51st Congress, 2nd Session, chapter 565, section 4, part 3; Musical Compositions, New Series (Government Printing Office, Washington, D.C. 1906) vol. 1, nos. 1-26, July-December 1906, p. 5.

[7a] *Florida Laws, 1935: General Acts and Resolutions adopted by The Legislature of Florida at Its Twenty-fifth Regular Session April 2 to and Including May 31st, 1935. Under the Constitution of A.D. 1885.* Published by Authority of Law (Rose Printing Company, Tallahassee, Florida) Vol. I, house concurrent resolution number 22, p. 1540.

melodies helped to break down the opposition given them by contemporary opera singers and their supporters.

In *The Swanee River,* the old darkey is reminiscing on the familiar scenes of his old plantation home.

Georgia

Georgia's State song, entitled *Georgia,* was selected by concurrent resolution number fifty-three, approved August 19, 1922. [8] The reason for choosing this song is given in the text of the resolution, which says:

"Be it resolved by the House of Representatives, the Senate concurring therein, the following:

"It appearing that Lottie Belle Wylie has set to music the beautiful poem of Robert Loveman, entitled 'Georgia' and that said poem expresses the highest and loftiest sentiment as to our beloved State, and that the music as composed by Miss Wyley [9] is tuneful, refined and beautiful, a copy of said song, as set to music being attached hereto,

"Be it resolved, That the thanks of this body be extended to Miss Wyley for her services to the State in composing this music and that the same be designated as Georgia's song."

Robert Loveman in the wording of this song, pictures Georgia's rolling rivers, meadows, vales and sky, and the contentedness, the peace, and the bravery of the people of the State.

Idaho

Idaho by an act of her legislative bodies, approved on March 11, 1931, adopted as the State song, *Here We have Idaho.* [10]

The act says:

"That the song 'Here We Have Idaho', sometimes known as 'Our Idaho', the music for which was composed

---

[8] *Georgia Laws, 1922: Acts and Resolutions of the General Assembly of the State of Georgia, 1922,* compiled and published by authority of the State (Byrd Printing Company, State Printers, Atlanta, Georgia, 1922) part IV, p. 1141.

[9] The correct form of the name of the composer of the music to this State song is Mrs. Lollie Belle Wylie.

[10] *Session Laws of Idaho, Regular 1931 and Extraordinary: General Laws of the State of Idaho, Passed at the Twenty-first Session of the State Legislature 1931,* published by authority of the Secretary of State (Capitol News Publishing Company, Boise, Idaho, 1931) p. 185.

by Sallie Hume Douglas, is hereby designated and declared to be the state song of the State of Idaho."

In the words to this song, the author, Miss Lula M. Huffman, emphasizes her love for Idaho, the wonders, silver, gold, and the romance of this State; Idaho, as a place where ideals may be realized; and the service of the pioneers in leaving this State as a legacy to future generations.

Illinois

An act of the Illinois legislature, approved on June 30, 1925, [11] selected the official State song, *Illinois*, the words of which were written by C. H. Chamberlain and the music was composed by Archibald Johnston. This song was copyrighted by the Clayton F. Sammy Company, Chicago, Illinois, on January 23, 1925.

Mr. Chamberlain builds the theme of this composition about the gently flowing rivers, the green prairies, the commerce of the State, the patriotism of its inhabitants, and the great men she has produced, naming Lincoln, Grant, and Logan.

Indiana

On the Banks of the Wabash Far Away, with words and music composed by Paul Dresser, was officially made the State song of Indiana by an act of the State legislature approved on March 14, 1913. [12] This song was copyrighted by the publishers, Hawley Haviland Company, New York, in 1897.

In this well-known lyric of a past generation, the composer tells of his homestead surrounded by cornfields, the woodlands, the moonlight, the sycamores, the candlelight,

---

[11] *Laws of Illinois, Fifty-fourth General Assembly, 1925: Laws of the State of Illinois Enacted by the Fifty-fourth General Assembly at the Regular Biennial Session Begun and Held at the Capitol, in the City of Springfield, on the 7th Day of January, A. D. 1925, and Adjourned Sine Die on the 30th Day of June, A. D. 1925* (Schnepp and Barnes, Printers, Springfield, Illinois, 1925) p. 601.

[12] *Acts 1913 Indiana, 68th Session: Laws of the State of Indiana, Passed at the Sixty-eighth Regular Session of the General Assembly, Begun on the 9th Day of January, A. D. 1913*, by authority, L. G. Ellingham, Secretary of State (William B. Burford, Contractor for State Printing and Binding, Indianapolis, Indiana, 1913) p. 693.

the river, and how he strolled with, and courted his sweetheart, Mary.

Iowa

The State song of Iowa, entitled *Iowa,* written by S. H. M. Byers in 1867, was at that time, and has been, sung to the tune of the old German song *O Tannenbaum.* This song, however, set to a different melody by Paul Lange, was published by Bollman and Schatzman, St. Louis, Missouri, in 1867.

Byers received the inspiration for writing this production while he was confined in Libby Prison, at Richmond, Virginia, after he had been taken by the enemy in the battle of Lookout Mountain, in 1863. His captors were accustomed to pass by his prison playing the air of *O Tannenbaum* or *My Maryland,* or singing it "set to Southern and bitter words." It was at this time that Byers resolved to put that tune "to loyal words." The song *Iowa* was the crystallization of his resolve. This musical composition was authorized to be recognized as the State song of Iowa by a house concurrent resolution of the Senate on March 20, 1911. [13] The resolution reads:

"*Whereas,* the patriotic song of Iowa by S. H. Byers, has, for years, been sung in all the schools of the State, and on thousands of public occasions, political and social, and wherever Iowa people come together in other States

"*Therefore, Be it Resolved by the House,* the Senate concurring, that it be hereby declared to be recognized as the State Song."

The theme of Byers' lyric centers about his love for, and praise of Iowa, the cornfields, prairies, purple sunsets, fair women, and the patriotic sons of his beloved State.

Three other songs about Iowa are great favorites; namely, *Iowa—Beautiful Land; Iowa, Proud Iowa;* and the *Iowa Corn Song.*

[13] *Senate Journal, 1911: Journal of the Senate of the Thirty-fourth General Assembly of the State of Iowa, Which Convened at the Capitol, at Des Moines, January 9, A. D. 1911, and Adjourned Sine Die April 12. A. D. 1911* (Emory H. English, State Printer, E. D. Chassell, State Binder, Des Moines, Iowa, 1911) p. 950.

The words of the first named of these were written by Tacitus Hussey in 1889 and the music was composed by Horace M. Towner of Corning, Iowa. This composition is a great favorite throughout the State with the school people and with quartette singers.

Iowa, Proud Iowa, was written by Virginia Knight Logan. The Iowa Federation of Music Clubs adopted this composition as their State song. It was published and copyrighted by Forster Music Publisher, Incorporated, Chicago, Illinois, in 1920. A bill was introduced in the State legislature in 1921 to use this as the State song "on all public and official occasions where the use of a State song is proper or advisable," but the bill was lost for want of action.

The *Iowa Corn Song,* written by George E. Hamilton about 1911 and sung to the tune of *Travelling,* was popularized by the Shriner Conclave held in Des Moines, Iowa, in 1921. This production is very popular throughout the State and is sung by the people on various occasions. [14]

Kentucky

My Old Kentucky Home, written and set to music by Stephen Collins Foster in 1850 [15] and published in 1853 by Firth, Pound, and Company, New York, was designated as the State song of Kentucky by an act of the legislature approved March 19, 1928. [16]

The act says:

"WHEREAS, the song, 'My Old Kentucky Home,' by Stephen Collins Foster, has immortalized Kentucky

[14] For a full and comprehensive discussion of these songs, see the article entitled *Songs of Iowa,* by Ruth Gallaher, in *The Palimpsest,* January to December, 1924, edited by John Ely Briggs (The State Historical Society of Iowa, Iowa City, Iowa, 1924) vol. v, no. 10, October 1924, p. 387-94.

[15] *The Encyclopedia Americana* (Americana Corporation, New York and Chicago, 1929) vol. 20, p. 655.

[16] *Kentucky Acts, 1928: Acts of the General Assembly of the Commonwealth of Kentucky, Passed at the Regular Session of the General Assembly, Which Was Begun in the City of Frankfort, Kentucky, on Tuesday, January the third, 1928, and Ended Friday March the sixteenth, 1928* (The State Journal Company, Printer to the Commonwealth, Frankfort, Kentucky, 1928) p. 851-2.

throughout the civilized world, and is known and sung in every State and Nation; therefore,

"Be it Resolved by the Senate of Kentucky, the House of Representatives concurring:

"That the song, 'My Old Kentucky Home,' by Stephen Collins Foster, be and is hereby selected and adopted as the official State song of the State of Kentucky."

This piece of music is a true melody of plantation life characteristic of the South before the Civil War. The composer sketches the old homestead, the bright summer days, the happy negro, the cornfields in tassel, the blooming meadows, the singing birds, and the cabin with children on its floor. Then comes the note of melancholy telling of the approaching hard times when the possum and coon hunting must cease, and the darkies' singing in the moonlight will be heard no more.

Louisiana

Louisiana by an act of her legislative bodies, approved on July 14, 1932, adopted as her official State song the musical composition entitled *Song of Louisiana*, the words and the music of which were composed by Vashti Robertson Stopher.

The act adopting this song says:

"Section 1. Be it enacted by the Legislature of Louisiana, That there shall be, and is, hereby adopted and established as the Official State Song for the State of Louisiana, a musical composition, with words and music by Vashti Robertson Stopher, and entitled: 'Song of Louisiana'; . . .

"Section 2. That all laws or parts of laws in conflict with the provisions of this Act be, and the same are, hereby repealed." [16a]

In the lyric of this song the composer sets forth her love for the State; speaks of the singing of the mocking

---

[16a] *Acts Passed by the Legislature of the State of Louisiana at the Regular Session Begun and Held in the City of Baton Rouge on the Ninth Day of May, 1932, Constitutional Amendments Adopted at an Election Held November 4, 1930, and a Special Session of the Legislature Held September 16, 1931,* published by authority of the State (Ramires-Jones Printing Company, Baton Rouge, Louisiana, 1932) p. 579-80.

bird, and of the blossoming of the flowers; tells of the reverence and loyalty of the Louisianans for their State, and proclaims that they will continue to sing her praises. Information about purchasing copies of this State song may be had from Vashti Robertson Stopher, Louisiana State University, Baton Rouge, Louisiana.

Nevada

Nevada by an act of her legislative bodies, approved on February 6, 1933, [16b] adopted as the official State song *Home Means Nevada* with words and music composed by Mrs. Bertha Raffetto. This song was published and copyrighted by Mrs. Bertha Raffetto in 1932, the publishing being done by the Pacific Music Press, San Francisco, California.

In the lyric of this musical production the author builds the theme about Nevada with its setting sun, its wild, free winds, the "Old Kit Carson trail," the gray desert, the colorings of the western sky at evening, the towering mountains, the glen lighted with moonbeams, and the spotted fawn and the doe. In the refrain she stresses the facts that Nevada means home, that the hills, the sage, the pines, the Tuckee river, and the sunshine, all belong to Nevada, the land she loves.

This song may be bought from Mrs. Bertha Raffetto, 629 Lander Street, Reno, Nevada.

New Mexico

O, Fair New Mexico was adopted as the State song of New Mexico by an act of her legislature, approved on March 14, 1917. [17]

[16b] A communication from V. M. Henderson, Librarian, Nevada State Library, sent from Carson City, Nevada, June 7, 1933.

[17] *Laws of New Mexico, 1917: Laws of the State of New Mexico, Passed by the Third Regular Session of the Legislature of the State of New Mexico, Which Convened at the City of Santa Fe, at the Capitol, at the Hour of Noon on the Ninth Day of January, 1917, and Adjourned at the Hour of Noon on the Tenth Day of March, 1917,* prepared for publication by Antonio Lucero, Secretary of State, published by authority (Albright and Anderson, Albuquerque, New Mexico, 1917) p. 306.

Both the words and the music of this composition were written by Elizabeth Garrett. It was published by Gamble Hinged Music Company, Chicago, Illinois, and copyrighted by Elizabeth Garrett, in 1915.

Stanza one pictures New Mexico as the home of the Montezuma, a land having azure skies, balmy breezes, and golden sunshine. Stanza two depicts the State with its rugged Sierras, deep canyons, and fertile valleys, with its fields of alfalfa, and with blooming apple trees. Stanza three tells of New Mexico with its days filled with heart-dreams, and its nights with their low-hanging moons,— the land of hope and tomorrow. The chorus rings with the grandeur of the State and the passionate love the New Mexicans have for it.

North Carolina

North Carolina by an act of her legislature, ratified on February 18, 1927, chose as the State song the composition *The Old North State,* the words of which were composed by Honorable William Gaston of North Carolina and by him adapted to a German melody. It was arranged for the pianoforte by P. Culver.

The act adopting this song says:

"WHEREAS, the last State convention of the North Carolina Daughters of the Confederacy appointed a committee to investigate the advisability of adopting 'The Old North State,' as the State's official song; and,

"WHEREAS, the said committee of the North Carolina Division of the United Daughters of the Confederacy has requested the General Assembly of the State of North Carolina, by appropriate legislation, to adopt said song written by Hon. William Gaston as the State's official song: Now, therefore,

"The General Assembly of North Carolina do enact:

"Section 1. That the song known as 'The Old North State,' as hereinafter written, be and the same is hereby adopted and declared to be the official song of the State of North Carolina." [18]

This song was published as a supplement to *The Minneapolis Tribune,* Sunday, November 29, 1903.

The Old North State is a patriotic song depicting North Carolina as being a leader in the cause of American liberty; a land of plain sons and graceful daughters; and a State of plenty, freedom, love, and peace.

Oklahoma

Oklahoma by house concurrent resolution adopted by the House on March 21, and by the Senate on March 26, 1935, adopted as the official State Song, *Oklahoma (A Toast),* the words and music of which were composed by Mrs. Harriet Parker Camden.

The resolution [18a] says:

WHEREAS, the State of Oklahoma has never adopted an official song; and

WHEREAS, Harriet Parker Camden composed the music and wrote the words to the song: "Oklahoma (A Toast)", in 1905, the words and music of which express in a beautiful manner the tradition, conditions and ideals of the State; and

WHEREAS, this song has been the unofficial anthem of this State since that time, a true and correct copy of which has been, and is now, on file and of record in the office of the State Library Commission;

. . . .

AND, WHEREAS, it is fitting and proper that the words and music of this song should be adopted as the official song of the State;

Now, Therefore, Be It Resolved by the House of Representatives of the Fifteenth Legislature of the State of Oklahoma, the Senate Concurring Therein:

FIRST: That the words and music of the song, "Oklahoma (A Toast)", by Harriet Parker Camden, 1905, be

[18] *Public Laws of North Carolina Session 1927: State of North Carolina Public Laws and Resolutions Passed by the General Assembly at Its Session of 1927, Begun and Held in the City of Raleigh on Wednesday, the Fifth Day of January, A. D. 1927,* published by authority (The Observer Printing House, Incorporated, Charlotte, North Carolina, 1927) p. 17-18.

[18a] *Harlow's Session Laws, Oklahoma, 1935,* Edited by C. W. Van Eaton (Harlow Publishing Corporation, Oklahoma City, Oklahoma, 1935) house concurrent resolution No. 19, Section 1261, p. 460-1.

and the same are hereby adopted as the official song and anthem of the State of Oklahoma.

SECOND: That the State Library Commission, where there is now on file and of record a true and correct copy of the words and music of this song be, and, the same is hereby designated as the depository of this official song. [18b]

. . . .

Oregon

Oregon, by senate joint resolution number three in 1927, adopted as her State song the composition *Oregon, My Oregon*. The resolution reads:

"WHEREAS the State of Oregon has never adopted a state song; and

"WHEREAS many civic and patriotic bodies have recommended that the song entitled 'Oregon, My Oregon,' words by J. A. Buchanon [Buchanan] and music by Henry B. Murtagh, be adopted as the State song of Oregon; and

"WHEREAS it is eminently proper that a State song should be adopted; therefore,

"Be It Resolved by the Senate of the State of Oregon, the House of Representatives jointly concurring: That the song entitled 'Oregon, My Oregon,' words by J. A. Buchanon [Buchanan] and music by Henry B. Murtagh, be and the same hereby is accepted and adopted as the State song of the State of Oregon." [19]

This production was published in 1920 for the Society of Oregon Composers by the Oregon Eilers Music House, Portland, Oregon. The copyright is owned by Henry B. Murtagh.

[18b] *Harlow's Session Laws, Oklahoma, 1935,* Edited by C. W. Van Eaton (Harlow Publishing Corporation, Oklahoma City, Oklahoma, 1935) house concurrent resolution No. 19, Sec. 1261, p. 460-1.

[19] *Senate and House Journals, Oregon, 1927: State of Oregon, Journals of the Senate and House of the Thirty-fourth Legislative Assembly, Regular Session, Beginning January 10, and Ending February 25, 1927,* published by authority, compiled by Sam A. Kozer, Secretary of State, abridged and bound in one volume by order of the State Printing Board under the provisions of section 2783 and 2790 of Oregon Laws (State Printing Department, Salem, Oregon, 1927) p. 35.

The lyric of this composition praises Oregon as the land of the "Empire Builders"; a western land conquered and inhabited by freemen; a land of roses, sunshine, fresh breezes, and of the setting sun.

South Carolina

On February 11, 1911, the South Carolina General Assembly adopted as the State Song the song *Carolina,* written by Henry Timrod and music composed by Anne Curtis Burgess.

The Senate concurrent resolution [19a] adopting this song says:

"Whereas, The Daughters of the American Revolution have memorialized the General Assembly to adopt as a State Song the beautiful poem written by the gifted Timrod, and set to music by Miss Curtis, a daughter of South Carolina; therefore,

Be it resolved by the Senate, the House of Representatives concurring, That the song "Carolina" be accepted as and declared to be the State Song of South Carolina.

On immediate consideration the Concurrent Resolution was adopted.

Ordered sent to the House for concurrence." [19b] The members of the House approved the resolution on the date given above.

Tennessee

Tennessee, by house joint resolution number thirty-six of her legislative bodies, approved on April 10, 1926, adopted as the State song, the production entitled *My Homeland, Tennessee.*

The resolution says:

"WHEREAS, The late George Fort Milton of Chattanooga, one of Tennessee's most highly esteemed and patri-

---

[19a] *Legislative Manual, 1936: Legislative Manual of the Eighty-first General Assembly of South Carolina, at Columbia, Second Session Commencing January 14, 1936,* Edited by James E. Hunter, Jr. Clerk of the House of Representatives (The State Company, Columbia, South Carolina, 1936), p. 198.

[19b] *Journal of the Senate of the General Assembly of the State of South Carolina, Being the Regular Session Beginning Tuesday, January 10, 1911.* (Gonzales and Bryan, State Printers, Columbia, S.C., 1910-11) p. 557

otic citizens, offered and awarded a prize for the best words and the best music submitted for a State Song, and,

"WHEREAS, The Committee headed by Mrs. John I. Meek and Mrs. George Fort Milton, worked for a period of three years upon said contest to secure a creditable and noteworthy State Song, and,

"WHEREAS, The Judges have awarded the prize for the best State Song that could be had to Miss Nell Grayson Taylor, poet, and to Roy Lamont Smith, eminent music composer, and,

"WHEREAS, The Women's Organizations of the State have adopted the same and the school children all over the State are singing it successfully and it is pronounced by the Music Clubs to be an excellent piece of music which may well be dedicated to the great old Volunteer State as its State Song,

"Be it resolved, That the House of Representatives, the Senate Concurring, do accept and adopt this song, 'My Homeland,' as the State Song of Tennessee." [20]

The words of the song named above were written by Nell Grayson Taylor, and the music was composed by Roy Lamont Smith. This composition was published by I. R. Summers, Chattanooga, Tennessee, in 1926, at the press of the Zimmerman Print, Cincinnati, Ohio. It was copyrighted the same year by the Chattanooga Writers' Club.

The first stanza of this song tells of pioneer Tennessee as the childhood land of its people. The second stanza recounts the coming of the forefathers and the fair land they found. The third stanza eulogizes the loyalty of the people of Tennessee and their memory of their heroes, designating Andrew Jackson by name.

By senate resolution number thirty-six approved on July 2, 1931, [20a] Tennessee adopted as the State song the musical composition entitled *My Tennessee.*

[20] *Public Acts of Tennessee, 1925: Public Acts of the State of Tennessee, Passed by the Sixty-fourth General Assembly, 1925,* published by authority (Printing Department, Tennessee Industrial School, Nashville, Tennessee, 1925) p. 602

[20a] *Public Acts of Tennessee, 1931: Public Acts of the State of Tennessee, Passed by the Sixty-seventh General Assembly, 1931,* published by authority (Printing Department, Tennessee Industrial School, Nashville, Tennessee, 1931) p. 490.

The resolution reads:

"WHEREAS, Frances Hannah Tranum has written a song which has been set to music, which beautifully describes the landscape of our State and the spirit of our people, which song she has given the title, 'My Tennessee,' *therefore,*

"*Be it resolved by the Senate of the Sixty-seventh General Assembly* That the song entitled 'My Tennessee,' written by Frances Hannah Tranum, be adopted as the State song for Tennessee."

This song, both the words and the music of which were composed by Frances Hannah Tranum, is yet in manuscript form.

The author builds the theme of this composition about Tennessee, its natural beauty, its streams and valleys, its rills, its wooded hills, its lowing herds, its humming bees, its battlefields, its fair daughters, and brave sons.

In the chorus, she speaks of the hills, valleys, mountains, fertile lands, and of her love for Tennessee, her native State.

Another song well-known and loved by the people of the State is *Tennessee,* the words of which were written by Reverend A. J. Holt. This composition may be had from the Division of Library and Archives, Department of Education, Nashville, Tennessee.

Although Tennessee has two state songs officially adopted by legislative action, it is the ruling of the Assistant Attorney General of the State that the State song adopted first is still the official State song of Tennessee. [20b]

Texas

Texas, by senate concurrent resolution number six, approved May 28, 1929, [21] designated as the State song,

[20b] A Western Union telegram from Mrs. John Trotwood Moore, State Librarian and Archivist of the Division of Library and Archives, Nashville, Tennessee, December 21, 1933.

[21] *Texas General and Special Laws, 1929, First Called Session: General and Special Laws of the State of Texas, Passed by the Forty-first Legislature at Its First Called Session, Which Convened at Austin, Texas, April 22, 1929, and Adjourned May 21, 1929,* printed under the authority of the State of Texas, Jane Y. McCallum, Secretary of State (The name of the publisher and the place of publication are not given on the title page of the law, 1929) p. 286-7.

Texas, Our Texas, the words of which were written by Gladys Yoakum Wright, and William J. Marsh and the music was composed by William J. Marsh.

The resolution says:

"WHEREAS, the 39th and 40th Legislatures passed resolutions authorizing the adoption of a State Song for the State of Texas, and

"WHEREAS, a Committee of seven members, three from the Senate and four from the House, was appointed to select a song, according to rules set up by the Committee, and

"WHEREAS, contests were held in each Senatorial District, and a final contest was held in Dallas for the purpose of selecting the song for adoption, and

"WHEREAS, 'Texas, Our Texas' by William J. Marsh and Gladys Yoakum Wright has been selected by the Legislative committee twice, proving the song was meritorious to the extent that it 'had sung itself into the hearts of the people,' now therefore be it

"RESOLVED BY THE SENATE OF THE STATE OF TEXAS, THE HOUSE OF REPRESENTATIVES CONCURRING:

"That, 'Texas, Our Texas' by William J. Marsh and Gladys Yoakum Wright be adopted as the State song for the State of Texas."

The composition named above was published by W. J. Marsh, Fort Worth, Texas, at the press of the Zimmerman Print, Cincinnati, Ohio, and was copyrighted by W. J. Marsh, in 1925.

The lyric of this production depicts Texas as the largest and grandest State of the Union, having a single star emblematic of Freedom. It also refers to historical San Jacinto and Alamo, and invokes God's blessings to keep Texans brave and strong.

Utah

The Utah State Song, entitled *Utah We Love Thee,* written by Evan Stephens, was adopted by the State Legislature on February 17, 1937, to become effective on February 24, 1937.

This act reads as follows:

"Be it enacted by the Legislature of the State of Utah:
Section 1. *State Song—Utah We Love Thee.*

The song entitled "Utah We Love Thee" by Evan Stephens is selected and designated to be the Utah state song.
Section 2. *Effective Date.*

This act shall take effect upon approval." [21a]

The author builds the theme of this song about Utah's mountains, sunny skies, State flag, pioneers, and closes by predicting that Utah will grow along the lines of wealth, peace, fame, and glory. He also stresses the great love of the people of Utah for their State.

This song with words and music written by Evan Stephens, was published by the Deseret Sunday School Union, Salt Lake City, Utah, in 1917.

Washington

Washington, by house concurrent resolution number thirteen, adopted on March 11, 1909, [21b] declared the song, *Washington Beloved,* to be the State anthem.

The resolution reads:

"Resolved by the House, the Senate concurring, That the song, 'Washington Beloved,' the words by Edmond S. Meany, and music by Reginald DeKoven, be, and the same is hereby declared the State anthem of Washington."

This musical composition was published and copyrighted by the John Church Company, Cincinnati, Ohio, in 1908.

In the lyric of this musical composition the author speaks of the renowned name of Washington, her glories, her fame, her purple pennant, the deeds of the Wash-

[21a] *Laws of Utah, 1937: Laws of the State of Utah at the Regular Session of the Twenty-second Legislature, Convened at the Capitol in the City of Salt Lake, January 11, 1937 and adjourned sine die on March 11, 1937* (Inland Printing Company, Kaysville, Utah, 1937) p. 226.
[21b] *Senate Journal, State of Washington, Regular and Extraordinary Sessions, 1909: Senate Journal of the Eleventh Legislature of the State of Washington, Begun and Held at Olympia, the State Capitol, January 11, 1909, Adjourned Sine Die, March 11, 1909,* compiled, arranged, and indexed by William T. Laube, Secretary of State (E. C. Boardman, Public Printer, Olympia, Washington, 1909) p. 1005-6.

ingtonians, and of their being noble sons, who love their State.

STATES HAVING NO OFFICIALLY ADOPTED SONGS

In several states, songs have been selected by vote of the school children, by popular consent, by the recommendation or by the vote of special organizations.

Investigation shows that in the case of the states not having official songs there are one or more productions which could be fittingly employed on occasions that require the use of a state song, but in the following development of this chapter it will hardly be advisable to attempt to discuss all of them. The writer had no intention of showing special favor to any in the choice of the songs selected; but in the light of the information which he has been able to gather, acting with an unbiased and impartial mind, he has attempted in the case of those states having no officially adopted state songs, to discuss those musical compositions which have been selected by any of the agencies named above, or which seem to him most fitted to be used as state songs. It is highly probable that from the compositions discussed under each of the following states, one will be officially adopted as the State song.

California

I Love You, California, with words written by F. B. Silverwood and music composed by A. F. Frankenstein, is very popular with the inhabitants of California. This production was published by Hatch and Loveland, Music Printers, Los Angeles, California, and copyrighted by F. B. Silverwood, in 1913, but it is not the State song.

This song enumerates the beauties and advantages of California; and makes reference among other objects to the ocean, the climate, fields of grain, honey, fruits, vineyards, wine, old missions, redwood forests, mountains, the Golden Gate, and the Yosemite Valley.

Connecticut

The *Connecticut State Song,* although it is not the official State song, is a popular favorite with the people of

Connecticut. The words of this song were written by Ida Townsend-Green and the music was composed by E. A. Leopold. It was published and copyrighted in 1913 by the Loomis Temple of Music, New Haven, Connecticut.

This song, consisting of three stanzas and a chorus, mentions the ruggedness of the State, the purple hills, the stately trees, the long rivers, the pioneers, Indians, patriots, the patriotism of her heroes, and Yale College.

The District of Columbia

The musical composition *Washington* is widely known and sung by the people in the District of Columbia. The lyric to this production was written by Mrs. Jessie I. Pierson and the music was composed by William T. Pierson.

It was published and copyrighted in 1919, by W. T. Pierson and Company, Washington, D. C.

This song pictures Washington as a city with its foundations rooted in the past, with its banner of freedom unfurled over the Nation, with its statue of Freedom towering high; a city standing where the Potomac river flows into the Chesapeake bay; a city with the power of state calling for law and order, with the magnificent dome towering over the Capitol's spacious halls, with men of high courage protecting the land, and willing to die for freedom.

The chorus expresses love for the city of Washington, praises its fame and its great Avenue, and designates it as the heart of the Nation and as the "Gateway to God."

Kansas

The composition *Kansas,* written and set to music by Humphrey W. Jones, was selected as the State song of Kansas by the schools of the State. It was published by W. F. Roehr Music Company, Topeka, Kansas, and copyrighted by H. W. Jones, in 1907.

This patriotic song makes reference to the State flag; to the pluck and bravery of the Kansans; to the sunflowers; and to the optimistic outlook of the State.

Maine

The six musical compositions expressing laudable sentiments about Maine are: *Maine, A State Song; Maine; State of Maine, My State of Maine; Dear Old Maine; A Song to Maine;* and *State Song Maine.*

Maine, A State Song, with words and music written by Harry A. Dinsmore, was published by the Milburn Music Publishing Company, Skowhegan, Maine, in 1931.

Maine, with words by Lester M. Hart and music by Alice Benedict Goodridge, was published by C. W. Thompson and Company, Boston, Massachusetts, in 1924.

State of Maine, My State of Maine, having words and music written by George Thornton Edwards, was published by the Underwood Music Company, Portland, Maine, in 1913.

Dear Old Maine is the State Federation song of the Business and Professional Women's Clubs of Maine. The words and the music were written by Mary Thompson-Green. This song, published by the Pine Tree State Amusements, Portland, Maine, was copyrighted by Mary Thompson-Green in 1922.

A Song to Maine, with words written by Louise Helen Coburn and with music composed by Elise Fellows White, was published and copyrighted by C. W. Thompson and Company, Boston, Massachusetts, in 1911.

State Song Maine, having words written by A. B. Andrews and music composed by Miriam Eunice Andrews, was copyrighted by Miriam Andrews in 1925.

Maryland

My Maryland, the State song of Maryland, was written by James Ryder Randall in 1861 while he was doing newspaper work on *The Sunday Delta,* published at New Orleans, Louisiana. It was set to the music of the German song *O Tannenbaum.* If *My Maryland* were ever officially adopted by the State legislature as Maryland's State song, the writer is unable to find any trace of such an adoption.

Matthew Page Andrews, in speaking of this song, says:

"On April 23, 1861, James Ryder Randall immortalized Maryland in what is generally conceded to be the most original and melodious verse dedicated to any State in the Union. In distant Louisiana, the young poet heard of the first bloodshed in the streets of his native city.

"Believing that his native State was wrongfully invaded, he rapidly penned the stanzas of *My Maryland,* a song that has now rightly become a heritage, not merely of the State, but of the Nation." [22]

The entire song is an appeal to the Marylanders to be courageous and to crush the invading foe.

Massachusetts

Massachusetts has no official State song, but the publication, *Massachusetts* with words and music written by C. W. Krogmann having been selected as the official club song by the Massachusetts Federation of Music Clubs, is very popular throughout the State.

This song was published by C. W. Krogmann, Boston, Massachusetts, at the press of John Worley Company, Boston, Massachusetts, and was copyrighted by the publisher, in 1928.

The author builds the message of this composition about the following ideas: praise of the *Old Bay State,* the harmony and melody of music, and the harmony of relationships prevailing throughout the State.

Michigan

There are two songs entitled *Michigan, My Michigan,* which are widely known and sung by the people of Michigan. "Shortly after the Battle of Fredericksburg in December, 1862, Miss Winifred Lee Brent, afterwards Mrs. Henry F. Lyster, of Detroit, wrote the song 'Michigan, My Michigan.' It was first published in the *Detroit Tribune* and early in 1863 made its way into the army

---

[22] *Tercentenary History of Maryland,* Matthew Page Andrews (The S. J. Clarke Publishing Company, Chicago, Illinois and Baltimore, Maryland, 1925) vol. I, p. 908.

at the front and became very popular with Michigan troops. [23]

This composition was sung to the tune of the German song, *O Tannenbaum,* written by Carl Anshutz, the royal musical director at Coblentz, Germany, and published at Coblentz, in 1840.

The second *Michigan, My Michigan* was written by Douglas Malloch of Muskegon, Michigan, in 1902. He wrote this lyric for the eighth annual convention of the Michigan State Federation of Women's Clubs which met in Muskegon that year. *Michigan, My Michigan* "has become the Federation song and is now widely used in schools as the Michigan song more suitable in times of peace." [24] The music was composed by W. Otto Miessner. It was published by Frederick W. Arbury, Detroit, Michigan, and copyrighted by W. Otto Miessner, in 1911.

The first is a war song stressing the bravery and the faithfulness of the Civil War heroes; the second is a song of peace telling of the greatness of Michigan with her thundering inland seas, her whispering pines, her historic lore, her wealth, and her famous men.

Minnesota

Minnesota has no State song in the true sense of the word; but the University song, *Hail! Minnesota,* consisting of two stanzas, one addressed to the University and the other to the State at large, is popularly considered to belong to the statewide campus, which embraces the people of the entire State. [25] The music was composed by T. E. Rickard; the first stanza was written by Truman Rickard; and the second, by Arthur Upson.

In the first stanza the writer hails the University as a light and a beacon, and says her sons and daughters will proclaim her far and near, guard her fame, and adore her name.

[23] *Michigan History Magazine,* George N. Fuller, Editor (Published quarterly by the Michigan Historical Commission, Lansing, Michigan, 1929) vol. xiii, p. 650-1.
[24] *Ibidem,* p. 651.
[25] *Our Minnesota, A History for Children,* Hester McLean Pollock (E. P. Dutton and Company, New York, 1917) p. 329-31.

In the second stanza he stresses the facts that the citizens of the State are strong and true, that they cheerfully come at her call, and that they hail her as their Northern Star.

Two other songs that should receive mention in this connection are *Minnesota* and *Minnesota, All Hail*.

The words and music of *Minnesota* were written by A. L. MacGregor. This song may be bought from Howard Farewell and Company, Fifth and Cedar Streets, St. Paul, Minnesota. *Minnesota, All Hail*, with words written by Gertrude Thomas and music composed by Margaret Zender Beaulieu, was published by The Northwestern Music Press, Minneapolis, Minnesota, in 1930, and copyrighted by Margaret Zender Beaulieu.

Mississippi

Mrs. Dunbar Rowland has written a popular song entitled *Mississippi* with music composed by Walter H. Aiken. It was published and copyrighted by the Willis Music Company, Cincinnati, Ohio, in 1925.

In the first stanza of this production Mrs. Rowland pictures the State as beautiful, with blooming magnolias and jasmines, and happy-hearted people clinging to the faith of their fathers. In the chorus she depicts Mississippi as a land where peace, plenty, and freedom reign.

Another favorite with the people of Mississippi is the song entitled *Mississippi,* the words of which were written by Perrin Holmes Lowrey and the music was composed by Mrs. De Witt Morgan. In 1925, this song was published by the Okolona Music Club, Okolona, Mississippi, and copyrighted by Mrs. De Witt Morgan.

Missouri

Missouri having no officially adopted State song, might use either of the three named as follows: *Missouri State Song; Missouri State Song;* and *Missouri.* The first one of the songs named above, with words written by Lizzie Chambers Hull and music composed by Julie Stevens Bacon, was adopted by the Missouri Daughters of the

American Revolution as their official State song. This composition was published by the Shattinger Piano and Music Company, St. Louis, Missouri, and copyrighted by Lizzie C. Hull, in 1913. The second named *Missouri State Song,* both words and music to which were written by Preston Kendall, was published by W. B. Allen Music Company, Columbia, Missouri, and copyrighted by W. B. Allen, in 1910. *Missouri,* with words and music written by Paul Fahle, was published by the Missouri Music Publishing Company, St. Louis, Missouri, and copyrighted by Paul Fahle, in 1911.

Montana

The song *Montana,* with words by Charles C. Cohen and music by Joseph E. Howard, is gaining in public favor. The title cover says that this production was approved as the State song by Governor Edwin L. Norris; A. N. Yoder, Secretary of State; and Attorney General Albert J. Galen. It has been approved and adopted by the Montana University Athletes, and approved for the State Militia by Adjutant General Phil Greenan.

This song was published and copyrighted by the Montana Children's Home Society, Helena, Montana, in 1910.

In the first stanza the author praises Montana, calling it the "Treasure State." In the second stanza he mentions the bitter root, the State flower; and in the refrain he emphasizes the blue skies and his intense love for Montana, calling it the "Glory of the West."

Nebraska

There are four musical compositions written about Nebraska which have marked characteristics of State songs; namely, *The Flag Song of Nebraska; Nebraska, My Native Land; My Nebraska, A Verse to the Cornhusker State;* and *Dear Old Nebraska.*

The Flag Song of Nebraska, with words written by Mrs. B. G. Miller and music composed by George H. Aller, was published by Mrs. B. G. Miller of Crete, Nebraska, and was copyrighted by Mrs. Benjamin G. Miller and George H. Aller, in 1931.

Nebraska, My Native Land has words written by Grace Welsh Lutgen and music composed by Leon Beery. This number was published and copyrighted by F. H. Jones and Son, Wayne, Nebraska, in 1924.

My Nebraska, A Verse to the Cornhusker State, having words and music composed by Theodore C. Diers, was published and copyrighted by Theodore C. Diers, Lincoln, Nebraska, in 1927.

Dear Old Nebraska, with words and music written by Harry Pecka, may be bought from Walt's Music House, 1240 O. Street, Lincoln, Nebraska. This publication is included among those found in the *University of Nebraska Song-book* of 1924

New Hampshire

The Daughters of the American Revolution and the Confederated Music Clubs of New Hampshire have chosen as their State song the production, *Old New Hampshire,* the words of which were written by John F. Holmes, Manchester, New Hampshire, and the music was composed by Maurice Hoffmann.

C. I. Hicks Music Company, Boston, Massachusetts, is the distributing agent for this song. It was copyrighted in 1926 by John F. Holmes, Manchester, New Hampshire. The cover page carries a sketch of the Great Stone Face.

This song features New Hampshire as the *Granite State,* rugged, majestic, and grand; a land of fields, woods, mountains, seashore, and inland lakes.

New Jersey

The *Legislative Manual of the State of New Jersey* says:

"Strictly speaking, New Jersey has no State song. However, there is what is known as an 'Ode to New Jersey' which was composed by the late Dr. Elias F. Carr, a professor in the State Normal School at Trenton, and which is frequently sung at school celebrations and exercises to the air of 'Maryland, My Maryland.' " [26]

The first stanza of this ode tells of New Jersey's rolling waves, azured mountains, and low-lying plains; the second stanza recounts her fame and battle-fields—Trenton, Princeton, and Monmouth; and the third stanza praises her literary and educational activities.

Another song which is especially liked by the people of New Jersey is *Jersey Land, My Jersey Land,* sung to the tune of the German song *O Tannenbaum.* The words to this musical composition were written by Elias F. Carr. A copy may be found in *Randolph's Songs That Will Live,* published by Oliver Ditson Company, Boston, Massachusetts.

New York

New York's lack of an official State song could easily be supplied by using any one of the following compositions: *New York, Our Empire State; The Empire State; New York State Song;* and *New York State Song.*

New York, Our Empire State, with words written by Etta H. Morris and music composed by Caroline Fitzsimmons and dedicated to the New York Federation of Music Clubs, was published and copyrighted by its producers in 1929.

The Empire State, the second song named above, having words written by John F. Howard and music composed by Charles P. Scott, was published and copyrighted by John F. Howard, Silver Lake Assembly, New York, in 1921.

The Empire State, the third song named above, with words and music written by Laura Sedgwick Collins, was copyrighted by Laura Sedgwick Collins both in 1909 and in 1926.

New York State Song, the fourth song named above, the words of which were written by Elliot Field and the music composed by A. F. Coca, was published and copy-

[26] *Fitzgerald's Legislative Manual, State of New Jersey, 1931: Manual of the Legislature of New Jersey, One Hundred and Fifty-fifth Session, 1931,* by authority of the Legislature, Josephine A. Fitzgerald, publisher, John P. Dullard, compiler (MacCrellish and Quigley Company, Trenton, New Jersey, 1931) ·p. 723.

righted by W. H. Boner and Company, Philadelphia, Pennsylvania, in 1899.

New York State Song, the fifth song named above, with words and music written by Henry W. Clark, was published and copyrighted by Henry W. Clark, Booneville, New York, in 1921.

North Dakota

North Dakota having no officially adopted State song, the State Federation of Women's Clubs adopted a composition called *North Dakota State Song* written and published by Margaret E. Plank, Valley City, North Dakota. It was copyrighted by its author in 1916.

This song is descriptive and patriotic in its appeal, depicting North Dakota as the Prairie State with blossoming roses, the mother of brave men and courageous women, and extolling her freedom, liberty, and unity.

Another musical composition that is well-known and frequently sung throughout the State is *Dakota,* having words and music written by Frank L. Gale. This song was published in the *North Dakota Parent-Teachers Association Song-book,* but is now out of print.

Ohio

Ohio has at least seven musical productions which could be used as substitutes for a State song: *Ohio, My Ohio; The Land Where the Buckeyes Grow; Ohio Home; Our Old Ohio State; The Buckeye State; The Buckeye State;* and *Beautiful Ohio.*

Ohio, My Ohio, with words written by Raymond Zirkel and music composed by Ross C. Coffman, was published and copyrighted by the Rialto Music Publishing Company, Columbus, Ohio, in 1912.

The Land Where the Buckeyes Grow has words and music composed by Kate D. Gordon. This song was published by the Gordon Publishing Company, Columbus, Ohio, and was copyrighted by K. D. Gordon, in 1907.

Ohio Home, with words written by William R. Fox and music composed by G. Larkin Fox, was published and copyrighted by William R. Fox, Cincinnati, Ohio, in 1907.

Our Old Ohio State, the words and the music of which were composed by Professor F. P. Porter was published and copyrighted by F. P. Porter, McConnelsville, Ohio, in 1917.

The Buckeye State, with words written by Walter J. Blakely and music composed by W. H. Pommer, was published and copyrighted by W. H. Pommer, St. Louis, Missouri, in 1899.

The Buckeye State, having words written by Robert C. Lemon and music composed by A. Leopold Richard, was published by Legters Music Company, Chicago, Illinois, and was copyrighted by Robert C. Lemon, in 1921.

Beautiful Ohio, with words written by Ballard Macdonald and music composed by Mary Earl, is a general popular favorite among people both within and without the State. It was published and copyrighted by Shapiro, Bernstein and Company, New York, in 1918.

Pennsylvania

Probably the best known and most widely used song of Pennsylvania is *Pennsylvania, Official Song of the Keystone State.* The words and the music of this composition were written by Edgar M. Dilley. It was published by George J. Brennan, Philadelphia, Pennsylvania, and copyrighted by E. M. Dilley, in 1908.

Rhode Island

Perhaps the five most familiar songs written about Rhode Island are: *Rhode Island; My Rhode Island; Rhode Island Song; My Rhode Island;* and *Rhode Island.*

Rhode Island, the song first named above, with words written by Dr. Charles Carroll and sung to the tune of *Materna* composed by Samuel A. Ward, is a great favorite of many people in the State of Rhode Island.

My Rhode Island, the words of which were written by Mrs. Marianna Tallman and the music composed by Mrs. Roscoe L. Chase, is the prize song of the Rhode Island

State Federation of Women's Clubs. It was copyrighted by the Rhode Island State Federation of Women's Clubs in 1923.

Rhode Island Song, with words and music composed by May Herrick Nichols, was published and copyrighted by May Herrick Nichols, Providence, Rhode Island, in 1931.

My Rhode Island, the fourth song named above, with words written by W. H. Peters and the music composed by George A. Slocum, was published and copyrighted by George A. Slocum, Providence, Rhode Island, in 1918.

Rhode Island, the last song named above, was written by Henry Sherin, he composing both the words and the music. This musical production was copyrighted by Henry Sherin, New York, in 1910.

South Dakota

The song entitled *South Dakota* is widely used on occasions necessitating the use of a State song by the people of South Dakota. Willis E. Johnson composed both the words and the music of this song. This composition may be found in the collection of songs called *Let's Sing,* published in 1922 by the State College School Printing Press, Brookings, South Dakota, and may be bought from the State College Book Store at Brookings.

This composition makes reference to the sunshine; the State motto; the social institutions, home, church, and school; the fertile plains and the prairies; and the mountains with their gems and ore.

Vermont

Four popular songs whose themes are built about Vermont are: *The Song of the Green Mountains; Song of Vermont; A Roundelay for Old Vermont;* and *Champlain.*

The Song of the Green Mountains, with words and music composed by John F. Howard, was published and copyrighted by John F. Howard, Silver Lake Assembly, New York, in 1916.

Song of Vermont, with words written by Wendell Phillips Stafford and music composed by Lillian H. Olzendam, was published by the Tremont Music Publishing Company, Boston, Massachusetts, and was copyrighted by Lillian H. Olzendam, in 1924.

A Roundelay for Old Vermont, with words and music written by Alice J. Rowell, was published and copyrighted by Alice J. Rowell, South Albany, Vermont, in 1926.

Champlain, with words written by Dr. D. D. Fisher and music composed by C. S. Putnam, may be found in the *University of Vermont Song-book,* published by Hinds and Eldredge, 31 West 15th Street, New York City.

Virginia

A musical composition often used in some parts of the Commonwealth at public gatherings or patriotic occasions is *Call of Virginia,* with words written by Lillian Smith and music composed by B. T. Gilmer. This song was published and copyrighted by B. T. Gilmer, Draper, Virginia, in 1926.

Another musical composition, very popular and widely used in Virginia is *Old Virginia,* the words of which were composed by Dr. John W. Wayland, and the music written by Will H. Ruebush. This song was first published by the Ruebush-Kieffer Company, Dayton, Virginia as a special feature for a collection of State and National songs entitled *Songs of the People.* The State Teachers College at Harrisonburg, Virginia, has published and is distributing free of charge for the use of their students, and for the use of teachers and pupils in Virginia, a special edition of this song.

One of the most familiar and best loved songs dealing with Virginia is the composition entitled *Carry Me Back to Old Virginny,* with music composed by James Bland. This production is found in many song collections; but it may be bought from Oliver Ditson Company, 179 Tremont Street, Boston, Massachusetts, or from Charles H. Ditson and Company, 10 East 34 Street, New York City.

West Virginia

The musical composition most frequently used by the people of West Virginia on occasions demanding a State song is *West Virginia Hills* with words written by Mrs. Ellen King and music composed by H. E. Engle.

It was first copyrighted in 1886 by H. E. Engle, and recopyrighted by H. E. Engle in 1913. Copies may be bought from H. E. Engle, Lloydsville, West Virginia.

In the lyric, Mrs. King praises the majesty and the grandeur of the West Virginia hills, and expresses her love for them with great tenderness.

Wisconsin

Four songs whose themes are built about the State of Wisconsin with a patriotic appeal are: *Hail Wisconsin, A March Song; O Fair Wisconsin; Hymn to Wisconsin;* and *On, Wisconsin!*

Hail, Wisconsin, A March Song, with words written by Albert E. Johnson and music composed by B. Halbrook Poucher, was published and copyrighted by the Midland Publishing Company, Incorporated, Milwaukee, Wisconsin, in 1922.

O Fair Wisconsin, with words written by Henry Barkenhagen and music composed by L. F. Needham, was published and copyrighted by Henry Barkenhagen, Watertown, Wisconsin, in 1908.

Hymn to Wisconsin, with words and music written by John Krause, was published and copyrighted by John Krause, Madison, Wisconsin, in 1928.

On, Wisconsin! with words written by Dr. Philip A. Forsbeck and music composed by W. T. Purdy, may be bought from the Flanner-Hofsoo's Music House, Incorporated, Milwaukee, Wisconsin. There is an earlier edition of this song having the same title with the words written by Carl Beck and the music composed by W. T. Purdy. This edition may be found on page four of *University of Wisconsin Songs, Collection of Songs of the University of Wisconsin,* published by the University of Wisconsin

Club of Chicago and the Class of 1910, University of Wisconsin, Madison, Wisconsin, 1920.

Wyoming

The two songs written about Wyoming that seem splendid substitutes for a State song are: *Wyoming, The Wyoming State Song;* and *Wyoming State Song, Wyoming.*

Wyoming, The Wyoming State Song, with words written by Charles E. Winter and music composed by Earle R. Clemens, was published by the Wyoming Publishing Company, Casper, Wyoming, and was copyrighted by Earle R. Clemens and Charles E. Winter, in 1913.

Wyoming State Song, Wyoming, with words written by Charles E. Winter and music composed by George E. Knapp, was published and copyrighted by the Richter Music Company, Casper, Wyoming, in 1920.

These two songs have the same words, but they have different music.

CHAPTER XII

MISCELLANEOUS ITEMS

Due to scarcity of material, these miscellaneous items do not justify treatment in separate chapters.

APIARISTS

Sixteen of the forty-eight states have apiarists. The states having officially chosen apiarists or bee inspectors are: Arkansas, California, Colorado, Idaho, Indiana, Iowa, Massachusetts, Michigan, Minnesota, Missouri, Ohio, Rhode Island, Tennessee, Utah, Vermont, and Wyoming.

Seven states have provided for bee inspection by means other than by official bee inspectors as follows: Arizona, which provides that the Commissioner of Agriculture and Horticulture appoint the bee inspectors; Montana, which requires that bee colonies be registered; Nebraska, which specifies that the Agricultural Department inspect bees; New Mexico, which obligates the county bee inspectors to do this work; South Dakota, which expects the Department of Agriculture to inspect bees; Texas, which has the State Entomologist to inspect bees; and West Virginia, which requires the State Commissioner of Agriculture to inspect them.

STATE COLORS

Arizona

Arizona by an act of her legislature approved March 9, 1915, [1] adopted the State colors blue and old gold. The act says:

---

[1] *Session Laws of Arizona, Regular, First and Second Special Session, 1915: Acts, Resolutions and Memorials of the Regular Session of the Second Legislature of the State of Arizona, Session Begun January Eleventh, 1915, Session Adjourned March Eleventh, 1915* (The McNeil Company, Phoenix, Arizona, 1915) p. 66.

"Be It Enacted by the Legislature of the State of Arizona:

"Section 1. The colors known and designated as blue and old gold are hereby adopted as and shall be the State colors. The blue shall be of the same shade as that of the flag of the United States."

Oklahoma

Green and white are the State colors of Oklahoma. These were adopted by house concurrent resolution number nine, passed by the House on January 21, 1915, and by the Senate on January 22, 1915.

The Resolution says:

"WHEREAS, It is a custom of the various States of the Union to adopt colors to be known as State colors, and,

"WHEREAS, The State of Oklahoma, in keeping with her sister States, desires to adopt colors to be known as her State colors, and,

"WHEREAS, The Ohoyohoma Circle, composed of the wives of the members of the Fifth Legislature, present and organized at the capitol of the State of Oklahoma, do recommend the adoption of the colors of Green and White as permanent and appropriate colors for the State of Oklahoma.

"*Therefore Be It Resolved by the House and Senate Concurring Therein* That the said colors of Green and White be adopted as permanent and appropriate colors for the State of Oklahoma."[2]

THE SWORD OF STATE

South Carolina

South Carolina has a sword of State which is the Senate emblem of authority. During the daily sessions of the Senate it hangs from the front of the Senate rostrum and is carried by the Sergeant-at-Arms on all state

[2] *Session Laws of Oklahoma, 1915: State of Oklahoma Session Laws of 1915, Passed at the Regular Session of the Fifth Legislature of the State of Oklahoma, Convened at Oklahoma City on the Fifth Day of January, 1915* (State Printing and Publishing Company, Oklahoma City, Oklahoma, 1915) p. 724.

occasions. Authorities say that the first mention of this sword of State is found in the *Journal of the Commons House of Assembly of South Carolina* for May 5, 1704. This journal, on the date mentioned above, says that about one hundred twenty-nine dollars was paid for it.

It is thought that this sword of State was made by a local silversmith at Charleston. [3]

AN OFFICIAL STATE BANNER

Kansas

Kansas adopted an official State banner by house joint resolution number three, approved by the members of the State Legislature on February 26, 1925, to become effective after the act had been published in the official State paper, which publication appeared in this paper on February 27, 1925.

The house joint resolution says:

WHEREAS, Our state law calls it a desecration of 'Old Glory' to have any flag, standard, color, ensign or picture representation on any substance of any size, showing the colors, and the stars or stripes in any number to represent the United States flag: therefore

Be it enacted by the Legislature of the State of Kansas:

SECTION 1. That a state banner be and the same is hereby adopted to be used on every and all occasions, when the state is officially and publicly represented, with the privilege of the use by all citizens on all fitting and appropriate occasions authorized by the state authorities.

SECTION 2. That the official state banner of the state of Kansas provided for in section 1 of this act shall be of solid blue, and shall be of the same tint as the color of the field of the United States flag, whose width shall be three-fourths of its length, with a sunflower in the center, having a diameter one-third of the space of the banner, enclosing and surrounding with its petals the state seal of

---

[3] *Legislative Manual of the Seventy-eighth General Assembly of South Carolina at Columbia, Second Session, Commencing January 14, 1930,* J. Wilson Gibbes, Clerk of the House of Representatives (State Company, Columbia, South Carolina, 1930) p. 171-2.

Kansas; above the sunflower is the word Kansas, in letters one-eighth of the length of the banner. Service banners may be made of bunting or other material of such sizes required, all conforming to the proportionate Specifications.

SECTION 3. That this act shall take effect and be in force from and after its publication in the official state paper.[4]

THE FLAG AND PENNANT OF THE GOVERNOR

Rhode Island by legislative action, approved on March 21, 1931, adopted the flag and pennant of the Governor. The act[5] reads:

"It is enacted by the General Assembly as follows:

Section 1. Chapter 5 of the general laws, entitled "Of the arms, the seal and the flag of the state," is hereby amended by adding thereto the following section:

"'Section 4. The flag and pennant of the governor shall be white bearing on each side the following: A gold anchor on a shield with a blue field and gold border; above the shield a gold scroll bearing the words in blue letters 'State of Rhode Island;' below the shield a gold scroll bearing in blue letters the word 'Hope;' the shield and scrolls to be surrounded by four blue stars; both the flag and pennant to be edged with yellow fringe."

Section 2. This act shall take effect upon its passage.

[4] *Laws of Kansas: Session Laws, 1925, Passed at the Forty-first Regular Session—the Same Being the Twenty-fourth Biennial Session—of the State of Kansas* (Printed by Kansas State Printing Plant, B. P. Walker, State Printer, Topeka, Kansas, 1925) p. 372.

[5] *Rhode Island Public Laws, passed at the January Session, 1931.* (E. L. Freeman and Sons, State Printers, Providence, Rhode Island, 1931) p. 81-2.

CHAPTER XIII

A List of the Leading State Histories

Oftentimes when one desires to gather historical information about any of the various states of the Union, he is handicapped by not knowing what reliable material is best suited to his needs. If he does not have access to a large library, he is frequently unable to get just the type of information he wants. The following list gives the names and publishers, in most instances, of four or more important histories discussing the facts relative to each state. The writer was guided in the selection of these histories by recommendations from the several State librarians. The prices listed, for the most part, are those of the histories now in print.

Alabama

Alabama History, Joel Campbell Du Bose (B. F. Johnson Publishing Company, Richmond, Virginia, 1908) 432 pages, price 75 cents
This book, having colored plates and a folded map, was written primarily for public school use. It traces out the growth and development of the State from its earliest exploration by Hernando De Soto in 1538 through its educational, industrial, and political history to the year 1908. It is written in a clear and easy style with important dates set in the margin. The chapter on Alabama literature is noteworthy. The appendix gives the names and the dates of important events in Alabama history, year by year from 1540 to 1908.

2.

History of Alabama and Her People, Albert Burton Moore, Author and Editor (The American Historical Society, Inc. Chicago and New York, 1927) three volumes, price $37

This history was printed in three volumes. Volumes Two and Three are biographical, and Volume One contains the history by periods, with an index to the whole work. A selected bibliography appears at the close of most of the chapters in Volume One. The author was assisted with the production of this book by an advisory council. The biographical material is attributed to a special staff of writers. All the volumes of this history have abundant illustrations.

3.

History of Alabama and Dictionary of Alabama Biography, Thomas McAdory Owen (The S. J. Clarke Publishing Company, Chicago, Illinois, 1921) four volumes, price $48

Volumes Three and Four of the book named above contain biographical material. Mrs. Marie Bankhead Owen completed the manuscript of this history after the death of the author.

4.

History of Alabama and Incidentally of Georgia and Mississippi from the Earliest Period, Albert James Pickett (Walker and James, Charleston, South Carolina, 1851)

The two volumes of this history deal with the following topics:

1. *Alabama History*
2. *History of the Gulf States*
3. *North American Indians of the Gulf States*
4. *The Creek War from 1613-1614*

The author of this book does not discuss any facts beyond the organization of the State of Alabama in 1818. This history was republished by R. C. Randolph, Sheffield, Alabama, in 1896, in one volume containing six hundred and sixty-nine pages. The approximate cost is three dollars.

5.

Alabama: A Social and Economic History of the State, Mrs. Marie Bankhead Owen (Dixie Book House, Incorporated, Montgomery, Alabama, 1937) This history containing five hundred and eighty-one pages, deals with the history and with the economic conditions of Alabama. It

was written to bring up to date the material contained in
the *History and Dictionary of Alabama Biography* by
Thomas McAdory Owen, which was published in 1921.
Nathan Glick of Montgomery, Ala., made the pen drawings of the illustrative material and line drawings of the
individuals pictured in Mrs. Owen's recent publication.
These drawings are especially noteworthy.

ARIZONA

*The History of Arizona from the Earliest Times Known
to the People of Europe to 1903,* Sydney R. Delong (The
Whitaker and Hay Company, Inc., San Francisco, California, 1905) 199 pages, price $1
The volume mentioned above was "written under the
auspices of the Pioneer Historical Society of Arizona."

2.

History of Arizona, Thomas Edwin Farish, Arizona Historian (Filmer Brothers Electrotype Company, Phoenix,
Arizona, and San Francisco, California, 1915)

The book was "printed and published by direction of the
Second Legislature of the State of Arizona." It is published in eight volumes, the First and Second of which
sell for one dollar and fifty cents each, and the remaining
volumes sell for one dollar and seventy-five cents each.

3.

Legislative History, Arizona, 1864-1912, compiled by
George Henderson Kelly, State Historian (The Manufacturing Stationers, Inc. Phoenix, Arizona, 1926) 399
pages

The volume contains three hundred and fifty-three pages
of tables and historical data and forty-six pages of
biography.

4.

*Pioneer Days in Arizona, from the Spanish Occupation to
Statehood,* Frank C. (Francis Cummins) Lockwood (The
Macmillan Company, New York, 1932). This history, containing three hundred and eighty-seven pages, is good for
the general reader. It costs $4.00.

5.

Arizona Prehistoric, Aboriginal, Pioneer, Modern; the Nation's Youngest Commonwealth within a Land of Ancient Culture, James H. McClintock (The S. J. Clarke Publishing Company, Chicago, Illinois, 1916) price $30
This history is published in three volumes, the last of which contains biographical sketches. The three volumes are illustrated and bound in one-fourth leather.

6.

History of Arizona, Honorable Richard E. Sloan, Supervising Editor, Ward R. Adams, author, assisted by an advisory council (Record Publishing Company, Phoenix, Arizona, 1930) This four volumed history in a leatherette binding sells for $40.00. Volumes one and two written by Ward R. Adams deal with the history of Arizona, and Volumes three and four written by a staff of writers are devoted to Arizona biography.

ARKANSAS

Biographical and Pictorial History of Arkansas, John Hallum (Weed, Parsons and Company, Printers, Albany, New York, 1887) 581 pages

The above-named publication gives historical and biographical material about Arkansas and her citizens.

2.

Historical Review of Arkansas; Its Commerce, Industry and Modern Affairs, Fay Hempstead (The Lewis Publishing Company, Chicago, Illinois, 1911)

The Second and the Third of the three volumes of this history include biographical material.

3.

A History of the State of Arkansas for the Use of Schools, Fay Hempstead (F. F. Hansell and Brother, New Orleans, Louisiana, 1889) 236 pages

This volume contains illustrative material, portraits, and maps in addition to historical data.

4.

A Pictorial History of Arkansas, from the Earliest Times to the Year 1890, Fay Hempstead (N. D. Thompson Publishing Company, St. Louis and New York, 1890) 1246 pages

The author discusses the following topics in this volume:

1. *The Indian Tribes Formerly Occupying What Is Now Arkansas*
2. *The French and Spanish Explorers*
3. *The Louisiana Purchase*
4. *The Territory of Arkansas*
5. *The Early Governors*
6. *Arkansas as a State*
7. *The Civil War Period*
8. *The Development of the State Since the Civil War, etc.*

5.

The High Lights of Arkansas History, Dallas T. Herndon (The Arkansas Historical Commission, Little Rock, Arkansas, 1922) 174 pages

This history was printed as a special edition for distribution by the Arkansas Historical Commission

6.

Centennial History of Arkansas, Dallas T. Herndon (S. J. Clarke Publishing Company, Chicago, Illinois, and Little Rock, Arkansas, 1922)

7.

Makers of Arkansas History, John Hugh Reynolds (Silver, Burdett and Company, New York, 1918) 365 pages, price $1

The book is written in story form.

8.

The History of Arkansas; A Text-book for Public Schools, High Schools, and Academies, Josiah H. Shinn (B. F. Johnson Publishing Company, Richmond, Virginia, 1905) 335 pages, price $1

This book reflects advanced historical and pedagogical methods, but the style is simple and clear so as to meet the needs of pupils in public schools, high schools, and academies. It gives the chronological development of the State of Arkansas from its exploration by Hernando De Soto in 1541 to the year 1903.

9.

Arkansas and Its People, a History, 1541-1930, David Yancey Thomas, Editor (The American Historical Society, Incorporated, New York, 1930) The Second, Third, and Fourth of the four volumes of this history contain biographical data. Volume Two has an extensive bibliography. This four volumed history, bound in buckram, sells for $37.50.

CALIFORNIA

California and Californians, Edited by Rockwell Dennis Hunt, assisted by an advisory board (The Lewis Publishing Company, New York and San Francisco, 1930). This four volumed history sells for $42.50. The Spanish Period was written by Nellie Van de Grift Sanchez. The American Period was written by Rockwell Dennis Hunt. The California Biography was written by a special staff of writers.

2.

The California Plutarch, John Stephen McGroarty (J. R. Finnell, Publisher, Los Angeles, California, 1935). Volume One, containing four hundred and thirty-six pages, is all of this biography which has been published so far. It contains biographical date on the lives of men and women who have contributed to the founding and the developing of California. This volume sells for $100.

3.

History of California, Hubert Howe Bancroft (The History Company, San Francisco, California, 1890)
This is a seven volumed history containing both historical and biographical material.

4.

A History of California: The Spanish Period, Charles Edward Chapman (The Macmillan Company, New York, 1921) 527 pages, price $4

The author gives the following reasons for publishing this history: First, "It presents a vast amount of new material, some portions of which have never before appeared in print, while others were not known or not utilized, by the general historians of the state. Secondly, an attempt is made to place the history of California in its proper perspective in relation to that of North America as a whole. This history employs many quotations from historical documents, has maps, and an appendix giving bibliographies, and the names of manuscripts, periodicals, essays, unpublished documents, and much other useful information about California history.

5.

A History of California: The American Period, Robert Glass Cleland (The Macmillan Company, New York, 1922) 512 pages, price $4

This history is written to complete *The History of California: The Spanish Period,* by Charles Edward Chapman. It stresses the national and traditional aspects of California and Californians.

6.

History of California, Zoeth Skinner Eldredge, Editor (The Century History Company, New York, 1915) price $30

There are five volumes of this history. The Fifth Volume is made up of special articles by various authors.

7.

History of California, Theodore Henry Hittell. Volumes One and Two were published by the Pacific Press Publishing House and the Occidental Publishing Company, San Francisco, California, 1885. Volumes Three and Four were published by N. J. Stone and Company, San Francisco, California, 1897

COLORADO

History of the State of Colorado, Frank Hall (The Blakely Printing Company, Chicago, Illinois, 1889 to 1895) four volumes

The author in these volumes discusses the following phases of Colorado history:

1. *The Pre-historic Races and the Remains of these*
2. *Early Spanish, French, and American Explorations*
3. *First Permanent American Settlements*
4. *The Discovery of Gold in the Rocky Mountains*
5. *The Beginning and Development of Cities and Towns*

2.

Colorado: Short Studies of Its Past and Present, Junius Henderson, E. B. Renaud, Colon B. Goodykoontz, and others (University of Colorado, Boulder, Colorado, 1927) 202 pages, price $2

This history discusses the following phases of Colorado history:

1. *The Pre-historic Peoples of Colorado*
2. *The Indians of Colorado*
3. *The Exploration and Settlement of Colorado*
4. *Early Range Days*
5. *The Gold Rush and after*
6. *Education in Colorado*
7. *Colorado Literature*

3.

History of Colorado, Wilbur Fiske Stone, Editor (The S. J. Clarke Publishing Company, Chicago, Illinois, 1918) Of the four volumes of this history, Two, Three, and Four contain biographical material.

CONNECTICUT

Connecticut Historical Collections, Containing a General Collection of Interesting Facts, Traditions, Biographical Sketches, Anecdotes, etc., Relating to the History and Antiquities of Every Town in Connecticut, with Geographical Descriptions. Illustrated by 190 engravings

Second Edition, John Warner Barber (Durrie and Peck
and J. W. Barber, New Haven, Connecticut, 1846) 576
pages

2.

*The History of Connecticut, from Its Earliest Settlement
to the Present Time,* W. H. Carpenter and T. S. Arthur,
Editors (Lippincott, Grambo and Company, Philadelphia,
Pennsylvania, 1854) 287 pages

The history named above is one of Lippincott's Cabinet
Histories of the States.

3.

A History of Connecticut, Its People and Institutions,
George L. Clark (G. P. Putnam's Sons, New York, 1914)
509 pages, price $3.50

The above-named book in addition to historical data has
maps and about one hundred illustrations.

4.

*Connecticut: The Public Records of the State of Con-
necticut . . . with the Journal of the Council of Safety . . .
and an Appendix, Published in Accordance with a Resolution of the General Assembly,* Charles J. Hoadly . . .
(The Case, Lockwood and Brainard Company, Hartford,
Connecticut, 1894-1922) three volumes

5.

*The History of Connecticut, from the First Settlement of
the Colony to the Adoption of the Present Constitution,*
Gideon H. Hollister (Durrie and Peck, New Haven, Connecticut, 1855) two volumes

6.

Connecticut, A Study of a Commonwealth-Democracy,
Alexander Johnston (Houghton, Mifflin and Company,
Boston and New York, 1887) 409 pages

7.

The Story of Connecticut, Lewis Sprague Mills (Charles
Scribner's Sons, New York and Boston, 1932) 414 pages

8.

Connecticut as a Colony and as a State; or, One of the Original Thirteen, Forrest Morgan, Editor-in-chief (The Publishing Society of Connecticut, Hartford, Connecticut, 1904) four volumes

9.

History of Connecticut in Monographic Form, Norris Galpin Osborn, Editor (The States History Company, New York, 1925) five volumes; price $37.50 bound in buckram, $45 bound in one-half leather

10.

General History of Connecticut, from Its First Settlement under George Fenwick, to Its Latest Period of Amity with Great Britain, Prior to the Revolution, Including a Description of the Country, and Many Curious and Interesting Anecdotes, with an Appendix, Pointing out the Causes of the Rebellion in America, . . . by a Gentleman of the Province, London, 1781, Rev. Samuel Peters, Additions to Appendix by Samuel Jarvis McCormick (D. Appleton and Company, New York, 1877) 285 pages

11.

A History of Connecticut, Reverend Elias Benjamin Sanford, Editor (The S. C. Scranton Company, Hartford, Connecticut, 1922) 450 pages

This book has maps and illustrative material in addition to the data dealing with Connecticut history.

12.

A Complete History of Connecticut, Civil and Ecclesiastical, from the Emigration of Its First Planters from England, in the Year 1630 to the Year 1764, and to the Close of the Indian Wars, Benjamin Trumbull (Maltby, Goldsmith and Company, and Samuel Wadsworth, New Haven, Connecticut, 1818) two volumes

13.

The Public Records of the Colony of Connecticut, 1636-1776, . . . transcribed and published (in accordance with a resolution of the General Assembly) J. H. Trumbull and C. J. Hoadly (Brown and Parsons, Hartford, Connecticut, 1850-1890) fifteen volumes

DELAWARE

History of Delaware, Past and Present, Wilson Lloyd Bevan, Editor (Lewis Historical Publishing Company, Inc. New York, 1929)

This history is published in four volumes, the Third and Fourth of which have biographical material.

2.

History of the State of Delaware, from the Earliest Settlements to the Year 1907, Henry C. Conrad (The Author, Wilmington, Delaware, 1908) three volumes

3.

A History of Delaware, Walter A. Powell (The Christopher Publishing House, Boston, Massachusetts, 1928) 475 pages, price $3.50

Part One of this volume deals with the general history of Delaware from its discovery to 1925; and Part Two deals with the history of education in Delaware.

4.

History of Delaware 1609 to 1888, J. Thomas Scharf and assistants (L. J. Richards and Company, Philadelphia, Pennsylvania, 1888)

The above-named history in two volumes deals both with the general history and with the local history of Delaware.

THE DISTRICT OF COLUMBIA

History of the National Capital from Its Founding through the Period of the Adoption of the Organic Act, Wilhelmus Bogart Bryan (The Macmillan Company, New York, 1916) two volumes. This is one of the best histories for reference use on the various aspects of The District of Columbia.

2.

The District of Columbia, Its Government and Administration, Laurence F. Schmeckebier (The Johns Hopkins Press, Baltimore, Maryland, 1928) 943 pages

This history is very full and comprehensive. It is divided into Part One, giving the history and general government of the District, and Part Two, giving the plan of organization and the operation of the government of the District.

3.

Origin and Government of the District of Columbia, William Tindall (Government Printing Office, Washington, D. C. 1903) 224 pages

4.

The Economic Development of the District of Columbia, Carroll D. Wright (The Academy, Washington, D. C. 1899) 187 pages

FLORIDA

Florida, Old and New, Frederick W. Dau (G. P. Putnam's Sons, New York and London, 1934). This three-hundred-and-seventy-seven-paged history sells for $5.00.

2.

A History of Florida from the Treaty of 1763 to Our Own Times, Caroline Hays Brevard, edited by James Alexander Robertson (Florida State Historical Society, Deland, Florida, 1924-1925) two volumes, price $15 per volume

3.

History of Florida from Its Discovery by Ponce de Leon in 1512, to the Close of the Florida War, in 1842, George Rainsford Fairbanks (J. B. Lippincott and Company, Philadelphia, Pennsylvania; C. Drew, Jacksonville, Florida, 1871) 350 pages

4.

School History of Florida, Edwin Luther Green (Williams and Wilkins Company, Baltimore, Maryland, 1898) 339 pages

5.

The Territory of Florida: or, Sketches of the Topography, Civil and Natural History, of the Country, the Climate, and the Indian Tribes, from the First Discovery to the Present Time, with a Map, Views, etc., John Lee Williams (A. T. Goodrich, New York, 1837) 304 pages

GEORGIA

The History of the State of Georgia from 1850 to 1881, Embracing the Three Important Epochs: the Decade before the War of 1861-5; the War; the Period of Reconstruction, Isaac Wheeler Avery (Brown and Derby, New York, 1881) four volumes

2.

Georgia History Stories, Joseph Harris Chappell (Silver, Burdett and Company, New York, 1905) 382 pages, price $1

3.

First Lessons in Georgia History, Lawton Bryan Evans (American Book Company, New York, 1913) 356 pages, price 84 cents

4.

A History of Georgia for Use in Schools, Lawton Bryan Evans (American Book Company, New York, 1908) 360 pages, price $1

5.

Stories of Georgia, Joel Chandler Harris (American Book Company, New York, 1896) 315 pages

6.

The History of Georgia, Charles Colcock Jones (Houghton, Mifflin and Company, New York, 1883)

The First of the two volumes discusses the Aboriginal and Colonial Epochs; and the Second, the Revolutionary Epoch.

7.

A Standard History of Georgia and Georgians, Lucian Lamar Knight (The Lewis Publishing Company, Chicago and New York, 1917) six volumes, price $30

8.

A History of Georgia, Containing Brief Sketches of the Most Remarkable Events, up to the Present Day, Captain Hugh McCall (Seymour and Williams, Savannah, Georgia, 1811-1816) two volumes

9.

The Story of Georgia and the Georgia People, 1732 to 1860, George Gilman Smith (G. G. Smith, Macon, Georgia, 1900) 634 pages

This book has illustrations, plates, and a list of the Georgia soldiers who fought in the Revolutionary War.

10.

A History of Georgia, from Its First Discovery by Europeans to the Adoption of the Present Constitution, in MDCCXCVIII, Reverend William Bacon Stevens (W. T. Williams, Savannah, Georgia, 1847) two volumes

11.

The Student's History of Georgia, from the Earliest Discoveries and Settlements to the End of the Year 1883, Lawton Bryan Evans (J. W. Burke and Company, Macon, Georgia, 1844) 352 pages

The volume named above has illustrations, charts, and maps.

IDAHO

History of the State of Idaho, Cornelius James Brosnan (Charles Scribner's Sons, New York, 1926) 260 pages, price $1.50

This history has illustrations, portraits, and a double-paged map.

2.

History of Idaho: A Narrative Account of Its Historical Progress, Its People and Its Principal Interests, Hiram Taylor French (The Lewis Publishing Company, Chicago and New York, 1914)

In this set there are three volumes, the Second and Third of which contain biographical material.

3.

Reminiscences: Incidents in the Life of a Pioneer in Oregon and Idaho, William Armistead Goulder (Timothy Regan, Boise, Idaho, 1909) 376 pages

4.

The History of Idaho, John Hailey (Press of Syms-York Company, Inc. Boise, Idaho, 1910) 395 pages, price $3

This history traces the exploration and settlement of the Northwest Territory before the beginning of the historical development of the State of Idaho, which is discussed through the year 1909.

5.

History of Idaho, the Gem of the Mountains, James H. Hawley, Editor (The S. J. Clarke Publishing Company, Chicago, Illinois, 1920)

The Second, Third, and Last of the four volumes of this set contain biographical material.

6.

An Illustrated History of the State of Idaho, Containing a History of the State of Idaho from the Earliest Period of Its Discovery to the Present Time, together with Glimpses of Its Auspicious Future . . . and Biographical Mention of Many Pioneers and Prominent Citizens of To-day (The Lewis Publishing Company, Chicago, Illinois, 1899) 726 pages

Idaho, The Gem of the Mountains, appears on the cover-title of this volume.

ILLINOIS

*The History of Illinois from Its Discovery and Settlement
to the Present Time (that is, 1844)* Henry Brown (J.
Winchester, New York, 1844) 492 pages

2.

Illinois History Stories for Use in Elementary Schools,
W. H. Campbell (D. Appleton and Company, New York,
1910) 247 pages, price 55 cents

3.

Illinois, History—Geography—Government, Revised Edition, Henry Victor Church (D. C. Heath and Company,
New York and Boston, 1931) 591 pages.

4.

*A Complete History of Illinois from 1673 to 1873; Em-
bracing the Physical Features of the Country; Its Early
Explorations; Aboriginal Inhabitants; French and British
Occupation; Conquest by Virginia; Territorial Condition,
and the Subsequent Civil, Military and Political Events
of the State,* Alexander Davidson and Bernard Stuvé
(Illinois Journal Company, Springfield, Illinois, 1874)
944 pages

5.

*A History of Illinois from Its Commencement as a State
in 1818 to 1847,* Thomas Ford (Published by S. C. Criggs
and Company, Chicago, Illinois, 1854) 447 pages. This
history discusses the Black Hawk War, the rise, progress,
and fall of Mormonism, the Alton and Lovejoy Riots, and
various other important and interesting events connected
with the historical development of the State of Illinois.

6.

The Making of Illinois, Revised Edition, Irwin F. Mather
(A. Flanagan Company, Chicago, Illinois, 1935) 274 pages.
This history covers more than two hundred years of the
discovery, exploration, settlement, and development of Illinois, and gives many helpful incidents and details.

7.

Illinois, Historical and Statistical, Comprising the Essential Facts of Its Planting and Growth as a Province, County, Territory, and State, Derived from the Most Authentic Sources, Including Original Documents and Papers, together with Carefully Prepared Statistical Tables, John Moses (Fergus Printing Company, Chicago, Illinois, 1889-1892)

The publishers put this work out in two volumes, which are paged continuously.

8.

History of Illinois and Her People, George W. Smith, assisted by an Advisory Board (The American Historical Society, Inc., Chicago and New York, 1927) price $42.50

This publication consists of six volumes, of which volumes Four, Five, and Six contain biographical material.

INDIANA

A History of Indiana, 1816 to 1856, John B. Dillon (Bingham and Doughty, Indianapolis, Indiana, 1859) 637 pages

This book is now out of print.

2.

Indiana and Indianans, A History of Aboriginal and Territorial Indiana and the Century of Statehood, Jacob Piatt Dunn (The American Historical Society, Chicago and New York, 1919) five volumes, subscription price $30

Of the five volumes of this history, Three, Four, and Five contain biographical material.

3.

A History of Indiana, Logan Esarey (Hoosier Press, Fort Wayne, Indiana, 1924) two volumes, price $8

This history may be bought from the Indiana University Book Store, Bloomington, Indiana.

4.

Indiana, One Hundred and Fifty Years of American Development, Charles Roll (The Lewis Publishing Company, Chicago and New York, 1931) five volumes, subscription price $37.50

Of the five volumes of this history, Three, Four, and Five contain biographical material.

Iowa

Iowa, Its History and Its Foremost Citizens, Johnson Brigham (The S. J. Clarke Publishing Company, Chicago, Illinois, 1915) three volumes

2.

A History of the People of Iowa, Cyrenus Cole (The Torch Press, Cedar Rapids, Iowa, 1921) 572 pages

Part One of this history discusses the discovery and possession of Iowa; Part Two, the Indians; Part Three, the Territory and Territorial government; Part Four, the first State Constitution; Part Five, the remaking of the State; Part Six, the Civil War and after; Part Seven, the years between 1765-1885; Part Eight, the social and economic reforms; Part Nine, the years from 1897-1920.

3.

History of Iowa from the Earliest Times to the Beginning of the Twentieth Century, Illustrated with Photographic Views of the Natural Scenery of the State, Public Buildings, Pioneer Life, etc., with Portraits and Biographies of Notable Men and Women of Iowa, Benjamin F. Gue (The Century History Company, New York, 1903)

This history consists of four volumes; the First of which deals with the Pioneer Period, the Second with the Civil War, the Third with the period from 1866 to 1903, and the Fourth contains biographical material.

4.

Stories of Iowa for Boys and Girls, Bruce E. Mahan and Ruth Augusta Gallaher (The Macmillan Company, New York, 1929) 365 pages, price 96 cents

KANSAS

Kansas: A Cyclopedia of State History, Embracing Events, Institutions, Industries, Counties, Cities, Towns, Prominent Persons, etc., with a Supplementary Volume Devoted to Selected Personal History and Reminiscences . . . Frank W. Blackmar, Editor (Standard Publishing Company, Chicago, Illinois, 1912) price $27.50

The three volumes are published in four books.

2.

History of Kansas, State and People, Kansas at the First Quarter Post of the Twentieth Century, written and compiled by William E. Connelley, *Kansas Biography,* by a Special Staff of Writers (The American Historical Society, Inc. Chicago and New York, 1928) five volumes

3.

History of the State of Kansas, Containing a Full Account of Its Growth from an Uninhabited Territory to a Wealthy and Important State; Its Rapid Increase in Population and the Marvelous Development of Its Great Natural Resources; also a Supplementary History and Description of Its Counties, Cities, Towns and Villages, Their Advantages, Industries, Manufactures and Commerce; to Which are Added Biographical Sketches and Portraits of Prominent Men and Early Settlers, William G. Cutler, Editor (A. T. Andreas, Chicago, Illinois, 1883) 1616 pages

4.

The Annals of Kansas: New Edition 1541 to 1885, Daniel Webster Wilder (T. D. Thacher, Topeka, Kansas, 1885) 1196 pages

KENTUCKY

History of Kentucky, Temple Bodley and Samuel M. Wilson (The S. J. Clarke Publishing Company, Chicago, Illinois and Louisville, Kentucky, 1928) five volumes, price $40

2.

Historical Sketches of Kentucky, 1797-1870, Lewis Collins (J. A. and U. P. James, Cincinnati, Ohio, 1847) 560 pages

This book embodies the following topics:
1. *Kentucky History*
2. *Antiquities*
3. *Natural Curiosities*
4. *Anecdotes of Pioneer Life*
5. *Geographical, Statistical, and Geological Descriptions*
6. *Biographical Sketches of More Than One Hundred Pioneers, Soldiers, Statesmen, Divines, etc.*

3.

Collins' Historical Sketches of Kentucky: History of Kentucky by the late Lewis Collins: Revised, Enlarged Fourfold and Brought Down to the Year 1874 by his son, Richard H. Collins (Collins and Company, Covington, Kentucky, 1874)

This work of two volumes takes up the following aspects of the history of Kentucky:
1. *Pre-historic*
2. *Yearly Happenings for 331 Years*
3. *Statistics*
4. *Curiosities both Antique and Natural*
5. *Geographical and Geological Descriptions*
6. *Incidents of Pioneer Life*
7. *Biographical Sketches, Almost Five Hundred in Number*

4.

The Discovery, Settlement and Present State of Kentucke: and an Essay towards the Topography and Natural History of That Important Country. . . . John Filson (James Adams, Wilmington, Delaware, 1784)

To the original copy of this book was added an appendix containing:
1. "The adventures of Col. Daniel Boon, one of the first settlers, comprehending every important occurrence in the political history of that province.

2. "The minutes of the Piankashaw Council, held at Post St. Vincents, April 15, 1784.
3. "An account of the Indian nations inhabiting within the limits of the thirteen United States.
4. "The stages and distances between Philadelphia and the falls of the Ohio; from Pittsburg to Pensacola and several other places. The whole illustrated by a new and accurate map of Kentucky and the country adjoining, drawn from actual surveys."

A single copy of an early edition of this history recently sold for thirty-four hundred dollars.

5.

A History of Kentucky, Thomas Dionysius Clark (Prentice-Hall, Inc., New York, 1937) 702 pages. This publication is a general History of the State. It stresses the historical events in the development of the post-Civil War Period of Kentucky, but it does not present this aspect of Kentucky history at the expense of other important historical data belonging to the development of this state. This history sells for $5.00.

6.

A History of Kentucky and Kentuckians: The Leaders and Representative Men in Commerce, Industry and Modern Activities, E. Polk Johnson (The Lewis Publishing Company, Chicago and New York, 1912) three volumes

Volumes Two and Three of this history contain biographical material.

7.

History of Kentucky, Judge Charles Kerr, Editor, compiled by William Elsey Connelley and E. M. Coulter (The American Historical Society, Chicago and New York, 1922) five volumes, price $35

Volumes Three, Four, and Five of this history contain biographical material. The Editor's Preface to Volume One says: "Those engaged in its composition have had but one purpose, and that was to give to the people of Kentucky a social and political account of their state, based

on contemporaneous history, as nearly as the accomplish
ment of such an undertaking were possible."

8.

Kentucky in the Nation's History, Robert McNutt Mc
Elroy (Moffat, Yard and Company, New York, 1909) 59(
pages, price $5

9.

*The History of Kentucky: Exhibiting an Account of the
Modern Discovery; Settlement; Progressive Improvement
Civil and Military Transactions; and the Present State o,
the Country,* Second Edition, Humphrey Marshall (G. S
Robinson, Printer, Frankfort, Kentucky, 1824) two vol
umes

LOUISIANA

*A History of Louisiana—Wilderness—Colony—Province—
Territory—State—People,* Henry E. Chambers (The
American Historical Society Incorporated, Chicago and
New York, 1925) price $37.50

The work consists of three volumes, the Second and the
Third of which contain biographies.

2.

A History of Louisiana, Alcée Fortier (Goupil and Com
pany, Manzi, Joyant and Company, Successors, Paris and
New York, 1904)

This publication was put on the market in four volumes
the First of which deals with the early explorers and the
domination of the French, 1512-1783: the Second, with the
Spanish domination and cession to the United States
1769-1803: the Third, with the American domination
Part 1, 1803-1861: and the Fourth, with the American
domination, Part 2, 1861-1903.

3.

*Historical Collections of Louisiana and Florida, Including
Translations of Original Manuscripts Relating to Their
Discovery and Settlement, with Numerous Historical and*

Biographical Notes; Second Series, Historical Memoirs and Narratives, 1527-1702, B. F. French (A. Mason, New York, 1875) 300 pages

4.

History of Louisiana, with City and Topographical Maps of the State, Ancient and Modern, Third Edition, Charles Étienne Arthur Gayarré (A. Hawkins, New Orleans, Louisiana, 1885)

The French, Spanish, and American dominations are discussed in the above-named order in the four volumes of this history.

5.

The History of Louisiana from the Earliest Period, by Francis Xavier Martin, . . . , *with a Memoir of the Author,* by Judge W. W. Howe, . . . ,*to Which is Appended Annals of Louisiana, from the Close of Martin's History, 1815, to the Commencement of the Civil War, 1861* by John F. Condon (J. A. Gresham, New Orleans, Louisiana, 1882) 523 pages

6.

A History of Louisiana, Revised and Enlarged, Harriet Magruder (D. C. Heath and Company, New York, 1922) 424 pages, price $1.44

7.

Louisiana: A Record of Expansion, Albert Phelps (Houghton, Mifflin and Company, Boston and New York, 1905) 412 pages, price $2.00.

8.

The Story of Louisiana, A Text-book for Schools, William O. Scroggs (The Bobbs-Merrill Company, Publishers, Indianapolis, Indiana, 1924) 324 pages, price ninety-five cents.

MAINE

The History of Maine, John Stevens Cabot Abbott: *Revised Throughout, and Five Chapters of New Matter Added* by Edward H. Elwell, Second Edition (Brown Thurston Company, Portland, Maine, 1892) 608 pages

2.

Maine: A History, Centennial Edition, Louis Clinton Hatch, Editor-in-chief (The American Historical Society, New York, 1919)

The three volumes of this history are paged continuously.

3.

Maine, Its History, Resources, and Government, Revised Edition, Glenn Wendell Starkey (Silver, Burdett and Company, Boston and New York, 1930) 249 pages, price $1.25

4.

The History of the State of Maine; from Its First Discovery, A. D. 1602, to the Separation, A. D. 1820, Inclusive, with an Appendix and General Index, William Durkee Williamson (Glazier, Masters and Smith, Hallowell, Maine, 1839) two volumes

MARYLAND

History of Maryland: Province and State, Matthew Page Andrews (Doubleday, Doran and Company, Inc. Garden City, New York, 1929) 279 pages, price $7.25

The edition is limited to two hundred and seventy-nine copies. It discusses Maryland politics and government, as well as Maryland history.

2.

The History of Maryland, from Its First Settlement, in 1633, to the Restoration, in 1660, with a Copious Introduction, and Notes and Illustrations, John Leeds Bozman (J. Lucas and E. K. Deaver, Baltimore, Maryland, 1837) two volumes

3.

An Historical View of the Government of Maryland, from Its Colonization to the Present Day, John van Lear McMahon (J. Lucas and E. K. Deaver, Baltimore, Maryland, 1831) 539 pages

The book discusses only the Colonial Period.

MASSACHUSETTS

The History of Massachusetts, John Stetson Barry (Phillips, Sampson and Company, Boston, Massachusetts, 1855-1857)

Volume One deals with the Colonial Period, up to 1692; Volume Two, with the Provincial Period, to 1775; and Volume Three, with the Commonwealth Period, which covers the time from 1775 to 1820. The work has bibliographical footnotes.

2.

History of Massachusetts, Alden Bradford (Richardson and Lord, Boston, Massachusetts, 1822-1829)

This history was published in three volumes. Wells and Lilly of Boston published Volume Two in 1825; and the author, Volume Three, which was printed by J. H. Eastburn, Boston, Massachusetts, in 1829. Volume One covers the period of time from 1764 to July 1775; Volume Two relates the events of Massachusetts history from July, 1775, to the year 1789, inclusive; while Volume Three gives the historical facts about Massachusetts during the years from 1790 to 1920.

3.

Commonwealth History of Massachusetts, Colony, Province, and State, edited by Albert Bushnell Hart, with the coöperation of an Advisory Board of forty-two learned bodies (The States History Company, New York, 1927-30) five volumes

At the end of each chapter there is a selected bibliography. Volume One, bound in buckram, can be bought for nine dollars and fifty cents.

4.

The History of Massachusetts, from the First Settlement Thereof in 1628, until the Year 1750, Third Edition, Thomas Hutchinson (Printed for Thomas and Andrews, Boston, Massachusetts, by Thomas C. Cushing, Salem, Massachusetts, 1795-1828)

Of the three volumes of this history, Volume Two was printed at Boston by Manning and Loving for Thomas and Andrews, in 1795; Volume Three was printed in London by John Murray in 1828.

5.

Massachusetts: A Guide to Its Places and People, written and compiled by the Federal Writers' Project of the Works Progress Administration for the State of Massachusetts, Frederick W. Cook, Secretary of the Commonwealth, Coöperative Sponsor (Houghton, Mifflin Company, Boston, Massachusetts, 1937) 675 pages, price $2.50

MICHIGAN

Michigan: A History of Governments, Thomas McIntyre Cooley (Houghton, Mifflin and Company, Boston and New York, 1905) 409 pages, price $2

This history, having a supplementary chapter by Charles Moore, is one of the American Commonwealth Series.

2.

History of Michigan, Lawton Thomas Hemans (Hammond Publishing Company, Limited, Lansing, Michigan, 1906) 278 pages

3.

The Story of Michigan, Claude Sheldon Larzelere (The Michigan Education Company, Lansing, Michigan, 1928) 424 pages, price $1.28

The volume named above has illustrations, and references appear at the end of most of the chapters. Twenty-two sections from this history, bound separately, are now obtainable at from ten to thirty cents each.

4.

Michigan as a Province, Territory and State, the Twenty-sixth Member of the Federal Union, Henry Munson Utley and Byron M. Cutcheon, Clarence M. Burton, Advisory Editor (The Publishing Society of Michigan, New York, 1906)

Volume One treats of Michigan as a province from the discovery and settlement by the French to its final surrender to the United States, and was written by Henry Munson Utley. Volume Two, by Byron M. Cutcheon, deals with Michigan as a territory, from its incorporation as part of the Northwest Territory to its organization as a state. Volume Three, by Byron M. Cutcheon, gives an account of Michigan as a state from its admission to the Union to the close of the Civil War. Volume Four, by Henry Munson Utley, treats of Michigan as a state from the close of the Civil War to the end of the Nineteenth Century. The whole work, under the advisory editorship of Clarence M. Burton, contains plates, frontispieces, portraits, and maps.

MINNESOTA

Minnesota and Its People, Joseph Alfred Arner Burnquist, Editor (The S. J. Clarke Publishing Company, Chicago, Illinois, 1924) price $40

Of the four volumes comprising this treatise, Volumes Three and Four contain biographical material.

2.

A History of Minnesota, William Watts Folwell (Minnesota Historical Society, Saint Paul, Minnesota, 1921-1926) price $5 per volume

Four volumes, of which Volumes One, Two, and Three may be obtained at five dollars each, while autographed copies of these volumes in three-quarter leather binding sell for ten dollars each.

3.

Minnesota in Three Centuries, Semi-Centennial Edition, 1655 to 1908. Board of Editors: Lucius F. Hubbard, William P. Murray, James H. Baker, and Warren Upham (The Publishing Society of Minnesota, New York, 1908)

The above-named work is published in four volumes, covering the following periods and subjects: Volume One gives a description of the State and of its explorations; Volume Two describes Minnesota as a Territory; Volume Three tells of Minnesota as a State up to 1870; and Volume Four covers the statehood of Minnesota from 1870 to 1908.

4.

The History of Minnesota, from the Earliest French Explorations to the Present Time, Edward Duffield Neill (J. B. Lippincott and Company, Philadelphia, Pennsylvania, 1858) 628 pages

5.

Minnesota, the Land of Sky-tinted Water: A History of the State and Its People, Theodore Christianson (The American Historical Society, Chicago and New York, 1935) five volumes. Volumes Three, Four, and Five of this history contain biographical material exclusively, written by a special staff of writers.

MISSISSIPPI

A History of Mississippi for Use in Schools, Robert Lowry and William H. McCardle (The University Publishing Company, New York, 1900) 265 pages, price $1

2.

School History of Mississippi for Use in Public and Private Schools, Franklin Lafayette Riley (B. F. Johnson Publishing Company, Richmond, Virginia, 1900) 421 pages, price 75 cents

3.

A History of Mississippi, the Heart of the South, Dunbar Rowland (The S. J. Clarke Publishing Company, Chicago, Illinois, 1925) price $25

This two-volumed set contains illustrations, plates, portraits, maps, and bibliographical material.

4.

Mississippi: Comprising Sketches of Counties, Towns, Events, Institutions, and Persons, Arranged in Cyclopedia Form, planned and edited by Dunbar Rowland (Southern Historical Publishing Association, Atlanta, Georgia, 1907) three volumes

MISSOURI

A History of Missouri from the Earliest Explorations and Settlements until the Admission of the State into the Union, Louis Houck (R. R. Donnelley and Sons Company, Chicago, Illinois, 1908) three volumes

2.

A History of Missouri: A Textbook of State History for Use in Elementary Schools, Clarence Henry McClure (The A. S. Barnes Company, Chicago and New York, 1920) 268 pages

3.

The History of Missouri from the Earliest Times to the Present, Revised Edition, Perry Scott Rader (The Hugh Stevens Printing and Stationery Company, Jefferson City, Missouri, 1922) 225 pages

4.

The Civil Government of the United States and the History of Missouri from the Earliest Times to the Present, Perry Scott Rader (The Hugh Stevens Printing and Stationery Company, Jefferson City, Missouri, 1904) 599 pages

This volume, in addition to the history of Missouri, contains "Civil Government of the United States and of the State of Missouri."

5.

A History of Missouri and Missourians . . ., Floyd Calvin Shoemaker (Lucas Brothers, Columbia, Missouri, 1927) 386 pages, price $1

A list of "reference books for a small working library of Missouri history" is given in this book.

MONTANA

History of Montana, 1739-1885, Michael A. Leeson, Editor (Warner, Beers, and Company, Chicago, Illinois, 1885) 1367 pages

In this work, the following are some of the subjects treated: *The Discovery and Settlement; Natural Resources; Their Exploitation and Use; Natural and Artificial Products; Indian Wars; Transportation*: *Social Agencies; Courts; The Press; and a History of Villages; Cities; Counties and Mining Camps.*

2.

An Illustrated History of the State of Montana, Containing . . . Biographical Mention . . . of Its Pioneers and Prominent Citizens, Joaquinie Cincinnatus Heine Miller (The Lewis Publishing Company, Chicago, Illinois, 1894) 832 pages

3.

A History of Montana, Helen Fitzgerald Sanders (The Lewis Publishing Company, Chicago and New York, 1913) 847 pages

This history contains thirty-four chapters. The first chapter deals with the name, the topography, the climate, and the scenery of Montana. The historical narrative goes through the year 1910.

4.

Montana, Its History and Biography; A History of Aboriginal and Territorial Montana and Three Decades of Statehood, under the editorial supervision of Tom Stout (The American Historical Society, Chicago and New York, 1921) price $40

Of the three volumes of this history, the Second and the Third contain biographical material.

NEBRASKA

History of the State of Nebraska, . . . (The Western Historical Company, Chicago, Illinois, 1882) 1510 pages

This large volume includes a military history with the roster of Nebraska regiments serving in the Civil War. It is a comprehensive account of the history and early State of Nebraska, with biographical sketches.

2.

*History of Nebraska: Illustrated History of Nebraska:
A History of Nebraska from the Earliest Explorations of
the Trans-Mississippi Region with Steel Engravings,
Photogravures, Copper Plates, Maps, and Tables,* Julius
Sterling Morton, succeeded by Albert Watkins, Editor-
in-chief, and George L. Miller, Associate Editor (Jacob
North and Company, Lincoln, Nebraska, 1905) three vol-
umes, price $25

This publication was copyrighted in 1905 by *The Western
Publishing and Engraving Company* of Lincoln, Nebraska.
A limited number of copies may be purchased from Mrs.
C. S. Paine, Lincoln, Nebraska. The history named above
is considered to be a scholarly, trustworthy treatise on
Nebraska history. These volumes contain articles on
aboriginal occupation, early travels and transportation,
Indians, Mormons, the organization both of the Territory
and State political history and church history; Volume
One has two hundred and six pages of biography; Volume
Two has two hundred and ninety-seven pages of biography;
and Volume Three has two hundred and sixty-five pages
of biography.

3.

History and Stories of Nebraska, Addison Erwin Sheldon
(The University Publishing Company, Lincoln, Nebraska,
and Chicago, Illinois, 1926) 321 pages, price 96 cents

4.

Nebraska, The Land and the People, Addison Erwin
Sheldon, Nebraska Biography (gratuitously published)
selected and prepared by a special staff of writers (The
Lewis Publishing Company, Chicago, Illinois, and New
York, 1931) three volumes
Volumes Two and Three are biographical.

5.

Nebraska Old and New, History, Stories, Folklore, Addison Erwin Sheldon (The University Publishing Company,
Lincoln, Chicago, Dallas, and New York, 1937) 470 pages,
price $1.28

NEVADA

History of Nevada with Illustrations and Biographical Sketches of Its Prominent Men and Pioneers, Myron Angel, Editor (The Thompson and West Company, Oakland, California, 1881) 680 pages

2.

History of Nevada, Colorado, and Wyoming, Hubert Howe Bancroft (The History Company, San Francisco, California, 1890) 828 pages

It is said that Bancroft wrote the first two chapters on Nevada, and that Mrs. Frances Fuller Victor wrote the other chapters.

3.

The History of Nevada, edited by Samuel Post Davis, . . . (The Elms Publishing Company, Incorporated, Reno, Nevada, and Los Angeles, California, 1913)

The Second of the two volumes includes biography.

4.

A History of the State of Nevada, Its Resources and People, the late Honorable Thomas Wren, Editor-in-chief (The Lewis Publishing Company, New York and Chicago, 1904) 760 pages

5.

Nevada: A History of the State from the Earliest Times through the Civil War, Effie Mona Mack (The Arthur H. Clark Company, Glendale, California, 1936) 495 pages, price $6.00.

6.

Nevada: A Narrative of the Conquest of a Frontier Land, Comprising the Story of Her People from the Dawn of History to the Present Time, James Grover Scrugham, Editor (The American Historical Society, Inc., Chicago and New York, 1935) three volumes, price $50.00. Volumes Two and Three of this publication are given over to Nevada biographies, written by a special staff of writers.

NEW HAMPSHIRE

A History of New Hampshire from Its Discovery, in 1614, to the Passage of the Toleration Act, in 1819, Second Edition, George Barstow (Little and Brown, Boston, Massachusetts; G. P. Putnam and Company, New York, 1853) 456 pages

2.

The History of New Hampshire, from a Copy of the Original Edition, Having the Author's Last Corrections, to Which Are Added Notes, Containing Various Corrections and Illustrations of the Text, and Additional Facts and Notices of Persons and Events Therein Mentioned by John Farmer, . . . Jeremy Belknap (G. Wadleigh, Dover, Delaware, 1862) 512 pages

3.

History of New-Hampshire, Containing a Geographical Description of the State; with Sketches of its Natural History, Productions, Improvements, and Present State of Society and Manners, Laws and Government, Jeremy Belknap (Printed for the author by Belknap and Young, Boston, Massachusetts, 1792, and by Robert Aiken, Philadelphia, Pennsylvania, 1784) three volumes

4.

History of New Hampshire from Its First Discovery to the Year 1830; with Dissertations upon the Rise of Opinions and Institutions, the Growth of Agriculture and Manufactures, and the Influence of Leading Families and Distinguished Men, to the Year 1874, Edwin Davis Sanborn (J. B. Clarke, Manchester, New Hampshire, 1875) 422 pages

5.

New Hampshire: An Epitome of Popular Government, Franklin Benjamin Sanborn (Houghton, Mifflin and Company, Boston and New York, 1904) 354 pages

NEW JERSEY

Historical Collections of the State of New Jersey, . . . John Warner Barber and Henry Howe (Published by B. Olds for J. H. Bradley, Newark, New Jersey, 1852) 519 pages

The book named above contains traditions, facts, anecdotes, biographical sketches, and geographical descriptions of every township in the State.

2.

A Brief History of New Jersey, Edward Sylvester Ellis and Henry Snyder (American Book Company, New York and Cincinnati, 1910) 274 pages

Maps, illustrations, and a bibliography are contained in this book.

3.

New Jersey as a Colony and as a State: One of the Original Thirteen, Francis Bazley Lee, and an Associate Board of Editors (The Publishing Society of New Jersey, New York, 1902) four volumes

4.

History of the Colony of Nova-Caesaria, or New Jersey: Containing an Account of Its First Settlement, Progressive Improvements, the Original and Present Constitution, and Other Events, to the Year 1721, with Some Particulars Since: and a Short View of Its Present State, Samuel Smith (J. Parker, Burlington, New Jersey, 1765) 573 pages

The book contains the original constitution of New Jersey, and is complete to the year 1721.

NEW MEXICO

History of New Mexico: Its Resources and People, . . . compiled by George B. Anderson (The Pacific States Publishing Company, Los Angeles and New York, 1907) two volumes

2.

History of Arizona and New Mexico, 1530-1888, Hubert Howe Bancroft (The History Company, San Francisco, California, 1889) 829 pages

3.

New Mexico History and Civics, Lansing B. Bloom, and Thomas C. Donnelly (The University of New Mexico Press, Albuquerque, New Mexico, 1933) 539 pages, price $2.50

4.

A History of New Mexico, Charles Florus Coan, assisted by a Board of Advisory Editors (The American Historical Society, Inc. Chicago and New York, 1925) three volumes, price $37.50

The Second and Third volumes have biographical material. A bibliography appears at the close of some of the chapters in the first volume.

5.

History of New Mexico from the Spanish Conquest to the Present Time, 1530-1890, with Portraits and Biographical Sketches of Its Prominent People, Helen Haines (The New Mexico Historical Publishing Company, New York, 1891) 632 pages

6.

A Concise History of New Mexico, Second Edition, L. Bradford Prince (The Torch Press, Cedar Rapids, Iowa, 1914) 279 pages, price $1.50

7.

Illustrated History of New Mexico, Benjamin Maurice Read (New Mexican Printing Company, Santa Fe, New Mexico, 1912) 812 pages, price $10

The book named above, having been first printed in Spanish, was translated into English under the direction of the author by Eleuterio Baca.

8.

The Leading Facts of New Mexican History, Ralph Emerson Twitchell (The Torch Press, Cedar Rapids, Iowa, 1911) five volumes, price $6 per volume

9.

History and Government of New Mexico, John H. Vaughan (C. L. Vaughan, State College, New Mexico, 1927) 377 pages

This book has a bibliography at the end of each chapter.

NEW YORK

History of the State of New York, John Romeyn Brodhead (Harper and Brothers, New York, 1853-1871) two volumes

2.

New York: the Planting and the Growth of the Empire State, with a Supplementary Chapter Dealing with the Period from 1885 to 1900 ... Ellis Henry Roberts (Houghton, Mifflin and Company, New York, 1904) price $10 per volume

The revised edition of this history is published in two volumes.

3.

History of New York State, 1523 to 1927, Editor-in-chief, Dr. James Sullivan, Associate Editors: E. Melvin Williams, Edwin P. Conklin, Benedict Fitzpatrick (Lewis Historical Publishing Company, Inc. New York, 1927)

The last of the six volumes contains biographical material.

4.

New York's Part in History, Sherman Williams (D. Appleton and Company, New York, 1915) 390 pages, price $3.50

NORTH CAROLINA

Biographical History of North Carolina from Colonial Times to the Present, "Old North State" Edition, Samuel A'Court Ashe, Editor-in-chief (C. L. Van Noppen, Greensboro, North Carolina, 1905-1917)

This set of eight volumes is limited to seven hundred and fifty registered and numbered sets.

2.

History of North Carolina, Samuel A'Court Ashe (Charles
L. Van Noppen Greensboro, North Carolina, 1908-25) two
volumes

3.

History of North Carolina, William Kenneth Boyd, R. D.
W. Connor, and J. G. de R. Hamilton (The Lewis Publishing Company, Chicago and New York, 1919)

The six volumes of this history discuss the following
topics:
Volume One:
The Colonial and Revolutionary Periods, 1584-1783,
by R. D. W. Connor
Volume Two:
The Federal Period, 1783-1860, by W. K. Boyd
Volume Three:
North Carolina Since 1860, by J. G. de R. Hamil-
ton
Volumes Four, Five, and Six:
North Carolina Bibliography, by a Special Staff
of Writers

4.

Young People's History of North Carolina, Daniel Harvey
Hill (The Stone and Barringer Company, Charlotte, North
Carolina, 1907) 410 pages

5.

*Historical Sketches of North Carolina from 1584 to 1851,
Compiled from Original Records, Official Documents, and
Traditional Statements, Jurists, Lawyers, Soldiers, Di-
vines, etc.,* John Hill Wheeler (Lippincott, Grambo and
Company, Philadelphia, Pennsylvania, 1851)

Volume One consists of two volumes in one with frontispieces. Volume Two is a history of the counties of North
Carolina.

NORTH DAKOTA

History of North Dakota, by Lewis F. Crawford; North
Dakota Biography by a separate staff of special writers
. . . (The American Historical Society, Incorporated,
Chicago and New York, 1931) three volumes

Volumes Two and Three of this publication contain biographical material.

2.

History of Dakota Territory, George Washington Kingsbury (The S. J. Clarke Publishing Company, Chicago, Illinois, 1915) price $25 per set

There are five volumes of this history, the last two of which contain biographical sketches. Volume Three, edited by George Martin Smith, discusses the history and the people of South Dakota.

3.

North Dakota History and People: Outlines of American History, Colonel Clement Augustus Lounsberry (The S. J. Clarke Publishing Company, Chicago, Illinois, 1917)

The last two of the three volumes of this set contain biographical material.

OHIO

History of Ohio, Charles Burleigh Galbreath (American Historical Society, Inc. Chicago and New York, 1925) price $37.50

The last three volumes of this history contain biographical material.

2.

Historical Collections of Ohio, . . . an Encyclopedia of the State: History both General and Local, Geography, . . . Henry Howe (H. Howe and Son, Columbus, Ohio, 1890-1891)

This publication, the Centennial Edition, contains three volumes in two with engravings. It consists of history, general and local; descriptions; sketches; and notes of a tour over the State in 1886.

3.

Fifty Stories from Ohio History, Clement Luther Martzolff (The Ohio Teacher Publishing Company, Columbus, Ohio, 1917) 254 pages

4.

History of Ohio: the Rise and Progress of an American State, Emilius O. Randall and Daniel J. Ryan (The Century History Company, New York, 1912) five volumes, price $25

OKLAHOMA

History of the State of Oklahoma, Luther B. Hill, with the assistance of local authorities. . . (The Lewis Publishing Company, Chicago and New York, 1908) two volumes

2.

Illustrated History of Oklahoma, Its Occupation by Spain and France—Its Sale to the United States—Its Opening to Settlement in 1889—and the Meeting of the First Territorial Legislature, Marion Tuttle Rock (C. B. Hamilton and Son, Topeka, Kansas, 1890) 277 pages

3.

A History of Oklahoma, Joseph Bradfield Thoburn and Isaac M. Holcomb (Warden Company, Oklahoma City, Oklahoma, 1914) 120 pages, price 75 cents

4.

A Standard History of Oklahoma, . . . Joseph Bradfield Thoburn, assisted by a Board of Advisory Editors (The American Historical Society, Chicago and New York, 1916)

This comprehensive publication covers the historical events from the early explorations to the present time, including discussions of the Indian tribes, cattle ranges and land openings, etc. The set comprises five volumes, the last three of which contain biographical sketches.

5.

Oklahoma: A History of the State and Its People, Joseph B. Thoburn and Muriel M. Wright (Lewis Historical Publishing Company, Incorporated, New York, 1929) four volumes, price $37.50 per set, or $65 for the de luxe edition

OREGON

History of Oregon, Hubert Howe Bancroft (The History Company, San Francisco, California, 1886-1888)

This history forms volumes xxix and xxx of the *Works of Hubert Howe Bancroft.* It was also published as Volumes Twenty-four and Twenty-five of the *History of the Pacific States,* in 1886-1888, and separately in 1890. The last-named work, *History of the Pacific States,* is still in print, and prices of the thirty volumes comprising the set may be had on application to the publishers, The Bancroft Company, 156 Fifth Avenue, New York City.

2.

History of Oregon, Author's Edition, Charles Henry Carey (The Pioneer Historical Publishing Company, Chicago, Illinois, and Portland, Oregon, 1922) 1016 pages

This history, of which the edition mentioned above constitutes Volume One, is published in three volumes; Volumes Two and Three being biographical.

3.

History of the Willamette Valley, Oregon, Robert Carlton Clark (The S. J. Clarke Publishing Company, Chicago, Illinois, 1927) three volumes, price $45

The author's name does not appear on volumes Two and Three, which contain biographical material.

4.

The Centennial History of Oregon, 1811-1912 (with notice of antecedent exploration) Joseph Gaston (The S. J. Clarke Publishing Company, Chicago, Illinois, 1912)

The last three of the four volumes of this set contain biographical material, and the work contains frontispieces, portraits, maps, and facsimiles.

5.

A History of the Pacific Northwest, Revised Edition, Joseph Schafer (The Macmillan Company, New York, 1918) 323 pages, price $2.50

This history contains illustrations, a double frontispiece, plates, portraits, and maps.

6.

History of Oregon, Philip H. Parrish (The Macmillan Company, New York, 1937) 254 pages, price $1.44.

PENNSYLVANIA

History of Pennsylvania from the Earliest Discovery to the Present Time, . . . William Mason Cornell (Quaker City Publishing House, Philadelphia, Pennsylvania, and B. B. Russell, Boston, Massachusetts, 1876) 575 pages

This volume includes "an account of the first settlements by the Dutch, Swedes, and English, and of the colony of William Penn, his treaty and pacific measures with the Indians; and the gradual advancement of the state to its present aspect of opulence, culture and refinement."

2.

Historical Collections of the State of Pennsylvania, Sherman Day (G. W. Gorton, Philadelphia, Pennsylvania, 1843) 708 pages, price $5

This volume contains biographical sketches in addition to trade and topographical descriptions of the cities and towns of each county.

3.

An Illustrated History of the Commonwealth of Pennsylvania, Civil, Political, and Military, from Its Earliest Settlement to the Present Time, . . . William H. Egle (De W. C. Goodrich, Harrisburg, Pennsylvania, 1877) price $3 per volume

The two volumes of this history were sold only by subscription. They contain material on the counties, towns, and industrial resources of the State.

4.

Pennsylvania Place Names, A. Howey Espenshade (Pennsylvania State College, State College, Pennsylvania, 1925) 376 pages

This volume is book number one, series number one, of the Pennsylvania State College Studies in History and Political Science.

5.

Pennsylvania, A Primer, James B. Ferree (L. Scott, New York, 1904) 256 pages, price $3

This book is especially valuable for history of the settlement of the State, and for its constitutional and political history.

6.

The Making of Pennsylvania, New Edition, Sydney George Fisher (J. B. Lippincott and Company, Philadelphia, Pennsylvania, 1932) 380 pages, price $1.50

7.

Pennsylvania, Colony and Commonwealth, Sydney George Fisher (H. T. Coates, Philadelphia, Pennsylvania, 1897) 742 pages, price $3

The political history of Pennsylvania is stressed in this volume.

8.

Pennsylvania, Colonial and Federal, from 1609 to 1903, Howard Malcolm Jenkins (Published by the Pennsylvania Historical Association, Philadelphia, Pennsylvania, 1903) three volumes, price $7

This history, valued highly by most students of history, covers well the settlement of the State, and it gives in detail many of the transactions that are usually found only in State records. It also treats in a thorough manner the Indian wars and the evolution of the political history of Pennsylvania.

9.

A History of Pennsylvania, Thomas Stone March (American Book Company, New York, 1926) 368 pages, price $1

At the end of each chapter of this book except the last are references together with illustrative material.

10.

Pennsylvania Keystone, Samuel W. Pennypacker (Christopher Sower, Philadelphia, Pennsylvania, 1914) 316 pages, price $1

This is a short history written by a former Governor of the State. It is condensed but accurate.

RHODE ISLAND

History of the State of Rhode Island and Providence Plantations, Samuel Greene Arnold (D. Appleton and Company, New York and London, 1859-1860)

The set contains two volumes covering the history of the State from the settlement in 1636 to the adoption of the Federal Constitution in 1790.

2.

Documentary History of Rhode Island, Howard Millar Chapin (Preston and Rounds Company, Providence, Rhode Island, 1916) two volumes, price $4 per volume

3.

State of Rhode Island and Providence Plantations at the End of the Century: A History, Illustrated with Maps, Facsimiles of Old Plates and Paintings and Photographs of Ancient Landmarks, edited by Edward Field (The Mason Publishing Company, Boston, Massachusetts and Syracuse, New York, 1902) three volumes

This work contains illustrations, portraits, maps, plans, and facsimiles. It consists of historical and descriptive articles by various authors.

SOUTH CAROLINA

Historical Collections of South Carolina; Embracing . . . Rare . . . Pamphlets, and Other Documents, Relating to the History of That State, from Its First Discovery to . . .

1776, edited by B. R. Carroll (Harper and Brothers, New York, 1836) two volumes

2.

A History of South-Carolina, from Its First Settlement in 1670, to the Year 1808, David Ramsay (Published by David Longworth for the author, Charleston, South Carolina, 1809)

The original of this history was issued in two volumes; but there is another edition, two volumes in one, published and sold by W. J. Duffie, Newberry, South Carolina, printed by Walker Evans and Company, Charleston, South Carolina, 1858.

3.

A History of South Carolina, by William Gilmore Simms; edited by Mary C. Simms Oliphant; Revised Edition with new maps and illustrations, specially adapted for use in schools (The State Company, Columbia, South Carolina, 1927) 305 pages, price 85 cents

This history is now in its fourth edition.

4.

History of South Carolina, edited by Yates Snowden, in collaboration with H. G. Cutler and an Editorial Advisory Board, including Special Contributors (The Lewis Publishing Company, Chicago and New York, 1920) price $30

The last three of the five volumes of this set contain biography.

SOUTH DAKOTA

In the South Dakota Country, Effie Florence Putney (The Educator Supply Company, Mitchell, South Dakota, 1922) 176 pages, price $1

2.

The Sunshine State: A History of South Dakota, Frank L. Ransom (The Educator Supply Company, Mitchell, South Dakota, 1912) 159 pages, price 90 cents

3.

A Brief History of South Dakota, Doane Robinson (Jonah Leroy Robinson) (American Book Company, New York, 1926) 232 pages, price 76 cents

The treatise devotes four pages to the "Bibliography of South Dakota History."

TENNESSEE

History of Tennessee, Its People and Its Institutions, William Robertson Garrett and Albert Virgil Goodpasture (Brandon Printing Company, Nashville, Tennessee, 1900) 351 pages

This book has, in addition to the subject matter proper, some biographical material, the Constitution of Tennessee adopted in 1870, and a bibliography of Tennessee history and biography.

2.

The Civil and Political History of the State of Tennessee, from Its Earliest Settlement up to the Year 1796; Including the Boundaries of the State, John Haywood (Printed for the author by Heiskell and Brown, Knoxville, Tennessee, 1823)

There is an 1891 reprint of this work having five hundred and eighteen pages, printed for W. H. Haywood by the Publishing House of the Methodist Episcopal Church South, of Nashville, Tennessee.

3.

Tennessee, the Volunteer State, 1769-1923, John Trotwood Moore and Austin P. Foster (The S. J. Clarke Publishing Company, Chicago, Illinois and Nashville, Tennessee, 1923) five volumes

4.

History of Tennessee: The Making of a State, James Phelan (Houghton, Mifflin and Company, Boston and New York, 1888) 478 pages

The above-named history covers the period of time from the settlement of the State to the outbreak of the Civil War.

5.

The Annals of Tennessee to the End of the Eighteenth Century, Comprising Its Settlement, as the Watauga Association, from 1769 to 1777; a Part of North-Carolina, from 1777 to 1784; the State of Franklin, from 1784 to 1788, a Part of North-Carolina, from 1788 to 1790; the Territory of the United States, South of the Ohio, from 1790 to 1796; Tennessee, from 1796 to 1800, James Gettys McGready Ramsey (Kingsport Press, Kingsport, Tennessee, 1926)

The reprint edition of this work is now obtainable. This edition contains eight hundred and thirty-two pages and stresses the various names of Tennessee. On pages 745 to 832 will be found Fain's Critical and Analytical Index and Genealogical Guide compiled by John Tyree Fail.

6.

Tennessee, Its Growth and Progress, Robert H. White (Robert H. White, Publisher, Nashville, Tennessee, 1936) 709 pages, price ninety-five cents, exchange price eighty-six cents. The State Textbook Commission fixed the price.

7.

Discovering Tennessee, Mary U. Rothrock (The University of North Carolina Press, Chapel Hill, North Carolina, 1936) 498 pages, price seventy-seven cents.

TEXAS

A Texas Scrap-book; Made up of the History, Biography, and Miscellany of Texas and Its People, compiled by D. W. C. Baker (A. S. Barnes and Company, New York and Chicago, 1875) 657 pages

The subject matter is the history, biography, and miscellany of Texas and its people.

2.

History of Texas, from Its Discovery and Settlement, etc., J. M. Morphis (United States Publishing Company, New York, 1874) 591 pages

This book contains "a description of the principal cities and counties, and the agricultural, mineral, and material resources of the state."

3.

A History of Texas from the Earliest Settlement to the Year 1885, . . . H. S. Thrall (University Publishing Company, New York, 1885) 244 pages

This book has portraits and illustrations. It is intended for use in schools, and for general readers as well. The State Constitution of 1875 and the amendments of 1883 are given in an appendix to the book.

4.

A Comprehensive History of Texas, 1685-1897, edited by Dudley G. Wooten (W. G. Scarff, Dallas, Texas, 1898)

These two volumes contain various illustrations, including maps, facsimiles, and tables.

5.

Texas Under Many Flags, Clarence R. Wharton, Author and Editor, Texas Biography by a Special Staff of Writers (The American Historical Society, Inc., Chicago and New York, 1930) five volumes

Volumes Three, Four, and Five of this history are biographical.

6.

Rise of the Lone Star: A Story of Texas Told by Its Pioneers, Howard Roscoe Driggs and Sarah S. King (Frederick A. Stokes Company, New York, 1936) 438 pages, price $2.75

UTAH

History of Utah, Hubert Howe Bancroft (The History Company, San Francisco, California, 1890) 808 pages

The book covers the period from 1540 to 1887 inclusive. Twenty-six pages are given to a list of authorities.

2.

The Story of the Mormons, from the Date of Their Origin to the Year 1901, William Alexander Linn (The Macmillan Company, New York, 1902) 637 pages

3.

Utah Since Statehood, Historical and Biographical, Noble Warrum, Editor, assisted by Honorable Charles W. Morse for Bench and Bar, and W. Brown Ewing, M. D. for the Medical Chapter (The S. J. Clarke Publishing Company, Chicago, Illinois and Salt Lake City, Utah, 1919)

The set of four volumes contains plates and portraits.

4.

Vermont, the Green Mountain State, Walter Hill Crockett *of All the Northern, Eastern, and Western Counties of Utah* . . . Edward Wheelock Tullidge, Proprietor and Publisher (Press of the Juvenile Instructor, Salt Lake City, Utah, 1889)

This publication contains the history of all the northern, eastern, and western counties of Utah, also the counties of southern Idaho.

VERMONT

Tullidge's Histories (Volume 11) Containing the History (The Century History Company, Inc. New York, 1921) four volumes, price $20 or $24 if bound in half-leather

2.

Vermont: A Study of Independence, Rowland Evans Robinson (Houghton, Mifflin and Company, Boston and New York, 1892) 370 pages, price $2

3.

History of Vermont, Natural, Civil, and Statistical, . . . Zadock Thompson (C. Goodrich, Burlington, Vermont, 1842)

The book is published in three parts embodying a new map of the State and two hundred engravings.

4.

The Natural and Civil History of Vermont, Samuel Williams (Printed by Samuel Mills, Burlington, Vermont, 1809)

This second edition, in two volumes corrected and much enlarged, was published according to an act of Congress.

VIRGINIA

Virginia: Rebirth of the Old Dominion, Philip Alexander Bruce, Virginia Biography by a Special Staff of Writers (The Lewis Publishing Company, Chicago and New York, 1929)

Of the five volumes comprising this set, the last three contain Virginia biography. Volume Two contains four pages of bibliography.

2.
History of the Colony and Ancient Dominion of Virginia, Charles Campbell (J. B. Lippincott and Company, Philadelphia, Pennsylvania, 1860) 765 pages

This book is considered to be one of the best general histories of Virginia covering the period of time from the colonization up to the Civil War. It has recently been reprinted.

3.
Virginia: A History of the People, John Esten Cooke (Houghton, Mifflin and Company, New York, 1891) 523 pages, price $1.25

The volume named above is edited by Horace E. Scudder.

4.
Old Virginia and Her Neighbours, John Fiske (Houghton, Mifflin and Company, Boston and New York, 1900) price $2.50 per volume

This history is published in two volumes, having illustrations, plates, portraits, maps, and facsimiles. Volume One deals with Virginia history to about 1649. Volume Two discusses Virginia history from about 1649 to 1753. This splendid book is considered a scholarly, reliable history of this period of time.

5.
A History of Virginia, from Its Discovery and Settlement by Europeans to the Present Time (1848) Robert Reed

Howison (Carey and Hart, Philadelphia, Pennsylvania, 1845 to 1848)

Volume One gives the history of the Colony up to the Peace of Paris in 1763. Volume Two deals with the history of the Colony and of the State from 1763 to 1847.

6.

The Story of Virginia's First Century, Mrs. Mary Mann Page (Newton) Stanard (J. B. Lippincott Companv, Philadelphia, Pennsylvania, 1928) 331 pages

This book contains twenty-seven illustrations.

7.

Virginia, The Old Dominion, Matthew Page Andrews (Doubleday, Doran and Company, Inc., Garden City, New York, 1937) 664 pages, price $6.00

WASHINGTON

An Illustrated History of the State of Washington, Containing . . . Biographical Mention of . . . Its Pioneers and Prominent Citizens, . . . Reverend Harvey K. Hines (The Lewis Publishing Company, Chicago, Illinois, 1893) 933 pages

2.

Washington, West of the Cascades: Historical and Descriptive: The Explorations, the Indians, the Pioneers, the Modern, Herbert Hunt and Floyd C. Kaylor (The S. J. Clarke Publishing Company, Chicago, Illinois and Seattle, Washington, 1917)

The Second and Last of the three volumes of this set contain biographical sketches.

3.

A History of the State of Washington, Edmond Stephen Meany (The Macmillan Company, New York, 1924) 412 pages, price $2.20

4.

History of Washington: The Rise and Progress of an American State, Clinton A. Snowden, Advisory Editors:

Cornelius H. Hanford, Miles C. Moore, William D. Tyler, Stephen J. Chadwick (The Century History Company, New York, 1909) four volumes, price $25

WEST VIRGINIA

Semi-centennial History of West Virginia, with Special Articles on Development and Resources, James Morton Callahan (Semi-centennial Commission of West Virginia, Charleston, West Virginia, 1913) 594 pages

2.

History of the Early Settlement and Indian Wars of West Virginia, Wills DeHass (H. Hoblitzell, Wheeling, West Virginia, Printed by King and Baird, Philadelphia, Pennsylvania, 1851) 416 pages

The above-named history has an account of the various expeditions in the West previous to 1795, also biographical sketches of distinguished actors in the border wars of West Virginia.

3.

A History of West Virginia in Two Parts, Virgil Anson Lewis (Hubbard Brothers, Philadelphia, Pennsylvania, 1889) 744 pages

Part One takes up the general history of the State from the settlement of Virginia to 1889. Part Two deals with the history of the counties of West Virginia.

4.

West Virginia and Its People, Thomas Condit Miller and Hu Maxwell (Lewis Historical Publishing Company, New York, 1913) price $21

The last two volumes of this three-volume work cover family and personal history.

5.

West Virginia, in History, Life, Literature and Industry, Morris Purdy Shawkey, assisted by an Advisory Council, West Virginia Biography by a Special Staff of Writers (The Lewis Publishing Company, Chicago and New York, 1928)

The last three of the five volumes contain biographical data.

6.

West Virginia: Stories and Biographies, Charles Henry Ambler (Rand McNally and Company, Chicago, Illinois, 1937) 600 pages, price $1.48

WISCONSIN

Wisconsin in Three Centuries, 1634-1905; Narratives of Three Centuries in the Making of an American Commonwealth, . . . Henry Colin Campbell (The Century History Company, New York, 1906) four volumes

This history is illustrated with numerous engravings, and includes historical scenes and landmarks, portraits and facsimiles of rare prints, documents, and old maps.

2.

The French Regime in Wisconsin and the Northwest, Louise Phelps Kellogg (The State Historical Society of Wisconsin, Madison, Wisconsin, 1925) 474 pages, price $3.50

3.

Wisconsin, Its History and Its People, 1634-1924, Milo Milton Quaife (The S. J. Clarke Publishing Company, Chicago, Illinois, 1924) price $40 per set

The book named above is published in four volumes, the last two of which have biographical material.

4.

Wisconsin, the Americanization of a French Settlement, Reuben Gold Thwaites (Houghton, Mifflin Company, New York, 1908) 466 pages, price $1.25

WYOMING

History of Wyoming, Ichabod S. Bartlett, Editor (The S. J. Clarke Publishing Company, Chicago, Illinois, 1918) three volumes

The last two volumes of this publication contain biography.

2.

History of Wyoming from the Earliest Known Discoveries, in Three Volumes, Charles Giffin Coutant (Chaplin, Spafford, and Mathison, Laramie, Wyoming, 1899)

Volume one, the only volume published as yet, gives the history of the state up to 1869.

3.

Collections of the Wyoming Historical Society, Robert C. Morris (Wyoming Historical Society, Cheyenne, Wyoming, 1897) 352 pages

Only one volume has been published so far.

INDEX [1]

---

[1] Figures in boldface type denote the more important entries.

Hanford, Cornelius H. See Snowden, C. A. joint author
Hanna, Charles A., 84
Hard-case State, nickname of Oregon, 141, 142
Hard Cases, nickname of Oregonians, 142
Harris, Joel Chandler, *Stories of Georgia*, 439
Harrisburg, Pa., 321
Harrison, President Benjamin, 140
Hart, Albert Bushnell, *Commonwealth History of Massachusetts, Colony, Province, and State*, 451
Hart, Lester M. and Goodridge, Alice Benedict, *Maine*, 410
Hartford, Conn., 63, 106, 301
Haskell and Wood, 308
Hatch, Louis Clinton, *Maine: A History*, 450
Hawkeye, Indian chief, 114
Hawkeye State, nickname of Iowa, 114-15
Hawkeyes, nickname of Iowans, 115
Hawley, James H., *History of Idaho, The Gem of the Mountains*, 441
Hawthorne, Missouri State flower, 342
Hay, Robert, 69, 167
Haywood, John, *The Civil and Political History of the State of Tennessee, from Its Earliest Settlement. . . Including the Boundaries of the State*, 471
Heard, Governor W. W., 195
Heath, Sir Robert, 25
Helena, Mont., 314
Helmet, depicted on State seal of, California, 247; Maryland, 197; Missouri, 200; New Jersey, 204
Heloïse, 24
Hemans, Lawton Thomas, *History of Michigan*, 452
Hemlock, Pennsylvania State tree, 356
Hemp State, nickname of Kentucky, 117, 118
Hempstead, Fay, *Historical Review of Arkansas; Its Commerce, Industry, and Modern Affairs*, 430
Hempstead, Fay, *A History of the State of Arkansas for the Use of Schools*, 430
Hempstead, Fay, *A Pictorial History of Arkansas, from the Earliest Times to the Year 1890*, 431
Henderson, James Pinkney, 89
Henderson, Junius, E. B. Renaud and Colon B. Goodykoontz, *Colorado: Short Studies of Its Past and Present*, 434
Henderson, Richard, 71
Hennepin, Father Louis, 57, 58, 93
Henrietta Maria, 20, 21, 40, 122
Henry IV of France, 20, 40
Here We Have Idaho, State song, Sallie Hume Douglas and Lula M. Huffman, 394-5
Here We Rest, used as Alabama State motto, 52, 170-1, 182
Hermit thrush, appropriate for Vermont avian emblem, 387
Herndon, Dallas T., *Centennial History of Arkansas*, 431
Herndon, Dallas T., *The High Lights of Arkansas History*, 431

Heyward, T. S., 348
High Lights of Arkansas History, The, Dallas T. Herndon, 431
High-holder, 359
Hill, Daniel Harvey, *Young People's History of North Carolina*, 463
Hill, Luther B., *History of the State of Oklahoma*, 465
Hills, depicted on South Dakota State seal, 212, 237
Hines, Reverend Harvey K., *An Illustrated History of the State of Washington, Containing . . Biographical Mention of Its Pioneers and Prominent Citizens, . . .*, 476
Hippolytus, Lucius Annaeus Seneca, 166
Historical Collections of Louisiana and Florida, . . . with Numerous Historical and Biographical Notes, Second Series, Historical Memoirs and Narratives, B. F. French, 449
Historical Collections of Ohio, . . . , an Encyclopedia of the State: History both General and Local, Geography, . . ., Henry Howe, 464
Historical Collections of South Carolina; . . . , from Its First Discovery to . . . 1776, B. R. Carroll, 470
Historical Collections of the State of New Jersey, . . ., John Warner Barber and Henry Howe, 460
Historical Collections of the State of Pennsylvania, Sherman Day, 467
Historical Review of Arkansas; Its Commerce, Industry, and Modern Affairs, Fay Hempstead, 430
Historical Sketches of Kentucky, 1797-1870, Lewis Collins, 446
Historical Sketches of North Carolina from 1584 to 1851, . . ., John Hill Wheeler, 463
Historical View of the Government of Maryland, from Its Colonization to the Present Day, An, John van Lear McMahon, 450
Histories, of the District of Columbia, 437-8; of State of, Alabama, 427-8, Arizona, 429-30, Arkansas, 430-2, California, 423-3, Colorado, 434, Connecticut, 434-7, Delaware, 437, Florida, 438-9, Georgia, 439-40, Idaho, 440-1, Illinois, 442-3, Indiana, 443-4, Iowa, 444, Kansas, 445, Kentucky, 445-8, Louisiana, 448-9, Maine, 449-50, Maryland, 450, Massachusetts, 451-2, Michigan, 452-3, Minnesota, 453-4, Mississippi, 454, Missouri, 455, Montana, 455-6, Nebraska, 456-7, Nevada, 458, New Hampshire, 459, New Jersey, 460, New Mexico, 460-2, New York, 462, North Carolina, 462-3, North Dakota, 463-4, Ohio, 464-5, Oklahoma, 465, Oregon, 466-7, Pennsylvania, 467-9, Rhode Island, 469, South Carolina, 469-70, South Dakota, 470-1, Tennessee, 471-2, Texas, 472-3, Utah,

R